The Kent & East Sussex Railway, 1974-2004

The Kent & East Sussex Railway, 1974-2004

Return to the Rother

Nick Pallant

AN IMPRINT OF PEN & SWORD BOOKS LTD.
YORKSHIRE – PHILADELPHIA

First published in Great Britain in 2025 by
Pen and Sword Transport
An imprint of
Pen & Sword Books Ltd.
Yorkshire – Philadelphia

Copyright © Nick Pallant, 2025

ISBN 9781036102227

The right of Nick Pallant to be identified as author of this work has been asserted by him in accordance with the Copyright, Designs and Patents Act 1988.

A CIP catalogue record for this book is available from the British Library.

All rights reserved. No part of this book may be reproduced or transmitted in any form or by any means, electronic or mechanical including photocopying, recording or by any information storage and retrieval system, without permission from the Publisher in writing.

Typeset in INDIA by IMPEC eSolutions
Printed and bound in India by Replika Press Pvt. Ltd.

Pen & Sword Books Ltd. incorporates the imprints of Pen & Sword Books: After the Battle, Archaeology, Atlas, Aviation, Battleground, Discovery, Family History, History, Maritime, Military, Politics, Select, Transport, True Crime, Fiction, Frontline Books, Leo Cooper, Praetorian Press, Seaforth Publishing, Wharncliffe and White Owl.

For a complete list of Pen & Sword titles please contact

PEN & SWORD BOOKS LIMITED
George House, Beevor Street, Off Pontefract Road, Hoyle Mill, Barnsley, South Yorkshire, England, S71 1HN.
E-mail: enquiries@pen-and-sword.co.uk
Website: www.pen-and-sword.co.uk

or

PEN AND SWORD BOOKS
1950 Lawrence Rd, Havertown, PA 19083, USA
E-mail: uspen-and-sword@casematepublishers.com
website: www.penandswordbooks.com

Dedicated to the memory of Michael Alan Williams

1947–2018

As good a friend as anyone could wish for

Contents

Foreword	9
Acknowledgements	10
Chapter 1 Historical Preface	11
Chapter 2	18
Chapter 3	25
Chapter 4	31
Chapter 5	41
Chapter 6	54
Chapter 7	60
Chapter 8	71
Chapter 9	80
Chapter 10	86
Chapter 11	91
Chapter 12	97
Chapter 13	105
Chapter 14	113
Chapter 15	122
Chapter 16	130
Chapter 17	138
Chapter 18	144
Chapter 19	152
Chapter 20	161
Chapter 21	164
Chapter 22	173
Chapter 23	176
Chapter 24	178
Chapter 25	182
Chapter 26	189
Chapter 27	193
Chapter 28	203
Chapter 29	210
Chapter 30	215
Appendix A Rolvenden Steam Enterprises	223
Appendix B (See Chapters 16 & 17) Summary of 1994 Business Plan	225
Appendix C	227
Appendix D 68078: Restoring a Locomotive in a Field	229
Sources and Suggestions for Further Reading	232

8   The Kent & East Sussex Railway, 1974–2004

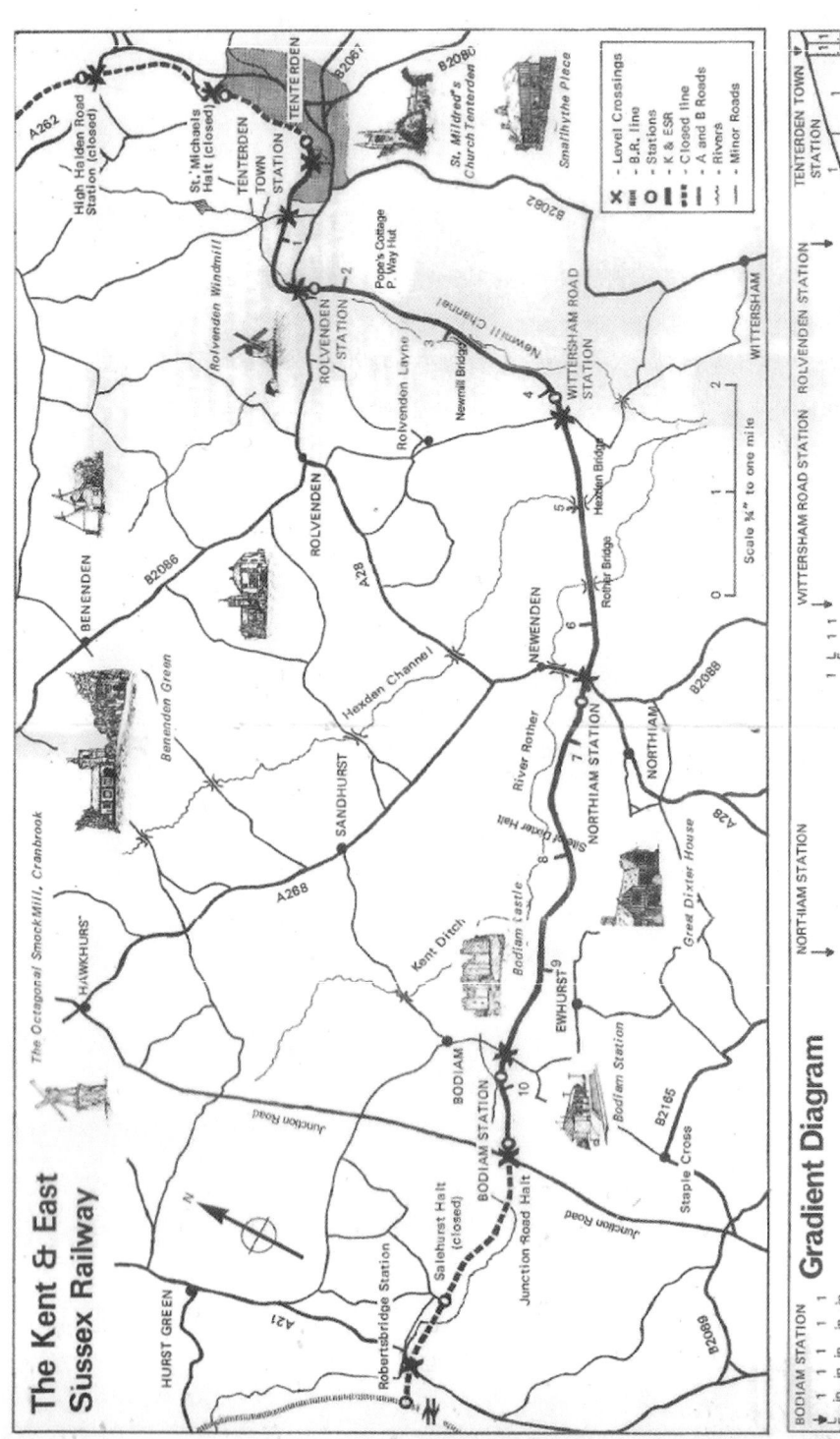

Foreword

My book *Holding the Line – Preserving the Kent & East Sussex Railway* was published in November 1993. It represented just under two years work, and provided my opportunity to rejoin the Kent & East Sussex Railway's (K&ESR) workforce after an absence of around 20 years. Its subject matter was the difficult, and previously often misunderstood, phase in the railway's history between closure in 1961 and partial reopening in 1974.

The reaction from both critics and readers was about as good as any writer could have reasonably hoped for. There were, and have continued to be, requests for 'more of the same' and that I should continue the story. I have resisted this, partly because of other commitments – mostly to the K&ESR – and partly because of the difficulties in being objective about an era whose resonance continues to be contemporary; it is difficult to write an account featuring people you may see a couple of days later. There was also the additional problem – which I had flagged up towards the end of the first book – that my absence through the 1970s and 80s would make it difficult to address the subject with the insight I might wish to employ.

Given these difficulties, it occurred to me that I should write this story in two parts. The first (chapters 2–12) would rely mainly on secondary sources (particularly the *Tenterden Terrier*) although including some personal experience and the recollections of others. The second (chapters 13–30) would cover the years after I returned as a volunteer in the early 1990s, and include more in the way of personal memoir – something not altogether absent from *Holding the Line*. That is what is now presented although, in Chapter 1, it has first been necessary to give some historical background and an outline account of the years between 1961 and 1974. I ask readers to indulge what is now included and what is not. The present work is a lengthy story, and I have had to be selective. If mention of a person, incident or development is omitted, please be assured that no disrespect or lack of interest is intended.

Acknowledgements

My thanks for the various ways they have helped in the writing of this book are due (in no particular order) to the following:

Brian Janes (Hon Curator, Colonel Stephens Railway Museum), Phil Edwards, Norman Brice, Alan Crotty, Carol Mitchell, Paul Wilson, Mark Stuchbury, Graham Bridge, David Morgan (of the Heritage Railway Association), Jon Elphick, David Brailsford, the Board of the Kent & East Sussex Railway Company (for permission to use copyright material), Alan Tebboth, Robin Moira White, Chris Fautley, Ian Scarlett, the late David Stratton, Malcolm Webb, Graham Williams, Chris Garman, Brian Stephenson, Bernard Sealy, Dave Hazeldine and (on behalf of the publishers) John Scott-Morgan.

The customary apologies are offered to anyone I have overlooked. 'CSRM' in the photo attributions of course refers to the Colonel Stephens Railway Museum.

Chapter 1

Historical Preface

Even in the twenty-first century, the area on the Kent–Sussex borders marked at its corners by Tonbridge, Hastings and Ashford remains one of the most beautiful and least populated parts of South East England. The boundaries of this triangular region of marshland and the High Weald are further delineated by the railways serving and connecting these three towns.

Although the earliest of these lines had been opened in the 1840s, railways were to make no advance into this varied landscape until late in the nineteenth century. As a result, the ancient town of Tenterden, federated to the Cinque Ports but subsequently land locked by some ten miles of marshland, was threatened with economic stagnation. However, plans for railways there had been. The most significant in the present context had been the Tenterden Railway which was authorised in 1895 and was intended to link Headcorn, Tenterden and Appledore.

Prior to this, the area had, in 1892, been connected to the railway network by a South Eastern Railway (SER) branch line from Paddock Wood to Cranbrook which was extended to Hawkhurst in 1893. Resident Engineer for the Hawkhurst Branch was Holman Fred Stephens, who was to make a career out of infilling the gaps in the railway system with light railways appropriate to these areas of modest traffic potential. He was greatly assisted in this by the passing of the Light Railways Act of 1896, which sought to bring the benefits of rail transport to rural areas. This statute enabled lines to be cheaply constructed with the minimum of heavy engineering and only basic facilities at passenger stations. A 25mph speed limit was usually imposed, and the weight of locomotives was often restricted.

Such simplification was ideally suited to the next scheme to bring a railway to Tenterden. This was the Rother Valley Railway (RVR), which was to start from Robertsbridge on the Tonbridge–Hastings line and follow marshy valleys of the eastern Rother and its tributary Newmill Channel. There is said to have been little enthusiasm for this scheme in Tenterden, as no-one in the town would have previously thought of travelling to the outside world via Robertsbridge. The line was originally authorised by the Rother Valley Railway (Light) Railway Act 1896. No sooner had this been obtained than the Light Railways Act was passed. This suited the RVR even better and the Company successfully applied for a Light Railways Order to build and operate its line, thus making it the first line to be authorised under the new Act. The contractors for this relatively level 12-mile-long line were the London & Scottish Contract Corporation. Holman Stephens was Engineer, General Manager from 1899 and Managing Director from 1900. In the fullness of time, Stephens came to manage sixteen minor railways from his offices in Tonbridge. The Rother Valley line was his first independent standard gauge line and, in extended form and under another name, was said to be his favourite. Goods services commenced on 26 March 1900 and passenger trains on 2 April, the present day Rolvenden station at that time being named Tenterden.

Although various extensions were proposed – including abortive schemes for lines to Pevensey, Rye, Cranbrook and Maidstone – only two actually became realities. The first was the famous short fierce climb, mostly at 1 in 50, to Tenterden Town station which was opened on 16 March

1903. Work had however begun on a part fulfilment of the Tenterden Railway scheme with a start to construction of a northward extension to Headcorn. This project relieved the South Eastern & Chatham Railway (SE&CR), as successor to the SER, of the obligation to build this line. In exchange the SE&CR guaranteed to subsidise the operation of the extension. To reflect these developments the RVR changed its name during 1904, becoming the Kent & East Sussex Railway.

The Headcorn extension opened on 15 May 1905. The K&ESR then began its Edwardian heyday, during which it was relatively prosperous and regarded as an efficiently run example of the independent light railway concept, often making economical use of locomotives and rolling stock bought second-hand from the main line companies. Not least in this respect was the purchase of two ex-London Brighton and South Coast Railway (LB&SCR) Terrier tanks – a type of locomotive which for many continues to symbolise the K&ESR. Passenger numbers reached 105,676 in 1913, a figure not to be approached again until 2000. All this ended, like so much else, in August 1914. Holman Stephens was a keen member of the Territorial Army and the appalling war which followed saw him achieve the rank of Lieutenant Colonel. He was thereafter addressed as 'Colonel', thus establishing one of the enduring elements of his mythos.

The end of the Great War brought many changes. Stephens used his not-inconsiderable influence to keep most of his railways, including the K&ESR, out of the railway Grouping of 1923, although it can be argued that the newly formed Southern Railway did not want it! The development of the internal combustion engine had benefited greatly from the conflict; large numbers of servicemen returning to civilian life had learned to drive during the war and army-surplus lorries were available at bargain prices. Freight traffic nevertheless held up comparatively well, particularly on the Rother Valley section, but the growth of competing bus services had a severe effect on passenger numbers. This was particularly true of the Headcorn extension, which was paralleled by what is now the A274. Stephens countered these developments with crude but ground-breaking railbuses, using adapted road technology. It was too late. Other economies and deferred maintenance led to an atmosphere of gentle decline and picturesque dereliction.

Stephens died in 1931. The K&ESR went into receivership, with Stephens' Assistant W.H. Austen as Receiver and General Manager. There was a clear-out of derelict rolling stock, with some replacement items coming from the Southern Railway. It was during these inter-war years that the Railway was discovered and its profile raised by railway enthusiasts. We owe a debt to these people, who doubtless never set out to give a misleading impression. Nevertheless, their photographs are of a period when the K&ESR, set in areas of great natural charm, had ceased to be prosperous but retained its individuality and contrasted markedly with the then-new homogeneity of the 'Big Four'. Such photos seem to have played a significant part in the growth of the legend which grew up about Stephens' 'empire' of ramshackle railways that had been poorly built and badly run. This happened despite the earlier view that the K&ESR had been economically built and well run. But whatever the historical truth, the K&ESR came to enchant all those who knew it.

The Railway carried on into the Second World War and this proved to be its salvation, as it was able to provide an important diversionary route. There was again a clear-out of derelict rolling stock in 1940–41, with further replacement items coming from the Southern Railway. Nationalisation and inclusion in the Southern Region (SR) of British Railways followed in 1948. Despite various improvements by the SR, traffic declined and passenger services ceased in January 1954; the section from Headcorn to Tenterden was closed altogether and the track lifted the following year. Hop pickers' specials – always an important source of K&ESR traffic – nonetheless continued on the southerly part on the Robertsbridge–Northiam section until 1958.

Meanwhile, growing affluence and leisure time for hobbies kept an ever-increasing number of enthusiasts aware of the K&ESR, and special trains sometimes appeared, including railtours in 1958 and 1959. It has been claimed that these trains did much to prepare the way for what was to follow.

The Railway was greatly simplified and deteriorated after 1954. The condition of the already weak bridge over Newmill Channel worsened. Wittersham Road station was demolished and the Rolvenden site, which had been the location of the locomotive shed, became a scene of particular desolation. The end came with the withdrawal of the freight service on Saturday, 10 June 1961 and the final farewell passenger special the following day. Earlier in the year, however, three senior pupils at Maidstone Grammar School – Tony Hocking, Gardner Crawley and Nick Rose – discussed the possibility of establishing a preservation scheme for the K&ESR. In this, they were inspired by the example of the Bluebell Railway, which had reopened the previous year. As mentioned in the Foreword, I told the tale of how the K&ESR was saved in my book *Holding the Line – Preserving the Kent & East Sussex Railway* (Alan Sutton Publishing); but an outline of the events described is appropriate before proceeding further.

Tony Hocking was contacted by an equally youthful Robin Doust and during March 1961 they laid their plans. A meeting was arranged at the Rother Valley Hotel, Northiam, on 15 April with about 125 people present. Maurice Lawson Finch, the K&ESR's first historian, was in the chair and a Steering Committee for the Kent & East Sussex Railway Preservation Society (K&ESRPS) was appointed. Robin Doust was appointed as its Secretary and became a driving force in the Society for the next few years. The aims were, at that stage, to run full passenger and freight services, winter and summer, with voluntary labour assisting a small full-time work force. It was a scheme to run, on the standard gauge, a functioning railway.

Rental of the Tenterden Town booking office was arranged and volunteer working parties began to appear from October onwards, work beginning with the clearance of undergrowth and track maintenance. No-one at that time had any notion of the battle that lay ahead. At the other end of the line, the proprietors of Hodson's Mill, Robertsbridge, had acquired ex-SE&CR P Class No. 31556 from BR to work the short section of line from Robertsbridge station to Northbridge Street to allow grain wagons continued access to their premises. The Railway has always tended to be somewhat 'Tenterden centred', despite repeated efforts to the contrary. The earliest of these was the arrival at Northiam Station of a group of younger members who were attending King's College School, Wimbledon. The adjacent former staff cottages were later also taken over and this established a presence which, with varying groups of people, was to continue right through to the eventual return of a train service to Northiam and allowed the station to remain in reasonably good order.

British Railways had agreed not to lift the track while negotiations were in progress and an offer to sell the Tenterden–Rolvenden section to the K&ESRPS in January 1962 was enlarged in June to include the whole of the route to Robertsbridge. It was not however until September 1963 that the purchase price become known – £36,000 (approximately £640,000 at 2023 values, or double that relative to earnings). Three locomotives had been donated to the Society by this stage although, being small 0-4-0s, none was suitable for serious traffic. The most unusual to many eyes was *Gervase*, a vertical boilered Sentinel rebuild of a Manning Wardle. *Dom*, a more conventional Sentinel that had once been part of a Jersey Eastern railcar, and *Marcia*, a very small side-tank Peckett. Potentially more useful motive power began to arrive during 1964 with the newly formed Kent & East Sussex Locomotive Trust's (K&ESLT) purchase of 0-6-0STs *Charwelton* (a Manning Wardle) and *Hastings* (a Hunslet). This rolling stock owning group, although made up of Preservation Society members, was independent of the K&ESRPS and today continues to provide valuable practical and financial support. It also set the pattern for other support groups which were to follow.

Most significantly, Terrier No. 32670 – otherwise the last surviving K&ESR locomotive, No. 3 *Bodiam* – was privately purchased and arrived at Robertsbridge under its own power. It was later joined by Terrier No. 32650 which became named *Sutton* in recognition of it being owned by the Borough of the same name. Both Terriers had initially to remain at the main line junction pending BR permission to move them up the line, whereas the other locomotives were firstly at Tenterden and from part way through 1964 at Rolvenden.

The first of the preservation-era rolling stock also arrived in the form of several three-plank open wagons which were acquired from Woolwich Arsenal. In August 1964, from the same source, came the first passenger vehicle – the Woolwich Coach. This ex-L&NWR North London line vehicle was to see some restoration and use on works trains (and as a 'board room'!) but it was to be the twenty-first century before it entered full passenger service. It is also worth mentioning a South Eastern Railway bogie coach body purchased from Ashford Works early in 1964, which went into use at the end of Tenterden platform as a mess coach. In this role it is remembered by the long-serving K&ESR members who fondly look back to it as a weekend home and centre for a growing volunteer railway community with its sights set firmly on a distant horizon.

With motive power, wagons and an enthusiastic workforce it was actually possible to run a works train during Whitsun Bank Holiday weekend in 1964. *Dom*, which was never restored to running order, acted as brake van. This train was, among other things, run in connection with (for those days) a major project to relay Northiam loop. Clearance, track maintenance, work on the locomotives and rolling stock, not to mention innumerable other tasks, went on during this period and, with some faltering brought about by the course of events, right up to the eventual reopening of the line. Conditions were, to say the least, rudimentary and work was often conducted with little more than hand tools. An early p-way vehicle was, famously, a pre-war Morris 20 fitted with flanged wheels. This was later replaced by Wickham trolleys. That much was achieved in these conditions is remarkable – although the difficulties themselves often contributed to the challenge!

Despite these upbeat sounding developments, progress towards acquiring the Railway had stalled. British Railways' statement that the asking price for the K&ESR was £36,000 had been accompanied by the news that a local member of the Society (who preferred to remain anonymous) was prepared to provide much of the necessary finance. This was matched by the Society's own efforts to raise money and the formation of a Kent & East Sussex Railway Company. The local backer then withdrew his offer, but it was replaced during 1964 by an alternative scheme proposed by another member, George Pickin. This was, however, on terms unacceptable to many of the Railway's supporters. One outcome of these events was that the preservation project lost, to the new prospective backer, the use of the Kent & East Sussex name for a registered company. This was not remedied until 2003. At one stage, the Society was given 28 days to complete purchase of the line, after which Mr Pickin would in effect have first refusal. This development led to the Society considering having to lift and sell the track between Northiam and Tenterden to raise the necessary money, it being intended that the track east of Northiam would be replaced as money and opportunity permitted. This dire possibility was avoided by the election in October 1964 of a Labour government which immediately halted the sale of disused lines, pending its revision of national transport policy.

This coincidence was remarkable, and has been commented on as typical of the close-run things which have characterised K&ESR history. I have previously noted elsewhere that difficulties in the 'politics' of the heritage-era K&ESR have often been the reverse of solid achievements at the practical 'coalface'. At this stage, when the continued existence of the Railway was far from certain, the Society had the foresight to purchase Pullman cars *Barbara* and *Theodora*, thus laying the foundations for the Wealden Pullman dining train – one of the most innovative and successful services of a then only dreamt of K&ESR future. Both were delivered to Robertsbridge in September 1964.

The scheme for purchasing the Railway which members found unacceptable effectively disappeared during 1965. Disagreements about which section of the line to reopen first, however, continued within the K&ESRPS, and were resolved at the time in favour of Robertsbridge–Bodiam. BR now offered the line to the Society again for £36,000. The Society accepted the offer although, despite a negotiated bank loan of £15,000, it would remain necessary to sell the track from the Northiam–Tenterden section. Finance generally was being raised by the Rother Valley Railway Trust Fund, which had been formed at the beginning of the year. A Special General Meeting to endorse the proposed purchase was convened on 18 December 1965. As if to emphasise this development, a rake of four Maunsell Restriction '1' coaches had during the previous month joined the growing collection in Robertsbridge yard.

On 1 January 1966, the K&ESRPS amalgamated with the Westerham Valley Railway Association, which lost its line because of plans for what would in time become the M25. Their members dispersed in various directions, but the core group went to the Kent & East Sussex and the combined organisation became the Kent & East Sussex Railway Association (K&ESRA). Also early in 1966, a further private company to own the line was formed as the Rother Valley Railway Company Ltd (not to be confused with the similarly named present-day company which is concerned with restoring the link from Bodiam to Robertsbridge).

The K&ESRA signed the contract to purchase the line from British Railways at a ceremony held at Tenterden Town Hall on 30 March 1966. The Association then had to make application for a Light Railway Transfer Order (LRTO) with a view to operating in the summer of 1967. Positive progress was to be seen in the trains run on 11 and 23 April and at the Whitsun Bank Holiday to move the stock berthed in Robertsbridge yard up to Rolvenden. The Terriers were used for this purpose and the relocated stock included GWR Railcar W20W, which had actually been delivered by rail – tipped to one side – as the widest vehicle ever to pass through the Hastings line tunnels between Robertsbridge and Tonbridge in their pre-electrification condition. A further historic diesel obtained during 1966 was the BTH Bo-Bo diesel electric locomotive which was donated by the Ford Motor Company. The locomotive arrived by road, in fact, and with some difficulty, by way of Tenterden's Station Road, a thoroughfare which was in part even narrower than it is today. Fifty years later 'the Ford' was still running on the K&ESR as the world's oldest operational diesel-electric.

Objections to the LRTO were not heard until March 1967, but when there had been no decision by August, re-opening was postponed until Easter the following year. The news was however brighter on the financial front where there was now sufficient available, or promised, for the threat of having to lift the Northiam–Tenterden section to have gone away. Work to prepare the Kent & East Sussex for reopening continued. Then, on 4 September, a letter was received from the Ministry of Transport. The LRTO had been refused on the grounds that the level crossings would possibly be a hindrance to traffic, particularly on the A21 at Robertsbridge, and that any future road improvements could result in bridges having to be built at the public expense. The point was also made that the Association had insufficient resources to cover unforeseen costs in the event of some emergency, and the river authority was concerned should any of the bridges over the various water courses collapse. That the preservation scheme survived this body blow and, against the odds, went on to succeed exemplifies the commitment and determination which have served the Railway so well through half a century. It should nevertheless be added that, although the K&ESR had been early in the field of standard gauge preservation, the scheme lost its original momentum. It took many years to fully recover and was a significant factor in many later difficulties.

A case was brought against the Minister of Transport, Barbara Castle, on the grounds that she had exceeded her powers in refusing the LRTO on the basis of arguments and evidence which had not been presented to the applicants. The Association's first move was to obtain an interim injunction preventing BR from lifting the track. There then also began a ferocious parliamentary lobbying campaign with many MPs receiving representations on the subject. This resulted in an adjournment debate in the House of Commons on 7 December 1967. The assistance of the Rt. Hon. William Deedes, the MP for Ashford, both at this time and subsequently, cannot be underestimated. A further personality of great importance was Peter Benge-Abbott, volunteer and businessman, who was appointed Chairman in early 1968. Not only did he take a firm control of what could have become a organisation in terminal decline but implemented two crucial changes. Firstly, he ensured that efforts towards initial reopening were concentrated on the Tenterden–Rolvenden section. Secondly, he saw through a policy change under which the objective of a full freight and passenger service was changed to the intention to run a tourist railway. After ten years of outstanding commitment, Robin Doust's involvement wound down at this time. He later emigrated, but often returned to Britain and stayed in touch with the K&ESR until his death in 2008.

The Association was not successful in obtaining a full injunction against British Railways, but in the event, BR agreed not to carry out any demolition until the court case against the Ministry of Transport had been heard. There was a long wait before the case was heard, and these were grim times for the Association. Eventually, in February 1970, the High Court decided in favour of the Association. BR immediately appealed, and the Court of Appeal overturned the decision.

But once again this was not to be the end. The long wait for the court case to be heard had been used productively to plan a way ahead. Prominent in this were Peter Davis, who had succeeded Peter-Benge Abbott as Chairman during 1970, and Philip Shaw, who was still actively involved at the time of writing. Negotiations with the Ministry and the local authorities had emphasised the change in policy to a tourist railway and also led to the agreement that the K&ESR would only run from Tenterden to Bodiam. This sacrifice of Bodiam to Robertsbridge was entirely necessary – the only other choice was failure. Understandably, this outcome was not universally popular and, although accepted for twenty years under the pressure of events, a desire to recover this 'lost territory' would linger and later resurface.

British Railways now valued the line at £60,000 and was prepared to take £20,000 as a down payment with a mortgage for the remainder. Work of course continued on the line and the rolling stock, and in March 1970 BR eased a ban they had imposed on train movements by allowing a 'steam up' within the confines of Rolvenden yard. Hodson's Mill had meanwhile stopped using rail traffic after a period during which both Terrier *Sutton* and the 'Ford' had covered these shunting duties. As a result, the K&ESR was able to acquire the mill's 'P' class locomotive in 1971. The same year also saw the arrival of the ex-Norwegian State Railway 2-6-0 tender locomotive which, like the 'P', was to become an increasingly popular resident of the K&ESR over the following fifty years.

Application could now again be made for a Light Railway Transfer Order and there were also significant changes to the K&ESR corporate structure under the guidance of Philip Shaw. The Rother Valley Railway Company, the Trust Fund and the Association were all wound up, effectively from May 1971, and were replaced by the Tenterden Railway Company, which was Limited by Guarantee and subsequently achieved the status of a Registered Charity. A wholly-owned private company, known today as Colonel Stephens Railway Enterprises, was later added to allow commercial trading in respect of books, souvenirs and catering. The K&ESR was not the first heritage railway to be Limited by Guarantee – the Welshpool and Llanfair was the inspiration for the idea – but it was the first to add charitable status. This corporate structure was innovative in the heritage railway movement and has been copied in varying degrees elsewhere.

In January 1972, the final clearance of Robertsbridge yard was carried out in anticipation of the demolition of the line to Bodiam. The stock moved included two ex-SE&CR Birdcage coaches and other items which had come from the failed scheme for the Longmoor Military Railway. The heritage-era K&ESR had first been used for location filming during the gloomy autumn of 1967, and this was followed by a TV comedy series in 1972 and a drama in 1973. Such film contracts would increase with the years and prove to be not only a useful money raising activity but a source of good publicity. Other work, both practical and legal, continued through 1972 and 1973 with the volunteers champing at the bit to run a service. The long march towards beginning to reopen the K&ESR was however drawing to a close. The British Railways Board (Kent & East Sussex Railway) Light Railway (Transfer & Amendment) Order came into force on 8 November 1973. There was a dress rehearsal members-only service on Boxing Day 1973, and a Railway Inspectorate visit on the section from Tenterden to a point some way past Rolvenden on 21 January 1974. Then, suddenly, it was not next year any more, it was next week; and on a bright and crisp Sunday, 3 February, without ceremony, the GWR railcar ran the first train. The second was the two Maunsell brakes hauled by Terrier *Sutton*, resplendent in the apple green livery at one time used by the old Company. The Kent & East Sussex Railway was beginning to reopen.

Chapter 2

'The Railway is ours.' Thus wrote the editor of the new in-house journal, *The Tenterden Terrier*, which in March 1974 replaced *The Farmers' Line*, the magazine which in various forms dated back to 1961 and the start of the preservation era. Sunday, 3 February, the date of the first public trains, had been the culmination of so much. The *Terrier* had nonetheless to remind its readers that the Tenterden Railway Company had 'acquired a whole host of responsibilities' and that this was 'a considerable challenge in itself'.

Having seen the Railway through to reopening, Peter Davis resigned as Chairman soon after 3 February and was replaced by Stephen Bennett. Writing in the July *Terrier* Peter nevertheless reminded the membership that 'the 2½ mile section just reopened is only the tip of the iceberg…' and that the 'effort expended on its preparation was minimal compared with what will be needed to restore the remaining 7½ miles'.

Otherwise, an enduring impression is of the Railway retaining much of its pre-reopening atmosphere until at least the end of 1974. At this point, I had been away from regular volunteering for several years, although I had kept in contact by way of continuing membership and irregular visits. The reasons were those usual for young volunteers – career studies and the pursuit of girls. The former was time consuming and ultimately proved of more use to the K&ESR than to the London Borough which paid for it! With regard to the latter activities, it says everything about the time it had taken to revive the K&ESR that I had first arrived in 1961 as 14-year-old schoolboy and travelled to the re-opening with my wife.

The Tenterden Railway Company did however now have new responsibilities and two enormous differences; passengers and all the obligations of running a public service. The initial three-train Sundays-only service lasted until just 23 March. Saturday running then commenced, with a maximum of five trains per day, a minimum of three on Sundays and use of the GWR railcar on first train of the day. The first timetable – a duplicated A4 sheet – had a most nostalgic feel to it; it was in the exact style of much K&ESR paperwork of the 1961–74 era. Early attempts at publicity included participation in 'Steam Lines South East', a joint marketing initiative with the Bluebell, Sittingbourne & Kemsley and Romney Hythe & Dymchurch railways. There was a perceived need to get the Railway much better known, and by implication bring it out from the shadow of more established lines. This was to be an ongoing problem for years to come.

There was notable stock movement from Northiam to Wittersham Road on 18 May, which was related in the Winter 1974 *Tenterden Terrier* by someone writing under the pseudonym of 'Cornerseat':

> It was in the summer of 1970 that we were successful in obtaining from the Longmoor Military Railway two SECR Birdcage coaches for use on the Kent & East Sussex. These coaches were delivered to Robertsbridge by rail, and then taken to Northiam on the very last train ever to run from Robertsbridge prior to dismantling of the section to Junction

Road, in February 1972. The need to be able to accommodate more passengers in each train – their seating capacity is 70 compared with a BSO's 36 – was the prime reason for getting these splendid coaches back in to use again, and before this could be done they had to be moved to Rolvenden, across three weak bridges. A civil engineer was called in for inspection and, following some remedial work, the bridges were passed fit to carry the proposed train, provided certain conditions were adhered to.

It was soon after 10.15am that *Arthur*, [Manning Wardle 0-6-0ST No 1601 of 1903. On the K&ESR 1967–85] the engine selected for the move, eased out of the yard and off down the line towards 'the barrier' which is the present limit of passenger operations. As a 10mph speed limit is in force beyond the barrier, it was nearly 11.30 am before *Arthur* chugged into the station, the first steam engine to visit Northiam for eight years. Her passage through the 'jungle' was evident by the varied assortment of wild flowers, grass and undergrowth on the motion and various other parts of the locomotive. She looked a strange sight, with a steel cable coiled around her smokebox door and a pump and hose perched on top of her boiler. In need of refreshment after the journey, *Arthur* moved to the end of the loop where the hose was uncoiled and connected to the main water supply in the cottages adjacent to the line. The move was to include a Maunsell coach and an ex-LMR brake van in addition to the two birdcages, and the shunting was quite a complicated manoeuvre. At about 2.30pm the procession moved on its way, crossed the A28 and plunged into the undergrowth. A gap in the vegetation indicated that we were approaching the 66ft span of the Rother Bridge and the train slowed to a crawl as we gingerly crossed the bridge. Another half a mile on we came to the Hexden Channel bridge, halting just short of it for an inspection. Our engineer had recommended that, in order to avoid placing too great a stress on the bridge abutments, we should tow each coach over individually – hence the steel rope carried lasso-style by *Arthur*.

It was all hands on the rope as *Arthur* moved across the bridge in readiness for the first pull. Shouts like 'Take the strain' and 'Slowly does it' were followed by 'Handbrake on, someone' until the first coach was safely over the bridge. The operation was repeated three times before the train was formed up again ready for the ascent of Wittersham bank. The thick hedges along the bank are quite a sanctuary for wildlife, and we disturbed the numerous small birds which flitted from bush to bush in front of us. As the gradient steepened, the train got slower and slower… until at last she lost her grip and stopped. The slope had proved too great for our 1903 veteran with her 120 ton load. Backwards we went, a few hundred yards down the track, while the crew sanded the rails in front of us. Then *Arthur* tried again, and once again failed. At the third attempt we moved slowly to the summit and coasted down the bank into Wittersham Road station, pausing first at the ungated level crossing on the road to Wittersham village.

The Shell tanker stabled here for the weed-killing gang to use as water storage came in very useful, and the pump and hose were again put to good use to replenish *Arthur's* water tanks. Soon we were off again, minus the Maunsell coach (left in the siding) along a track which, thanks to the stalwart efforts of many clearance gangs, was now virtually devoid of vegetation. The final pause came at Newmill Channel bridge, and the same procedure of one vehicle at a time was adopted. At about 6.30 pm we were able to report to the signalman at Tenterden that the mission was complete. He arranged for the staff to be brought out to the barrier quickly and so, as we rounded the final curve, we saw *Bodiam* – which had earlier been handling the scheduled passenger service – whistling and coming head-on for us on the single track. However the barrier separated us and 20 yards short of it we halted. The padlock was unfastened, the barrier swung open and *Bodiam* backed on to Arthur for a double-headed run into Rolvenden in fine style. Thus ended an unforgettable and nostalgic journey which particularly reminded the writer of the wanderings of Manning Wardles on the overgrown tracks of the Wissington Light Railway in the Fen country of East Anglia, and other rural byways now gone forever.

Saturday, 23 March had originally been chosen as the date for the official reopening, but this had been postponed as a consequence of the coal shortage caused by the miners' strike of that winter. The ceremony finally took place on Saturday, 1 June as the bunting fluttered, the crowd bustled and the warm summer sun shone. The event was described in the *Tenterden Terrier* No. 5, Spring 1974, by Roger Crawford who had been Secretary during the years when the tide of fortune had begun to turn in the Railway's favour.

For anyone who has been associated with the struggle to save the Kent & East Sussex Railway, Saturday, 1 June 1974 was a memorable occasion. It did not matter that public services had restarted last winter; this day was the real climax to a long and unique battle, a battle whose full and intriguing story has yet to be told. There, against all the odds, was proof positive of victory – an elegant white card conveying the joyous nature of the occasion in formal phrases, 'The Directors of the Tenterden Railway Company Ltd. cordially invite . . . to the official re-opening of the Kent & East Sussex Railway by the Rt. Hon. William Deedes, M.C., D.L., M.P.' What a privilege to be asked! When my wife and I walked down Station Road that day, we found the Station in festive mood. There was the Cranbrook Town Band, bunting, crowds in shirt sleeves and summer dresses, cars, officials protecting the platform, the bustling yard and, of course, the guests. Inside the Booking Office, railway books and souvenirs were on sale, and outside in the sun a special table had been set up for the elegant first day postal covers to be carried on the train. On the platform, seated, in rows, were the invited guests, including Robin Doust (Founder of the Preservation Scheme); Reuben Collison, resplendent in Mayoral robes and chain; David Barham, High Sheriff of Kent and owner of the Norwegian Mogul; Peter Brown, the Appeal organiser; Sir Peter Allen, the Chairman of the Transport Trust; Lord Dundonald and, perhaps most appropriate of all, Bill Deedes, who helped the railway in its hour of need and without whose efforts it would surely not have survived. After being introduced by Company Chairman Stephen Bennett, Mr Deedes delivered an eloquent and kindly speech praising the small band of determined men who would not take no for an answer, who had defied government, objectors and all manner of obstacles to keep alive the hopes of preserving at least part of the K&ESR. Commending their success as an example of true democracy at work, Bill Deedes then moved to the platform edge, and *Sutton* steamed quietly up the platform to allow him to perform the opening ceremony in the accustomed way. Mr Deedes' enthusiastic audience joined him on the special train. I travelled on the now familiar first mile and a half, accomplished in grand style with *Sutton* at the front of the train and *Bodiam* at the rear. During the journey, the passengers were given a progress report by Company Directors Derek Dunlavey and Simon Green on the plans for the restoration of the remainder of the line. After the train ride, everyone was taken to the newly restored elegance of the Town Hall in a London double-decker bus. Negotiating the narrow station yard gate through a large crowd of spectators was not the least exciting event of the day, but this was accomplished without mishap. At the Town Hall, guests were given wine and an excellent buffet luncheon, and the Chairman and Directors moved among the party making everybody most welcome. Throughout the rest of the day special trains carried the public on this official opening day – a day which formally ended one era for the preservation movement of the Kent and East Sussex, and opened another. The Railway is alive again, and we wish it a long and successful life.

I managed to miss the official opening having moved house the previous day. In a way I didn't mind because at that time, and even looking back now, the unofficial opening in February had seemed, appropriately, to be a part of the early years and not the era that was to follow. It however set a pattern for the next two decades when family life and other priorities just did not seem to provide an opportunity to return to volunteering on the K&ESR. This is now widely recognised as a pattern in the world of heritage railways – 'You've got them until they discover girls and then you don't see them until they're 40.' My membership of TRC nonetheless continued, the *Tenterden Terrier* kept me informed, and there were, of course, those occasional visits to see what had been, and what was being, achieved.

A journey on the Railway was, with hindsight, an intriguing mixture of past and future. Two-coach trains hauled by a Terrier looked very like the K&ESR of legend but, as already mentioned, the Railway still felt much as it had in the later pioneering years. Perhaps this was inevitable; life tends to have few abrupt divisions and, give or take the sort of reverse which had occurred in September 1967, the K&ESR usually evolves. Arriving at Tenterden, it could feel odd having to obtain tickets to get on to the platform – even if one's own was a member's concession. People one knew were not just working, they were actively involved in running an operational railway controlled by the remorseless clock. After so many years of minimal use, the earthworks had to reconsolidate and the smaller locomotives were much used at first. I remember one trip, not long after reopening, with a Terrier in charge and a train made up from amongst the original four Maunsell coaches. The trip out was routine enough. Rolvenden was now firmly re-established as the loco depot, the initially open-ended shed being built towards the end of the first season. For the first couple of years trains were either 'topped and tailed' (a loco at each end) beyond Rolvenden or the loco ran round on Rolvenden loop, propelled out to the limit of operation and then hauled the train back. It hardly needs to be said that there was a widespread desire both for something more professional and to open more of the Railway, and beyond Rolvenden work to that end was well under way. But the most splendid part of the whole journey was, as ever, the ascent of Tenterden bank. The Terrier barked its way up the 1 in 50 climb and the familiar townscape came into view. The tower of St. Mildred's soared skywards and the fine peal of eight bells rang out in counterpoint. It was glorious.

The Summer 1974 issue of the *Tenterden Terrier* had seen editorship change to Philip Shaw who, as mentioned in the preface, had had a prominent role in the reopening of the line and was destined to have a very long and notable association with the K&ESR. The design of the journal changed from that of the initial three issues, No. 4 being visibly the ancestor of its evolved descendant of the twenty-first century. The Editorial included some passages which both pointed the way ahead and anticipated troublesome issues in the years to come:

> This is also the first issue of the magazine under your new Editor, and naturally there will be some changes of emphasis in editorial policy … and articles will be written to stimulate comment and contribution from those who have knowledge of the Kent and East Sussex and also of the other small railways formerly operated by the late Lt-Col H.F. Stephens. Increased emphasis on the historical side will be matched by attempts to achieve better communications between the members, and in particular between those who wish to take an active part in the running of our railway.

Communication within the Railway was to prove a continuing problem for decades to come, and a further effort to improve this aspect was under way at the time of writing. The matter of increased historical emphasis was if anything to prove even more pernicious. The same issue of the *Terrier* also included the following item:

> The Directors of the Tenterden Railway Company have decided that, in principle, a museum dedicated to the memory of the late Lt-Col H.F. Stephens should be established at Tenterden. The objectives of the museum will be to collect for public display relics relating to light railways in general and in particular to those with which Colonel Stephens was intimately connected. It must be emphasised that this is essentially a long term project, in that the more immediate financial priorities for the Company must be to restore the railway and provide the necessary facilities for its successful and profitable operation. However, the directors feel that the company should attempt to collect items as and when they may come available, and a small amount of money will be set aside for this purpose. Any member who has in his possession letters, old unpublished photographs, documents, relics etc. relating to any of the following railways which he feels he would like to donate to this cause or is prepared to sell for a small sum, is invited to contact your Editor, Philip Shaw, who is acting as liaison officer for this purpose. Progress will be fully documented in subsequent issues of *The Tenterden Terrier*.
>
> Ashover Light Railway
> East Kent Railway
> Kent & East Sussex Railway
> Rye & Camber Tramway
> Shropshire & Montgomeryshire Railway
> Snailbeach District Railways
> Weston, Clevedon & Portishead Railway
> West Sussex Railway
> Colonel Stephens' close connections with the Welsh Highland and Festiniog Railways are well known, but in view of the existence of companies specifically concerned with the preservation of these lines, it is felt inappropriate to include them on the list at this stage.

On the one hand, a heritage railway is by definition involved in the study of history. On the other, the formative years of the K&ESR project had given rise to a necessarily pragmatic attitude; and I recall that a preference for the Railway rather than the Colonel had arisen during this process. The requirements of regulatory authorities have progressively increased since the 1970s, as have the expectations of the public and commercial pressures generally. Furthermore, volunteers attracted to heritage railways may not always be motivated by a sense of history. Ego and ambition may also play their part, and for some it may be more convenient to travel to a railway nearer to home than a preferred one further away. Although a Museum did come to be seen as a valued additional visitor attraction, a division quickly emerged between 'traditionalists' (often armchair members) and 'pragmatists' (often volunteers) although the line between the two has been more blurred than this generalisation suggests. In addition, there is the allied question as to whether a railway exists to provide a hobby for its members or whether the hobby side of the organisation supports the existence of the railway. On the K&ESR all these things led, as we shall see, to tensions which have never been fully resolved.

As the 1974 season progressed, other locomotives came into use, although all had been on the line prior to reopening. First came USA No. 22 *Maunsell* on Easter Sunday, a move which supplemented the two Terriers and the Manning Wardle *Arthur* which had been operating the service since February. I remember discussing the USA's debut with a volunteer not long after the event. The loco had taken over from a Terrier at Rolvenden and was said to have 'walked' its train up the hill – such was the contrast with the Brighton veterans.

On August Bank Holiday came an indication of the future when Austerity No. 23 (later named *Holman F. Stephens*) worked a train for the first time. This was the first use in revenue earning service of a type that was to become almost as much associated with the K&ESR as the Terriers. In the first instance, Hunslet's rugged Austerity tanks were restricted to working between Tenterden and Rolvenden, but this restriction was eased as civil engineering improvements, particularly to bridges, raised the axle loading above the 10 tons in force since 1900. The organisation now long associated with the use of Austerities is Rolvenden Steam Enterprises. Rather than fragment the record of their significant contribution, an account of this locomotive owning group is to be found in Appendix A.

The first trial runs were also made with ex-Stewart and Lloyds RS&H No. 56. This massive 0-6-0ST – a further development of Hunslet's Austerity design – was so large it had to run with a reduced coal and water supply. Popularly known as Ugly, No. 56 had a shattering exhaust blast which was said to make the locomotive sound much closer than it actually was.

A notable career began at this time when Mike Hart, a K&ESR volunteer who had joined in 1967, was appointed as Mechanical Department Manager. Although known as a 'doer' and with no small hint of a charismatic personality, how many would have guessed at the significant and accomplished role this young man would play in the heritage railway movement in the decades to follow?

During these years the largest engine seen at Tenterden up to that time rested in the siding behind the station platform. This was Southern U Class 2-6-0 No. 1618. She was owned by the Southern Mogul Preservation Society, which had been formed in 1966 by some of the active K&ESR members, to preserve either an N or a U class Mogul. At this time, it was mainly small tank locomotives or large express types that were being acquired by preservationists and it was felt that a Mogul, being a medium-sized loco, would fill a gap between these extremes. Five were located in the soon-to-be-famous scrapyard of Woodham Brothers at Barry. After an inspection, No. 1618 was found to be in the best mechanical condition, and in January 1969, following purchase, she was moved by rail to a private siding near Maidstone, only the second engine to leave Barry. In 1972, after two years of restoration, it became necessary to find a new home for the engine. As virtually all of the working members of the Society also worked for the K&ESR, and had done so for a considerable time, it seemed natural that the railway should be considered as a permanent location for No. 1618. The Society knew that the engine would be too heavy for regular use on the K&ESR due to the line's axle loadings at the time, but it was felt that she would attract a great deal of attention from the general public at Tenterden and at the same time she could be well looked after. The tender was moved by low loader in June 1972, but transfer of the engine was a far more complex matter as the weight and length meant hiring a multi-wheeled transporter, which took place in late October. This heavy vehicle and its load caused a great deal of interest in Tenterden. Following further restoration work, No. 1618 was successfully steamed for the first time on 15 May 1974. While at Tenterden the Mogul always looked splendid in her Maunsell era green and showed this magnificent livery off to advantage. Movements continued to be restricted to Tenterden Station limits as the infrastructure improvements necessary to accommodate a Maunsell Mogul were years away, and No. 1618 relocated to the Bluebell Railway in 1977 – a move which some regret to this day.

There were stirrings of important developments for the future during that first season. June and July had seen an increasing number of special workings. Some of these were filming jobs – although this had also occurred during the closed period – but others including a firm's outing and a wedding involved the use of Pullman Car *Barbara*. This was the acorn from which a great oak would grow – but more on this in a moment. Santa Specials were also seen for the first time at 12.15pm on 15, 22 and 26 December. This also highly successful formula soon spread elsewhere. The Keighley & Worth Valley Railway was the originator of this idea, but it may be that the K&ESR was the first to feature Santa Claus doing his rounds on a moving train.

38,833 passengers were carried during that first year – less than the 50,000 aimed for, but that had been a guess. More disappointing was the poor response to an Appeal, launched in October 1973, to raise £50,000 towards reopening the remainder of the line over a period of seven years. By the autumn of 1974, only £11,766 had been promised. With the national economy threatening to go into meltdown, this could have been a reflection of the times and, in a foretaste of things to come, the reopening of most of the Railway was postponed. These were not good years in Britain and, with the industrial unrest, inflation and political uncertainty, the bright hopes of the 1960s faded. Ironically, the early 1970's were the same years in which, nationally, the heritage railway movement built the firm foundations on which it has since rested.

It is worth pausing for a moment to look at the K&ESR in the wider context of the heritage railway scene in Southern England. Mention has already been made of the 'Steam Lines South East' initiative, and it should be remembered that the arrival of the K&ESR as an operating line had ended the Bluebell's long monopoly on standard gauge in the region. Something of an exception to this monopoly at that time was the short-lived Ashford Steam Centre, which operated on the site of the former loco shed between 1968 and 1976. It was from here in April 1974 that Merchant Navy Class No. 35028 *Clan Line* departed to work the first railtour of the Southern contribution to the 'Return to Steam' programme. This highly symbolic event was repeated the following October, No. 35028 taking over at Stratford-upon-Avon a special which had come across country from the Welsh Marches line. Even here there was a K&ESR connection when Alan Crotty, whom I had known as a volunteer at Tenterden, turned up as one of the support crew. Forty years later we were still able to reminisce about *Clan Line*'s infamous slipping start out of Stratford-upon-Avon Station.

Chapter 3

1975 marked the 75th anniversary of the K&ESR, or the Rother Valley Railway as it had been in 1900. The Spring issue of the *Tenterden Terrier* featured a plea by Eric Tonks – a well-known authority on industrial railways – for the retention of lineside trees, and a Peter Davis article about Hunslet Austerities. Both writers had expressed views on either side of the debate already referred to and which would gain momentum as the years went by – authenticity versus upgrading. That same issue of the *Terrier* stated that the limit of operation was 1¾ miles from Wittersham Road, but on 18 May it was extended further on to the 'Pope's Cottage' permanent way hut. Meanwhile, another development, albeit of a non-operational kind, was the agreement with Tenterden Council for a section of the Town Museum, which had been created by local historian Hugh Roberts, to be used for the planned collection relating to Colonel Stephens and his railways. This too would grow into greater things in later years. Meanwhile, the site used was most appropriate – the Town Museum had once been the Railway's stables. The Spring 1975 issue of the *Terrier* also reported that the locomotive shed had been completed at Rolvenden (the first stage of the one still extant in the third decade of the twenty-first century) and was proving a very valuable addition to repair facilities. An inspection pit had been constructed in load-bearing brickwork, it being intended to construct another pit on the second road when the shed was extended and when funds permitted. The same issue of the journal also mentioned that coach No. 57 was receiving an exterior repaint. This vehicle is of some interest in the ex tempore development of volunteer accommodation on the K&ESR. This had grown from chaotic occupation of the booking office at Tenterden to the arrival of the famous and fondly remembered SE&CR coach body at the rear of Tenterden platform and to the use of an old van body in Rolvenden Yard. No. 57 had been a First Corridor built for the Hastings Line in 1929. The vehicle had been a work study coach (081621) from 1961 to 1971, in which latter year it had arrived at Tenterden with the interior gutted. It was quickly converted for use as the S&T Department mess and sleeping coach.

The K&ESR's 75th anniversary was celebrated on Saturday, 22 March (the actual date was 2 April). Only people in late Victorian costume were allowed on to the platform at Rolvenden to greet the Terrier and two birdcage coaches of the special train. This was perhaps the first manifestation of a tendency for dressing up which was to affect some, although by no means all, areas of the Railway. The limit of operation duly reached Pope's Cottage on 18 May 1975. By August it was reported that the Wine & Dine specials were very popular and fully booked.

The *Terrier* for Summer 1975 included details about the proposed extension to Wittersham Road, the reader having had this emphasised from the start by the editorial on page 2:

Forward to Wittersham

Included in this issue is an article by our Chairman, outlining the development programme for the Railway over the next two years. If all goes according to plan we shall be running four miles of railway through to Wittersham Road station during the 1977 season, giving us for the first time a terminus at both ends of the line from which passengers may alight or join the trains. The capital expenditure necessary to achieve this objective is considerable, and under present economic conditions our best hope of raising the revenue is to increase the number of passengers travelling on each train. Although we carried 37,833 passengers last year, and we have hopes of a slight improvement this season, the average number per train was only 91 and we had the capacity to carry at least twice as many within the framework of the existing service. We certainly need to publicise the attractions of our railway and perhaps we need to provide additional amenities to encourage more visitors to come to Tenterden. The proposed 'Colonel Stephens' museum is one amenity which is being actively pursued, and an important announcement concerning the siting of the museum will be made in our next issue. If you have an idea which could help us to increase passenger numbers, write to the Editor about it. All suggestions will be carefully examined by the Company management and a selection will be published in the *Tenterden Terrier*.

The item by the Chairman told members that the Board had considered two main options as a result of the experience gained during the first season. One was to continue the steady advance south-westwards from Rolvenden and the other was to reinstate the Bodiam end as a separate entity. Probably wisely, the Board adopted the first option. The prohibitive cost was given as the reason, although one is reminded of the conventional wisdom about fighting on two fronts. Public services to Wittersham Road were planned for March 1977.

An integral part of the scheme was signalling at Tenterden Town and a temporary installation at Rolvenden. These improvements were necessary to permit a half hourly interval service but, even without distant signals, involved installations on a scale unknown on the K&ESR. This was to cause comment and neatly illustrated the growing pragmatic pressures on more traditionalist views. Less controversially, plans were in hand to replace the undermined Newmill Channel Bridge, the Army having already conducted geological and soil surveys. Having long vanished, Wittersham Road station would need to be rebuilt, five-coach loops being planned both for that location and at Rolvenden. It is interesting to note the 'front line' participation of Area Groups at that time; Tunbridge Wells was to build the platform while the South East London Group was to undertake the trackwork. We shall be meeting the South East London Group (or at least its successor) again, and in a quite far-reaching context.

Occasional insights into life on the K&ESR were sometimes to be found in the pages of the *Terrier*, one such example being an item by driver Norman Denty in the Winter 1975 issue:

The Railway's first engine failure since reopening happened on Saturday, 5th July. I came on duty at Rolvenden at 3.40pm and worked No 19 (The Norwegian Mogul) which was heading the 3.30pm train, back to Tenterden. The engine was run round and coupled up in readiness for the 4.30pm departure, which was fully booked. At about 4.18pm there was a loud bang, followed by steam and smoke entering the cab by way of the fire-hole door. The water level in the gauge glass started to fall alarmingly and the steam gauge pointer began to move towards zero. I put on the injectors to try to maintain the water level in the boiler, but a boiler tube had burst and it was impossible to even move the locomotive. Fireman Brian Muston was sent to Rolvenden by car with the 'staff' in order to summon relief locomotive No. 3 and, in accordance with Kent & East Sussex Railway rules, detonators were put down on the line, 100 yards from Tenterden station, to protect the disabled train in the platform. My main concern was that that the firebox crown plate would become uncovered through lack of water in the boiler and hence damaged, but in the event most of the water from the boiler entered the firebox by way of the burst tube, which in turn almost put the fire out. Off duty fireman Chris Mitchell was at hand and dropped the fire into the ashpan; fortunately No. 19 has a lever which opens up part of the grate area. Within 20 minutes the boiler was empty and the steam gauge almost at zero. The explosion of detonators heralded the arrival of No. 3 and driver Colin Edwards and fireman Paul Wilson came over to give us assistance. The 4.30pm train left Tenterden at 4.50pm, with No. 3 piloting the now 'dead' No. 19. At Rolvenden No. 19 was shunted off and the train proceeded with No. 3 to the limit and back to Tenterden, arriving only 20 minutes late.

I was pleased that we had maintained our tradition of never having had to cancel a scheduled steam train. Later, I examined the disabled locomotive with Mechanical Department Manager Mike Hart. We could see that one of the six small tubes next to the larger flues had split. As the superheater tubes are inside these large flues, the six tubes were left in place when the locomotive was re-tubed last year, as replacement would have meant taking out the superheaters. However the work has now been put in hand, and No. 19 is likely to be back in service before the season ends.

A significant innovation encouraged by the use of a Pullman Car during the previous year was the introduction of a 'Wine & Dine' service, again making use of *Barbara*. As received in September 1964, the vehicle had been configured as a buffet car. It was thanks to the efforts of Paul Ramsden and Alan Castle of the Carriage & Wagon Department that tables were available for the new service – the beginning of a process that eventually led to *Barbara* being restored to parlour car condition. A Pullman train first ran on 5 July 1975 and then on alternate Saturdays through that summer. This was the first such service on a heritage railway (later much emulated) and, despite the very 1970s title, the beginnings of the Wealden Pullman service. The years after reopening saw a continuing and marked growth in popularity of the Pullman trains, which at first offered a 'Chef's Cold Collation' but later became the Wealden Pullman when hot food began to be served.

Two contemporary accounts of the early Pullman service are worth quoting, the first by K&ESR volunteer, and later Board member, John Liddell:

We are certainly most fortunate in having two lovely Pullman cars in which to entertain our guests, but it was with some trepidation that I arranged for a party of 14 to sample the first 1975 Special on 5th July. As a largely voluntary organisation, would we be able to offer 44 members of the public a four-course dinner representing value for money at £4 per head? [approximately £30 at 2023 values]. First impressions are always important and my initial fears were quickly dispelled when, peering through the windows of 'Barbara' it was apparent that our tables had been meticulously laid. White table cloths, printed menu cards, table napkins and attractive floral arrangements all combined to give a favourable impression and the 'Pullman Bar' was equally well arranged and obviously well stocked. Promptly at 7.45pm *Bodiam* gently descended the bank, and within seconds waitresses appeared with hot soup. Fresh cold salmon or cold beef and salad followed, while our 'Maitre de Train', Donald Wilson, went up and down the gangway ensuring that our wine glasses remained filled. Before long the train reached the 'limit' and here we remained for some time, in a truly rural setting with just a few cows nearby, curious to see what was going on. Strawberries and cream followed the main course and then a selection of cheeses. Coffee was served as the train came back to Rolvenden and we then returned to the limit once more, as the sun was setting, to enjoy our liqueurs. Time no longer mattered as *Bodiam* climbed the bank back to Tenterden and, as we drew into the station, it seemed to have acquired a completely different character from daytime, with the brightly lit platform and signal box. Our thanks to Catering Manager Terence Mann, and to everybody who contributed to such a memorable evening; my only criticism – it was too cheap a price to pay!

The second account was from the well-known railway historian and photographer Dr Ian C. Allen, who concluded an item about his travels on the K&ESR which had begun in 1932:

Last August I visited the Railway again, on one of the Wine & Dine specials, and what a memorable occasion it was. I shall never forget arriving at Tenterden on that glorious evening to find that No. 3 was to have the train – I had so hoped that it would be her; and then the consummation of a boyhood ambition – to travel in the complete comfort of a first class Pullman. I shall never forget that glorious sunset down the track, apparently miles away from anywhere, with no house, road or car visible. It cannot have been easy to produce such a good dinner; everybody was so cheerful, flowers on the table, spotless silver and glass and the excellence of the meal.

The Pullmans in fact proved to be so successful that it is no exaggeration to say that they have underpinned the subsequent operation of the K&ESR. Through the 1975 season the shape of difficulties faced by, and likely to be faced by, the Railway were becoming apparent. These were summed up in the Editorial in the Winter issue of the *Terrier*.

The Tenterden Railway Company Ltd recorded a surplus of income over expenditure amounting to £1445 in 1974, its first operating season. This is a modest enough achievement and, as the Chairman noted in his report accompanying the accounts, 'has allowed for little to be re-invested in restoring the 7¼ miles of railway which still remain derelict'. Until comparatively recently any new railway preservation project appeared to be assured of instant financial success, but in the current economic climate the realities are very different. Nevertheless the proliferation of new schemes continues unabated, many involving hundreds of thousands of pounds. Do the promoters of these schemes really study the economics of railway operation before launching forth with their ambitious prospectuses? 1975 is proving to be an even more difficult year for the Kent & East Sussex Railway, but the most pressing need is also a comparatively modest one. £7000 is required for the Newmill Bridge project by next March if the Railway is to reopen to Wittersham in 1977. This is equivalent to a mere £5 from every Company member. Surely this is a small sacrifice that everyone will wish to make to enable us to take the next leap forward?

This theme was continued in the Spring 1976 issue of the *Terrier* which stated that the Railway carried 33,535 passengers in 1975, an 11 per cent reduction on 1974, although the figures were not necessarily comparable as numbers were swelled in February and March 1974 by the 'novelty' aspect following reopening, and in addition the 1975 season did not commence until March.

Passenger numbers for the latter months of 1975 had however shown an improvement on the corresponding period of the previous year. The result of a 1975 Bank Holiday traffic census suggested that there were large areas of potential business which still remained untapped, in particular the South Coast towns. This was to prove a continuing problem in the twenty-first century, the cause being variously attributed to competition from the Bluebell Railway and the East Sussex road system.

Despite these worrying trends, a positive aspect was the activities of the Area Groups, and since before the initial reopening these had been a feature of the preserved K&ESR. It is worth quoting a 1975 *Tenterden Terrier* report to illustrate their activities:

News from Area Groups

London. The London Area Group is an expansion of the Blackheath Youth Group which, under the leadership of Gordon Laming, covers South and South East London and Thames-side. Until the opening of the line the Group looked after the section from Rolvenden to the former limit of operation, but the Group has now left this section to keep the boys away from moving trains. The present work is in the vicinity of Wittersham Road station. This first involved the clearing of undergrowth and stacking the heavy metal sleepers stored there. The culvert has had to be extended to make way for the new passing loop and the laying of new pipes. The work coincided with recent flooding, but the boys – in this case from St Dunstan's College, Catford – worked willingly with their feet in water. The trench was filled in with ash from the old goods platform by boys from Welling and Bexley with some help from the Tunbridge Wells Group. Over Easter most of the earthwork was completed and the points are now ready for reinstatement further up the line. The Group has also cleared a space in Rolvenden yard for three new containers, near to the site of Jimmy Norton's notorious ticket printing hut.

During the excavations a few pieces of type and a bottle of (Stephens) ink were discovered. The Youth Group, which is affiliated to the Inner London Education Authority, now has a following of nearly 200. To help with transport they have secured two buses; one is a 56-seater double-deck Southdown Leyland and the other a 35-seater 'Lincolnshire' Bristol. Both buses have been restored to original condition, and last year the 'Southdown' attended a few bus rallies. London bus driver Dick Deacon gives his services free, which reduces costs considerably. The Group has also been busy at 2 Railway Cottages, Northiam, repainting three rooms and making structural repairs. The area round the cottage has been tidied up and the outside is to be painted this year. In the old days, this cottage used to be occupied by ganger Dickie Hills.

Maidstone. A very lively committee has been formed and during April the first open meeting was held. It is planned to have meetings on the last Thursday of every month – the venue being the Methodist Youth Centre, Brewer Street, Maidstone, at 7.30pm. The pattern of meetings is a short talk on a specific subject, a film or slide programme and a panel discussion where questions from the floor are answered. Other activities include working parties, publicity and exhibitions. In March and April an attractive display was mounted in the offices of the Hastings and Thanet Building Society in Maidstone. Officers of the Group are Simon Green (Acting Chairman), John Liddell (Secretary),

David Felton (Treasurer and Sales Officer) and Jack Fox (Publicity Officer). Although the main objective of the Group is to encourage membership of the Tenterden Railway Company, all are welcome to attend meetings and there is no admission charge.

Surrey. The Surrey Group has made a flying start to the 1975 exhibition season and its members have attended events in Chelmsford, Greenwich, Grayshott, Eastleigh and Eltham, in addition to their own Holy Trinity Halls Model Railway Exhibition in Guildford. It should perhaps be explained that Surrey Group regard their title as applying to a base of operations rather than a limit on the area covered. The 1975 Holy Trinity Model Railway Exhibition was an even greater success than usual, with an attendance of well over 1800 people. Our thanks are due to all the clubs and individuals who put in so much hard work to raise the £300 profit which this event realised. In particular the model layouts themselves are largely provided by clubs and individuals having no direct link with the K&ESR. Notable exceptions this year were Alan Dixon with his O Gauge Tinplate and Jim Wilson with an O Gauge model of Bodiam Station. [This layout no longer exists.] The door and refreshment sales are also largely manned by non-members and our thanks are due to all these people, without whom there would have been no exhibition. The Surrey Group publicity and sales stand is active at model railway exhibitions, traction engine rallies etc. throughout the spring, summer and autumn, and at the time of writing bookings have been received for future events at Andover, Mayford, Knowle Hill (Berkshire), Dorking and Reading. The formula for success at these events is to carry an ever-widening range of sales goods appropriate to steam and railway interests and to ensure that those goods represent value for money. In addition to sales the Group's activities help to publicise the railway and bring details of its operation to people who may not otherwise know of its existence.

Tunbridge Wells. The Tunbridge Wells Group was given approval last November to proceed with Stage I of its plan to build a station at Wittersham Road. After an exhaustive but unsuccessful search for a building in Southern England and East Anglia, the Group has purchased for £30 a potentially suitable building from Borth station, seven miles north of Aberystwyth. The building is of wood weatherboard construction with an asbestos panelled roof, complete with finials. It measures approximately 20' x 10' x 10'. The Group already has a glass 'pigeon hole' booking office window, and plans to partition off one end of the building to make a booking office which could be manned by one clerk. Several rare Southern Railway posters and pictures will be put up on the walls. Volunteers are needed to take part in this project. Members were up at Borth from 28th May to 2nd June, working on demolition and preparing the sections for removal. The Group's Annual General Meeting, at which Robert Searle was re-elected Secretary, was held on 8th April.

Chapter 4

On 16 June 1976, BBC Radio's long running programme *Down Your Way* came to Tenterden, and Commercial Manager Donald Wilson was interviewed by Brian Johnston on the history and future plans for the Railway. The interview, which lasted for about five minutes and was broadcast nationwide on Friday, 18 July and repeated the following Tuesday, included records of trains leaving Tenterden Town Station. It concluded with the music *Elizabethan Serenade* – which might not be a universal choice to evoke the K&ESR, but each to their own.

1976 saw the 200th anniversary of the United States' Declaration of Independence. Possibly as a consequence of 4th July that year falling on a Sunday, this was celebrated on both sides of the Atlantic, including at the K&ESR. As a struggle for independence from an obstructive British government followed by westward expansion had a certain resonance for a Kent & East Sussex supporter, I had decided to spend the day at the Railway. I duly drove to Tenterden on what proved to be one of the warmest days of a very warm summer. The train was appropriately headed by USA Class No. 22 *Maunsell*, a miniature Old Glory mounted on each front lamp iron. My main memory of the event however is of the local retained fire fighters being transported to near the limit of operation to deal with a lineside fire started by sparks from the loco's chimney! Also during July, locomotive No. 12 *Marcia* attended the Kent County Show on a low-loader to publicise the Pullman Wine & Dine service. This was to be the first of several such trips off the Railway for the little Peckett 0-4-0T.

A major event of the 1976 season was the centenary of Terrier *Sutton*. At 1.30pm on 25 September, a coupled cavalcade of nine steam locomotives, together with the 'Woolwich' coach and a Southern Railway brake van, left Rolvenden for Tenterden. At Cranbrook Road the locomotives were uncoupled and then proceeded individually up Tenterden Bank to the station. The cavalcade, which was arranged as the highlight, was repeated at 10.30am on the following day, when it was preceded by a ceremony with civic dignitaries of the London Borough of Sutton, the owners of the locomotive, in attendance. Also present were the Town Mayor of Tenterden and K&ESR Company Chairman Stephen Bennett. Five thousand visitors came to the Railway over that weekend, by far the greatest number that had been achieved over any two-day period since reopening and, compared with 1975, passenger numbers were up by 18 per cent by the middle of the year. A footnote to this, which should perhaps be noted, was that HM Railway Inspectorate subsequently pointed out that splitting the cavalcade in section had produced, in effect, two locomotives in section at the same time and we were not to do it again. Later similar cavalcades have been organised with this in mind.

The editorial in the *Tenterden Terrier* for spring 1976 had stated that the working atmosphere was 'relaxed and informal'. The following issue spoke, however, of the 'JCP taking the strain off volunteers'. This was a reference to the Job Creation Programme, a scheme devised to enable voluntary organisations or local authorities to employ staff on a temporary basis on projects which were deemed to be socially beneficial and in the interests of the community. The cost of the wages and a contribution towards materials was paid by the Manpower Services Commission (part of the Department of Employment). It was a reflection of the rising unemployment of the time, and one of the final gasps of the Keynsian economics which had dominated government policy since the 1930s and was about to become discredited. In January 1976, an initial approach was made to the MSC – without too much confidence, as previous applications for grant-aid had failed because South East England was not in a Development Area. Rapid progress was nonetheless made and on 9 April the Company was told that it was to receive a grant of £13,770, to employ twelve full time staff for twenty-six weeks to assist in the extension of the Railway from Newmill Bridge to Wittersham Road by Easter 1977. One of the main activities of the project would consist of assisting in bridge construction and working side by side with Tonbridge Wells Area Group in the reconstruction of Wittersham Road. Essential full-time staff would not work as a separate entity but alongside volunteers. Only registered unemployed could be taken on. In the event, the Job Creation Programme continued on the K&ESR, the personnel involved taking part in many projects, both large and small, until 1981. It established two things: the employment of paid staff on the Railway and the use of finance from outside bodies. In addition to the projects mentioned above, the JCP staff undertook the relaying of the Railway for the mile between Newmill Bridge and Wittersham Road using steel sleepers from the Bodiam to Junction Road section. Work also started on the installation of a loop at Wittersham Road.

The K&ESR negotiated a contract with W.F. Smith & Co Ltd of Sheffield to supply 258 36ft panels of 75lb flat bottom rail complete with concrete sleepers from MOD Kineton, to replace the majority of track between Wittersham Road and Northiam. This was to be exchanged for an equivalent length of existing 91¼lb rail together with chairs from the same section and from Bodiam to Junction Road. The aim was to ensure that the Railway was not faced with the cost of purchasing some 5,000 wooden sleepers to replace defective ones. Track laying was undertaken by the Job Creation Programme. No. 2 carriage siding at Tenterden was also to be relaid. Use of this concrete-sleepered track for the running line did not last, particularly not until the time of the re-opening to Northiam, and later came to be regarded as a mistake.

Newmill Bridge remained, of course, critical to any further progress. The old bridge was demolished, volunteers undertaking removal of the rails and breaking out the tops of the concrete abutments. The remainder of the allegedly 'weak' abutments were blown up by the Army's Junior Leaders using several ever-larger charges. By November 1976, demolition had been completed and the Southern Water Authority was driving sheet piles for the new abutments. They did this free of charge, as the bridge was to be raised and lengthened to meet their requirements. Further savings had been made thanks to help from the Junior Leaders Regiment of the Royal Engineers, but £7,000 was still needed to meet the cost of the second-hand Callender-Hamilton Bridge, provided by Kent County Council and previously at Aylesford – another bridge had earlier been obtained from Woolwich Arsenal but it was decided not to use this. The total span of the Aylesford bridge was to be 60ft which at the time was thought to have been the largest bridge designed and built by a heritage railway.

The replacement structure was lifted into place on 1 December 1976. Torrential rain however caused the crane hired for the task to slide part way into the river. It was recovered on 8 January.

With more complex train operation anticipated, signalling was being developed accordingly. Wittersham Road itself was to have a signal box, but initially a ground frame was installed pending completion of this part of the project. Tenterden Town signal box, previously at Chilham and re-erected at its new location in 1973, was fitted out for the Tenterden signalling scheme and had been brought into full operation on 17 July 1976. Details of this scheme were described by volunteer David Yorke in the *Tenterden Terrier* during 1975, and extracts from this are appropriate at this point in the story.

> Some readers may be surprised at the idea of signalling the K&ESR at all, but it is worth remembering that when the railway is fully re-opened it will be 10 miles in length, and the round trip from Tenterden to Bodiam will take approximately 2 hours. It will therefore be impossible to operate the line in one section if we are to maintain an hourly service, and at least one, and possibly two or three, passing loops will be required. These loops must be fully signalled to conform with Department of the Environment regulations, and it is clearly desirable to signal the terminal stations as well. The S&T Department has so far been mainly concerned with signalling the Tenterden area, and work commenced on rebuilding the signal box (originally sited at Chilham) in 1972. Earlier this year we agreed the form of the signalling for the Tenterden area with the DoE, and it is the aim of this article to give some idea of the installation that will be made at Tenterden in the next few months.

Although the layout at Tenterden seems very simple, consisting only of a run-round loop, a level crossing and a few sidings at the north end of the station, the signalling has presented a number of headaches in the design stages. Basically the problem arises from the curious track layout adopted by Colonel Stephens, apparently as a standard, as it is very similar at Rolvenden, Northiam and Bodiam! At all these locations the points leading into the loop are situated along the short station platform, and are adjacent to a level crossing.

From a signalling point of view, it is difficult to imagine a more inconvenient layout. The position of the level crossing gates not only makes run-round movements awkward, but also means that the level crossing gates have to be interlocked with the signals, thus requiring a length of point rodding to be laid under the road to operate the gate lock. Furthermore, as the tips of the point blades are only about 10ft from the gate, it is impossible to install the conventional 40ft lock bar usually fitted along the inside edge of the rail approaching a set of facing points, which prevents the signalman moving the points as a train is approaching them. A track circuit on the approach to the points would be one answer, but the DoE has agreed that we can omit the lock bar altogether providing that a regulation is included in the rule book forbidding the signalman to replace the home signal to danger until the train has passed over and is completely clear of the points. The interlocking of the lever frame then prevents him from moving the points. This relaxation is possible at Tenterden because the points are immediately in front of the signal box, and it is most unlikely that a signalman would attempt to move them whilst a train is standing on them or about to pass over them.

Another complication arises from the position of the points, which occupy about one quarter of the platform length. This means that if the whole length of the platform is to be occupied by a train, the engine must stand on the points close to the gates. A profusion of starting signals, very close to one another, then becomes necessary; one at the crossing gates where a train about to depart will normally stand, an advanced starting signal, about

30 yards along the single line towards Rolvenden, to prevent an unauthorised movement along the single line towards Rolvenden by a train that has shunted across the crossing, and a third signal (or a STOP board) situated along the platform at the fouling points to prevent a movement originating in the yard from fouling the loop points without the signalman's permission. Yet another starting signal (a ground disc signal), must be provided to authorise movements from the loop on to the main line.

The home signals are rather more conventional. A shunt signal will be situated close to the crossing gates on the Rolvenden side, which will read into either the main line or the loop, to facilitate run-round movements. The interlocking will require this signal to be cleared before either of the main home signals can be cleared, so that a passenger train can never approach it at danger; a small ground signal is adequate. The main home signal will be a two-doll bracket reading into both the platform road and the loop, and will be situated about 250 yards towards Rolvenden from the advanced starter. Generally a distance of about 440 yards would be required here, but this has been reduced to 250 in view of the 1 in 50 gradient approaching Tenterden, and the very low speeds on the line. A bracket is not strictly required, but it has been decided to install one from the outset in case two platform working is ever instituted at Tenterden, in which case it would become essential. Because of the low speeds on the line and the very steep gradient, the DoE has agreed that no distant signal is required providing that there is adequate sighting of the home signal. However, if time and labour permit, a fixed distant signal may be installed close to the Cranbrook Road crossing [this was never carried out].

A word now on equipment. The lever frame is a Saxby & Farmer 23 lever 'Duplex' locking frame which was originally installed in the box at Chilham. It is catch-handle locked – that is, the interlocking is operated by means of the catch handles rather than by the levers themselves. Although this makes the interlocking very strong, it has the disadvantage that each lever has two tappets, resulting in twice as much work in making new interlocking. Work on the new interlocking should be well advanced by the time this article appears. The signal posts to be installed at Tenterden are all ex-SR lattice posts with upper quadrant arms (very tedious to restore), whilst the bracket home signal will be a two-doll balanced bracket with lattice dolls, originally a platform starter at Epsom Downs. Unfortunately the original lattice main post was too short for use at Tenterden, and a new rail post is under construction, involving some fairly heavy engineering by S&T standards. Standard channel rodding and fittings are being used for the gate locks and point connections, and the ground signals will be the standard SR disc type, possibly fitted with miniature arms rather than the more modern disc. The existing 'butterfly' type economical facing point lock, now quite a curiosity on passenger lines, will be replaced by a standard FPL and signal detector, as it is rather worn, but it is hoped to preserve at least one of these locks in use somewhere on the line.

Those 'surprised by the idea of signalling on the K&ESR' were not necessarily placated by this explanation and, although the scheme described can, with modifications, still be seen at Tenterden today, much more came to be said on the subject in due course.

A further item worth quoting from the *Terrier*, which gives a flavour of the Railway in the mid-70s, is John Weller's article 'One Year's Hard Labour'.

On the first Sunday in March last year [1975] I resolved to give a helping hand in lengthening the operational section of the railway, which at that time extended to a point some two miles and twelve chains from Tenterden Town station.

A further one hundred and fifty yards of track had been the subject of sleeper renewal, and the immediate aim was to make this length operational by the Spring Bank Holiday with the rest of the section to Pope's Cottage permanent way hut, some 350 yards beyond.

Progress was steady but slow during the following weeks as the relaying gang, which varied between five and nine members, had to carry out the task of removal and replacement of chair screws by hand. Additionally a retaining work had to be completed in order that a small earth movement which was threatening to foul the loading gauge could be contained.

The job in hand was not simply a question of replacing each defective sleeper. We had to ensure that replacement sleepers were available when needed and as the section of line currently receiving attention had latterly been relaid with 91¼lb rail this necessitated each new sleeper being drilled six times in order to take the 91¼lb chairs. Then, each of the original six screw holes had to be plugged with lengths of dowel in order to prevent the ingress of water which would inevitably result in the premature onset of rot.

These tasks were usually accomplished during the loading of the wagons at Tenterden Town station yard using a heavy duty electric hand drill, a template and a 5lb hammer. When loaded the wagons were taken to Rolvenden after the last passenger train of the day and forwarded to the site for unloading early the next day.

Before the return trip to Tenterden the wagons were loaded with sleepers which had been removed. These sleepers were subsequently sold, and provided a welcome source of income. The movements of sleepers to and from the site required careful planning in order to ensure that wagons, motive power and train crews were rostered in the right place at the right time.

Each movement into and out of Tenterden Town yard was complicated by the need to shunt stock which was the subject of current restoration by the Carriage and Wagon Department.

On 18th May the 'Limit of Operation' was duly moved to Pope's Cottage, some 360 sleepers having been replaced at a rate of 30 each weekend. At this time the absence of a suitable supply of replacement sleepers resulted in a lull in re-sleepering, so attention was concentrated on improvement of the newly opened section in order that the 10 mph speed restriction could be raised.

Following the receipt of a fresh supply of sleepers work recommenced on renewals. At this time the newly restored Matissa chair bolt screwing machine (known as 'Neddy the Knurdler') became available, and its use brought about a substantial increase in the rate of replacement. Between July and September 760 sleepers were replaced at a rate of more than 70 per weekend.

In September assistance was given with the removal of some 13 tons of rail from Bodiam to Wittersham Road, where it is to be used in the construction of the new loop. Later the same month the track and decking of Newmill Bridge were removed as the first stage of the replacement of the structure. Subsequently the bridge beams were exposed and the mass concrete abutments removed to the level of the lower edge of the beams. This work was accomplished mainly with the assistance of an air drill but also, perhaps rather surprisingly, by the use of a shovel to remove the dry lean mix concrete which had either never set or had subsequently been broken down by the action of weather and time.

From October to February this year work was concentrated mainly on the renewal of defective sleepers and point timbers in the operating section. The point from the main line to the carriage siding at Tenterden proved to be particularly taxing, as virtually all the timbers required renewal and in the three days needed to complete the task work continued into the winter evening by the light of Tilley lamps on two occasions, and through a snowstorm on the third.

The track between Tenterden and Rolvenden was the subject of a detailed scrutiny to check for and correct minor fluctuations in alignment and levels of the rails. On non-operating days use was made, on every journey to and from the work in hand, of a Wickham Trolley and flat wagon to collect wood for the lighting of engines and to otherwise carry out work necessary to tidy up station areas as well as alongside the running line.

Following substantial correction of the alignment of the curve at Pope's Cottage a satisfactory conclusion to the year's work was achieved on 29th February 1976 when a further length of track was opened for operational purposes, making a total of 52 chains for the year. This leaves some 2,300 sleepers to be replaced between the new Limit of Operation and Wittersham Road which at current rates amounts to roughly 33 weekends' work. The time period will, of course, be reduced by the efforts of the Job Creation Programme employees, but we still need a substantial increase in the number of volunteer helpers.

Meanwhile I look forward to a second year's hard labour, to meeting fresh and familiar faces, and to the pleasure of the company of the swans, partridges, rabbits, hares and other fauna which abound in the sections of the line which cannot be currently appreciated by paying passengers.

As explained in a later chapter, John Weller was subsequently both Mayor of Tenterden and a Director of the Kent & East Sussex Railway.

At the end of December 1976, Mike Hart left to become General Manager of the Nene Valley Railway. By this time had he added the paid post of Job Creation Project Manager to his volunteer position of Mechanical Department Manager. In addition to keeping the locomotive fleet running, he had demonstrated his considerable abilities in supervising the extension to Wittersham Road and the rebuilding of Newmill Bridge. Over the decades to follow, Mike's achievements in the railway industry both as a components manufacturer and as a leader of the heritage sector were to be outstanding.

The end of the 1976 season provided an opportunity for the *Tenterden Terrier* to compare the passenger figures for two 'normal' years (1974 having been the 'abnormal' reopening year). The total carried in 1976 showed an overall increase of 17 per cent over 1975 (39,741 against 34,059) although the Railway had only operated for one more day. This was regarded as highly satisfactory result, despite the summer having been one of the hottest for years – the conventional wisdom was that the public preferred the beach on a warm day. Summer Wednesdays were however very popular, and passenger numbers on those days were up 52 per cent. November, as in 1975, proved to be very poor. 61 per cent of passengers were adults, as opposed to 63 per cent in 1975. It was observed that this was a high ratio of adults to children, in view of the large number of school parties which had been carried during the year. Santa Specials improved by 7 per cent. In retrospect, it comes as no surprise that the biggest growth area in 1976 was 'Wine & Dine Specials' (i.e. Pullmans) where the number of diners increased by no less than 310 per cent. An interesting aspect of these published figures was that they contained trends which, with varying but overall increasing numbers, are still identifiable at the time of writing. The major exception is the influence of hot weather which has since 2001 been supplanted by the Bodiam traffic – or 'Bodiam Beach Effect' as it has sometimes been called.

The proposed museum referred to earlier came into being in the early part of 1977 as the Colonel Stephens Railway Museum. At this stage it was located some 300 yards from Tenterden Town Station in the two-storey weather-boarded town museum, at the rear of the car park in Station Road. Built about 1850, it had originally been a stonemason's, with stabling at one end, and had once housed the Kent & East Sussex Railway horse bus (as of 2023 still at the National Railway Museum in York). The space made available to use was inevitably small, as the museum premises themselves could not be opened in their entirety at that time, in particular the upper storey, pending completion of structural alterations in order to comply with fire regulations. The museum also housed items relating to Tenterden's 1,200-year history. A small collection of railway items was quickly established, including certain of Colonel Stephens' personal effects and a photographic study of the various lines in the 'Stephens empire'. Philip Shaw and Eric Fletcher redecorated a suitable area and soon afterwards John Miller joined as de facto curator. Part of the upper storey of the premises, then in use as a store, was reported as likely to become available for display purposes and it was hoped that the railway exhibits would be moved there. This would give an area of about 400sqft. Most of the exhibits lent themselves to wall displays, but it was intended to introduce a series of models to illustrate both the K&ESR and the other lines represented. Admission was free to members of the Tenterden Railway Company.

With the bridge complete, services to Wittersham Road commenced on Saturday, 5 March 1977. Historian Stephen Garrett, writing under his pseudonym of 'Morous' reported the event in the *Tenterden Terrier*:

> At 11.30am … the first passenger train since January 1954 left Tenterden Town Station for Wittersham Road. Aboard were approximately 100 invited guests, including as Guest of Honour Councillor Tucker, Chairman of the Amenities & Countryside Committee of the Kent County Council. The train paused at the newly-rebuilt Newmill Bridge for Councillor Tucker to perform a brief reopening ceremony; in introducing the Councillor Company Chairman Stephen Bennett said that this was a very historic occasion for the Railway, as the extension of services had not only involved rebuilding the bridge, but also added over one mile to the operating length of the line. The work could not have been carried out without the help of both the Kent County Council, which had donated the bridge, and the Manpower Services Commission, which had been responsible for

the grant under the Job Creation Programme. He then called on Councillor Tucker to perform the opening ceremony.

Councillor Tucker said that the Amenities & Countryside Committee had been particularly anxious to assist voluntary organisations in the County, and that the Railway was a prime example of this. He therefore had much pleasure in declaring the bridge and extension open. The train then moved across the bridge and proceeded to Wittersham Road. There, Project Director Simon Green explained how tight the deadline had been to get the project finished by March 1977. In December 1975 the Company heard from Kent County Council's Surveyors Department that the bridge structure was to be donated to the Company. In May 1976 the first 12 employees taken on under the Job Creation Programme arrived, and the bridge parts started arriving in August. Rapid progress was made on the re-assembly, which also involved substantial modifications to the structure. In addition, a mile of track was relaid in the record time of one month. Three weeks ago, the first crossing of the bridge had been made by a small Wickham trolley, and last Tuesday the works were inspected by Major Rose of The Railway Inspectorate, who declared himself satisfied that trains could run. However much work remained to be done, including the reconstruction of the station itself, fencing, car parking and landscaping. Furthermore, another six miles of railway still had to be rebuilt. Thanks were extended to all of those who had helped with the project, many of whom were on the train.

The first train, a VIP Special hauled by Terrier No. 10 and the Norwegian Mogul, arrived at what was effectively a building site. A major task was to move the platform mound (all that remained of the platform) back by one road width to allow for the installation of a run-round loop. This could have been achieved by leaving the mound in its original, historic, position and creating an island platform; it was, however, claimed that, on safety grounds – passengers having to cross the line – this would never be acceptable to the Railway Inspectorate. It is said that when, after much effort, the new platform was inspected by Major Rose he turned to the K&ESR officers and asked 'Why didn't you build an island platform?'! [Something similar to what might have been created exists, suitably protected, at Haven Street on the Isle of Wight Steam Railway]. The new station building, erected end-on to the line in the manner of the original, was that which the Tunbridge Wells Group had found at Borth in Wales. Some of the platform coping slabs were recovered from Junction Road Halt, while railings from Cranbrook on the Hawkhurst branch provided a link with another Colonel Stephens line. A unique feature for the heritage era K&ESR was the lower quadrant signals which had originated with that fascinating railway, the Great Northern of Ireland.

Despite the usual euphoria at the extension of a heritage railway, the summer 1977 issue of the *Terrier* sounded a note of caution – by mid-June passenger numbers were down 20 per cent against the previous year. By the end of the year this had 'improved' somewhat with the minus figure down to 6 per cent, 37,360 having been carried against a slightly revised figure of 39,764 for 1976. The reasons were explained in the house journal by Chief Booking Clerk Colin Deverell.

> This is somewhat better than had been anticipated earlier in the season, following the almost disastrous months of March, April and May, but still a little disappointing in view of the eight additional operating days, which were introduced mainly to extend services

over the peak holiday periods. In consequence the average daily passenger total fell by 16 per cent from 385 to 322. The extension of services from Newmill Bridge to Wittersham Road at the beginning of the season appeared to bring little or no extra traffic, except for members travelling on privilege tickets. Unfortunately the station platform at Wittersham could not be completed during the year as had originally been intended, and therefore passengers were unable to join or alight from trains at this point, which would have added considerably to the variety and interest of the journey. The inclement summer weather and a general preoccupation with the (Queen's Silver) Jubilee may have been factors affecting the numbers carried, but the decline was fairly consistent until very late season when the Santa Specials got under way. These trains were a great success, and numbers carried were 37 per cent up on 1976.

The higher number of promotional and pass tickets was mainly accounted for the issue of 596 'go places' tickets by arrangement with Cadbury's cakes. The Awayday scheme with British Rail was discontinued at the end of 1976 due to lack of support. The number of passengers coming to Tenterden by public transport since reopening has always been negligible. The Wine & Dine trains continued to flourish, with the number of diners up no less than 39 per cent – a great credit to all those who help with these trains. 1977, then, did not come up to our best expectations; but the economy remained depressed and many leisure industries, including private railways, suffered from the lower levels of consumer discretionary spending power. This year should see the platform at Wittersham Road complete and the attractiveness of the journey considerably enhanced; with personal incomes likely to rise in real terms in 1978 as North Sea oil gathers pace, we shall look forward to a more prosperous season both for our customers and for ourselves.

Work to rebuild Wittersham Road went on apace during the early months of 1978. It had been decided to ask a 'big name' to officiate at the re-opening, and the task had fallen to former prime minister the Rt Hon Edward Heath MP. At this distance in history this seems to have been an odd choice. Ted Heath was then, as indeed now, seen as a disgruntled figure much associated with the infamous Three Day Week crisis of 1973/74. He had ceased to be Conservative Party Leader three years previously when the position had gone to Margaret Thatcher – the implications of which development were not yet fully realised, although change was in the air. Still, Ted was a Man of Kent, born in Broadstairs, and in parliament he represented Bexley, part of an area on the borders of Kent and London which has over the years been home to quite a few K&ESR members. It had been planned to formally re-open Wittersham Road on 26 May, but this was postponed to 16 June due to Mr Heath's commitments. The event was described for the *Terrier* by Paul Sutton, who had been Project Co-ordinator during the latter stages of the scheme.

The 16th dawned bright and sunny and remained so for the rest of the day. Mr Heath arrived unavoidably late and the welcoming party was rushed into Tenterden Station, where invited guests were already assembled and Bill Austen had earlier named locomotive No. 24 William H. Austen in memory of his father, the former general manager of the Railway; No. 23 simmered at the other end of the train and we were soon on our way to Wittersham Road. The five coach formation including Pullman Barbara arrived with a sizeable crowd waiting and the flags and bunting flying. Chairman Stephen Bennett made a short speech and introduced Mr Heath who gave a very entertaining response. After photographs, autographs, chats, introductions and a buffet lunch he returned to Tenterden for a quick visit to the museum. The whole event had gone very well and received excellent coverage on TV and in the Press. Everyone had combined to make the project a success, something which at one time seemed impossible. Mike James and his group were responsible for the majority of the work, and it should not be forgotten that without the JCP grants we almost certainly would not be running over the Newmill Channel, let alone into Wittersham.

Like many railways, the K&ESR had organised what were called 'Steam Ups' – a sort of gala day during which anything and everything that could move did so. In 1978, after two years of these, the K&ESR replaced its successful 'Steam Ups' with the first of the almost legendary Steam & Country Fairs. In essence these were an expanded traction engine and classic vehicle rally with country crafts and a steam railway attached.

The organising committee was John Miller, Derrick Bilsby and Mark Yonge, and the fair was planned for the weekend of 16 and 17 September. This was the 'shoulder' period of the season, a time when the normal service traffic tails off rapidly. Planning had begun as early as the spring, when a decision on the site area was made. Farmers with fields adjacent to Tenterden station generously gave permission to use their land. Much of the main event was held on the field adjacent to the level crossing (now known as Morph's Field). Another field provided most of the car parking. A small fair was hired from a contractor to provide sideshows, small roundabouts and a bouncy castle, in addition to a galloper roundabout and a showman's organ. Invitations were extended to the owners of traction engines, vintage cars, vans and motorcycles to parade regularly in a roped-off area in the field and to receive the customary attendance plaque. An exhibition of rural crafts enhanced the atmosphere of the event, including beekeeping, spinning, horticulture and straw handicrafts.

Publicity was handled by Tony Hocking, who booked space on 100 Southern Region railway stations and advertising in every local paper in Kent and Sussex. Although the weather in August and September had been poor, Saturday morning dawned bright and the forecast was promising. In the event, it was one of the best weekends of the year, with mainly cloudless skies and warm temperatures. Some 2,300 visitors came through the gates on Saturday and traffic congestion was kept to a minimum. Sunday, however, attracted no fewer than 4,500, and by mid-afternoon traffic stretched right up Station Road and into the High Street. This was due to the necessity for continuous opening and shutting of the level crossing gates, either to let the trains pass or for the engines to run round. Admission was 60p for adults and 30p for children, but for all the effort that was put into the fair, the profit was small – only amounting to £450 on total takings of £5,000, not taking into account train revenue or bookshop takings which were considerable. It was nonetheless decided that the Fair was to be repeated on 15 and 16 September 1979.

Chapter 5

Following the rebuilding of Newmill Bridge, the Company Chairman had, in 1977, written about the possibility of reaching Bodiam by 1980. This was admittedly tempered by consideration of whether the Job Creation Programme would continue, and the economics and practicalities of attaining such an objective. The realities – not least the commercial realities – of running a heritage railway had begun to set in. This period had seen a steady increase in passengers, with 50,148 being carried in 1978 – an improvement of 34 per cent over the previous year. The implications of both immediate and future policy were nonetheless emotive.

By the end of the 1970s, the Terriers were out of use awaiting overhaul and services were having to be maintained with Austerity 0-6-0 saddletanks and ex-British Railways Mark 1 coaches. At the beginning of 1977 it had become clear that, following three years continuous service, the Maunsell rolling stock would require major restoration work. In addition, *Barbara*, obviously an essential element of the developing Pullman service, needed external renovation. Various other Carriage and Wagon work was in hand and, to enable services to continue in 1978, the Company had successfully tendered for three 64-seat Mark 1 coaches, on behalf of private owners who were prepared to lend them to the Railway. Getting these into service was therefore top priority.

At this point, divisions of opinion had one of their periodic flare-ups. To put it at its simplest (perhaps most euphemistic) a body of opinion felt that the light railway atmosphere of the 'old' Kent & East Sussex had been lost. A more robust view might be that the Arcadian dream of the K&ESR was finally vanishing in the cold light of day. Conversely, the Railway had attracted a number of volunteers who, greatly welcome though they were, had little interest in a debatable view of the past. Somewhere between these two positions was a third view that the K&ESR was developing within its pragmatic traditions. The strength of feeling that was being generated is best illustrated by quoting in their entirety three letters published in the *Terrier* in the spring and summer editions of 1978. Although these were ostensibly about signalling, they illustrate the issues nicely. The first of these came from former Chairman, Simon B. Green.

> Sir – The S&T notes in the Winter 1977 issue raise a number of points of principle which demand wider discussion of our objectives than internal debate within the S&T Department or even the Operating Division. Two items reported upon serve to illustrate what I believe to be an entirely wrong approach to signalling a light railway:
>
> The new bracket home signal is not only of massive dimensions but it is in my view entirely unnecessary. The 'temporary' signal erected in 1976 was quite adequate and was in fact in character, featuring two home signals (platform and loop) one above the other on the same post. The new bracket even includes a fixed distant signal which I am told indicates that Tenterden is a terminal station: surely any driver who is unaware of this fact is unfit to be in charge of a train!

It is said that the point run to the up loop points at Wittersham is 'lengthy'. In fact the distance is some 600 feet and if the rodding followed the eastern side of the old main line it would be absolutely straight. Properly constructed (and our S&T Department has been widely praised for its high standard of installation) this would require little effort to operate. An electric point motor is entirely out of place in a tiny, rustic station in the middle of a light railway and the suggestion that one should be used is symptomatic of the attempts to run our railway as though it was British Railways 20 years ago. The much abused raucous loudspeaker system at Tenterden was an early manifestation of this attitude. Quite apart from this 'philosophical' objection, electrical controls require power supplies – in the form of an unfortunate pointsman to wind them if the electrical source fails.

Other ideas surface from time to time. A second phase of signalling is mooted for Tenterden to cover the splay of points at the Headcorn end. I am sure most other enginemen and guards would agree that this would certainly waste time in shunting, even with the faster and more alert signalmen who are sadly in the minority, and as track curvature makes these points invisible from the signalbox, additional safety hazards would be introduced with no apparent benefit.

There is a feeling in some quarters that these developments reflect a desire for gimmickry; in itself undesirable and in effect diverting scarce labour resources from jobs which are less popular such as manning, maintaining and even painting crossing gates. (It is notable that the majority of those splendid people who man the gates at Cranbrook Road are not signalmen!)

Stephen Whiteman, Manager of the Signals and Telecommunications Department, was given a right of reply which immediately followed Mr Green's letter:

The bracket signal was on the plans passed by the Board which were then submitted to the Railway Inspectorate for approval. The signal was not ready for installation when the signalling was commissioned, so permission was obtained to put the temporary signal up. The bracket signals were commissioned on 29th January this year and the system now complies with the plans lodged at the DoE. The distant signal does not denote to the driver that he is approaching a terminal station and an amendment to the rule book explaining the reason will be issued shortly.

The points at Wittersham Road are to be operated by motors as they are on the fringe of the distance from the signal box which may be worked by rodding. Points at this distance are greatly affected by changes in temperature even when compensators are installed in the run.

The signalling at the eastern end of Tenterden was cancelled some time ago although some levers in the signal box were allocated to work that end of the station. The remarks about the loudspeaker system I do agree with; the speakers were installed for the opening ceremony of the Railway and left so that special announcements could be made, rather than to give a history of the Railway and of the train before it departs. The crossing gates at Cranbrook Road are mostly manned by members who wish to help the Railway but are unable to do other work. [This has long since ceased to be the case]

Finally, I would like to say that our equipment is bought at a very nominal rate, which I am sure Colonel Stephens would have approved of and would have used wherever it was wanted, 'in character' or not.

The argument continued in the subsequent issue of the journal. The first letter this time came from member Peter Clark:

Sir – What an extraordinary letter from Mr Simon B. Green in your Spring (No. 15) edition! As he has been so adequately answered from the signalling point of view, there is little I can add except to say that I can't help wondering why he is a member when we have, for example, 'Wine & Dine' trains, 'Santa Specials' and The Buffer Stop Shop. For a light railway, these are surely felonious compared with the misdemeanour of a bracket signal. However, let me be the last to spoil his enjoyment of trains. Although I have a feeling one can no longer obtain those engines which were motivated by the winding of a key, the electric train sets are quite safe in the hands of boys of most ages. An engine, two or three trucks and an oval of track around the hearth rug make a jolly good light railway.

This was followed by a contribution from Tom Lewis:

Sir – I applaud Simon Green's attempt to provoke thought and discussion about the future appearance and fabric of our railway, but feel that his letter leaves much unsaid. Now that the railway has reached what is to be a period of consolidation, it seems that the time has come for us all to stop and think about the appearance that we wish it to take on in the years to come. Are we prepared to let the railway become a completely functional affair, or do we wish to retain some of the character and charm of a branch line light railway that we are still able to create with the materials at our disposal? Even before I put a full stop to this sentence, I can hear the 'functionalists' shouting from afar that it is 'impracticable', in their words, to run a railway without such and such a piece of equipment or gadget, such as the proposed electric point motor at Wittersham, and to some extent I sympathise. It will never be possible to recreate the K&ESR of the past, and a degree of modernity and mechanisation is absolutely necessary to make the most of our limited labour resources.

However, between this uncontested level of modernity and the complete austerity (no pun intended) that some wish to create, there is a wide margin for decisions that depend, quite simply, on whether we, the working members, can be bothered or not to make the effort required to create something that conveys the atmosphere of a branch line earlier this century, or rather than that of 'British Railways 20 years ago'. The functionalists, those who are unwilling to make this effort and can see no further challenge at Tenterden than to operate 'a railway service', whatever its nature, will immediately answer that the average passenger knows little or nothing about railways and is happy if his train is drawn by a 'steam loco'. If this is so, why, then, does the railway's sales line mention centenarian Terriers and Edwardian Birdcage coaches rather than saddle tank locomotives of 1953 vintage, that can still be seen working in collieries, and coaches of a similar age that still run on BR in vast numbers? Why then does the splendid 'Wealden Pullman' publicity paint an attractive portrait of the Pullman coach and not of the 'Elizabethan' splendour of the Mk. I in which the unsuspecting diner may find himself?

If this argument fails to cut ice, the functionalist will, alas, repeat once again that all-time favourite non-argument, that if Col. Stephens had had access to this, that, or the other modern gadget, he would have used it; let it be said in reply, that the prices of coal and scrap iron having reached the heights of the last 20 years, this admirably practical man would have sold his railway and purchased a fleet of buses. Is this what those apparently dedicated to the spirit of Col. Stephens want, or is it merely the best argument available to defend the modern and practical in one of the few places where these qualities are inherently undesirable? The truth is that while the average passenger, it is true, knows little about railways, he is sensitive to an impression and atmosphere of aged authenticity, such as is so excellently marketed by our nearest competitor. In the Chairman's speech to the AGM two years ago, Stephen Bennett expressed a desire to see ours become an outstanding example of that species, the preserved railway; if this admirable ambition is to stand any chance of fulfilment, it seems to me that the railway must make an effort along the above lines, lacking as it does the breath-taking scenery or express locomotives, for example, that may lend considerable attraction to some of our competitors.

Allow me to close by stating the obvious in the belief that it has been overlooked yet again. The preserved railway is, by definition, whimsical and impractical through and through, and it is precisely these qualities, which are so notably absent in contemporary life, that our passengers expect to find and take delight in when they visit our railway; those who seek to rationalise and modernise therefore misunderstand it completely. If the coaches we ask our passengers to ride in are those which they may use on BR to ride through considerably more attractive and varied countryside than ours and at less expense, then it is up to us to provide the maximum possible interest in our locomotives, stations, signalling installations and all the other paraphernalia that went to make up a branch line earlier this century.

As I implied earlier, these and allied matters will occur again in the course of this account.

Pullman passenger numbers were however continuing to rise and the 'Wealden Pullman' (as the Wine & Dine Train had now been renamed) was establishing itself as one of the Railway's ongoing success stories. 'Where do we go from here?' asked the *Tenterden Terrier* winter issue for 1978. The answer emerged by the middle of the following year.

The line as it now stood was a compact railway of reasonable length, and the Board duly considered the options – extension or consolidation. They chose consolidation. The potential market associated with Bodiam Castle and Northiam's location on the A28 were tempting, but tapping this potential traffic was problematic. A major difficulty was the perennial issue of finance. The cost of restoring Wittersham Road to Bodiam was estimated at £70,000 for materials (1979 values) including £30,000 for ballast and £30,000 for sleepers. Once other costs were included, including renovating Northiam and Bodiam stations and work on the Rother Bridge, it was thought that the total would be nearer to £100,000.

Finding the necessary labour was an additional difficulty. If a ten-man gang was employed for a year this would cost a further £50,000. Government finance, as had been used for Wittersham

Road, could not be relied upon. Such monies were described as politically vulnerable at the time, which was something of an understatement. This was the summer of 1979 and the Thatcher government had recently come to power. The Board therefore decided on a policy of consolidation until the end of 1981 and possibly longer. A major factor in the decision was an awareness that in many areas of staffing and maintenance, the Railway was only just managing. There was a serious risk of overstretch to a degree which was unacceptable. Instead, the Board decided on a group of projects intended to develop the Railway as it then stood and which would enhance it when it was further extended:

1. A catering building at Tenterden with toilet facilities. This was to be sited on the eastern side of the Tenterden Station buildings. Plans were well advanced for work to begin in 1980. This would replace the facility provided in the unrestored Pullman Car *Theodora* in the back road behind Tenterden. This scheme was of particular interest as it involved re-erecting, in Tenterden yard several years later, the former Maidstone Bus station which had stood in Mill Street, Maidstone. This attractive building, which had been the first bus station in Britain, had been dismantled piece by piece and was in store pending the start of the project.
2. A Carriage and Wagon building. This emerged as the first part of the present C&W workshops at Tenterden.
3. A Signals and Telecommunications workshop, again at Tenterden. This was initially achieved by taking over a wooden building previously used by C&W and which stood adjacent to the present Buffet site. It lasted until the late 1990s.
4. Modification of track layouts to provide extra carriage berthing, and extend both the platform and the loop at Tenterden to accommodate five-coach trains. Substantial improvements were also planned at Rolvenden. These would include track modifications, the provision of inspection pits, a coal dump, an ash dump, concreting of the remainder of the locomotive shed floor, a new oil store and a workshop and general store.
5. A Permanent Way Department base at Wittersham Road.
6. Completion of the signalling at Wittersham Road and plans to signal Rolvenden to be drawn up.
7. Care and maintenance of the railway west of Wittersham Road to prevent further deterioration. Only relatively minor work appeared to be necessary on the Rother Bridge. This structure was not as bad as had once been feared, it at one time having been thought to need either rebuilding completely or replacing. It had however been surveyed by a professional railway bridge engineer, who had concluded that the general state of the structure and abutments was very good and only required some minor repairs to the platework and a thorough cleaning down and repainting.

Despite the reluctance to overstretch the Railway's resources, it did prove possible to make some advance towards Northiam during 1979 when work started on the reconstruction of Hexden Bridge, the first watercourse crossing beyond Wittersham Road. This was, however, a much less complex task than the Newmill scheme, as Hexden continues to be a very basic Colonel Stephens type structure of much shorter span.

The winter 1979 issue of the *Tenterden Terrier* included two items further addressing the future direction of the K&ESR. The first was Philip Shaw's editorial, which is quoted here in full.

Donald Wilson's enlightening article on the workings of the commercial division brings into focus the problems that we face as we move into the 1980s. With some 30 preserved railways operating around the country, we cannot hope to survive if we merely wait for passengers to arrive and then travel from A to B and back on a steam train. The 'novelty' aspect of the 70s is giving way to a more competitive environment in the 80s. 1979 has shown that special events and attractions continue to attract unprecedented numbers of visitors, and the rewards are high although the risks are correspondingly greater. Both marketing and financial planning will play an ever increasing role in deciding our future – particularly as the economy moves into recession. Then, problems will arise when hard economics have to be equated with our primary and original role of preserving a light railway. In this respect we are fortunate in that we possess ten miles of line, half of which still remains to be resuscitated. This should give us the flexibility that we need to combine the objectives of the purist with the benefit of a healthy bank balance.

The article referred to in the Editorial outlined the workings of the Commercial Division and the Commercial Manager's personal views about the future. He first referred to the list of projects listed above and that an extension of passenger services beyond Wittersham Road was unlikely before 1985. He continued:

With this in mind, the Commercial Division's job must be to generate as much profitable business for the Railway as possible.

When the K&ESR was constructed 80 years ago, the pace of life was far slower than it is today and the little stations catered for only a few hundred passengers a year. 'Marketing' and 'Sales potential' as far as railways were concerned did not exist. Passengers used the railway to get from A to B, albeit rather slowly. Today the K&ESR is reborn with nearly 50,000 people visiting us, mostly at weekends, as part of other leisure activity. The public at large have been educated towards steam railways over the last decade, ever since steam trains ceased to be an everyday sight in Britain.

Today there are nearly 30 private railways on which one can take a steam hauled train, not to mention the 'steam centres' and private excursions on BR lines! So whether one likes it or not, we are part of the massive tourist industry, plying for trade like any other attraction, so we must 'sell' the Railway effectively in our main market area, which is roughly a 50 mile radius from Tenterden.

Donald then explained the Commercial Department's annual planning and budgeting process before making the following observations on the state of the Railway at the end of the 1970s. A number of them have continuing resonance:

Our main source of income is from running the trains themselves. The object is to get as much revenue as possible from the minimum number of services, as running costs are the same whether the trains are empty, half full or overcrowded. In days of spiralling costs, we should always aim to increase our load factor and eliminate unprofitable services. Secondary to the trains is the operation of the Buffer Stop shop, where many passengers 'browse and buy'. The enthusiast market is now well catered for with a good selection of railway books and models as well as sales of rare tickets. The shop area has been enlarged and improved considerably in the last two years, and this has resulted in a very satisfactory increase in turnover.

The Catering Department cannot fully exploit the potential of the Railway due to the cramped access to and inside *Theodora*, but our planned new building will, it is estimated, treble our present turnover and be a useful profit centre for the future. Meanwhile our on-train refreshment trolley continues to trade briskly to our 'captive' market.

When the first 'Wine & Dine' train was run in 1974, no-one envisaged that six years later we would be running 60-seater trains every Saturday from April to October. Not only are these trains fully booked months in advance, but customers are booking a year ahead to be sure of a seat in high summer! With an income of around £500 per train, and demand unsatisfied, we could easily fill the train two or even three times a week. However to do so would involve the introduction of an outside caterer as well as overcoming the difficulty of obtaining footplate crews willing to work late midweek. This is a case where the potential for a substantial marketing exercise exists, but to attract more business could endanger our present scope of operations. However, it is possible that we will introduce Friday night charter trains in July and August 1980. To improve the quality of the on-train facilities, a Restaurant Kitchen Car has been bought from British Rail and it is hoped to have this in use for next season.

The Railway has received tremendous publicity from the success of the Steam & Country Fair which is now an established annual event, although not without considerable financial risk. The sun shone, as it has done for the last three fairs, and a good profit has been realised from this very worthwhile commercial activity. Popularity with the public is again noted during the month of December when upwards of 5000 people descend on us for the Santa Specials. A lot of organisation goes into the running of these services … having established the commercial framework and attracted custom, we must ensure that visitors enjoy themselves and tell their friends what a good afternoon they have had on the Kent & East Sussex Railway. First impressions count a lot, and to see a smartly turned out locomotive sitting at the head of its train, with the crew enlightening enquirers on the technicalities of their steed, the guard and ticket inspector in smart uniforms, all piece together to give an air of authenticity and professionalism. At present we have a major disappointment for visitors in that they are generally not able to inspect our locomotives. I would like to see some of our unserviceable locomotives stored at Tenterden and some form of activity in which to interest our visitors in between trains.

… it is worth a few lines to speculate on how the Railway could be developed without spoiling its character. The prospect of reaching Bodiam is a very exciting one as the K&ESR will become a very interesting line, linking two centres of considerable tourist interest. The line will become a major attraction to coach tour operators who are anxious to take the rush out of tourism and the idea of marketing one-way journeys is a very viable proposition – provided not all groups want to travel in the same direction! However, how do we retain our 'light railway' atmosphere and at the same time cope with the crowds? The purist will remember the line as one with short, infrequent trains, hauled by diminutive tank engines, with small stations and delightful lower quadrant (of course) signals controlled by ground frames. To meet demand, today's trains are longer, more frequent and hauled mostly by big (by light railway standards) engines and standard upper quadrant signals controlled by signal boxes are in evidence. These features are in my view more in keeping with a SR branch line. With our remaining six miles we should investigate methods of train control more compatible with light railways – radio control, divisible train staffs etc. – and so give ourselves flexibility of operation without the need to build yet more signal boxes.

In the meantime it would be an interesting development, as a prelude to opening the line to Northiam, to run a shuttle service between Wittersham and, say, Hexden Bridge. Such a move would bring added publicity and would enable us to give a practical test to recently laid concrete track panels. However it should not be forgotten that if a second train is in operation, this means a doubling of operating staff, doubling of locomotives in steam, doubling direct operating costs while not necessarily doubling our passengers or indeed our profit! With the ever-increasing price of coal – now almost £1,000 per lorry load – I believe it essential to our future success that we acquire at least one pair of diesel multiple units to operate 'land cruise' trains in off-peak times. Other preserved railways, such as the West Somerset and the North Yorkshire Moors, operate these trains successfully and, by running a similar operation ourselves, we would be carrying on the Stephens tradition of economical motive power. Looking to 1980, a determined effort is to be made to increase our revenue from filming and advertising contracts. Such work is obtained at short notice but large contracts are very difficult to secure, as we are unable to offer producers the full range of railway requirements.

Commercial success was certainly possible, and the following are extracts taken from Mark Yonge's report in the winter 1979 *Terrier* on the success of the 1979 Steam & Country Fair.

The [Fair] is now a major event in the County's calendar and this year attracted more than twice the number of visitors than in 1978. Mistakes were made in the organisation of the 1978 fair and as a result our final profit was a mere few hundred pounds despite glorious weather and satisfied customers, and this did not justify the months of effort that were put into the preparations. Although we set out to give value for money, the primary objective of this, by far the largest event in the Railway's calendar, is to raise money for the restoration of the line. With a fairly disappointing season of weekend traffic behind us, it was all the more vital that this should be a financial success.

The organising committee was strengthened from eight to ten for 1979 and planning commenced as far back as last January. We took a decision right from the beginning to keep the fair in a traditional mould and to avoid, as far as possible the use of modern attractions. We were, for example, offered a modern fairground complete with dodgem cars and loud pop music, but we felt it alien both to the Railway and to the town of Tenterden and that it would not be attractive to the type of family visitor that we wished to come. All the attractions were to be either steam, vintage vehicle or livestock and country crafts – chosen with great care to ensure that they conveyed the rural flavour that we were seeking to promote. Having set the tone, the next phase was to obtain permission from the various landowners for both fair space and car parking, to arrange the printing of posters and leaflets and the drawing up of site plans. In the light of generally an inadequate number of volunteers to man the events in previous years, we decided to farm out as many amenities as possible to outsiders. This would also act as an 'insurance policy' in the event of bad weather and restrict our potential losses. Despite excellent weather in 1978, we did not achieve the takings at the gate that we had expected and it was clear that a large number of people had entered without paying, due to an inadequate number of people issuing tickets on the gate. As ticket receipts represent an overwhelming proportion of our total takings we had to ensure that this was tightened up in the future.

… We felt that some people could be deterred from coming by high petrol prices (in the event this was not a problem) and arrangements were made for special buses to link Ashford station with Tenterden at hourly intervals.

… The total number of visitors for the weekend was 16,739 and we could hardly have coped with any more … total cash receipts were in the order of £15,000 (excluding, of course, those events franchised to outsiders) and the net profit to the railway is expected to be in the order of £6,000, excluding revenue from the running of the trains. During the course of the weekend a visitor survey was carried out and this produced some interesting observations. Two thirds of our visitors had come from a range of between five and 40 miles and 30 per cent had heard about the event from our own posters; 77 per cent came by car and 5 per cent by the special bus. Finally, when asked what they particularly liked to see, the number one choice for both men and women was 'steam trains'!

The winter 1979 *Terrier* also included an article by Steve Whiteman entitled 'Why Signals at Wittersham Road?' Various of its passages are reproduced here:

One may wonder why a signal box and passing loop should be needed at Wittersham Road. In fact it will be essential, if an hourly service is to be introduced between Tenterden and Bodiam, as trains will need to pass at about the halfway point, which is Wittersham Road. Additionally, in the event of trains having to be terminated short of their destinations, facilities have to be available for run-round movements. If we are to run an even more frequent service, passing loops will have to be put in at Rolvenden and Northiam in order to give greater flexibility to the service when trains get behind time. Why should we signal Wittersham Road before Rolvenden? The answer is that passing loops need to be 120 yards long to accommodate five coaches and our longest engine, and there are difficulties in extending the Rolvenden loop to this length. In order to provide continuity of work, it was decided that work should commence at Wittersham Road; and this is already well under way.

Most of the running signal posts, which are of the standard Southern Railway lattice type, have been erected. The arms will be of the lower quadrant type and are from the Great Northern line of the CIE. One ground shunt signal will be of the G.N. pattern … and will be the 'Loop to Up Starting' signal. Permission was given for a shunt signal to be used at this location owing to the limited clearance. Other shunt signals will be of the Southern Railway type... The signal box structure was originally at Deal Junction, between Kearsney and Dover Priory, and (was) removed to Tenterden later that year.

The frame will be of 22 levers, which may seem more than is necessary but ... the signalling has been designed to cover all movements in the event of a second platform being needed.

The level crossing gates will not be interlocked with the signalling, as this would cause complications when the box is switched out of circuit. A yellow light will be installed over the 'stop' boards on each side of the crossing and will be illuminated when the box is open; this will denote to the driver that, providing the gates are open to the Railway, he may proceed without stopping at the 'stop' boards.

The two 'Down' stop signals are mounted on the same post as, owing to the unstable ground in this area, it is not possible to install a half bracket. The top arm on this post will be a subsidiary arm until it is possible to run 'Down' passenger trains to the 'Down' line. The lower arm is for movements to the 'Loop' line. In the 'Up' direction, it will only be possible to run into the 'Loop' line as it was considered unnecessary for trains from the Northiam direction to run to the 'Main' line.

A 'Limit of Shunt' board will be used for shunt movements towards Rolvenden, and a driver must not pass this board unless he is in possession of the Train Staff.

The Engineers siding will be controlled by a ground frame released by the Annetts key attached to the Train Staff. These points will be fitted with an Economical lock which moves and locks the points with one lever. This type of lock is usually called a 'Butterfly' owing to its similarity to a butterfly with its wings open.

The Block Instruments will be Tyers No. 9 Electric Key Token, and will be installed both at Tenterden and in this box.

Electric locks will be put on Tenterden Down Advance Starting and on No. 8 signals, and interlocked with the instruments. The Loco siding points at Rolvenden will also be released by the Annetts key on the Train Staff.

It is hoped to commission this box by July 1981, but in the meantime work will start on some preliminary preparations for the signalling of Rolvenden.

Comment was promptly sent to the next issue of the K&ESR's journal for spring 1980, once again by Simon B. Green.

Sir – I was interested to read the article Why Signals at Wittersham Road? (Tenterden Terrier, Winter 1979) which attempted to explain the massive installation at that site. Accepting the need to pass trains at this point some signalling was required, but the number of individual signals could have been limited. In particular shunt signals would only be used for running round trains terminating there, very unusual when the Northiam extension is open.

As I understand it, shunt signals are used to permit trains to pass main signals which are on – in other words they save time, but that does not mean the permission to pass signals could not be given by flag or verbally. Elimination of shunt signals (which are, of course, a different type to the Great Northern Railway (Ireland) and not the CIE Great Northern line, please!) would have made a much tidier site and a more consistent appearance.

Can we now debate the situation at Bodiam and Northiam before secret decisions are made without consideration of the wider views of the membership? Firstly, would it be generally agreed that no signalling whatsoever is needed at Bodiam, which is a terminal station of very limited complexity and operational activity?

Northiam is more complicated as passing facilities will be needed combined with access to sidings, and in addition this could become a major point of origin for passengers. Having said that we must avoid destroying the character of the site by building a high signal box and posts which dominate the area as they do at Wittersham Road. There are only limited locations for the lever frame at Northiam, and they are very sensitively sited. As has been said before, a ground frame would be sufficient, and could be housed in a low, single-storey structure similar to Robertsbridge 'A'. The number of starting signals should be minimised by avoiding assumptions that trains must be able to leave either platform in either direction. Provision can always be made for later conversion if this proves essential. By the same decision it will be necessary to have only one home signal from each direction, as trains will always arrive in the same platform. N.B. The installation would not be commissioned while Northiam was a terminus, so the problem of departing from a platform having no starter for Tenterden would be avoided.

So far as shunting is concerned, I see no reason why this should require ground signals for the reasons given in the first paragraph. Indeed, consideration might be given to devising a system whereby the Bodiam end of the yard could be operated independently of the signal box when the latter is unmanned when no passenger trains are running.

Those of us who advocate a low-key approach to signalling a light railway do not pretend such an approach does not need careful planning and discussion with the DTp. However, the result of such forethought could not only produce a much better result but also reduce the amount of installation work to a minimum. Let us avoid using another sledgehammer to crack a small nut as has been done at Wittersham Road.

Mr Green's letter was answered in due course by Simon Marsh in the summer 1980 *Terrier*.

Sir – I would like to reply to some of the points made by Simon Green in his letter in the Spring 1980 issue. First, the signalling at Wittersham is designed to permit flexibility of operation, which is essential in view of the nature of the site and the uncertainty currently surrounding the future pattern of train services. It should be obvious that the platform road has to be signalled for traffic in both directions, while both run-round and crossing movements will also have to be provided for, as well as facilities for switching-out the signal box when circumstances permit. It would therefore be very difficult to reduce the number of individual signals as suggested; giving shunting instructions by flag or verbally would be unproductive in terms of staff utilisation and also very time-consuming, both factors which we will have to bear in mind when we are running a full service to Bodiam. Moreover, Mr Green appears to be labouring under a misapprehension in his understanding of the use of shunt signals. That said, however, I certainly agree that the size of the as-yet uncompleted signal box does rather spoil the character of the station and that especial care will have to be taken when selecting structures for Northiam and Bodiam.

As far as I know, no decisions have yet been made regarding the signalling of the latter two locations; when work at Wittersham is (eventually) finished the present intention is to move back and do Rolvenden, where aesthetic factors will not matter so much. When we do come to consider the Sussex end of the line the probable pattern of train service will of course be the main determining factor, although I hope that strenuous efforts will be made to preserve the 'light railway' atmosphere at those as-yet unspoilt places. I must confess I do not fully understand Mr Green's proposals for Northiam, but they do seem to overlook the fact that a signalling strategy can only be decided in the light of the overall operating requirements of the Railway; he seems to err a little too much on the side of aesthetics as opposed to more practical considerations. That is not to say that I do not respect his views however – free and open debate is an essential and often very worthwhile feature of an organisation such as ours.

And finally, while on this subject, may I endorse the implicit pleas in Mr Green's second paragraph for more openness wherever possible in decision-taking on the Railway. I am aware of at least one instance recently where unnecessary secrecy is in danger of leading to possible discontent among volunteers. After all, we are all in this – I hope – for our own enjoyment!

On the third page of the following *Tenterden Terrier* (spring 1980) the reader found the following editorial with the headline 'Things don't change, do they?'

As the years go by, more and more locomotives and rolling stock continue to arrive at Rolvenden, the rusty sidings full of silent relics hopefully waiting their turn in the restoration queue. The scene is now reminiscent of the late 1930s, when the railway was similarly fated, the yard being finally cleared in the wake of the wartime drive for scrap. Owning a locomotive has a magnetic attraction for the average volunteer, but making it work seems to be of secondary importance after the initial enthusiasm has faded. Surely the time has now come to call a halt – indeed maybe numbers should already be reduced to more manageable proportions before we become engulfed in a work programme that we cannot possibly complete, with the effort spread so thinly that nothing works at all.

This immediately caused controversy, two of the letters on the subject appearing in the summer 1980 issue of the journal illustrating the feelings of the membership. The first came from Keith Cook.

Sir – Your Editorial hit the nail on the head; my recent visit to the line drove the nail in and the subsequent comments of my friends finally drove the nail right home. In short, I believe that the Railway is in danger of not knowing where it is going. Is it simply to be preservation of anything, no matter how small the workforce and how long the time span, or are there specific objectives? If the latter, do they now need reappraisal and public stating?

The impression I get is that we are playing at full-size Hornby train sets, accumulating whatever we can find to spend our pocket money on. I know that this is probably an unfair appraisal of our colleagues on the Railway and I admire their enthusiasm and devotion, but are we overdoing this 'Colonel Stephens would have bought it if it had been going' philosophy? Are we fulfilling our duties as an educational, historical Trust?

The second was received from volunteer Alastair Forbes:

Sir – 'The steam trains at Tenterden are living history' – so runs the first sentence of the 1980 timetable leaflet. Would it not be a good thing, then, if visitors to the line in summer were able to see locomotives of some historical interest at the head of these trains? Although I appreciate the fact that the 'Austerities' are useful because of their tractive effort, they can hardly be described as interesting, being uninspiring in appearance and of relatively recent construction. Few steam locomotive enthusiasts would be prepared to travel a long way to see an Austerity in action when they can be seen all over the country. If instead of buying two further examples of this type, the Company had invested in a pre-war engine of suitable weight and power for use on four- and five-coach trains, more people might have been encouraged to make the trip to the K&ESR to see it. My suggestion would be a GWR locomotive of one of these three classes: 45XX (2-6-2T) 57XX, 74XX (0-6-0PT). However, various other types would fit the bill; the yards at Barry are not empty yet!

Alastair was prescient in his motive power suggestions, although it would be decades before they were to be fully realised. The Austerities were indeed useful locomotives, but feelings about them ran high in both directions and have continued to evoke emotional reactions. The signalling controversy continued in parallel with all this, further contributing to the febrile atmosphere that was building up.

Nature had in the meantime taken a hand in respect of Wittersham Road. Historically, spectacular flooding was far from unknown in the Rother Valley, and on at least one occasion during the preservation project's formative years in the 1960s. On these occasions, the valley regained much of its medieval appearance from the centuries when Tenterden had been a coastal town and the sea came up to where Rolvenden Station now stands. On 26 and 27 December 1979, almost 48 hours of continuous rain allowed several million gallons of water to find their way through a breach in the Newmill Channel flood wall and into the fields around Wittersham Road station. As the gap deepened and widened the waters rose, creating a vast lake covering many thousands of acres, bisected by the Railway and broken by a few clumps of trees. It seemed at first that the train service on Sunday 30th would have to be cancelled, but some rapid reorganisation enabled the diesel railcar to maintain services as far as the accommodation crossing at the end of the Oxney straight (named after the erstwhile island which was temporarily again separated from the mainland!) By the early morning of New Year's Day, the waters had receded sufficiently for the scheduled steam service to operate. Luckily the rise and fall of the floods was slow enough not to have caused any apparent damage to the permanent way. The K&ESR was able to assist the Southern Water Authority (then responsible for Newmill Channel) by transporting a load of sandbags out to the Oxney straight to make a temporary repair to the breach in the flood wall.

This was a foretaste of the climate change to be experienced in later decades.

Chapter 6

The *Tenterden Terrier*'s editorial for the summer 1980 issue was in buoyant mood as it looked ahead into the new decade, although reflecting the continuing uncertainty in the affairs of the nation. It was headed 'The next leap forward':

> The exciting new plans for extending the line from Wittersham to Northiam by 1982 should add impetus and enthusiasm to all who look forward to the day when trains will once again run through to Bodiam, for it is not until then that the traffic carrying potential of the line will be fully realised. Of course, there are those who will say that the time is not right and that we face the danger of stretching our resources to the point that the very existence of the Railway could be prejudiced. The crux of the matter is finance and, as the economy lurches from one crisis to another, unfortunately there never is a good time for raising money. Very shortly proposals will be announced for the raising of some £40,000 to finance the capital works. The scheme will be both novel and attractive to those who wish to participate in the success of the longer term aims of the Company. Let us hope that not only will members give this their whole-hearted support, but also the local populace which shares in the additional prosperity that the Railway has brought to Tenterden and will bring to the surrounding communities.

In the meantime, May 1980 provided a publicity opportunity when the 150th anniversary of the Canterbury & Whitstable was celebrated. The K&ESR, as one of Kent's youngest railways (opened 1900), participated with enthusiasm in this commemoration of one of the world's oldest, even if it had been closed since 1952. Cash was provided by the very active Maidstone Group which enabled the Peckett *Marcia* and Terrier *Bodiam* to be hauled through Canterbury on low loaders as part of the event.

One of the biggest success stories for the K&ESR continued to be the growth in popularity of the 'Wealden Pullman'. The number of diners served (or 'covers' in the jargon of the hospitality industry) had increased eightfold since these trains were introduced in 1975 and a major problem, which has never been entirely resolved, was one of unsatisfied demand. Until the middle of 1979, up to 75 covers per night were regularly being served, but during 1980 it was decided to restrict numbers to 64 on each train to improve standards and in particular to provide for more serving space throughout the train. To increase overall capacity, the Pullman was now to run on some Friday evenings as well as Saturdays in the high season, despite the problems that this would present with food preparation and laundry.

At this stage, the train itself consisted of two coaches, together with Pullman car *Barbara* which served as a bar and also contained the kitchen. A number of major improvements were made to the Pullman set after the close of the 1979 season, both for the benefit of the staff, who had to work very quickly in cramped and difficult conditions, and also for the diners. In the light of modern day requirements, the Railway was advised to install a hot and cold running water system in *Barbara*'s kitchen, and a double bowl sink and hot water in the bar. Previously, staff had managed with a caravan-type hand water pump, a single sink and a Calor gas stove for heating water. The practical problems of putting in this new system were considerable but overcome with a multi-point gas water heater, operating from the existing propane supply, and a 24 volt electric pump for drawing water from the original tank and fitted with an automatic pressure switch energised only when either the hot or cold taps were turned on. The interior was also generally smartened up at the same time.

A further improvement was the introduction into the set of a Maunsell BNO coach, K&ESR No. 53, in place of the identical No. 54. No. 53 had been out of service for major restoration and would now be kept exclusively for Pullman trains. The exterior had been repainted in what was then thought to be Kent & East Sussex livery – similar to Pullman – and the vehicle returned to service on 26 April, the first day of the 1980 season. The livery was in later years changed to the correct Southern Railway Maunsell-era dark green and lettered accordingly. It was further intended that in 1981 the Mark 1 RU restaurant car, purchased from British Rail at York the previous year, would replace the TSO then in the formation and provide much greater kitchen accommodation. During 1980 the vehicle was undergoing refurbishment at Tenterden.

The 'Wealden Pullman' was the flagship of the Company's operations; it was popular with the public and a very profitable source of revenue to the Railway as well, as it was then being run entirely by volunteers. The idea of such a service dated as far back as the purchase of the Pullman cars in 1964, and it is an undeniable fact that its commercial success has underpinned the continued existence of the K&ESR through five decades. It nevertheless has to be said that, being far removed from the basic concept of the preserved Railway, the tail has at times appeared to wag the dog – ungrateful though this statement sounds. Although the train has in later years been regarded as an integrated part of the organisation, looking at it from the outside in the 1980s there appeared to be two distinct operations on the Railway – the Pullman (almost 'open access' in later parlance) and everything else – with the former taking precedence and priority. For a short while the Pullman even had its own newsletter, which was included with the *Tenterden Terrier*. Years later, I discovered that there had been an undertone of dissent among some volunteers at the time although it would of course have been heresy for either volunteer or armchair member to have voiced this. A more charitable summary would be that the Pullman has performed a 'Robin Hood' function.

An innovation during 1980 was the entry into service of a vintage four wheel-coach which was believed to have once been owned by the District Railway. Known as No. 100, this vehicle had for many years been serving as a shed at Dungeness. It was rescued by a member and restored at his expense on its new, shortened, underframe which had previously been beneath a Southern Railway Parcels and Miscellaneous van (PMV). There has been much debate as to whether this vehicle is in fact a 'District' coach. At one time, it was thought that it was actually a section cut from a Metropolitan Railway rigid eight-wheeler of the 1860s, but opinion has since swung back in favour of a District Railway origin. Whatever the truth, it had, since the early days of the preservation scheme, been intended to run a vintage train, and this now began to look like becoming a reality.

The Steam & Country Fair was, like the Pullman, a big potential source of income for the Railway. It was, however, vulnerable to the weather and, in view of the heavy financial commitment, a particularly wet weekend could spell disaster for the K&ESR. For the first four years of the event the weather had been favourable and a substantial profit had been made in 1979.

Unfortunately, on the Friday night before the 1980 event, an inch of rain fell on the Tenterden area and it seemed likely that no movement of vehicles would be possible, particularly in the lower arena field. Saturday was nonetheless dry, albeit cloudy, and the opportunity was taken to spread straw over the most vulnerable areas. Traction engines were unable to access the arena, but the day was a success with a total of 5,429 visitors, 1,096 also travelling on the Railway in trains of seven coaches. These were the longest that have ever run in the heritage era, and would rarely be a K&ESR formation today. The Sunday enjoyed much better weather and the number of visitors rose to 10,654, of which 1,604 travelled on the trains. The total number over the weekend was down by 4 per cent compared to the previous year. This was regarded as a very satisfactory outcome in view of the weather pattern, the economic situation – which was still not the British 'economic miracle' of later years – and the Biggin Hill Air Show only 30 miles away. Gross takings at the gate were £18,500.

Despite this result and the optimistic outlook of the previous issue of the journal, the winter 1980 *Terrier*'s editorial struck a much more downbeat and cautionary tone. It was headed 'Look before you leap'.

> It is a pity that the plans for extending the line from Wittersham to Northiam by 1982 have had to be tempered before they even got under way, but a scheme backed by hope alone could have little chance of success. Indeed, it could have brought bankruptcy to the K&ESR for the second time in its history. In the event, a more gradual approach will be adopted, utilising the core of voluntary labour that we can realistically rely upon, with Wittersham to Hexden as a starter and concurrently some remedial work on the Rother bridge. In the meantime the bond issue will go ahead, initially for £20,000, with details being circulated to members shortly. At £25 a throw, a pretty certificate plus a guarantee of your money back in 15 years hence should be an investment worthy of a place over everybody's fireplace; with interest at 8 per cent it looks like being a real winner. First orders please!

It had been decided during the year to press on with restoring the line as far as Hexden Bridge and to raise the necessary finance by issuing the Bearer Bonds referred to above – investments on which fixed interest was paid and the principal sum was repaid after a set number of years. This was in itself an innovative approach, as it was believed that this was the first occasion on which such bonds had been issued since the Second World War.

To round off the year there was a change of leadership when, after six years, Mark Yonge replaced Stephen Bennett as Chairman. In the meantime, with the possibility of services beyond Wittersham Road seeming as far away as ever, the new Chairman addressed the membership via the *Terrier* in the same backtracking tone as the editorial.

> Much has been achieved on our Railway since it was reopened in 1974; over one-third of the track and three stations are now fully operational, and at the time of writing income in 1980 is running comfortably ahead of expenditure. In some areas we outshine our competitors – particularly with the Wealden Pullman, our Santa Specials and the Steam and Country Fair; in others we are less fortunate and as a result of either staff shortages or friction and disagreement amongst the workforce we are proving to be seriously unproductive. Nevertheless we are on the verge of an exciting new venture with the big push towards Northiam. The Directors are of the opinion that the cost of restoring the

line to Northiam utilising mainly voluntary labour and charging materials and services at 1980 prices is of the order of £40,000, but in view of our limited resources it has now been decided to tackle the work in two stages. The first is proposed for completion by the late summer of 1982 at a cost of £20,000. In order to finance this initial stage, which involves laying suitable sidings at Wittersham Road, renovating the track from there to Hexden Bridge and repairing the bridge over the Rother, the Directors are proposing an issue of Bearer Bonds in multiples of £25, carrying an interest entitlement of 8 per cent. Each bond will be attractively designed and it is hoped that every member will participate to the extent of at least one bond. A second Bond issue will be launched at a later date to finance the remainder the programme.

I cannot over estimate the importance of supporting the issue; if it were to fail the chances of getting to Northiam would be negligible and the line will almost certainly have to be abandoned and the track lifted. This would mean the railway terminating forever at Wittersham Road and the traffic potential from Bodiam Castle being lost irrevocably. Finally, may I refer once again to a subject that has been discussed many times in this journal – voluntary labour. The costings for the bond issue have been made on the assumption that the bulk of the work will be carried out by the efforts of our own members. If a sufficient number of people do not participate enthusiastically the project will not succeed, even if the necessary money is raised. We have appealed many times in the past for volunteers – this time your efforts are crucial.

One wonders if the dire warnings, reminiscent of some of the K&ESR's darkest days in the 1960s, were totally appropriate. Mark Yonge was however no bad hand at the dark art of spin, so the heavy selling approach may not have been out of place. Even less happy, if honest, is the frank admission of counterproductive friction among the workforce. It does not sit well in an appeal for support. This was something which unfortunately came to cloud many people's view of a group of volunteers – to whose influence on the Railway our attention now turns.

Although reopening to Bodiam might have seemed a very distant dream, for a few years from 1981 something like it did happen and a major digression is necessary into the activities of the successor to the South East London Group. The emergence of the Thameside Area Group, which covered South East London and North West Kent, was arguably one of the most significant developments in the history of the heritage era K&ESR. The inaugural meeting took place in March 1978 in Welling. Meetings were quickly established on a six-weekly cycle. October brought a foretaste of Thameside 'get up and go'. Here the legendary name of George Wright entered the story. George organised the recovery of an LB&SCR fruit van from an isolated section of track in Belvedere on 29 October, having persuaded ten volunteers to take part. The van reached the K&ESR on 11 November.

George Wright remains a highly regarded figure. In 1978 he had been a BR driver with a total of 24 years railway experience; he had been with the K&ESR since 1974. I believe that I only met him once, on a cold December day when we as a family were at Tenterden for a Santa Special. A giant of a man leaned out of *Maunsell* and asked my then small children if they would like to visit the loco's cab. Years later I deduced this to have been George Wright. Despite his imposing presence there was something kindly in his manner and, from an adult point of view, something else – charisma.

A sponsored pump trolley marathon held on 30 March 1979 raised £700 for the K&ESR. The election of a new Group Committee, with Charlie Masterson as Chairman, was followed by the Thameside Group taking over responsibility for the care and maintenance of Rolvenden Station. This scheme included recreating the façade and canopy of the old station building together with a small hut should the station be manned. This happened, but it has been far from consistent. Use of the station by the public has not been promoted and it mainly sees use as a staff halt and by enthusiasts wishing to see the locos. The official reopening took place on 5 July 1980, actress and local resident Joanna Lumley – who at that time was appearing in the *New Avengers* – officiating. One wonders if *Ab Fab*'s 'Patsy Stone' of later years would have been as welcome at an organisation which at times seemed to be trying to distance itself from its turbulent 1960s origins.

The dawn of the 1980s saw the Group begin work on two landmark projects. The first of these was the restoration of a GER six-wheel coach for the K&ESR at premises in Plumstead. It was to be a crucial step in the eventual establishment of the Victorian (later Vintage) train. The second was the notable innovation of Steam at Bodiam.

George Wright's item told the detailed story in his own words in the winter 1980 *Tenterden Terrier*:

> The idea of a steam event at Bodiam over the Sunday and Monday of the 1980 August Bank Holiday was first discussed at a Thameside Group meeting in December 1979. Major Rose of the Railway Inspectorate was approached and, after an inspection, gave his approval to the plans. The general idea was for a sponsored pump trolley to run from the station platform at Bodiam to Northiam at hourly intervals; in addition a steam engine and coach would run alternately with a pump trolley along ¼ mile of track in the other direction towards Junction Road. Resco Railways kindly agreed to loan their recently restored District Railway coach, and the Board gave permission for *Marcia* to provide the motive power. On 17th August we fought our way through the jungle between Northiam and Bodiam with a diesel-hauled supply train and a start was made on cutting back the heavy undergrowth which had grown up on both sides of the track. The problem of water supply at Bodiam was solved by running a pipe 150 yards from the station to a private house, connected up to a primitive but very effective water column which consisted of a sleeper-built trestle surmounted by three 45 gallon drums coupled together and emptied by means of a three-inch rubber pipe.
>
> On Saturday 23rd August *Marcia* and a train consisting of two wagons, the District coach (heavily sheeted) and a brake van left Rolvenden at 9.00am and proceeded to Northiam without incident, assisted over Wittersham summit by the diesel, which then returned to Rolvenden with the train staff. From there the jungle was tackled by means of a flat wagon propelled ahead of the train with four men on board armed with chain saws. Sunday dawned bright and sunny and by 11.00am a continuous stream of visitors were arriving; by 6.00pm more than 700 passengers had ridden on the train. Nine pump trolley trips had been completed to Northiam and 15 towards Junction Road. On Monday a similar number of passengers were carried and 57 members were recruited over the two day period.

The Thameside Group did well merely in persuading HM Railway Inspectorate (HMRI) to allow an event of this kind. The need to use both the operating and non-operating sections of the Railway raised a few eyebrows 'in-house', and a dispute took place over the locked barrier which then existed beyond Wittersham Road. This became very 'political', and the issue was ultimately resolved through negotiations carried out by George Wright in person with the departments involved. Whatever obstacles had to be overcome, Thameside Group was becoming a force to be reckoned with, and in addition to the restoration of the GER coach became involved in much other work around the Railway.

Major Rose of HMRI had approved running an ex-BR four-wheel AC railbus, W79978, which the K&ESR had bought from the North Yorkshire Moors Railway in June 1980, between Bodiam and a new halt near Great Dixter house. This was built in an eight-week period, the first working party arriving on site on Sunday, 1 March. A flail was hired during April and the line flailed between Northiam and Bodiam. Dixter Halt was opened in pouring rain on 23 May 1981. During the Spring Bank Holiday (24 and 25 May) *Marcia* and the District coach worked towards Junction Road and the railbus to Dixter Halt. The whole event was repeated on 30 and 31 August. The regular meetings were well attended by that time and one account of activities was able to point out to the general membership that the Group 'helps your railway'. Thameside was riding high, and it is unsurprising that at the 1981 Tenterden Railway Company AGM, George Wright was elected to the Board.

At the Group meeting in October 1981, it was decided to assist the Permanent Way Department with the extension to Hexden Bridge, with Thameside Group working as a self-contained unit. By March 1981, half a mile had been completed. Work was delayed by weather conditions in December and January and by the breakdown of the crane but re-started in mid-January using sleepers and rails recovered from Batchelors' private sidings at Ashford. All this had been achieved by a work group averaging seven people – a most creditable achievement considering the other K&ESR commitments of most of the Group. But even Thameside was not immune from staff resource problems, and only a handful of new faces had been seen. Work on the six-wheeler was also still proceeding, but with only two people working on this project, one of whom was David Stratton – whose eminent name we record for the first time in this account.

During the spring of 1982 the Thameside Group had started re-sleepering the Northiam to Bodiam section from the Bodiam end. Steam at Bodiam was again planned for August, but a worrying undertone about volunteer numbers reappeared and it was stated 'New faces always welcome as Group's activities are carried out by small number of very dedicated enthusiasts'. Were Thameside running out of steam or trying to do too much? In the event, the August Steam at Bodiam failed to materialise due to the state of the track. Thameside Group had other important commitments and were unable to complete the work. They tried again and on 29/30 May 1983 *Marcia* and the District coach again provided a service. An hourly railbus trip was operated from 1.30 to 4.30pm on all Sundays in July and August. The steam train planned for August had to be cancelled due to 'the lack of a suitable steam locomotive' – at least that was the official reason given. The abandonment of steam at Bodiam has remained the subject of uncertainties (controversy would be too strong a word) for years afterwards. Alternative explanations given were concerns (TRC or HMRI?) about what was, with respect to the professionalism of those involved, a somewhat improvised operation. There is also a suggestion that the popular nature of the events tended to draw traffic from the main service at Tenterden, with the consequent dangers of dividing one's forces. Or was it, one wonders, that some of the more abrasive personalities in Thameside had rubbed people up the wrong way, and this was an opportunity to retaliate?

Chapter 7

We return to the main course of the story with a look at the passenger figures for 1980, which for some reason were not published until the winter 1981 *Tenterden Terrier*. These showed that 50,501 people travelled, an increase of 10 per cent over the previous year, although only returning to the levels of 1978. Average per-train figures were published for the first time and, excluding the Santa Season, these indicated the very low average of 53 per train. By contrast, the Pullman and Santa trains could not satisfy demand. It was realised that the Railway was running too many ordinary service trains, or, in commercial terms, over-trading.

Plans to extend the Railway were nonetheless detailed by Board member John Miller in the spring 1981 issue of the *Tenterden Terrier* in an article titled 'Pressing on to Northiam'. After first reminding members of the Board's decision in May 1980 to further extend the line he continued:

> In the first instance a professional report was commissioned on the state of the track and the various bridges. This concluded that about £40,000 at 1980 prices would be required to open to Northiam, taking into account upgrading of the track for the axle loading of 'Austerity' class locomotives and fairly major repairs to Rother Bridge.
>
> The work will be tackled in six stages, of which the first three are planned for completion by late 1982, at a cost of £20,000. These are:
>
> 1. Finishing off the Wittersham Road station site, including the provision of engineers' sidings.
>
> 2. Upgrading the track between Wittersham Road and Hexden bridge.
>
> 3. Renovation of Rother Bridge itself.
>
> 4. Completion of the approaches to Hexden Bridge and upgrading the track from there to the Rother bridge.
>
> 5. Upgrading the track between Rother Bridge and Northiam Station.
>
> 6. Repairs to Northiam Station and change in the layout of the site to meet the requirements of passenger services.
>
> Finance for the first three stages has proved to be no problem. On 26 November 1980 the Company launched a £20,000 issue of 8 per cent unsecured bearer bonds ... the issue was fully subscribed within eight weeks of the lists opening, and the company has

subsequently had to return money to those applicants who sent their forms in after 24th January. 273 of the successful applications came from company members for a total of 544 bonds, and the remaining 256 from 153 members of the public. The uniqueness of the issue has ensured that the bonds will rapidly increase in value; already bond No. 001 has changed hands at auction for £130 and bond 007 (signed by Mr Roger Moore) for £42.50. A further bond issue is contemplated in about two years time to finance the remaining three stages of the programme.

The Railway can therefore be well satisfied with its most successful fund raising operation ever and the fact that it has achieved yet another 'first'. Members will recall that just as the Rother Valley (Light) Railway Company was the very first to be granted an order under the 1896 Light Railway Act ... a great deal of hard work will be needed in 1981 if the ambitious expansion plans are to be completed in time; much will depend on how suitable recruits can be seconded to the labour force. A more detailed look at the work involved under each of the six stages will give a better idea of the task ahead:

(1) Wittersham Road Station

The earthworks behind the platform have to be completed and seeded with grass. The area between the north boundary fence and the slope behind the platform needs to be levelled, have drainage put in, and a hardcore roadway laid from the car park to the lower end of the site where the engineers' sidings will be constructed. The area for the sidings has to be levelled and drained, and a drain provided from the former Shrewsbury Abbey water-tower, installed in 1980. All this work is scheduled to be completed during the spring of 1981. In particular, the pointwork giving access to the new engineers' sidings has to be laid into the running line by the water-tower during the 'closed' season (i.e. by the end of March). The hardcore roadway is to give access for contractors' lorries bringing in ballast, sleepers and other materials needed for the extension work.

(2) Wittersham Road to Hexden Bridge

This section, amounting to nearly a mile in length, includes Wittersham Bank which is second only to Tenterden Bank in its gradients. Most of the section is on wooden sleepers, virtually all of which will have to be replaced. About 150 yards short of Hexden Bridge the track changes to the 75lb per yard concrete sleeper track panels, which continue all the way to Northiam crossing. There is one minor bridge to be repaired and, as on the entire route, the track requires ballast. Accommodation crossings and fences need repairs and the lineside must be cleared of undergrowth. This work is scheduled for completion during 1981 so that in the 1982 season a railbus service can be introduced between Wittersham and Hexden Bridge as the first extension of public services. (There was of course to be no platform at Hexden Bridge)

(3) Rother bridge

With a span of 66ft, this is the largest engineering structure on the Railway. It is planned that work will start on this during summer 1981, concurrently with the work on section (2).

The bridge has to be cleaned, de-rusted, treated and then primed. New stages will have to be welded in to repair the metalwork of the side members, and the decking will have to be repaired and strengthened. The whole bridge will require painting, and some repairs will be necessary to the concrete abutments. Up to £10,000 has been allowed for this work. At one time it was thought that the bridge would have to replaced as being beyond repair, but it is now thought that this remedial work will extend its life by 15 years, at which time the bridge will have to be re-considered for replacement.

(4) Hexden Bridge to Rother Bridge

Hexden Bridge was replaced in 1979, with the height raised nearly 5ft in order to be consistent with other local flood defences. There is still some minor work to complete at Hexden, and the approaches on either side have to be brought up to correct levels. All the concrete sleeper track panels on this 3/4 mile section will be dismantled, re-assembled and aligned; broken sleepers will be replaced and extra sleepers inserted to give more support under rail joints. Three minor bridges and various culverts and drains require some attention. It is hoped that work may start on this section during 1981 and be completed in 1982.

(5) Rother Bridge to Northiam Station

This section is a little over a mile in length and consists of a long curve between two straights. There are a further three minor bridges and various culverts and drains needing attention. Included in the work on this section will be the installation of crossing gates over the A28 road at Northiam, probably the busiest road crossing on the Railway.

(6) Northiam Station

A small working party will be set up to consider the overall future development of the site. This station (and Bodiam) remain much as they were in 'the old days' and while the present day commercial and operational requirements will have to be considered it is hoped that we may retain (and restore) the essential atmosphere of the 'light railway' station. Certainly the station building and existing platform will have to be repaired, and perhaps extended. Finally, completion of work already in hand on the signalling system at Wittersham Road this summer will allow the movement of engineers' trains between passenger workings, and in due course enable us to use the railbus for passenger services on the restored sections as we gradually push the limit of operation towards Northiam.

Building projects during 1981 included a start to the Carriage and Wagon shed at Tenterden, which was paid for from the earnings of the Steam & Country Fair, and Wittersham Road signal box which was nearing completion. Concrete sleepers, which, outside station areas, have in the years since have been much used on the K&ESR, began to appear at this time. The first purchased had been for use in the 'wet' cutting on Tenterden Bank. A further supply was to be obtained, using some of the Bond issue money, for the above-mentioned replacement of the existing wooden section between Wittersham Road and Hexden Bridge. As mentioned in John Miller's article, just on the Wittersham side of the bridge began another group of concrete sleepers, this time forming ex-Army track panels which ran as far as Northiam. These had been part of a deal with a scrap merchant which involved the exchange of the existing bullhead rail for the lighter section ex-military track. At the time it seemed a good idea. The Railway was to come to regret it.

The motive power diet during the year was varied somewhat by the re-entry into service following overhaul of USA No. 22 *Maunsell*. The use of 'loan' locomotives reached the K&ESR September 1981 when, rather bizarrely, the National Railway Museum's replica of Stephenson's *Rocket* ran during the Steam & Country Fair and actually proved capable of tackling Tenterden Bank, even hauling its replica Liverpool & Manchester vehicles. The Bluebell Railway's *Fenchurch* made up for the absence of the K&ESR's own Terriers during the same event. Locomotive variety continued into 1982 with return of Manning Wardle *Charwelton* after several years away receiving an overhaul and working elsewhere.

There is in the company archives a report about an error-filled day in July 1981 which nonetheless, and by the standards of the time, did not involve anything actually dangerous. The background was that, due to procedural and communication shortcomings, a filming job had been arranged for 4.30pm on Wednesday, 8 July, at the same time as a 'Q path' afternoon tea party booking. To complicate matters, the Loco Department had arranged for Austerity No. 23, required for the filming, to have a boiler washout. Fortunately, a members' special for an Area Group the same evening had been cancelled.

The day dawned very warm and was to remain hot and oppressive. The service locomotive was USA Class No. 22 and the crew signed on at 6.00am. No. 23 was in the shed awaiting its washout. The fireman lit up No. 22 for the first train at 10.30; this was not in the public timetable but was run on Wednesdays for school parties. Shortly before 9.00, the Line Manager at Tenterden asked what bookings there were for the day. (The 'Line Manager' was roughly equivalent to 'Person in Charge' – not an actual post and involving different individuals from day to day.) At that point he discovered that there was a party booked for the 4.15pm train and the realisation dawned that this would clash with the filming session. The initial reaction was to cancel the party booking, although he quickly realised that this would be impossible at such short notice.

Meanwhile, at Rolvenden, the boiler washout and examination of No. 23 had commenced. Having discovered the clash of bookings, the Line Manager asked No. 22's driver (a board member) for advice. It was then that he found out that No. 22 was in steam, and not No. 23 as he was expecting. He gave instructions to terminate the washout and prepare No. 23 for service as soon as possible. The fitter concerned however dug his heels in and insisted on continuing – he had already removed 40 plugs and mudhole doors. He would have the job completed by 3.30 and the loco could be in steam two to two-and-a-half hours later. Repeated enquiries from Tenterden during the course of the morning hindered progress.

The light engine arrived at Tenterden at 9.58, about the same time as the guard, who only found out about the filming on arrival – the film unit vehicles were already in the yard – and gathered that there could be difficulties about the wrong locomotive. It was to be lunchtime before he also found out about the 4.15 tea party train. The train formation until the 4.15 was not what was required for the filming, and a shunt would be needed during the afternoon. Seven school parties had pre-booked. The number of non-pre-booked passengers through the day was very small, a mere 42 persons. Even at this relatively early stage in the K&ESR's heritage era, the value of pre-booked parties and film work was becoming apparent.

Services then proceeded to run behind time. The late departures of the 10.30 and 11.45 services could be attributed in part to the time involved in getting parties aboard. The 1.45pm was delayed, in part because the locomotive was coaled at Rolvenden at lunchtime and also because this train and the 3.00 service were affected by the knock-on consequences of late-running preceding trains. Lack of crossing keepers at Cranbrook Road and at Rolvenden (coupled with the difficulty of opening the latter whilst being repaired!) accounted for much of the slow running. Quick turnrounds at Wittersham Road were prevented by the disconnected level crossing end points which required unclipping and barring over. The stop at Cranbrook Road in the Up direction slowed No. 22's steaming rate, resulting in very slow progress for the rest of the way into Tenterden. There were also priming problems later on, and the ticket inspector reported that several passengers complained about the stopping and starting and general lack of progress.

22's driver requested that Cranbrook Road gates be manned to help trains maintain time, and that a coach be detached. The latter request was not possible as 140 passengers were pre-booked on the next return trip from Wittersham Road. Lack of staff prevented the manning of the level crossing.

At 12.59pm, No. 22, as mentioned above, left for recoaling at Rolvenden, necessary as five round trips were being run that day. Coaling was delayed while someone was summoned from Tenterden to drive the coaling tractor. The loco returned to Tenterden at 1.52, being stopped at the home signal by the signalman who advised the driver that the platform was blocked. This was technically correct, although it would have been possible to run into the loop and then shunt onto the train. As a consequence, the 1.45 service did not depart until 1.55, and returned late. At about 2.00pm, two catering volunteers arrived at Tenterden to organise the tea on the 4.15 train. They were aware of the film unit's presence but were not advised of any difficulties. They were asked to be ready to board the tea party as soon as possible, and as the coach to be used was empty on the 3.00pm service they prepared the carriage for tea during the journey.

The fireman for the film job arrived at Rolvenden around 3.20, expecting to take over from the daytime crew, and was amazed to be told, in view of the work in hand, that No 23 was required that evening. He changed and gave a hand with a faulty blow-down valve. Tenterden phoned again and asked whether No. 23 was in steam; the reply was that it would not be possible to light until the repair was completed. 23's fireman asked who his driver was, but no-one knew. It took an hour to replace all the plugs and fittings and remove No. 23 from the shed, the loco being lit up around 5.15 and permitted to warm up at the normal rate. The Line Manager had stressed the importance of running the 3.00pm service to time but it returned at 4.02, 12 minutes late.

The 36-strong tea party arrived before the return of the mid-afternoon train and were 'enchanted' by the sight of it ascending the Bank into Tenterden. Sadly, they were soon to be disillusioned. The party was ushered aboard their Mark 1 TSO in accordance with the earlier instructions, many being elderly and infirm and requiring the assistance of the boarding steps. Upon arrival of the train, a heated discussion ensued on the platform about what to do next. It had been decided earlier in the day that it would be impracticable to make up a Maunsell set and it was agreed with the film unit that two Birdcage coaches (plus No. 23) would do. By this time, the film crew were ready to shoot and were becoming agitated.

There were then difficulties deciding on the shunting moves required. If the two Birdcages were left in filming position, minus engine, while the tea party travelled to Wittersham Road it would not be possible to return the party to Tenterden since the Birdcages would be blocking the platform. Various ideas were put forward (including leaving the tea party in a siding without a ride!) and before shunting could take place the party had to alight from the train, the catering volunteers being advised about this as they were about to serve tea. A number of these passengers then had to stand on the platform as there were insufficient seats and, as the film unit was near

USA Class K&ESR No 22 Maunsell with a three coach set at Rolvenden on 12 May 1974. *John Wickham*

Terrier K&ESR No 3 *Bodiam* at Rolvenden on 12 May 1974. *John Wickham*

Tenterden Town Station in the 1970s after reopening. The buildings are in the Southern style green and light stone used before the original company colours were rediscovered. *Photographer not known / Tenterden Terrier Archive*

Junior Leaders at work at Newmill Channel in 1976. The sheet steel piles had been driven in by the Southern Water Authority. *John Liddell / CSRM*

The Rt. Hon. Edward Heath MBE MP talks with K&ESR members during the opening ceremony at Wittersham Road Station on 16 June 1978. *Brian Stephenson*

Edward Heath and driver George Wright on the footplate of No. 23 at the reopening of Wittersham Road Station. *Brian Stephenson*

AC Railbus on a Thameside Group organised service at Dixter Halt. *Brian Stephenson*

Marcia with the District Coach and ex-L&NWR brake van during one of the Thameside Groups Steam at Bodiam events. *Gordon Young / Phil Edwards Collection*

A Steam & Country Fair of the first series. *Brian Stephenson*

From the September 1981 Steam & Country Fair. The area on the left beyond the hedge is now Morph's Field, used by the K&ESR for car parking during special events. *Phil Edwards*

The Lord Warden train which carried HM the Queen Mother on 9 June 1982. *Brian Stephenson*

HM Queen Elizabeth the Queen Mother, accompanied by K&ESR Chairman Mark Yonge, unveils a plaque commemorating her visit on 9 June 1982. *CSRM*

HM Queen Elizabeth the Queen Mother signs the visitors book whilst speaking with TRC Director Tim Stanger on 9 June 1982. *Doug Lindsay Collection*

Ivatt 2MT No 41241 at Cranbrook Road on 2nd January 1983 following overhaul by Resco Ltd. *Brian Stephenson*

Visiting GWR 0-4-2T No. 1466 with the Pullman set in 1984. *Brian Stephenson*

Northiam Station during the early stages of restoration and the rebuilding of the platform. *John Liddell/CSRM*

Wittersham Road during the 1989 Northiam extension works with prepared track panels ready for installation on the running line. *John Liddell/CSRM*

Works train at Northiam in 1989 headed by Class 14 D9525. *John Liddell/CSRM*

Track laying at Northiam in the summer of 1989. *John Liddell/CSRM*

The visibly contrived climax to the *Challenge Anneka* episode in July 1989. *Brian Stephenson*

Electro Diesel 72126 *The Kent & East Sussex Railway* descends Tenterden Bank on 27 May 1991. *Brian Stephenson*

K&ESR No. 19 *Norwegian* with the Vintage Train on Tenterden Bank. *Chris Fautley*

Relaying track on the 'Rabbit Warren' rebuild in the early months of 1993. *Ian Scarlett*

The extensive repairs needed at the 'Rabbit Warren' are to be seen in this view. *Ian Scarlett*

Class 25 D7672 *Tamworth Castle* during its visit to the K&ESR in 1992. *Chris Fautley*

Visiting Hastings Diesel at Tenterden Town in 1993. *Chris Fautley*

Bodiam Station slumbers among the weeds circa 1984. *Chris Fautley*

Bodiam in 1997. The overgrowth has been cleared but the work necessary for reopening has yet to begin. *Chris Fautley*

Bodiam Station on 23 July 1998. The extension to the platform is underway. Note the new concrete facing. *John Liddell/CSRM*

Chritopher Fildes speaks at the Bodiam reopening ceremony. Dr Heather Couper, representing the Millenium Commission, is to the left of the microphone with Patron Admiral Sir Lindsay Bryson to her left. K&ESR Chairman Robin Dyce is on the right hand side of the picture. *Brian Stephenson*

Terrier No 32678 heads the VIP Train at Bodiam on 2nd April 2000, the day the Northiam–Bodiam section reopened. *Brian Stephenson*

HRH the Duke of Gloucester accompanied by K&ESR Chairman Norman Brice exchanges a word with Station Master Harry Hickmott before boarding the Royal Train on 5 July 2000. *Brian Stephenson*

No. 19 *Norwegian* and mixed train at Bodiam during a Hoppers Weekend. Note the hop bines decorating the canopy supports. *John Liddell/CSRM*

Mill Ditch 8 November 2000. The damage caused by the washout. *John Liddell/CSRM*

Reconstructing the Mill Ditch wash out. *John Liddell/CSRM*

Flooding at Wittersham Road in the early months of 2001. *Phil Edwards*

The excavation of the Colonel Stephens era weigh bridge at Tenterden by Museum volunteers. *Henry Edwards/CSRM*

Following a major overhaul, Pullman Car Barbara with Carriage & Wagon staff on 24 May 2001. Left to right, John Brice; the author; Alan Brice; Clive Lowe; Ron Nuttman; John Millward; Gordon Young; Frank Kent; John Weller. *John Liddell/CSRM*

No 32670 at Robertsbridge Junction with carriages from the Vintage Train on 20 September 2013. This formation worked a push-pull service to Northbridge Street. *Alan Crotty*

A view of the K&ESR that went round the world via television. The Vintage Train at Cranbrook Road during the English stage of the 2007 Tour de France cycle race. *John Liddell/CSRM*

the Booking Office, they were unable to spread down the platform or shelter from the sun under the station canopy.

A complicated shunt followed which resulted in the necessary coaches being marshalled for the service train but with both Birdcages also coupled on at the 'Headcorn' end. There were then a number of problems including four attempts to join up buckeye couplings between the Mark 1s (this task taking more than 15 minutes) and the handbrakes proving very difficult to release. The report following the subsequent investigation commented that the shunting should not have required at least an hour to complete and that the discussions leading up to them were obviously unsatisfactory. The guard had a particularly onerous task, working in temperatures of over 80°F.

The tea party was eventually permitted to re-board and finally served tea, although their coach was now uncomfortably warm. The party members were, unsurprisingly, disappointed about the delay and not least the need to get on and off the train. Shortly after re-boarding, the party organiser was told that, because of the filming, they could only travel one way to Wittersham Road where their coach would collect them. The organiser was 'unhappy' about this change in plan and was 'extremely concerned' about any extra payment that the coach driver might demand for the additional mileage.

After No. 22 had been coupled on to the train, there was a further series of stop and start movements to place the Birdcage coaches in the required location for the film unit, this shunting adding to the discomfort of the party. The 4.15 train eventually departed from Tenterden at 5.29 and ran at no great speed to Rolvenden, where the closing of the gates delayed a volunteer on his way home to Tenterden. Shortly after arriving home, he received a telephone call asking him to drive No. 23 that evening. At some personal inconvenience he agreed and almost immediately went back to Rolvenden.

At Rolvenden, where No. 23 was now in light steam, the train stopped for 15–20 minutes. It was decided not to leave the coaches on the running line at Wittersham Road because of the gradient and the risk of vandalism. Instead, it was proposed to return with the empty stock to Rolvenden, attach No. 23 to the rear, and take carriages and engine up to Tenterden, dispose of the carriages and attach No. 23 to the Birdcages when fully in steam (estimated at a further one-and-a-half to two hours). The Line Manager was informed but he opposed the plan as it would entail wasting more time shunting. The train proceeded to Wittersham Road where the probably bemused tea party disembarked, joined their coach and the driver/board member apologised for the delay and inconvenience caused. One wonders whether any of them ever returned and what they may have said to their families and friends.

After some time had been spent at Wittersham Road, the engine ran round and a fast trip to Rolvenden promised. Leaving the carriages at Rolvenden was now favoured. The return trip was unhurried although possibly faster than previous trips that day. On arrival at Rolvenden it was found that No. 23 was 'on the boil', a thick fire having been built up and the blower turned on. Pressure built up rapidly and by the time the train returned from Wittersham Road, 50lbs was showing on the gauge, although concern was expressed about raising steam so quickly.

The film crew were becoming very agitated, not believing that an engine was being prepared for them. Around 6.30 a film unit representative was driven to Rolvenden for him to see progress and No. 23's driver promised all possible assistance to speed matters along. Once the service train arrived at Rolvenden the carriages were berthed on the running line and protected with detonators, No. 23 was released from the shed siding and No. 22 was disposed of in the normal way. The crew on the service train went their various ways except for the catering volunteers, who had been overlooked and abandoned! They eventually found a lift, the dirty crockery having to remain overnight on the train. No. 23 finally arrived at Tenterden at 7.00pm, was coupled up to the Birdcage coaches and commenced the required movements within station limits. The unit had one hour to film with the loco; union agreements prevented filming after 8.00pm without excessive costs being incurred. In fact, it did not finish until 8.15 and a further session would be needed.

Neil Rose (who had formerly been Company Secretary) investigated this tragi-comedy, his recommendations including administrative improvements, which I recognise in the systems of more recent times, and better communications. The latter point has continued to echo down the years and appears elsewhere in this book. Forty years later, this episode is of historical interest and can be written about, although not in any sense of finger-pointing criticism. The intention is rather to illustrate how the K&ESR has learned from such episodes and evolved the professional approach and operating practices it enjoys in the twenty-first century.

The 1981 Steam & Country Fair was held over the weekend of 19/20 September, once again on the site at Tenterden that now includes Morph's field. Although the weather was generally cloudy with occasional showers, Saturday saw the arrival of 6,000 visitors which exceeded the first day's footfall the previous year. With 9,500 attending on the Sunday, the grand total was 15,500, only 1,000 down on 1980. The weather had once again threatened the event with heavy rain on the Friday night, but this was as nothing compared with the storm which arrived on Saturday night. Sunday morning revealed the large marquee partially collapsed, several stands blown away, awnings blown down and BR's Sealink tent in a different field! But railway volunteers are not easily defeated, and after the application of several sledge-hammers things had been sufficiently righted for the public to be admitted on time. Takings were up to expectations but the vulnerability of these events to the fickleness of the weather had been illustrated.

After a concerted effort by the Carriage & Wagon Department, Mark I Dining Car No. 69 entered service in the Wealden Pullman on Saturday, 1 August, looking a credit to those who had worked on it. Painting and lettering had been completed during the weekend of 18/19 July, which in those pre-carriage shed days had been under a plastic 'tent' erected against the weather. Internal varnishing had been finished by additional volunteer weekday input. During the following weekend, the bogies were run out and the centre castings changed, both being broken when the vehicle arrived.

At the beginning of August, the C&W department had also started work on the renovation of Mark 1 BSO No. 73 which, like No 69, was to be much used on service trains. Both sides were stripped back to bare metal, an arduous task as most of the old paint had to be ground off. This revealed a situation with which C&W would become all too familiar in the decades to come – bad patches of rust along the bottom of the doors and the need for new metal to be welded in and ground off flush. In addition, three passenger doors and both sets of luggage doors had to be replaced. As most standard gauge heritage railways were to discover, this was an awkward job as there is no such thing as a 'standard' Mark 1 door! Inside the vehicle, all paintwork and varnish was renewed and the plumbing overhauled.

In the subsequent period, work on the restoration of coaching stock was suspended and all efforts concentrated on constructing the new C&W shed at Tenterden. At the end of October, the services of a bricklayer were employed to construct the 4ft high double-skin wall on the station side of the building. 'Down the hill' the balance of the Rolvenden shed fund was being used to brick up the end of the shed, complete with a pair of arched doors. This work was also being carried out by a professional bricklayer; a member was giving financial and practical help for some of the electrical tasks in the workshop and getting some of the machine tools into working condition. These developments of course represented a significant step in improving the primitive working conditions which Loco and C&W staff had been used to since the 1960s.

'One Loco in Steam' operation had been in use on the Railway since reopening (and under BR since 1954). It was hoped to introduce two train token working from 1982, and to this end work continued on the construction of Wittersham Road signal box. Further woodwork was in hand, and a start had been made by Kevin Fulcher and Paul Vidler on the mechanical interlocking and also by Peter Lawrence on the electrical locking fittings. A set of electric key token instruments, together with an intermediate instrument at Rolvenden, had been tested. A further pair of telecommunication wires was being run back to Rolvenden where a multi-core cable had been installed to carry telephone and signal repeater circuits for the new installation. Work continued on the renovation of the former Herne Bay lever frame.

Publication of the 1981 passenger figures in the spring 1982 *Terrier* (with adjustments to the previously circulated 1980 totals) contained some ominous indications: there had been a drop of 15 per cent compared with the previous year (43,441 against 50,516). Even the Pullman showed a slight drop, although this was not seen as significant. The average number per train remained low and rarely exceeded seventy. The fall had been consistent throughout the year and was attributed to the weather in the early months, together with the recession and the state of the economy. Although this was the early period of the Thatcher government, the economy had not improved markedly (as it would do in the post-Falklands War era); there was pressure on incomes and nationally the grey down-at-heel atmosphere of the late 1970s lingered on. On the K&ESR, the *Tenterden Terrier* ('Tickets Please!' item in the spring 1982 issue) was suggesting greater flexibility and questioning why four-coach trains were being operated when two coaches or even one would have been sufficient and would have resulted in cost savings.

Restoration of Wittersham Road to Hexden Bridge continued through 1982. Peter Davis was in charge of the permanent way work both on the extension and the existing running line, and his first problem was people. Despite much work of this nature over the years, there was no department as such, and Peter had to borrow volunteers to tackle a number of critical defects. A major difficulty was that weekend operation was under way with daily operation due to begin a month later so a 'blockade' was out of the question at virtually any time when volunteers were likely to be available.

A start was made on the running line by laboriously hand packing the dropped joints above and below Cranbrook Road, three Sundays being spent on this. This was a far cry from the mechanised operation of the twenty-first century and used 15 tonne ratchet jacks, which were positioned under one rail at intervals of about four to five sleepers. The rail was then jacked up to the required level, which was determined by sighting along the railhead. The resulting voids under the sleepers were filled from both sides simultaneously by forcing ballast into them with shovels. When one rail had been lifted and packed the same procedure was applied to the other. All this had to be carried out between trains, and every 30 minutes or so all equipment had to be moved clear and the track made safe. Other reported dropped joints were sometimes dealt with on weekday evenings by volunteers, but two paid employees spent six weeks at the end of the summer doing emergency packing.

After an abortive mechanical tamping exercise in the spring, ash ballast remained for ½ mile from Wittersham gates to the Oxney Straight. It was particularly important to clear this from the loop at Wittersham in order to restore an orderly appearance to the station area. This piece of track was the original running line, and when the platform road was constructed to an easier gradient, it was left at a lower level by some three feet. It had been intended to lift the loop to the level of the platform line in easy stages as material became available. Use of a Matissa on-track machine was to have been the first stage of the lift, but it proved unsuitable and resort had to be made to hand packing using power station ash.

Throughout the year, development continued on the permanent way depot at Wittersham Road. The installation of a siding and road access was financed by the Northiam Extension Fund, as it was considered essential before work could be started on the relaying project. The notorious landslip near Morghew Curve (popularly known as Laming's slip after a volunteer who had valiantly grappled with it) was removed in early June by a Hymac operator who was able to work from the adjacent field by passing the arm of the machine under the telephone wires and over the fence, without damage to either. Further drainage and stabilisation work was required to complete the job. Away from the operating section, Northiam level crossing had been rebuilt in 1980 but by the following summer the rails had worked loose, causing the tarmac to break up. The Railway met its obligations to put this right during 30 September and 1 October when Dave Levett, Paul Hatcher, Jo Roesen and Peter Davis carried out the necessary repairs. East Sussex County Council provided traffic lights so that each half of the road could be dealt with in turn without undue disruption to road traffic.

By the end of 1981 much had been achieved towards reopening the three-quarters of a mile to Hexden Bridge, it was hoped by the spring. Total reconstruction was required. For the first 300 yards out of Wittersham Road, the line climbed at 1 in 80 through a cutting which had become completely waterlogged because the drainage had become unserviceable. Having successfully drained the formation it was found that the ash bed was in quite good order and it was possible to start relaying with chaired concrete sleepers. Beyond that section, the Thameside Group were making good progress installing wooden ones and a redundant culvert at the beginning of Hexden straight had been demolished and back-filled with minestone.

As mentioned earlier, the mile previous to Hexden Bridge was laid with the ex-Army 75lb flat bottom rail on light, siding standard, concrete sleepers. The unsuitability of these as part of the running line had now been realised, and it was decided to reclaim them for the carriage shed sidings at Tenterden. There they remained for many years; No. 3 siding in particular was widely regarded as one of the worst on the Railway. As also mentioned previously in the account of the Thameside Group, the 95lb bullhead rail recovered from Batchelor's sidings at Ashford was to be used in replacement. It would be necessary to raise and reshape the approach embankment at Hexden Bridge before relaying and another redundant culvert immediately after Hexden needed to be removed. Much more needed to be done, and the spring 1982 target was not to be achieved.

1982 was especially significant for the entry into service of the coach *Petros*, a Mark 1 Brake Second Open which had been converted at the Southern Region's Stewarts Lane workshops for use by people with disabilities, the project being led by K&ESR volunteer Dave Sinclair. The coach was donated by British Rail and numerous firms and voluntary organisations made contributions, which are still recorded on a plaque inside the vehicle's saloon. This project had been part of the International Year of the Disabled. *Petros* entered service on 9 June, being named on that occasion by no less a person than HM Queen Elizabeth the Queen Mother who honoured the Company by making the first royal visit to the Kent & East Sussex Railway. The conversion of *Petros* was also significant because it proved that a disabled toilet could be fitted into a C1 vehicle profile. British Rail took note and the disabled toilets now running on the national network owe their origins to *Petros*.

By this point in time, the animosity that had once existed between the 'pioneering' Bluebell Railway and the 'upstart' Kent & East Sussex had largely evaporated in the growing spirit of co-operation between heritage railways generally. It was against this background that Austerity saddle tank No. 25 *Northiam* paid an extended visit, starting in June, to the K&ESR's then-nearest standard gauge neighbour. The occasion was the cavalcade to mark the centenary of the Lewes–East Grinstead Railway of which the Bluebell was of course a part. *Northiam* represented industrial steam locomotives at this event, and reciprocated the loan of Bluebell Terrier *Fenchurch* at the time of the Steam & Country Fair in 1981. It was said that an 'industrial' was not entirely welcome at Sheffield Park (even if on a line which had, during its history, seen everything from a contractor's Manning Wardle loco to Bulleid's Leader and early diesels).

Northiam was nonetheless well received by the Bluebell crews, the loco itself benefiting from a longer uninterrupted run than the K&ESR could offer, the then-five mile Bluebell having neither intermediate stops nor level crossings. During the visit, *Northiam* was fired on Welsh steam coal from Lady Windsor colliery. So impressed were the K&ESR 'minders' that this fuel was brought into use at Rolvenden. Although its price per ton was higher than Rossington cobbles, it was more economical in use and caused less damage to firebars and tubes. No. 25 worked the normal passenger service on Friday, 18 June and, despite being a very wet day, had no trouble hauling five Bulleid-era coaches. The locomotive returned home during July having in the meantime double headed on normal services with the Adams Radial tank, No. 488, a loco once owned by Colonel Stephens' East Kent Railway; with Caledonian tank No. 419; and in the more familiar company of a USA Class, in this case the Bluebell's No. 30064.

The BTH Bo-Bo diesel electric locomotive, known as 'The Ford' after its previous motor manufacturer owner, had been on the K&ESR since 1966. It had been under restoration for several years, progress being related in the *Terrier* by Andrew Webb who had been involved with the restoration since 1976 and project co-ordinator since 1977. Assistance had been received from W.H. Allen Ltd, manufacturer of the loco's diesel engine. This was followed by enthusiastic aid from Dowding & Mills (Southern) Ltd which provided advice from their staff members George Gannon and Bill Phillip. They also involved retired employee Tom Stack as well as organising much useful press coverage via their publicity agents. Andrew Webb's view was that without this assistance the project would probably have ground to a halt.

Once the generator had been overhauled and re-installed, attention turned to the bodywork, and the corrosion which was discovered resulted in extensive renewal of the metalwork. The electrical control gear was the next area to be overhauled. Tom Marshall worked with Andrew on this, Andrew's background as a telephone engineer no doubt proving useful. Around 650 man-hours were spent stripping all five relay contactor panels, two of which were burnt and had to be replaced. All components were re-installed and other electrical work undertaken.

'The Ford' had been built with an air brake system, but as the K&ESR was a vacuum-braked line, an exhauster would have to be added. An electrically driven one previously used in the Southern's Bulleid–Raworth electric locomotive 20002 was obtained and installed, end-on to the existing electric motor driven compressor, thus concentrating braking apparatus and its electrical contactor control in one area. The need for some springs in the coupling between motor and exhauster led to one of those fortunate occurrences that seem to happen on heritage railways. After Compair Revell (which had built the exhauster around 1946) had actually located the relevant drawing, the next problem was to find Standage Power which made the springs. Some more investigations revealed that they were, appropriately, located in Newhaven, a town which had seen boat trains hauled by the Southern's 'Hornby' electrics. Probably not expecting success, a phone call was made to the firm. Much to everyone's surprise, the answer to the enquiry was, 'Yes Sir, we can do it – 96 P4 springs at 28p each!' In later years, there was a similar occurrence when the German manufacturer of the Norwegian's air brake pump was asked (allegedly by telephone!) if some small spare parts were available. Despite two world wars since the pump had been made the surprising answer was, 'Yes, how many do you want?' The 'Ford's' existing brake pipework was either replaced or altered to allow the locomotive air brake to work in conjunction with the train vacuum brake, the installation being designed by Derek Dunlavey. Attention was also required to the cooling system; although this was carried out it was not entirely successful, and it was to be the twenty-first century before the problem was finally resolved.

The final job was the overhaul of bogies, traction motors, wheels and brake gear. A suitable crane was provided by Mike Hart, who by this time was running Resco (Railways) Ltd, which lifted both of the 1 ton 8 cwt traction motors. The bogie frame was lifted off the wheels and two buckled main stretchers (cross members) replaced. British Rail reprofiled the tyres and skimmed the journals at Ashford. The traction motors were overhauled by British Electrical Repairs, thanks to financial assistance from Mike Hart's business partner Rick Edmondson. It was hoped to get the locomotive back into service by 1983.

Mike Hart and Rick Edmondson had set up Resco Railways, a professional restoration company, as a result of a friendship forged while volunteering on the K&ESR. Their non-rail-connected premises were in Plumstead, South East London. The Plumstead site where restoration of the GER brake had commenced was Resco's works. A major contract taken on by Resco during 1982 was boiler work on the Keighley & Worth Valley Railway's Ivatt Class 2 tank No. 41241. Once work was complete, test runs were needed prior to the locomotive returning north, and the Kent & East Sussex just happened to be convenient. This was to be the largest locomotive officially known to have operated on the K&ESR up to that time. There are rumours of a Schools having, in an emergency, reached Bodiam with a hop pickers' train during the 1950s, and no-one knows what may have appeared on the line during the Second World War when exigencies might have thrown weight restrictions to the wind.

No. 41241 was delivered to Tenterden late in the afternoon of Wednesday, 29 December and moved to Rolvenden behind Hunslet diesel No. 42. After the P.Way Department had considered the matter, it was decided that No. 41241 could be allowed up Tenterden Bank at limited speed. The following day, the loco was lit up and taken up to Tenterden at a sedate pace. Three successful return trips to Wittersham Road were made with a five-coach train. The Ivatt was next used on the Saturday (New Year's Day) for shunting at Wittersham Road and Hexden Bridge before taking the steam crane up to Tenterden in the afternoon. The major event of the loco's visit was however to be Sunday, 2 January. Local TV and radio stations had mentioned the presence of the loco on the K&ESR and, of course, word had gone round on the enthusiast grapevine (now supplanted by social media). The weather produced one of those brilliant blue-skyed days which can brighten an English winter. The three trains worked by the Ivatt tank were filled to a high-summer-like degree, and in addition the last Wealden Pullman of the operating year and the first of 1983 was hauled by the Ivatt. Enthusiasts were everywhere and the fields adjacent to Orpin's Curve at Rolvenden were crowded. More than 580 people travelled in the trains, with photographers travelling from as far away as Leicester and Bristol. The K&ESR's footplatemen were most impressed with No. 41241 and would have liked something similar for their own railway.

Chapter 8

The visit of the Ivatt tank had made a very good start to 1983, but this was to be a year of very mixed fortunes. Already the winter 1982 *Tenterden Terrier* had sounded a warning note in its editorial:

> The visitor numbers and financial outcome of the Steam & Country Fair may have disappointed some optimists. It is true that the level of support was well down on 1981, and even without the inclement weather would not have matched last year's total. One of the problems facing the Fair is increasing competition from other events – this year the West Malling Air show and another 'country fair' at Beltring – nevertheless a profit of £6,000 is probably more than could be obtained from staging any other single event at Tenterden. Lack of growth in passenger numbers on the normal service trains is a situation that we have faced ever since the line reopened, and special events have helped to alleviate but not solve the problem. For this reason the Show will go on, but this does not mean that it cannot change. The Steam & Country Fair Committee, who put in much hard work in planning the event over nine months, would welcome new ideas for 'Fair 1983', in order to persuade the visitors to keep on coming.

The same issue of the journal also contained an article by the Editor, Philip Shaw, titled 'Why do the Numbers Keep on Falling?' together with some observations raised in letters to the Editor.

> Excluding Pullman services, numbers of daytime passengers last year were only 5 per cent up on 1974; and perhaps most disturbing of all, the number of passengers per operating day reached an all-time low. Even in the peak year of 1980 the numbers carried were only 25 per cent higher than in the opening year, and comparisons are not strictly valid as in 1974 services were only operated over the short section of line from Tenterden to Rolvenden.

> The accounts of the Tenterden Railway Company Ltd highlight the problem of running trains with such low average passenger densities. The Railway achieved an excess of income over expenditure amounting to £7,681 in 1981, but this included a surplus of £12,500 on the Wealden Pullman trains (equivalent to £6 per passenger carried) and £10,278 on the Steam & Country Fair. Without these sources of income, the Railway would have clocked up a staggering loss of some £15,000, despite the fact that most of the operational tasks are carried out by volunteers. Losses of this order could not be sustained, and without the income from Pullman trains in particular we would have had to drastically curtail the whole field of our existing operations and possibly give up all hope of getting to Bodiam.

The objectives of management must therefore be to increase our passenger loadings to a level which makes them viable in their own right, rather than relying on a subsidy from specialist activities. The question is, how can this be best achieved?

The attractiveness of the line itself is unquestioned; steep gradients, curves, level crossings and a friendly informal atmosphere all contribute much to the wellbeing of both the passengers and the volunteers who operate the line. Factors missing in the equation are adequate catering and toilet facilities (soon to be remedied) and, perhaps most of all, a variety of vintage locomotives and rolling stock in operable condition for all to see and enjoy. The pulling power of vintage equipment is exemplified by the continuing success of the Bluebell Railway, which carries huge numbers of passengers each year over a line certainly no more attractive than the K&ESR.

The sad fact is that the ingredients are there – Terrier locomotives, Birdcage and Maunsell coaches, but with an enormous backlog of restoration and maintenance, hampered by a shortage of manpower and funds. This has meant that the Railway has had to rely for several years on a service operated by relatively modern and unlovely locomotives hauling a rake of British Rail coaches, the like of which can still be seen in service all over the country. Furthermore, between services there is little or nothing to do at Tenterden. Is it surprising, therefore, that the numbers keep on falling? The irony of the situation is highlighted by the outstanding success of the Pullman trains. Here we have to offer a service which is unparalleled in its style and excellence. As to the secret of its popularity, a regular customer, asked for her views on our relatively limited choice of menus and why she kept on coming, remarked 'I come for the occasion, not for the food.'

How can we therefore bring that sense of 'occasion' to our normal service trains? It is doubtful if an extension of services to Bodiam would make much difference at the Tenterden end. It would certainly increase the expense of travelling, and might even prolong the boredom for those passengers who decided to make the whole journey. The majority of our daytime passengers are not enthusiasts; they are families with children out for the day. The distance that they travel will largely be dictated by the depth of their pockets and what is offered in addition to the ride. Bodiam Castle may ultimately prove to be an attraction, but why travel there by train? The distance on foot from the station to the Castle will undoubtedly be a deterrent to some families used to travelling by car over even minor distances. Some traffic will, of course, originate from the Bodiam end, but passengers will need encouragement if they are to travel the whole way to Tenterden.

Publicity is important to any organisation and the K&ESR has had plenty of coverage over the last 12 months. Nevertheless, even the privilege of a visit by a much-loved member of the royal family last June failed to stimulate any significant increase in numbers this summer.

Action is required now. If we do not have the manpower resources to carry out the heavy work programme of restoration, then we should explore the feasibility of contracting out more of the work and thereby invest in the future. A limited amount of progress in this respect has already been made and our historic Terrier locomotive *Sutton* is now undergoing heavy repairs at Resco (Railways) Ltd, with money raised from last year's Steam & Country Fair. Another vintage locomotive, *Charwelton*, is currently on loan to us, through the courtesy of Resco. [Ownership of *Charwelton* had by this stage passed from The Kent & East Sussex Locomotive Trust to Rick Edmondson]

So much for the longer-term remedies, what of the short-term palliatives? Firstly, a small engine in steam at Tenterden, whether it be *Marcia* or any other, will do much to add to the variety and interest of the station environment. The recent loan of *Baxter* – a 105-year-old locomotive from the Bluebell Railway – for two weeks in September, was an immensely popular attraction shunting at the station. Properly attired staff (something of a rarity) will also be visually more attractive to visitors. Finally, special events at weekends, on the adjacent fields, will encourage people to come to Tenterden Station; and past experience has shown that this does increase railway passengers when taken as part of the package of a day out.

Philip concluded by thanking all correspondents for their contributions on this subject. A selection of their 'very helpful suggestions' followed:

- Run *Marcia* with a single coach for passengers over an extended headshunt, charging a separate fare.
- Remove scruffy rolling stock from public gaze at Tenterden and at Rolvenden, where 'passengers can only see a line of rusting junk standing on the loop'.
- Extend the line to Northiam, which has a lot to offer visitors in the form of Great Dixter, Brickwall Manor and a church with some of the oldest stained glass in the country.
- Improve publicity and marketing, particularly as back-up 'for the dedicated stalwarts of the Ashford & Maidstone Area Groups' who attended the Kent County Show with *Marcia*.
- Some train crews appear to show as much PR ability as a lump of fish on a fishmonger's slab. Send engine crews on public relations courses in order to make the public and volunteers welcome on the Railway.
- Increase newspaper and local radio advertising. Hire, exchange or borrow a large tender engine from another operator. Put engines on static display at Tenterden. Install PA systems in trains and describe the line to passengers as they travel. Introduce lunchtime Pullman trains.
- Provide camping coaches for holidaymakers at Wittersham Road and Bodiam.
- Introduce two train running.
- Do away with unswept platforms, full litter bins, dusty window sills, grimy carriage floors.
- Encourage staff to be smart in appearance, courteous and helpful.
- Increase publicity and keep *Marcia* on the road as a static exhibit at shows and exhibitions.
- Give the public better value for money by pegging or reducing fares and also provide additional entertainment in the form of a 'special' every four to six weeks. This could include a 'Railway at work' weekend, with demonstrations by the steam crane and footplate rides, and photographers' weekends with facilities for lineside photography.

In the first 1983 (spring) issue of the *Terrier*, Commercial Manager Donald Wilson further emphasised that something was wrong. The annual 'Tickets Please!' item showed that passengers in 1982 had declined to 42,454 from 43,441 in the previous year.

The past year has seen a fall in the number of passengers carried, but our special trains continue to attract custom in almost embarrassing proportions. The 'Wealden Pullman' continues to feature prominently and it is a great credit to the dedication of our regular helpers that we continue to attract more bookings than we can in fact accept. Already nearly half the (Pullman) trains in 1983 have been provisionally booked and relief trains will run on certain Fridays in the peak season. The highlight of the year, after the honour of the royal visit, must be the special operating day arranged on 2nd January when the K&WVR's Ivatt Class 2 tank locomotive hauled three special trains over the line.

The pattern of train operation will be similar to last year, but with the added run of ¾ mile to Hexden Bridge from 1st May. The 11.45am train on Saturdays – which has always been lightly loaded – will not run, to give more line time for works trains on the extension. Daily running will be for the month of August, and Wednesday and Thursday trains will operate mainly for schools in June and July. An enthusiasts' weekend is planned for 1st/2nd May when it is hoped that at least four locomotives will be in steam and displays will be set up at each station. The Thameside group will again be organising 'Steam at Bodiam' on 29th/30th May and 28th/29th August, but publicity for these fundraising events will be kept to a minimum so as not to take visitors (and working members) from Tenterden.

The Board was obviously aware of these concerns and an article by Chairman Mark Yonge addressing some of these also appeared in the spring 1983 *Terrier*. This outlined plans for the improvement of visitor facilities at Tenterden Town. The K&ESR's principal station lacked a number of basic amenities including adequate lavatories, catering facilities and something for visitors to do between train services. It was reasonable to suppose that this had affected visitor numbers and discouraged coach parties. It had now been possible to buy the coal yard on the town side of the station, which had not been included in the 1973 purchase and had only been rented from British Rail. The cost of this had been offset by the sale of one acre of surplus land adjacent to the Railway by the home signal. This was to form part of what is now the Rogersmead housing development.

A typically K&ESR reaction was then to form a group to look into what was needed. After consideration it was decided to purpose build lavatory and catering blocks to match as nearly as possible the style of the existing station building. Included in the plans was the re-erection of the former Maidstone Bus Station as a museum to accommodate the display at that time situated in the Town Museum at the top of Station Road and the K&ESR's other archives relating to the Stephens lines. The plans also allowed for limited parking facilities for people with disabilities, special occasions and deliveries. An impressive artist's impression accompanied the article describing all this. Neighbouring land owner Henry Edwards had agreed to lease a parcel of land immediately to the north and west of the carriage shed for a new car park to accommodate 130 cars and coaches, an arrangement still extant at the time of writing. This has proved to be of considerable benefit, and one wonders what passenger figures in later years might have been if visitors had had to reply on street parking and the town car parks.

As will be apparent to any present-day visitor to Tenterden Town Station, these ambitious proposals did not emerge in the form intended. Nevertheless, outline plans had received approval from Tenterden Town Council and planning permission was granted by Ashford Borough Council. Detailed planning approval had been obtained for the lavatory block and work was soon due to commence. The Company was exploring the possibility of obtaining grants towards the cost of the whole programme, and the English Tourist Board had already authorised a grant of £2,600 towards the cost of the new lavatories.

The extension to Hexden Bridge opened on 25 April, slightly earlier than planned. As it turned out, it was just as well that the originally planned date of 1 May was not kept to. As often seems to happen for K&ESR opening days, the weather was kind and produced one of the few sunny days in in one of the wettest Aprils on record. At lunchtime, the Pullman ran between Tenterden Town and Wittersham Road. Guests included Robert Neame, Chairman of the South East England Tourist Board (who was to perform the opening ceremony); Councillor and Mrs S. Brown, the Mayor and Mayoress of Tenterden; Councillor Mrs Winnifrith, Deputy Mayor of Ashford Borough Council; Councillor Linklater of Rolvenden Parish Council and Mrs Keith Speed, wife of the local Member of Parliament.

Once at Wittersham Road, Company Chairman Mark Yonge addressed those present and said that this was a very historic day for the Kent & East Sussex Railway as it would be the first official passenger train over the newly restored section of the line for nearly 30 years. Robert Neame replied that the British tourist industry was notoriously under-financed and that the revenue earned by tourist attractions from overseas visitors was of great benefit to the balance of payments. It gave him great pleasure to witness the expansion of the K&ESR. He wished the Railway every success for the future and hoped that trains would soon be running through to Bodiam. At about 2.30pm, Mr Neame boarded *Charwelton* and 'drove' the train through the tape to the applause of the assembled guests on the platform.

Operating normal service trains to Hexden Bridge, where there was of course no run-round loop, involved a push-pull style operation with the locomotive running round at Wittersham Road and the guard in effect controlling the train by holding a green flag out of the window. When approaching the barrier, this would be changed to red. On one set the guard was able to observe progress through a small window in an adapted gangway shield. Although this procedure of course continued to be necessary, after a while the drivers knew exactly where to stop. This extension was a psychological boost for those aspiring to extend to Northiam, but any euphoria arising from the Hexden reopening lasted all of six days. Public services began on Saturday 30 April; it was not raining, but there had been a prolonged wet period over the previous days. That May Day weekend, the operating procedure was for one train to arrive at Wittersham Road, the loco to run round and then propel its coaches to Hexden. While that was going on, the second train would depart Tenterden and arrive at Wittersham. The first (Up) train would then pass the second at Wittersham and head for Tenterden. There were therefore two Down trains and then two Up trains, and when the second train reached Tenterden the procedure started over again.

The following day, Sunday, 1 May, while returning to Tenterden with the first of a pair of trains, *Charwelton's* leading wheels left the road near Pope's Cottage permanent way hut west of Rolvenden. There was a length of track near Pope's which was something of a switchback and rather rough. It is said that the loco crews knew of it and hung on while the loco rolled around, except this time the rough section seemed longer, so they stopped to have a look. What they found was broken rail chairs over a distance of about 200 yards. The formation had also been undermined by the recent wet weather. Services on the Railway were immediately suspended.

In Wittersham Road signal box, Trainee Phil Edwards was on his passing-out turn. The first he knew of the incident was when Signalman Clive Norman came back into the box and told him that *Charwelton* was derailed near Pope's. Phil looked at Clive's face and seeing it was white realised that this was not the railway equivalent of a driving examiner tapping the dashboard for an emergency stop.

Quite apart from the affected train and the second train which was now coming back from Hexden, there was a freight in Wittersham yard plus two other locomotives. This being a Bank Holiday weekend, the public were being given variety and engine changes were being made at Wittersham Road. One loco was sent to rescue the coaches of the failed train – they at least had stayed on the track – and buses were organised to get all the passengers from both trains back to Tenterden. At Wittersham Road, the third loco was coupled to the permanent way van, which contained jacks and packing, which it then propelled towards Pope's Cottage. The position was far from good, with two empty passenger trains and three locomotives marooned on the west side of the obstruction. The Wittersham Road staff however decided to couple the trains together, put an engine on either end and run shuttles to Hexden Bridge at 50p a head.

There were now two imperatives. Firstly, the line had obviously to be cleared and repaired and, secondly, the repairs had to be done quickly. The following day was a Bank Holiday and with the parlous state of its finances the K&ESR could neither afford to lose the day's traffic nor attract the adverse publicity likely to arise from anything more than a very short period of closure. The *Tenterden Terrier* reported in its Summer issue:

> The heartening thing was the immediate and total response from volunteers on the Railway to remedy the situation that weekend, with the result that some 20 people worked through most of the night and others restarted the work at 6.00am the next morning. Due to the magnificent efforts of everyone we were able to resume scheduled services on the Bank Holiday Monday.

This was of course all true, but as so often in these situations it does not tell the whole story. Although a workforce of 20 people is quoted above, as many people as possible were needed to re-rail *Charwelton*, repair the track and probably for many other tasks as well. As a consequence Andrew Webb and another volunteer sat in the booking office at Tenterden with a copy of the membership register and phoned everyone who might be able to help. I heard about this years later but have no idea if an attempt was made to call me. In any event, if I remember rightly, I was away from home that day. The situation was desperate and emotions were running high – there was a near fight between a member of the Loco Department and someone from C&W over the need to pool all the compressed air hoses on the Railway. Local haulage company boss Laurie Woodcock of Headcorn got to hear about the accident and agreed to provide a mobile compressor to supplement the Railway's equipment and speed the efforts along. Work stopped in the early hours when there was an apparent injury – which turned out not to be as serious as feared – and someone was taken to hospital. The marooned locomotives, having dropped their fires, were kept at Wittersham Road overnight. In the early morning, after work had recommenced and the fires were re-lit, Driver Colin Edwards brought the first locomotive over the reinstated track. The Company treated those who had achieved this to breakfast in the café that was then some way up the hill from Rolvenden Station. As the *Terrier* reported, the Bank Holiday Monday service ran as advertised.

Charwelton had, unsurprisingly, sustained damage, not least to its axleboxes, and had to be withdrawn from service. Rick Edmondson as owner was less than pleased and took the locomotive away again for repairs. The way the derailment had been coped with and the general esprit de corps was the stuff of heritage railway legend, but was it anything to be proud of?

This had happened to a passenger train and was reportable to HM Railway Inspectorate. The subsequent inquiry laid the blame on track maintenance and there were consequent changes in the management of the P.Way Department. Locomotive Department Manager Bob Forsythe subsequently made further modifications to the horn stays on *Charwelton* to allow better vertical movement of the axleboxes in the frames. The locomotive had been reported as riding rough in places on the Railway quite apart from the Pope's Cottage stretch. The alignment of the leading springs was also straightened by the creation of a large dimple in the smoke box and a new spring hanger link. The incident has, understandably, left an ambivalent recollection in the collective memory of the K&ESR. Ten years later people could still be heard quietly recriminating about both the derailment and the performance of individuals, although four decades after the event time has softened memories.

The carriage shed at Tenterden was sufficiently complete to be brought into use and evolved from being simply covered accommodation to the largest workshops on the Railway. The opening in September of a modern toilet block at Tenterden Town was a revolution from the visitors' point of view. Incredibly, eighty-three years after the Railway first opened and nine years after re-opening, this was the first advance beyond the primitive gents urinals of Colonel Stephens' day and the chemical toilets installed by BR. The latter were out of use in the heritage era and visitors had had to be directed to the Council conveniences at the top of Station Road. It seems unbelievable today, but a letter was published in the *Terrier* from a member complaining about such modern facilities spoiling the 'bumbling' nature of the K&ESR. He was duly answered in the following issue. The grant to cover the cost obtained from the English Tourist Board was, like the Job Creation Scheme, an example of the K&ESR using public finance – a concept which, with the remorseless advance of Thatcherism, was then rapidly going out of fashion.

Work commenced in August on the overhaul of the Rother Bridge. Also, during the same month, work started to place minestone on Wittersham bank where the clay soil had deteriorated over a 400yd length because of defective drainage. The Wittersham–Hexden Bridge section had as a consequence to be closed from September 1983 to April 1984 for the civil engineering of the bank to be rebuilt. This needed a significant capital investment. 1983 was not proving to be a good year financially.

Although much money had been raised in earlier years at the Steam & Country Fair, the organising committee felt that a change in concept would increase public interest and improve attendances. Renamed the Tenterden Country Show, the 1983 event was held on the weekend of 10/11 September but the weather was not kind. In fact, it was the worst ever experienced, with continuous rain for both days and attendances down to 5,826 compared with 11,250 in 1982 and the record 15,400 in 1981. This was a pity, because a 1920s village scene was re-created in the 25 acre field to the north of the Railway, including a green with a cricket match, a pub and a cottage with Kentish weatherboarding. A band and village fete were featured, together with agricultural and country craft displays plus a traditional fairground.

The Fair only just broke even, and it was not possible to contribute anything towards the cost of restoration of Terrier No. 3 *Bodiam* which was the main aim of the weekend. Unreliable weather, variable profit margins and competition from similar events resulted in this being the last of the first series of Steam & Country Fairs. It was thought too great a risk to continue, despite the positive publicity and goodwill generated.

Despite the increasingly gloomy note being sounded through 1983, thoughts were turning to the Railway's next extension and a Northiam Study Group had been set up at the beginning of the year. The station would for an unknown length of time act as terminus and the Group considered issues such as station buildings, water supply and track layout. As things then stood, Northiam consisted of a two-coach length platform, a timber and corrugated iron station building, two sidings, a six-coach run-round loop and two staff bungalows. The Waiting Room had already been fitted with a new floor and was open as an information point during the summer. The Parcels Room housed the two machines and typesetting tables of the Tenterden Railway Company's Printing Department. This group did not print the *Terrier*, but it did produce many other items before the advent of desktop publishing and the Railway's printing going out to contract.

Tourists were of course now the Railway's traffic, and requirements were entirely different from when Northiam had last seen passengers in 1954. It was correctly anticipated that the existing building would accommodate the Booking Office, and a shop and refreshment area. New toilets would have to be built. A signal box would be needed and the level crossing over the A28 would have to be gated. Any new buildings would have to be designed to suit the location. It was also decided that the second platform would be reinstated. At this stage providing adequate car parking was seen as a problem. The sidings would have to be adapted to make more room for the storage of both operational and static rolling stock. With the K&ESR's perennial financial situation, it was hoped to obtain grants similar to those obtained for Tenterden Station.

The AGM, held on 1 October 1983, was significant for the growing influence of the Thameside Group. Mark Yonge announced his retirement as Company Chairman and no less a person than George Wright took over as Acting Chairman until a permanent appointment could be made. The top job subsequently went to John Miller, the *Tenterden Terrier* commenting that the holder of that post always got the blame when things went wrong but did not always get credit when they went right! Particularly significant for the future of the Railway was the election of David Stratton to the Board – a step he took at the urging of working volunteers. An interesting aspect of the 1983 AGM was the outgoing Chairman's report. He noted that there was 'friction in some departments', that 'enthusiasts tend to be intolerant of the views of others which may deter potential volunteers from active participation' and that there was 'a closed shop mentality in some departments'.

Much of this was, of course, human nature, and hardly unknown in the heritage railway movement. The retiring Chairman had more to say in an item titled 'The Way Ahead' in the Winter *Tenterden Terrier* published a few weeks later. As the reader will realise, it included a number of themes with which he or she will already be familiar:

> As many of you will know, I resigned from the Board of The Tenterden Railway Company in October after four years as a director and three years as Chairman. I have greatly enjoyed the task, but with the effects of the recession it has been for the most part a difficult period of trading.
>
> A criticism often levelled at me and my fellow directors is that we are guilty of poor communication and this has led to ignorance amongst some members of where we are going, apart from the obvious destination of Bodiam. I felt, therefore, that it would be appropriate to outline our future policies for the development of the Railway, although without reference to any particular time scale.
>
> It is the Board's intention that the Railway will continue to be presented as a small independent line, operated as far as possible in the Colonel Stephens tradition. Powerful locomotives and modern rolling stock are necessary to ensure commercial viability, but these will be augmented by vintage trains hauled by small historic locomotives to

maintain authenticity. Buildings will be designed and constructed in sympathy with their surroundings, as has been the case with the new toilet block at Tenterden and decorated in the recently adopted maroon and cream livery.

It has been felt for some time that the Railway as presently run is predictable and boring. In order to increase passenger appeal it is intended to introduce a variety of train formations, including mixed trains, hauled by a more varied selection of motive power. The facilities at Tenterden will be improved by the construction of the new catering block and museum, and there will be increased activity in the form of both the frequency of the service and light locomotives in steam between trains. It is important that we should have the ability to run up to four passenger trains at any one time and also incorporate works trains into the timetable.

With this in mind a loop will be installed at Rolvenden as soon as possible and, at a later date, similarly at Bodiam. The existing platforms here and at Northiam will be lengthened and at the latter the second platform, which has long disappeared, will be reinstated. Signalling on the present length of operating line will be expanded and a semaphore installation at Rolvenden will control the station and works. Signalling at Northiam and Bodiam will be minimal, to preserve as far as possible the light railway atmosphere, and the whole system designed so that train crews can operate it in the absence of rostered signalmen.

As far as the trains themselves are concerned, when the sidings at Tenterden are complete, coaches will run in sets, each carrying an individual livery. This, it is felt, will encourage volunteer help as well as heighten public interest. And now a word on liveries; as a general guideline all pre-1923 coaches will be restored to their original livery, including lettering and lining, whilst those post this period will be restored in their original livery, but with K&ESR numbering, lettering and lining.

Exceptions to this rule are that Mark 1 coaches currently in use will be of standard brown and cream, complete with lettering and lining as at present. However, it is hoped that an additional set of three Mark 1 coaches will be purchased and restored in British Railways maroon. All Pullman cars will be restored in the livery appropriate to that company and the GWR railcar, BR railbus and all goods vehicles to their original liveries and markings, providing that these are known.

With regard to locomotives, there will be no standard colour and engines of historical interest will be restored to their original livery, but with K&ESR numbering and lining out. We shall not, as has been the case in the past, collect engines merely because the owners are seeking a home for them.

Workshop facilities at Rolvenden will be given high priority; it is also planned to build a viewing gallery in the works to enable the public to see work in progress.

The way ahead may take ten years or even longer – much will depend on the level of volunteer support, but to those who have supported me over the last three years a very special thank you.

Chapter 9

As so often on the K&ESR, the problems of the business seem to have been in a parallel universe compared with life 'at the railhead', and the *Terrier* for spring 1984 announced that the Thameside Group had adopted a half-mile section of the operating line and undertaken to re-sleeper and maintain it. In this instance, practicalities and politics might not be so far removed from each other and it becomes increasingly difficult to disentangle Thameside efforts and influence from the overall scene. Financial stringency however was the order of the day in 1984 and the AC Railbus had to be sold to raise finance. As always, 'Tickets Please!' looked back on trading over the preceding year and tried to be moderately upbeat:

> Total passengers carried increased by a modest 2 per cent in 1983 (43,627 against 42,454) although this was still slightly below the 1981 achievement. An encouraging feature was the 13 per cent increase in average loadings per train, particularly in respect of the mid-week school trains in June and July. The 'Wealden Pullman' once again ran to full capacity and the importance of this service to our viability should not be underestimated. All commercial activities exceeded their financial targets thanks entirely to the hard work and innovations carried out by the individual departments.
>
> The most exciting prospect for our 10th Anniversary Year is the introduction of a two-train service on holiday weekends and Sundays in July and August. [The two-train service described in connection with the Pope's Cottage derailment had of course been a special event in connection with the Hexden Bridge extension and the Bank Holiday weekend.]
>
> This operation calls for strict timekeeping and it is hoped that all operating staff will rise to the challenge! Following an increase in the number of prospective customers on summer Saturday mornings, it has been decided to introduce, experimentally, an 11.45am service in July and August.

The next two *Tenterden Terrier* editorials however saw the glass as being half empty as opposed to half full. Firstly, in the spring edition:

> Ten years on – it seems a lifetime since Bill Deedes broke the champagne bottle over the then 98-year-old *Sutton*'s frames and a mile of the Kent & East Sussex Railway was launched into a new era, after a decade of dereliction, hopes first dashed and then raised. And now, in 1984, the Railway is a bit longer, the Terriers a little bit older although in fine fettle, but basically nothing has changed. It is a pity that Bodiam is still so far away – will the economics of running a ten-mile stretch ever make sense? Furthermore, steam fairs are now two a penny in Kent and this, together with the vagaries of the weather, suggest

that the expensive field events, which we so successfully pioneered in the 1970s, can no longer be justified. So we look for continued innovation in the next decennium, but at a price – engine swaps with other societies, plenty of unusual movement… coupled with an even better Wealden Pullman.

And in the summer:

The 1983 balance sheet does not make cheerful reading, showing as it does the biggest loss in the Railway's history. 1984 will almost certainly see a return to the black as a result of good marketing, more profitable special events, tighter controls on costs and an even better result from the Pullman. So with a return to modest prosperity, should consolidation still remain the name of the game or should 1985 be the year to raise more capital and push on to Northiam?

The same issue of the journal ruminated on special events.

Every year since 1976, the Railway has organised a major two day event in adjacent fields at Tenterden during the month of September in order to raise income when the traditional season is drawing to a close. This year it was decided that the size of the operation would have to be scaled down substantially and a low budget 'Summer Steam Spectacular' was mounted over the weekend of 8th/9th September in the station yard and on a small grassed area adjacent to the line. For a total capital outlay of some £4,000 a profit of nearly £3,000 was realised and in addition, net proceeds from the draw amounted to approximately £1,000. Attendances over the weekend totalled 4,500.

However, those who remembered the great Steam & Country Fairs of past years were disappointed and it may well be that 1984 has seen the last of the late summer shows. Perhaps we should concentrate on developing a more interesting service on the Railway itself in future – thanks for the memory, it was fun while it lasted.

With that final comment this is perhaps a good point in the narrative to look at the way in which this era in the history of the K&ESR is now remembered by working members of the time and to add some of my own observations. During research into the Pope's Cottage derailment, a long-serving officer wryly commented that many still yearn for those times. Some former members of station staff have looked back nostalgically on Saturday evening gatherings in the local Chinese restaurant. Alternatively, a pint in the pub after signing off was not unreasonable and for others the Vine Inn in Tenterden High Street at one time functioned as an unofficial mess room. Indeed, one bar area was known as 'the Railway Room'. It was here that forceful personalities presided Falstaff-like; surrounded by their admirers they ran 'the Vine Operating Committee' – an unofficial power base rivalling the management structure.

Any present-day difficulties can give rise to reminiscences about 'comradeship', 'co-operation between different groups' and a general impression of 'hail fellow well met'. All this is at variance with the concerns about disagreements, friction and intolerance which have appeared earlier in this book. Apart from the obvious rose-tinted spectacles, some of this can probably be explained as the existence of desirable team-working qualities within close-knit groups of staff. As in many organisations, loyalty tends to focus on one's immediate unit and colleagues, although this can in turn lead to myopic 'silo culture'. I would also draw comparisons with the formative years in the 1960s – a period of which I personally have the fondest memories. In both eras many volunteers were young and were looking for an outlet for youthful energy. But in retrospect the '60s were an imperfect time, a foundation on which later, better, things were built, not a time in which one would wish the Railway to remain. Maybe the late 1970s and early '80s should be viewed in the same way.

A visit to the Railway at this time, forearmed with what one read in the *Terrier*, could leave me with an unsatisfied feeling. Its most concrete form was in the experience of being propelled out of Wittersham Road only to stop at Hexden while knowing that Northiam was tantalisingly close. The area around 'Witt Road' has left a memory, possibly distorted across many years, of an atmosphere akin to South East England in the immediate post war era – bleak and austere improvisation, bonfires and morose-looking workmen. An uncomfortable memory is of standing on the platform at Tenterden Town waiting to travel on a down-at-heel Mark 1. My wife looked across to the immaculate Pullman standing in No. 1 siding and asked 'When can we go on that?' Not having the foresight to reply '2014 on the Sunday Lunch train' I felt embarrassed and mumbled some non-committal reply. How could I say 'We're not quite the market segment it's aimed at'?

It was on that or some similar occasion that a teenage Travelling Ticket Inspector, seeing my concessionary ticket, asked how long I had been a member. Having given him the answer he replied that it could not possibly have been since 1961 as preservation only began with the formation of the Tenterden Railway Company. This was one of the incidents that made me think that I really ought to write a history of the heritage era on the K&ESR.

Keynsian-style state aid was not yet quite finished, and there was a major task for staff provided by the Manpower Services Commission Community Programme. (Nationally, the MSC, which organised schemes to alleviate unemployment, was to last until as late as 1987.) It had now been finally realised that the 75lb track between Hexden and Northiam was unsuitable and the MSC staff's task was to remove these lightweight panels and take them back to Wittersham Road. They would be replaced with 95lb rail at a later date, but in the meantime the formation would remain empty.

Much work had to be done to reorganise Wittersham Road yard to take the lifted track panels. This included disposal for sale of various scrap metal that was contributing to the bomb site appearance. Longer sidings were laid in to accommodate works trains and steam cranes. Once the track panels were at Wittersham Road, they were dismantled and the rail sold to the Ffestiniog Railway. The redundant concrete sleepers were used for various purposes round the railway including forming a roadway leading into the car park at Tenterden Town – as will be apparent today to anyone driving over these home-made speed bumps.

Towards the end of October 1984, following heavy rain and on the 'town' side of the line, a serious problem occurred about 150 yards uphill from Cranbrook Road level crossing. At that point, a large area of ground formed a huge bowl shape, with the railway embankment acting almost as a dam. Within this were two springs as well as run-off from the surrounding fields, which was supposed to be piped under the embankment and into the drainage system. The heavy rain continued into November with the 'bowl' rapidly filling to the point where it was possible that it might damage the embankment. Several unsuccessful attempts were made to clear the water, but the level continued to rise as the Santa season approached. After a drain clearing firm failed to dislodge the blockage, a large pump, capable of handling 650 gallons a minute, was hired and taken to the site on a Flatrol wagon. It nevertheless still took three weeks of 24-hour running to clear an estimated 15 million gallons of water, success finally being achieved on Christmas Eve. In the New Year, the pipe was dug out, 4ft down, and was found to be partially covered by an old bucket. Temporary measures were then taken to ensure that it could not become blocked again. Later in 1985 there was a major civil engineering exercise to rebuild the culvert on a relatively massive scale. The resulting cast concrete structure is now one of the features of Tenterden Bank, and the flooding has not recurred. Publication of the preceding year's passenger figures in the early months of 1985 showed an increase of 7 per cent. This was attributed to the additional number of trains run during 1984, although average loadings remained constant. The only passenger type which had declined was the group return, which was down by 20 per cent despite an effort to promote its availability. This seems odd for a class of traffic which has been a staple of the K&ESR over many years. At the time, this was in part attributed to industrial action by teachers leading to fewer school parties, but more particularly to the lack of an educational aspect which was deterring some schools. This was corrected in 1985 with lectures being offered on the K&ESR and railway history generally. The educational aspect of the heritage era Kent & East Sussex Railway has received periodic attention since, not least because the Railway is an educational charity and there has been a perceived need to clearly focus on this.

A further issue was the reduction in passengers commencing their journeys at Wittersham Road. These now only amounted to 1 per cent of the total and represented an ongoing problem which had originally been identified by the Preservation Society in the 1960s. Tenterden was known far and wide as the place to go when visiting the K&ESR. A similar problem arose when services were extended to Northiam. In the twenty-first century, Tenterden Town Station continues to be the starting point for most of the traffic.

A notable happening during 1984 had been the appointment of David Stratton as TRC Vice-Chairman. David was one of those characters which only heritage railways can produce. Employed with great success by a City insurance firm, he habitually wore an expression of Churchillian resolution and it is even said that when he first worked in the City of London he was known among his colleagues as 'Young Winston'. All this disguised a most generous nature. A man of contrasts, he was both a former rally driver – his driving style was fast, precise and legendary – and a committed Christian. A famous eccentricity was his unique use of English which he himself came to refer to as 'Strattonese'. This was to be much lampooned, but it said a very great deal about David that he could see the funny side of the satire. The shape of the K&ESR management in the late 1980s was beginning to emerge.

David was among the volunteers who took part in a notable Thameside exercise over the weekend of 17/18 November – the recovery of 20 lengths of bullhead rail from the disused Gravesend West branch at Southfleet. This event was the precursor of the much bigger operation several years later when much of the remainder of the branch was lifted and taken to the K&ESR for re-use between Wittersham Road and Northiam. It was on the first of these occasions that something strangely prophetic happened. Proposals for a Channel Tunnel Rail Link were not being widely discussed at that time, but when a local resident asked what was going on Charlie Masterson, mischievous as ever, replied 'We're getting ready for the Channel Tunnel line.' Early in the next century, the Southfleet to Fawkham Junction section of the Gravesend West line was incorporated into the first phase of High Speed 1.

Over the next couple of years, Thameside Group put much work into alterations at Rolvenden. From early 1985 the track layout was remodelled, a signal box was constructed and a five-coach length passing loop was installed. It had been recognised for some time that Rolvenden would need to become a passing place in order to provide passengers on the existing service to

Wittersham Road with a more attractive and flexible timetable. In addition, waiting time between trains at Northiam, once it was reached, would be cut to a minimum. The previous track layout only allowed three-coach trains to pass. The work was divided into five phases:

1. Widening the formation over the culvert at the Wittersham end of the yard sufficiently to take double track. This was completed, as a separate job, without interruption to services, by mid November 1984.
2. Re-aligning and lengthening the passing loop using the existing platform.
3. Slewing the track away from the platform to the new alignment, and refacing the existing three-coach platform to suit.
4. Installing the signalling system and box.
5. Extending the platform to five-coach length.

This new layout was brought into use on 5 April, HM Railway Inspector having approved the completed works two days earlier. Around the same time, what has remained known as the 'wet cutting', below Cranbrook Road crossing on Tenterden Bank, also received considerable attention to clear blocked culverts, install new drains and realign the track. This however was not to be the end of problems in that location.

1985 had a somewhat military undertone. This was not entirely new, Military Spectaculars featuring preserved military vehicles having been held in 1982 and 1983 in co-operation with the Invicta Military Vehicle Preservation Society. 'Steam to Victory' held in June 1985 was altogether more ambitious; it involved the Railway, as well as a field event, and reappeared as 'Steaming Home' the following year. In varying forms, military and Second World War themed events were to continue into the twenty-first century.

Another, albeit more tenuous, military connection was the purchase from the Transport Trust of three coaches, 'the Blue Saloons', which had spent many years on the Longmoor Military Railway in Hampshire. Of London & South Western, South Eastern & Chatham and London & North Western origins, these coaches were to play an important role in later developments. Carriage preservation was also furthered the following year by the recovery of two London Chatham & Dover Railway designed four-wheeled bodies: three-compartment brake second (later brake third) No. 3062 of 1888 and SE&CR four-compartment second No. 2947 of 1901. Remarkably these were still in pre-grouping livery. Both came from a bungalow in Ashford which had been built from four vehicle bodies. This was being demolished prior to redevelopment of the site. The remaining two bodies were considered irrecoverable, although a third class compartment was taken to Tenterden and eventually used as a display in the Colonel Stephens Museum.

There was nonetheless cause for negativity in the way the Railway was perceived. Following what was obviously a visit by someone from the influential *Which?* Publications (the Consumers' Association) the following editorial appeared in the summer 1985 *Tenterden Terrier*.

> The *Holiday Which?* report on Britain's Nostalgia Railways hardly makes flattering reading for K&ESR supporters; whilst there is some praise for smartly painted stations and for the 'cheerful' buffet at Tenterden, there is little of cheer elsewhere in this report. Harking back to the early days, there is reference to the line being a backwater, once owned by a champion of lost railway causes. As of today, there is some disappointment with the carriages, presumably Mark 1s, which are seen as being of limited interest; flat countryside, together with a lack of lineside attractions also scores low marks. Perhaps

more disturbing is the comment on Rolvenden shed 'packed with locos which you can only see by appointment'. Holiday Which? is a respected publication, independent of commercial interests; we must take note of the survey findings even if we do not entirely agree with them. Clearly, more ideas and more events are needed including, perhaps, a more 'open house' policy at Rolvenden.

Uncomfortable as this undoubtedly was, it reflected some of this writer's impressions mentioned earlier. There was nonetheless a steady improvement in the Railway's fortunes through 1985, and John Miller in his final year as Chairman left the post with the Railway in possession of a healthy financial surplus which will be outlined shortly. Despite the perceived problems, passenger numbers were rising sharply as the combination of improved marketing and a better product took effect. The Chairman's report as presented to the AGM did, however, end on a cautionary note: some departments were well behind target with maintenance and planned programmes, which was more a reflection of lack of volunteer manpower than financial considerations.

October 1985 can be seen as the point at which Thameside Group influence reached its peak, as it was then that David Stratton became Chairman and he and George Wright were joined on the Board by Andrew Webb. An appraisal of the Railway in the heritage era must conclude this to have been the beginning of one of the K&ESR's dynamic periods. The negative views summarised by *Holiday Which?* and John Miller's report were in many ways shared by David Stratton, who viewed various aspects of the K&ESR as a mess – typified by the medieval toilet arrangements for staff at Rolvenden. John Miller's time as Chairman had indeed seen the Railway turned round, and that achievement should not be underestimated. The Stratton era was however to take the K&ESR up another level, or, to put it another way, to see a change of gear. One has to record that David's approach, often through the application of his singular personality, was not always popular or even understood. It divides opinion to this day, although his status as respected elder statesman grew with the years and was undiminished when he passed away, aged 80, in 2023.

1985 ended with a record number of passengers carried and reflecting a 7 per cent increase on 1984 to 45,232. Average loadings were again not significantly changed and it was seen as a wise decision to have increased the number of trains, particularly in the peak operating months of August and December. The improved marketing already noted was in large part due to the efforts of Mark Toynbee, a professional in this field who, working as a volunteer, never seemed to miss an opportunity to bring the K&ESR to the public's attention. For the first time, family tickets were made available, and on this basis over 10,000 passengers travelled. To some extent this mitigated the effect of a substantial 26 per cent increase in basic fare levels at the beginning of the year. Rover tickets, which were to be of great importance in later decades, fell sharply from 124 to a mere fifty. Discount schemes advertised in local newspapers and tourist publications only led to 942 vouchers being presented, though this exercise proved useful in identifying the areas from which traffic originated. As ever, the 'Wealden Pullman' had worked to capacity during the year. The surplus of £39,901 was very much higher than anticipated although in 1985, as in many later years, the surplus was a reflection of underspending by departments. Once again, the Pullman had been a major source of income (£30,976). The financial position allowed total net borrowings to fall from £83,861 to £31,515, and the Board was able to look forward to the future with cautious optimism.

Chapter 10

The 1980s generally were enlivened by locomotive developments including loans and exchanges with other heritage railways, a number of which have already been mentioned. Terriers *Sutton* and No. 3 *Bodiam* both received overhauls, although No. 3's time in traffic was short before being withdrawn again with boiler problems. This was, however, not before she had visited no less an establishment than the Great Western Society at Didcot. Great Western locomotives visiting the K&ESR were 0-4-2T No. 1466 from the GWS and Pannier Tank No. 7752 from Tyseley. Austerity No. 25 *Northiam* also went on its travels again, its visit to the Great Central Railway from December 1984 to April 1985 being occasioned by a motive power shortage. It is very difficult to imagine that mighty heritage main line asking for such assistance today! From the Bluebell came Fletcher Jennings 0-4-0T *Baxter* as well as Terrier *Fenchurch*.

During 1985 K&ESR drivers and firemen were privileged to take charge of the replica broad gauge Great Western 4-2-2 locomotive *Iron Duke*, when it was undertaking trials in, of all unlikely places, London's Kensington Gardens over a 200yd section of specially laid track. The building of the engine was undertaken by by Resco (Railways) Ltd, although the tender was built by British Rail at its works in Cathays, Cardiff. *Iron Duke* was constructed largely from components obtained from two former National Coal Board Austerities. K&ESR crews were of course well acquainted with the original standard gauge product. Accompanied by a replica broad gauge coach the locomotive arrived in Kensington over the weekend of 30/31 March and stayed until 9 April. The locomotive is the property of the National Railway Museum and is now on the broad gauge lines at Didcot.

Although one of the South Eastern & Chatham Birdcage coaches and the District Coach had been used in service trains there remained the unfulfilled ambition, dating back to the 1960s, of running a complete vintage train. This possibility was becoming closer as work progressed on the Great Eastern six-wheeler which had by this stage been moved from Plumstead to Tenterden. Work was progressing on the project under the guidance of Thameside member Bob Gilbert assisted by members from Croydon and Sutton – indicative of the wide range of area groups operating at that time.

Publicity for the Railway continued in some novel and sometimes fee-earning ways. One morning in the spring of 1986, I was cycling to work when I was held up in the heavy traffic which, then as now, accumulated in the vicinity of St Mildred's Road railway bridge, site of the tragic Hither Green derailment in November 1968. While waiting for the traffic lights to change, I noticed on an adjacent hoarding a large poster for a well-known chocolate bar. It featured a 12 ton LMS ventilated van painted in a scarlet livery with a large representation of said chocolate bar's logo on the side. Nearby sleepers had been covered to appear like fingers of chocolate. The setting of this scene seemed familiar. The plastic coverings were still on the sleepers at Orpins Curve, Rolvenden, in 1992 and van No. 515184 (K&ESR No. 128) has, although long repainted in an authentic livery, been known as the Kit-Kat Van ever since.

Infrastructure improvements were under way as 1985 became 1986. In the carriage shed there had been a concentration on 'squaring up' the workshop before the end of the year, and lighting was being progressively installed in the storage area on the mezzanine that was built on the north side of the shed. In the weeks leading up to Christmas a methodical sorting and tidying of the workshop floor had created much more working space (and not for the last time!) In January the workshop area was shunted and for the first time it was possible to stable four bogie coaches. In later years this was much reduced when part of the No. 3 road area was converted to workshops. During the three-month closed season, work was concentrated on light body repairs and repainting the Mark 1s. Progress on the GER six-wheeler continued steadily with compartment partitions being reinstated.

The rebuilding of the bus station kit of parts had been progressed during the 1985/86 winter months. The original intention to use it as a museum had now been abandoned, despite the museum team leading the reconstruction, and a more immediate need met – it was to be the Tenterden Station Buffet. This vast improvement over the facilities offered in *Theodora* opened on 2 August.

The upgrading of the track following the Pope's Cottage incident in 1983 was a continuing issue and in February 1986 Paul Wilson was appointed Permanent Way Manager. Dave Hazeldine was his assistant, responsible for organising civil engineering projects, with Lawrence Brydon acting as Civil Engineering Consultant.

It was agreed that all projects from then on would be engineered to the highest possible standards, with the objective of long life and minimal maintenance. A report on the then operating section was submitted to the Board emphasising the most urgent defects. The outcome was a three-year programme, costing over £100,000. As part of this reorganisation the Civil Engineering Department and Permanent Way Department were amalgamated.

With the ever-present problem of volunteer numbers and the scale of work on the soon-to-expand operating section a policy of mechanising as much work as possible was put in hand. This could be something as straightforward as a second-hand cement mixer, but it was the beginning of the developments which led to the acquisition of the track maintenance machines that later became an integral part of P.Way work on the K&ESR.

The various projects on Tenterden Bank have already been described. These were complemented with the installation, also on the Bank, of proper drainage in the lower part of what was, and still is, known as the Wet Cutting. That winter's work programme had been ambitious. The old timbers in the sewage works siding turnout at Rolvenden had been exchanged for jarrah hardwood replacements, and after the end of the running season on 1st January a collapsed culvert immediately west of Rolvenden Yard was replaced. This was completed shortly before a heavy snowfall, which was a prelude to a number of weeks of wintry conditions. Despite this, 700 sleepers were replaced at Rolvenden and at Wittersham Road; the record was 300 sleepers put down over one weekend, with up to 50 volunteers making this possible. In addition, a brand new point was built at Rolvenden, a more complicated and precise task than those not familiar with permanent way work might suppose. In the months before Easter, some 2,000 tons of ballast and minestone were deposited on the newly relaid stretches, as well as in some sidings. There nonetheless remained much to be done on the Tenterden–Hexden Bridge section before the challenge of the Northiam Extension could be tackled.

The publication of the passenger figures for 1986 showed it to have been a record year, with an increase of nearly 14 per cent on the previous year (57,370 against 50,645). There had been nine additional operating days. The 'Wealden Pullman' had, as ever, run to capacity, while the Santa Specials had enjoyed a 5 per cent increase and were said to have 'just about reached saturation point'. Thought was being given to how to address this, including how to run two Santa Trains (and therefore have two Santas) without destroying the illusion for the young audience. Fares during 1987 were to be maintained at 1986 levels despite an expected rise in costs, and it was seen as essential that higher net income was generated through a marked increase in train loadings – which, despite the overall numbers, had remained remarkably consistent for some years.

The Railway had reached a point where its direction over the coming 25 years began to be determined. I have heard it said that at one particularly crucial Board meeting, David Stratton asked something to the effect of 'Gentlemen, the question is whether or not we go to Northiam. I want an answer this evening'. The answer was evidently in the affirmative because the spring 1987 issue of the *Terrier* was able to announce that plans were in hand to cross the Rother into East Sussex by 1990.

The need both to attract more passengers and to finance the Northiam extension was increasing the pressure for a more commercial approach. This of course pointed up a major tension in the heritage railway world which was expressed in two letters to the summer 1987 issue of the *Tenterden Terrier*. The first came from Dr Gerald Siviour, a railway historian and photographer of some note, who was at the time the K&ESR's Education Officer:

> I wonder how many members share my distaste at this year's Easter festivities at Tenterden Town. The sight of the station building dwarfed by a plastic castle, swings and a candy floss stall in the yard and advertisements for a newspaper attached to fences at Cranbrook Road crossing brought home how far we have moved away from our aim of preserving a quiet country railway.
>
> We will be told that we must provide this kind of entertainment to attract the public. This is a total fallacy. During the same weekend the Bluebell Railway doubled last year's takings and ran two full six-coach trains every hour by selling itself as nothing more than a historic railway. At Tenterden we may have attracted the public in large numbers, but we had to accommodate them in Mark 1 coaches little different from those in daily use on BR lines in Kent. Two were even in BR livery and in a condition that left much to be desired.
>
> With an extension to Northiam in prospect the Tenterden Railway Company has to consider what it is and where it is going. Are we to grow bigger and risk stretching ourselves beyond our resources, or would we do better to remain small, placing the emphasis upon high quality and an authentic recreation of Pullman travel and the old Kent and East Sussex Railway?
>
> For my part I am appalled at the thought of yet more tatty Mark 1 coaches pushing our historic vehicles ever further back in the queue for restoration, while bigger funfairs have to be laid on because we feel we have to attract the masses. Let us have a full and open discussion about our future now, before hope of seeing again the attractive trains of historic vehicles which we used to run not so long ago is lost completely. The choice is between being bigger and being better; our limited labour and financial resources really will not allow us to have it both ways.

The second came from a member, Mr NC Langridge.

> I am concerned that it is the intention to repaint the 'P' Class locomotive No. 31556 in SR lined black. Also disturbing is the comment by Paul Sutton in the Spring edition of the *Tenterden Terrier* (page 43) that a rake of 'blood and custard' stock may be an improvement. I say that such moves would stray from the intention to preserve the K&ESR image and would make the railway no different from many other preserved lines with a motley assortment of liveries. Irrespective of former ownership or usage all locos and rolling stock, with the exception of the Pullmans and short term visitors, should be in K&ESR Livery, thus preserving the proper image.
>
> If people want to see SR locos or 'blood & custard' coach sets then there are plenty of other places where they can go after visiting our railway with its engines and coaching stock resplendent in K&ESR livery. The need to adhere to this livery should be one of the terms of acceptance that the owner of stock or locos should agree to if the K&ESR is to be their home.
>
> We are not just a preserved railway, and my comments would apply even if we were ever to have a West Country loco in the fleet. This would, I am sure, be Col. Stephens' policy.

This second letter brought forth a response from the Chairman, David Stratton. He stated:

> Although this is a highly emotive issue, we have to respect the wishes of locomotive owners and volunteers, especially where significant private funds are involved. Furthermore there has to be a balance between the purism of a Col. Stephens Railway and the perceived requirements of visitors and their families.

The above opinions and the reply echo similar views which had appeared in the *Terrier* a few months earlier. These concluded an article by former Chairman John Miller about the project to re-erect the Maidstone Bus Station building for use as Tenterden Town Buffet. Having described the completion of the scheme John added:

> With so much achieved, it is sad to end on a discordant note. Without discussion with any of those involved with the construction project, an arbitrary decision was approved by the Board to call the building 'The Colonel's Kitchen'. Whilst no doubt a splendid name for a trendy hamburger bar, it does not fit in with the image of a traditional teashop in a railway setting. A huge sign board proclaiming this title was fixed to the building, which totally filled the space between the dormer timbers. It is hoped that further thought will be given to this issue, as the building deserves a greater degree of sensitivity both in the context of its own history and in the development of the station site. Possibly the simple word 'refreshments' in the style of the Maidstone & District Bus Company's old logo, but in Tenterden Railway Company colours of maroon and cream, would create a suitable identity.

Commercial Director Donald Wilson commented at the end of the article:

> I am sorry that the bus station project has ended in controversy. The large name board between the eaves has now been removed and replaced by a smaller one positioned to

the side of the building. Whilst 'The Colonel's Kitchen' will be used as a marketing logo for the catering services on the Railway generally, the Tenterden building will be known simply as the 'Station Buffet' and all the signs and publicity material will reflect this.

This appears to prove that the workforce was occasionally listened to, and also implies that John Miller's views were held by others. Various wits, the K&ESR never being short of these, made the scatological suggestion that the toilet block should perhaps be named 'The Colonel's Khazi' to match. A 'Colonel's Kitchen' sign (presumably the one mentioned above) with a representation of Colonel Stephens was at one time fixed to a tree adjacent to the Buffet. This provided further opportunities for the wits who pointed out that it might give the public the impression that the Buffet was a franchise of a well-known brand of American deep-fried chicken. The sign was later taken down, or perhaps fell down. It was certainly gone by 1992.

Chapter 11

The Thameside Group, and the whole Railway, was greatly saddened when on 22 July 1987, after a short illness, George Wright died at the age of 47. The loss of such a man to the Kent & East Sussex was immense. Thameside seems to have subsequently faded out, less through lack of interest than because a number of members moved away – many to the vicinity of Tenterden. The Group was in effect absorbed into the main effort. Its former members continued to have great influence however, an influence which has continued down to the time of writing and if anything again strengthened during the second decade of the twenty-first century.

It is appropriate to mention here the Sussex Area Group's interest in Northiam Station during the long slumber of the line west of Wittersham. This evolved into the Friends of Northiam Station, a group which continued to show a keen interest once services resumed. Before that could happen, the station itself would require the construction of a toilet block, the reinstatement of the second platform and a car park; and the line from Hexden Bridge would have to be relaid. In order to raise the necessary finance, the Board decided upon another Bond issue, an item about which, penned by Philip Shaw, appeared in the winter 1987 issue of the *Terrier*. After recounting the story, of the first Bond issue In 1981, Philip continued:

> The sum of £20,000 required for the purpose of completing Wittersham Road station and bridge rebuilding was modest by today's standards. This was raised quite quickly, a small oversubscription of £500 being returned to unlucky applicants. The 1987 issue of £175,000 unsecured bearer bonds 1998–2007 as a contribution towards the cost of £225,000 to rebuild the railway from Hexden Bridge to Northiam is a much more formidable task, but does come at a time when the public at large are more aware of shares and bonds than ever before, following the various Government privatisation issues.

In the 1981 issue, the single bond denomination was fixed at £25, but this time a wider variety are being issued, carrying different benefits, in order to broaden the appeal. The bond numbers and denominations are as follows:

This article then described various incentives to purchase, such as the availability of fifteen Bonds at £1,000 each providing first class travel on the official opening train to Northiam and two tickets each year on the Wealden Pullman train for the first five years subsequent to the date of purchase. It concluded:

> The bond issue was launched on 29th September at Tenterden Town station with a press reception and special train. We arranged for a limited amount of paid advertising, but the K&ESR publicity machine moved into top gear thanks to Mark Toynbee and a considerable amount of news coverage was obtained, both in the national press, local papers and on television, including the breakfast time programme complete with City

comment. The £1000 bonds were sold out in two days and the £500 in two weeks, the minimum subscription of £35,000 being achieved almost before we had time to think about it! At the time of writing, a total of £80,000 has been raised, with more coming in the post every day. This still leaves us with the majority of the £100 and £25 bonds to sell, but it is felt that these will make ideal Christmas presents and a stand will be set up at the station in order to interest travellers on the Santa Special trains. We could therefore find virtually the whole issue sold out by the end of the year, with the distinct possibility that the bonds will become highly prized collectors' items. Meanwhile, work is in hand on the extension itself; we have already secured suitable track for the job – Northiam here we come!

The Bond issue occurred against the background of 1987 which had been one of the most successful seasons the Railway had seen up to that time. Passenger numbers using the basic services rose by 15 per cent to 59,302 and, more importantly, the average number of fare-paying passengers carried per train rose from 84 to 94, the former being the previously mentioned statistic that had remained virtually unchanged for a number of years. The season concluded with a 28 per cent increase in the Santa Special trains.

The track mentioned in Philip Shaw's article was the result of a second recovery effort on the Gravesend West Branch. Work on the extension continued apace through 1988, the formation of the line between Hexden and Northiam being upgraded and, in particular, the drainage rebuilt. The progress of the project is remembered for the esprit de corps in the workforce which heritage railways invariably produce on these occasions. It also brought a renewal of the traditionalists versus pragmatists controversy. Not all proposals for the extension were accepted; for instance, a plan to straighten out the curve in Northiam's platform was rejected by the Board as unacceptable. This scheme was referred to in a controversial article by former Chairman Peter Davis in the summer 1988 *Terrier*, and the following is a particularly pertinent extract:

> The promoters (of the preservation scheme) envisaged a revived Colonel Stephens railway serving both the community and tourists. Of course, subsequent less-than-happy circumstances dictated that the line should be further truncated and would rely solely on tourist traffic for its revenue. It should be remembered that the fight to reopen the line lasted 13 years, during which time hundreds of members remained loyal to the project. The frustration of years of painfully slow negotiation and obstructive bureaucracy were borne by a handful of directors and members. Both volunteer workers and directors were driven by the vision of a revived K&ESR as a living memorial to the light railway age and to Holman F. Stephens in particular.
>
> Looking back, can it be said that the vision has been realised? I am afraid not. From the earliest days it was understood that longer trains, extended platforms, heavier engines and even signalling would be necessary for viable operation and generation of funds sufficient to rebuild the line. Indeed, all this has taken place, but unfortunately without proper regard for the character and correct practices for a Colonel Stephens railway. Apart from characteristic fencing at Tenterden and an awning at Rolvenden, scant attempt has been made to re-create the K&ESR. In fact, the tendency has been to impose South Eastern & Chatham Railway, Southern Railway and even British Railways character on new developments and reinstated facilities. This is understandable, as equipment from

these concerns is most readily available in our part of the country. Also, in the formative years, expedience was paramount, aesthetics being given low priority.

Now, it seems, we are in a much better position to give more thought to the authentic recreation of a Colonel Stephens railway. Bodiam and Northiam are the only remaining examples of his many wayside and passing stations. Without question they should be carefully restored, perhaps to immediate post-war condition. Allowances for present day traffic requirements must be sympathetic and in the Stephens idiom.

The planned 'development' at Northiam is totally unacceptable. There is no case for re-aligning the permanent way, a footbridge, a South Eastern Railway signalbox, water columns or additional buildings. If the present layout creates operating difficulties, then so be it.

This led to a response from David Stratton in the Winter 1988 issue of the house journal:

The Directors and members who fought to re-open the line are held in the highest esteem, but please do not think that the present members, including Directors, do not work as hard. As Chairman, I am only too well aware that their output is colossal.

This year some 100,000 visitors will come to the Railway; at a conservative guess 80 per cent of them have no interest whatsoever in our antecedents. I would suggest also that it is good housekeeping to budget for a surplus, however small. Moreover, in the 1980s we are required to work within strict health and safety regulations which did not exist in former days; as well as to operate in accordance with the stringent requirements of the Railway Inspectorate.

At Northiam, road traffic has increased many fold since the line closed in the 1950s; anyone standing at the crossing will be acutely aware that traffic speeds have risen substantially since that time. I must also add that visitor safety is of paramount importance.

Water storage for locomotives at Northiam is essential. A different water composition there creates priming in boilers, which is potentially dangerous and causes many of the operating problems.

In conclusion, the funds raised towards the Railway's extension are thanks to diligent hard work by colleagues and members who have brought reality to past emotions with sensitive planning for Northiam. Dreams will be realised in 1990.

A second letter supporting Peter Davis was received from leading railway photographer Mike Esau, an associate of Dr Gerald Siviour:

Peter Davis's article 'A Matter of History' gives much to think about, and highlights the case for the conservation of the archetype Colonel Stephens K&ESR Light Railway which has miraculously survived at Northiam and Bodiam, virtually unchanged from the 1950s.

The contrast between the open and closed sections of the Railway perhaps underlines its problem of identity which has developed since re-opening in 1974 – the Bluebell recreates the LB&SCR and Southern Railway scene, the Mid Hants Southern Region steam, the Severn Valley the GWR, and so on, but the K&ESR? Is it now simply another pleasant but unremarkable steam ride for the family, or should it exploit the quaint and delightful Colonel Stephens Light Railway atmosphere which cannot now be found anywhere else in the UK in genuine standard gauge form?

The K&ESR Prospectus says that the second purpose of the issue is 'to recreate at Northiam a country station scene reminiscent of some 50 years ago'. This can mean anything, but if in reality it was the despoliation of what, with Bodiam, is now a unique period piece, this would surely be condemned as insensitive and short sighted by future generations, and against the trend to greater authenticity in the museum and preservation world, readily appreciated by a more discerning public.

Lack of enthusiasm and the need for greater volunteer effort was mentioned in the last issue of the Terrier… could it be that these problems are being exacerbated by a lack of purpose, and disillusionment for a Railway whose primary aim often seems to be for ever higher passenger figures to the detriment of its special light railway character and pressure on resources of all kinds.

Before it is too late the Railway must I feel now ensure that over the western end of its route, the essence of the old K&ESR is not lost forever and with it, the ability to fire the imagination of volunteers and visitors alike.

This was not of course to be the last word on this subject. Two further letters from around this period are worth quoting, and these pointed the way to developments which were to become significant in the decades which followed. The first came from Paul Sutton who had been most active on the K&ESR since the period preceding reopening and who had also been Assistant Editor of the *Terrier* for some years:

Surely a lucrative marketing opportunity was missed this season when the ex-GER 6-wheeler was removed from the Carriage & Wagon shed in January. 1987 is this vehicle's centenary year and, had the restoration team been encouraged and assisted to finish the renovation work quickly, the public would have had the rare opportunity of riding in a coach 100 years old. Quite naturally those involved with No. 87 have said they will not restart work until it is under cover again. Meanwhile much of their earlier efforts are being weathered away while it stands in the open.

This brings me to ask: when may we be told the Company's latest policy regarding our coaching stock? In the Boardroom notes in *Tenterden Terrier* No. 42 [spring 1987] it was stated that 'a small committee was set up towards the end of last year' – surely they must have concluded their deliberations by now. Some of the ex-Departmental stock acquired has now been on the line for over 20 years and, should they ever reach the head of the queue for restoration, they will be then be totally beyond redemption. It would appear that the Railway does not want historic coaches, but prefers Mark 1s and perhaps two or three token Maunsells.

In view of the foregoing, I suggest we either scrap these unwanted relics (approximately 14 in number) or give them away to other railways who will restore and look after them. We certainly never will.

Paul Sutton's views doubtless reflected concerns more widely held among the membership and anticipated developments regarding vintage coaches in the 1990s. Sadly Paul would not live to see these for, like George Wright, serious health problems led to his passing at far too young an age.

A further letter, this time from member Jonathan Dalton, reopened a subject many had considered closed for ever. It was headed 'Bodiam to Robertsbridge?'.

Now that the Kent & East Sussex Railway is hopefully extending to Northiam and later Bodiam, should we not consider the purchase of the trackbed between Bodiam and Robertsbridge as it becomes available, in order to allow a future link up with the national railway system?

The trackbed should be quite easy to acquire and we should object to any obstruction of the right of way by the proposed Robertsbridge bypass and other developments. The breach in the embankment to the west of Bodiam could perhaps be repaired using spoil from the Channel Tunnel.

A link with British Railways would make the K&ESR more accessible, especially as rising petrol prices restrict private motoring, and enable us to provide a proper public service to the local area as well as the tourist steam train service.

Three decades later it would be cynically easy to point out that this letter was imbued with the kind of optimism which has so often accompanied proposals for preserved railways; it nevertheless proved to be the proverbial acorn from which great oaks grow. Initially support came by way of several 'Letters to the Editor' and also in incidental comments in an article by founder member Robin Doust. Robin had been estranged from the preservation project when the original public service proposals had been abandoned in the late 1960s but later become reconciled to the tourist railway which emerged. He nonetheless saw in a Robertsbridge extension some hope of a broader role for the K&ESR. Eventually, the Board took the idea seriously enough to commission a feasibility study. But we are anticipating ourselves – there will be much more on this subject in due course.

Rolvenden signal box was also built at this stage, although not commissioned until December 1989. Also during 1988, another Terrier arrived on, or rather returned to, the K&ESR. This locomotive was No. 32678, also known by its LB&SCR name of *Knowle*, an old friend which had been loaned to the old company by the Southern Railway and which had worked on after nationalisation until the passenger service was withdrawn in 1954. After working on the Hayling Island branch and at Newhaven, withdrawal came in 1963. In 1964, *Knowle* was sold to Butlins and put on display at their Minehead holiday camp. Subsequently it moved to the nearby West Somerset Railway, from where the loco was acquired by Resco (Railways) Ltd. *Knowle* later came into the ownership of Rick Edmondson who moved to the K&ESR what was by then a kit of parts. An early return to traffic was not anticipated.

Passenger figures for 1988 had not reached the 100,000 predicted by David Stratton, although the 'ever higher' figures were maintained with 73,529 being achieved, an increase of 12.8 per cent which was well above budget. The two-train Santa Special service had been run, apparently without doppelganger Santas causing confusion, there again being an increase of business in this market segment. In the ordinary service, Wittersham Road figures were nearly 200 up on 1987 and mystification continued as to why Tenterden, a neat little station set in one of the most charming market towns in England, continued to attract vastly more passengers than an obscure halt-like platform located in one of remotest spots in the South East. Slightly worryingly, Pullman trains and charters were down on 1987, the reason being given as reduced train numbers due to 'staffing difficulties' of an unspecified nature.

Chapter 12

When planning for the Northiam extension started in the mid-1980s, the spring of 1990 seemed very far distant, but as ever the available time soon seemed to melt away. In the early stages of the extension scheme, it had been realised that Northiam Station as it stood was totally unsuited to the requirements of the K&ESR in the late twentieth century. Car parking was non-existent, the platform was too short and too low, and platform 2 needed to be reinstated. The toilet provision was a repeat of that at Tenterden – a primitive gents urinal flushed by the rain and draining into a ditch.

Doing something about all this, as we have already seen, provided 'fissile material' to the 'critical mass' which was building up between traditionalists and pragmatists.

The answer for Northiam was not revolution but evolution – a notion which could arguably be adopted generally as the way forward for a railway which was reviving its independent heritage and not trying to represent a segment of a much larger company. This approach could address the paradox that in preserving the K&ESR of legend a railway designed as a rural byway had to carry vastly greater numbers of passengers if it were to survive. It was stated at the time that mixing the past with the economic demands of the 1980s was no easy task. Those managing the extension would have liked to see brick-faced platforms without concrete coping stones, but the platforms had to be built in the most economic manner, using modern-day materials. That was not to say that the old K&ESR style was to be ignored; the prime example of this was the toilet block which was built alongside the existing building and faced and roofed with corrugated iron to match.

Two grant applications were made to assist in raising the planned cost of over £225,000. The first, £45,000 from the English Tourist Board, was eventually achieved. The second application was to the Department of Environment for a Derelict Land Grant. Andrew Webb, having looked at grants and fundraising, described the government grants system as a 'snake pit'. This appeared designed to put off all but the most determined and required lateral thinking to penetrate the labyrinth of Whitehall. Unperturbed and in a very determined mood Andrew went off to be 'interviewed' at the Department of the Environment as a preliminary to making an application. Once he had determined what the 'officialese' used by the Civil Service meant in plain English, an application was duly made based on the acreage of Northiam Station alone.

Andrew then realised that the linear length of the railway between Wittersham Road and Northiam also counted as brown field land, due to it having ash ballast laid along its length. He quickly asked for another copy of the relevant form, and he re-wrote the application with the additional linear land included! In today's money, this added the equivalent of approximately £200,000 in grant aid. Andrew had the bit between his teeth by this time and politely asked what other grants the K&ESR might be eligible for and which would not subtract from what had already been requested. (Andrew had by this time been given a tentative nod that the Railway would get the money.) The Webb determination worked again, and further monies were granted for drainage work under a scheme which previously was completely unknown.

Work started on the extension in mid-August 1988 – some four and a half months later than planned, due to bureaucratic delay. The Railway had no option but to start work or risk losing the ETB grant, which required completion of the project by June 1990. To help make up lost time, volunteer John Durrant joined the paid staff on a short-term contract as Site Foreman. The team responsible for the extension was led by Paul Wilson as volunteer Project Manager, with Dave Hazeldine again looking after the civil engineering. Due credit was given at the time to 71-year-old Rex Stirling-Baker who almost single-handedly dismantled the track at Northiam so that work could start as soon as the ETB aid was confirmed. Rex had also acted as 'site caretaker' for some months, his presence helping to discourage light-fingered visitors. It was not stated whether these were routine law-breakers or the type of railway 'enthusiast' who seems to think that their private collection is a more deserving location for historic items than a heritage railway. In the first instance, work concentrated on clearing about 400 yards of the boundary fence towards Bodiam and regrading part of the adjoining field to ease drainage problems at that end of the station site. In early September, and at the urging of the Southern Water Authority, it was decided to concentrate on rebuilding the culverts and to temporarily halt to work on the station site. The need to focus on this type of work where the surrounding countryside, in great contrast to the Wealden landscape of Tenterden Bank, resembled the flatlands of East Anglia, showed that the K&ESR was literally 'returning to the Rother'.

Two derelict culverts were soon demolished, piped and filled with minestone to give access via the trackbed to the major drainage channel known as the Petty Foreland Sewer. Excavating the culvert for this water course to the new levels required by the Water Authority fell foul of the remains of wooden foundations which Colonel Stephens had presumably used as an economy measure. Once the girders at the top of the culvert had been removed and excavations made below foundation level, one of the abutments collapsed. This was cleared, the other abutment demolished and reinforced concrete pipes laid on a concrete invert. About £7,000 was spent on this one project.

Two other culverts between Hexden Channel and the Rother Bridge were demolished and piped in late September, but there still remained much work on the trackbed to clear vegetation, clean out ditches and fill soft spots prior to relaying track early in the following summer. At Northiam Station, the two platforms were to be approximately 350ft in length to allow for five-coach trains. A water tower was to be erected at the Bodiam end of platform 1. It had been intended to install a footbridge between the station building and the road but this item, a cause of much controversy, was deleted from the scheme. The idea did not however go away and, with the likely location moved to the other end of the station, is active again at the time of writing.

At New Year 1989 and with less than 18 months to go before the planned reopening date, there still seemed to be a mountain to climb. By the early months of the year, income from the Northiam Bond issue and the grant from the English Tourist Board was enough to financially secure the project. Much volunteer effort went into this work, which took place in very hot weather and, as might be expected, additional labour arrived from around the Railway to assist the Permanent Way Department. The story of relaying the track between Hexden Bridge and Northiam was related in an article by Gary Barker in an article in the summer 1989 *Tenterden Terrier*. Gary (inevitably and stereotypically known as 'Bruce') was a qualified civil engineer with the Australian Army on a two-year secondment to the UK who had been 'volunteered' to help with the extension by David Stratton. As the P.Way Department had everything under control this was a little awkward to begin with, but Gary is remembered as a 'great guy' who, best of all, managed to arrange for the Army to do some of the civils:

It was around 9pm on Friday 19th May that the phone rang yet again. However this call was different; the 'P' class locomotive had just steamed over the A28 level crossing on to temporary track at Northiam Station. Somehow, through a combination of hard work, co-operation and good luck, our efforts during the working fortnight had been realised. We had laid 176 pre-assembled 45ft long track panels, representing 1.5 miles of railway and a labour effort of more than 500 man days (which also includes a significant number of lady days); truly a magnificent effort for a volunteer railway!

It is very easy to view the track now and be lulled into the false sense that we did all this in two weeks; our success was also due to prior preparation. I am not only referring to planning, but also to the dedicated efforts of two groups who over the last 15 months or so have prepared the track formation. Alan Tebboth and the Clearance Gang, and David Hazeldine, ably assisted by Kevin Hickmot, deserve credit for their work, much of which remains unseen and therefore difficult to appreciate – they prepared the foundations!

Our plan was to do the maximum preparation before the fortnight, spend the first five working days building up a stockpile of track panels, then use the remaining time to both lay and build panels. Panels were to be constructed and stockpiled in Wittersham Road Permanent Way yard, using the railway's three steam cranes, loaded on to a panel train and propelled to the railhead where a hired crawler crane would lay them. While one panel train was at the railhead a second train would be loaded to ensure a rapid turn round at Wittersham Road. Mainly because of resource limitations, the aim was to lay all the straight track from Hexden Bridge to Cysters Curve, which is about 700 yards from Northiam Station. Not only was this achieved but we also managed to get through to the station itself! [The panels for Cysters curve were fabricated to bespoke orders received directly from the railhead.]

By the end of the first week, including two days of track laying, we were just off Rother Bridge, and although panel production was slightly behind schedule all was going well. Then came the news that one of the steam cranes was out of action and would take days to fix. [The Grafton crane had run a bearing.] As the crawler crane was on contract, and volunteers had taken time off from work, we had to press on, although the remaining steam cranes would be unable to keep up with the panel building. The decision was then made to hire a rough terrain mobile crane and position it at Wittersham so that in conjunction with one of the two remaining steam cranes it could both make and load panels. On Monday morning we had our crane and by that afternoon we were over the Rother Bridge and a steam locomotive was in East Sussex. (The replacement crane was a monster – the jib could be seen from the railhead on the other side of Wittersham Bank.) Then came the shock news that an expected load of ballast would he delayed for at least a fortnight because of fire damage to the crushing plant in Scotland. This was critical, as we had already contracted for a track tamping machine to arrive on 20th May after the ballast had been laid. Apart from financial penalties, there would be a significant delay with the project. Luckily we had a 1600 tonne stockpile of ballast at Northiam; all we had to do was get to it – and we did! In the process we received excellent press coverage on radio, in newspapers and on two television networks.

As a civil engineering project, the scheme was relatively straightforward. For it to be achieved by a volunteer group in a short time, shows the dedication, endurance and sacrifice that a large number of people are prepared to make for this railway. From this 'Colonial Engineer' you have my heartfelt thanks. To those who did turn up and could not be employed all day please understand that at times we were overwhelmed by volunteers. Rather than turn people away in advance we decided that those who wanted to help would be allowed to do so.

Work at Northiam Station has continued and the majority of earthworks are now complete. The car park had been levelled, drains installed, platforms shaped and the track bed prepared for re-laying. We were fortunate to receive plant assistance from the Royal School of Military Engineering for a two-week period and we are grateful for their assistance. It does not take much imagination to visualise the finished job, particularly if one stands near the level crossing. It would be nice to say the job is finished, but although we are well on the way we are not there yet.

Mention of the number of volunteers who turned up reminds me that this was the point at which I might have returned to the Railway. It was not to be however – I was still recovering from a serious cycling accident and felt very frustrated when I realised what was going on. For those who were there much food – particularly cake – was produced on an industrial scale by wives and girlfriends. Signalman Gerald Beck was of the opinion that he had never worked Wittersham box so hard for an astonishing service of panel trains, and Paul Wilson recalls stumbling along the track from Rolvenden with a hurricane lamp at 5am to light up the cranes.

As Gary Barker pointed out, there was quite widespread media coverage of the relaying effort, this being focused on Thursday, 11 May when Mark Toynbee briefed journalists at what was then the Rother Valley Hotel, adjacent to Northiam Station, prior to the departure of two minibuses which conveying the party up the trackbed, over the Rother Bridge and on to the railhead. Coverage was subsequently received from Television South, the BBC, seven local newspapers and four railway enthusiast publications.

Although not subsequently used, provision was made for connections to bay platforms on both Up and Down sides. There was also a long siding designed for use by engineers' trains for whenever work commenced on the Bodiam extension and which led away from Northiam. On the running line, adoption of a railway industry standard of 300mm ballast depth was not justified for the K&ESR (and would have cost around £100,000). A depth of 200mm, which was suitable for concrete sleepers and mechanical tamping, as well as being reasonably economical, was used instead.

Meanwhile, 'back at the *Terrier*', the dispute about the project produced another round of correspondence which led the Editor to state that this was to be the last word on the subject and to summarise the arguments in his editorial for the spring 1989 issue.

The controversy over the style of the Northiam project seems to have crystallised within two camps. There are those, directly involved with its management, budgeting and execution, who prefer to upgrade the line, in the interests of solvency, and in the anticipation that at least 80 per cent of the visitors will not care too much about historical authenticity. No doubt many less active but no less committed members will agree. In the other camp there are the purists, some of whom re-started the railway in the first place, devised the constitution and feel that the past should play a greater part in planning the future. This is the dilemma that the Board faces, given that the whole scheme now spans two generations and includes members with different memories, interests and loyalties.

Perhaps a detailed statement from the directors on the Railway's future identity would help to clear the air. After all, everybody who donates time and money to a charity expects to know what it is all leading up to.

The project received a considerable boost when it was featured in the *Challenge Anneka* TV programme on 23 July 1989, transmission being on 20 October. David Stratton has told me that it was the K&ESR's very proactive publicity machine which made initial contact with Mentorn, the company which produced the programme for BBC1. The series featured TV celebrity Anneka Rice attempting to complete a task, usually for a charitable cause, within a given period of time, typically two or three days. The audience were given to believe that Ms Rice had no prior knowledge of the task and that she would persuade individuals and organisations to donate as appropriate. A notable feature of the programme was Anneka Rice's constant use of a mobile phone long before they became commonplace, were still the size of a brick, and definitely the preserve of the accomplished and upwardly mobile.

About three weeks after transmission, the *Tenterden Terrier* reported what happened:

Originally it was planned to complete track laying from Cysters Curve to the level crossing as well as work at the station. In retrospect, the task of rebuilding the station and laying track for a train to enter the platform, all within 48 hours, made a more attainable project.

Some preparatory work was undertaken. This included platform walls completed three blocks high throughout and a short length finished with oversail blocks and coping slabs, a task impossible in 48 hours. Ballast stone, plant and sleepers were pre-ordered and waiting in lorries not far away, ready for Anneka to decide how to do the job; hopefully her advisers would give her the right tips!

The challenge was set on Friday 21st July, Northiam becoming a hive of industry over the next two days. In a long hot summer, this must have been the hottest weekend of all. For muscle power Anneka turned to the Scots Guards as well as enlisting the help of Northiam Brownies. Six camera crews recorded the transformation, the site having been first made artistically untidy!

Over the weekend the trackbed between the platforms was graded, ballasted and approximately 200 yards of rails laid on new jarrah sleepers. Much of the platform was backfilled and the surface outside the building tarmacked, as was the approach road to the A28. The area between the building and the main road was landscaped, covered in topsoil, turfed and fenced in, turning it into a picnic enclosure. A length of fencing was installed on the Newenden boundary. Paint was applied to the building and fencing, as well as liberal measures over the Brownies themselves. From the crossing for a distance of about two coach lengths along the platform, and hence within camera range, a thorough job was performed,

Memorable incidents included Anneka blocking A28 traffic on a roller, Brownies undeterred by a lack of brushes (hands doing just as well), ever increasing crowds of spectators, and an upset production crew on discovering that the locomotive to haul the inaugural train faced the wrong way and that it was not possible just to lift and turn it around, at least not when it was already in steam!

6.15pm on the Sunday evening, or so it said on the station waiting room clock, and the P-class had brought its special train over the Extension into Northiam station; locomotive whistle sounded, detonators exploded, a ribbon bow over the track broken, crowds cheered and the Scots Guards Pipe Band struck up a welcome. Stirring stuff, Anneka had made it! It was perhaps appropriate that Jack Hoad, our former K&ESR driver, should be on the footplate.

It was a memorable weekend for everyone involved. The Railway benefited with new materials worth perhaps £30,000 and Northiam station now looks almost ready to open for services next year, although a lot more work is needed.

Screening is scheduled for 20th October and whatever the critical verdict about its programme, 40 minutes of prime viewing is invaluable publicity in getting the Railway known by the public. Inevitably there were difficulties, mainly arising from the secrecy beforehand, but overall the Railway must have gained immeasurably from the Challenge. Thank you Anneka, and well done!

Valuable income 'in kind' resulted from *Challenge Anneka*, together with the kind of publicity that is beyond price. Positive as all this was, there were instances when the frantic haste of the *Challenge Anneka* format left the recipients with work to be done or repeated. Such recipients included the K&ESR and, together with other work remaining to be done on the extension, it was to be a further ten months before services to Northiam began. From what has already been said, the reader will probably have gathered that the whole affair was more contrived than a naïve TV viewer might have supposed. Inevitably this leaked out and came to the attention of the *Sun* newspaper.

An account of how this was responded to was reported in a piece entitled 'Challenge Anneka – the Hype Goes On' which appeared in the *Rooter*, a newsletter which accompanied the *Terrier* for many years. It was signed 'MT', presumably Mark Toynbee.

11 million people watched our 'Challenge Anneka' programme on 20th October and were left in no doubt as to what we are and where we are.

The following week some 2 million readers of 'The Sun' newspaper [?] learned that the whole show was a sham – a 'con'-test in their own inimitable words. An embarrassment to us? Not a bit of it. Funny how the local papers and radio stations had copies of the appropriate page arrive on their Fax machines, to be followed shortly afterwards by an official statement from the Railway decrying 'The Sun's shameful accusations. The result? More press coverage – more publicity – more business!

In the past we've been tagged 'The Farmers line', 'The Colonel's line', now the press call us 'The Anneka line'. Wonderful! Personally I think she's much more attractive than an old man in wellie boots sucking on a piece of grass or a middle–aged bachelor purporting to be in the army. So for once it's a nickname I'm glad to see our railway linked with!

Highlights of the nine programmes in the *Challenge Anneka* series were shown on Friday 10th November, resulting in yet more exposure for the Railway.

The reaction to the *Sun* article now seems, like the huge mobile phone, typical of the era in Britain. 'Tough it out' as the then Prime Minister might have said. Although this incident might have been seen as a problem that could be turned into an opportunity, this was not the case when HM Railway Inspectorate found cause to comment. The ribbon breaking train on the Sunday evening had not been a mere works train – it had carried passengers and HMRI was less than pleased.

Whatever its rights and wrongs, the *Challenge Anneka* episode has to be viewed within the context of the need to raise the K&ESR's profile and in that it was undoubtedly successful. Twenty years later members of the visiting public would still mention that long-ago TV programme. 1989 had seen a slight increase in passenger numbers – 69,958 against 67,289 in 1988 – although Pullmans and Charters were down by 766 as a result of the Mark 1 restaurant car *Diana* having to be taken out of service for essential repairs for several months. The pattern of previous years was repeated and the main traffic was generated during August and by the Santa Specials. Together they accounted for 42.5 per cent of the total.

The efforts of 1989 were crowned with an award to the K&ESR for an 'outstanding contribution to railway preservation' by the Association of Railway Preservation Societies. The spring 1990 *Tenterden Terrier* said that this was:

> …a tremendous boost to morale at a time of immense activity. The award, given for the professionalism of its voluntary marketing and also engineering staff in the construction of its extension, is timely, given that passenger numbers continue to grow at a time when we most need them – for the main line from Tenterden, shortly to be extended to Northiam.

But much remained to be done. The extension works programme was running very tight regarding time and the Board and Managers were monitoring progress and costs. The Tenterden Railway Company Limited Northiam Station Level Crossing Order 1990 was signed by authority of the Secretary of State for Transport on 26 February. This allowed TRC to install and operate level crossing gates at Northiam.

The railway engaged the services of level crossing consultant Tom Craig for the necessary negotiations, as the requisite expertise was not available at short notice in-house. The platform blockwork and the toilet building were in an advanced state during March, and the Wittersham-end point had been laid and track panels were being laid down to the Bodiam-end point. Also in respect of the permanent way, ballast and tamping between Wittersham and Northiam had achieved an excellent ride, this work having been completed during February. March was also the month scheduled for the installation of the ground frames and the water crane.

The HMRI inspection of the Northiam extension by Major Peter Olver took place on 14 May 1990. The K&ESR representatives included Chairman David Stratton, Extension Director Andrew Webb, Operating Director Derek Dunlavey, Operating Manager Neil Sime, S&T Manager Peter Lawrence, Civil Engineer Lawrence Brydon and Project Foreman David Hazeldine as well as a class 14 diesel, two guards, three signalmen and the three operating department inspectors. At Hexden, the then limit of operation, the train went ahead and Major Olver, together with Messrs Brydon, Webb and Hazeldine, walked the track to Northiam. Various items were inspected including fencing, trespass notices, 'close the gate' notices, culverts, occupation crossings, general civil engineering, bridges and the state of the track. Once the foot party arrived at Northiam, a platform gauge was used to verify that platform horizontal clearance was adequate and that the vertical height of the platform from the track was within tolerance. The ground frame was tested and the level crossing inspected.

During the return journey to Wittersham, Major Olver requested that the train travel above the normal 25mph line speed to allow him to fully judge the condition of both the track and the vehicles although the normal speed restrictions over the bridges were observed. The revised signalling arrangements at Wittersham Road and Rolvenden were inspected before Major Olver congratulated the railway on the high standard of workmanship – an unexpected, though welcome, compliment.

Services to Northiam commenced with an unofficial opening on Saturday, 19 May 1990. This was followed by an official opening on Monday, 4 June when the Kent & East Sussex Railway received its second royal visit. The arrangements for this had begun in April 1989 when the support of the Lord Lieutenant's Office at East Sussex County Council was secured. Although a member of the Royal Family was very much hoped for, a 'Plan B' list of alternatives was drawn up 'just in case'. It was not until March 1990 that the Lord Lieutenant's Office indicated that His Royal Highness the railway-minded Duke of Gloucester had said that he would be delighted to attend on Monday, 4 June. This caused some degree of consternation as it was by no means guaranteed that the extension would be ready. Nevertheless, His Royal Highness's offer was accepted. An impressive guest list was prepared of appropriate local dignitaries and others from the private and public sectors, which was rapidly acted on once Major Olver had given the all-clear.

As had occurred – and was to occur again – on K&ESR opening days, Monday 4 June dawned fine with a forecast of dry weather. The locomotives (P class No 1556 and Terrier *Sutton*) and rolling stock (Maunsell BNO 53, Restaurant Car *Diana*, Pullman Car *Barbara* and Maunsell BNO 54, were brought up to an exceptionally high standard of presentation. At length the train took the guests off to Northiam where the arrival of the Duke of Gloucester was awaited. He duly arrived at 3.30pm in a helicopter from the Royal Flight which landed adjacent to the station. The Duke was welcomed by K&ESR President Lord Deedes and was introduced by Chairman David Stratton to members of the Railway who had made an outstanding contribution to the extension project.

In the Booking Hall, the Duke was presented with a leather pass for free travel on the railway by Company Secretary Raymond Williams and signed the visitors book before proceeding to the platform. There, Lord Deedes made a short speech and paid tribute to the determination of the Railway's supporters to save the line (an effort in which he himself had of course played a not insignificant part.). The Duke then welcomed the Railway back into the local community and drew a parallel with the project to restore the locomotive *Duke of Gloucester* (named after his late father) in which he had maintained a keen interest. His Royal Highness then unveiled a brass plaque, which was at that time located on the outside of the building but is now to be found in the Booking Hall.

With the publicity surrounding first *Challenge Anneka* and then the reopening, passenger figures began to climb to unprecedented levels. I made my first journey over the extension, together with my wife and children, in August. In all the years I had known the Kent & East Sussex Railway, I had never arrived in Tenterden from the outside world by train. I had long promised myself that one day I would do just that and this proved to be the fulfilment of that small ambition – and although I didn't clearly realise it, I was taking a hesitant step towards re-engaging with the Railway as a volunteer. It seemed slightly strange boarding a K&ESR train at the newly restored and still raw Northiam Station, but the Railway was pleasingly busy and crowded. The Kent and East Sussex had reached another of its milestones, it was across the county boundary and had truly returned to the Rother. But there was one more challenge to meet. The remaining three and a half miles to Bodiam.

Chapter 13

1990 was another excellent year for the Railway, as had been anticipated following the reopening to Northiam, with overall numbers of fare paying passengers increasing from 69,958 to 81,934 – an improvement of 17 per cent. The number of trains run increased by 100 with the average loading rising from 86 to 90. *Challenge Anneka* had further stimulated public interest, and the increase in business was most noticeable during May, June and July. There was, surprisingly, a slackening off in August although the month was as ever busy, this trend continuing for the remainder of the season with the overall increase during the latter part of the year being only 4 per cent. The number of Santa passengers had decreased slightly, although this was the result of the decision to reduce the number of trains from 80 to 66 in order to provide a less hectic and more enjoyable run for all concerned and not least the 'main man' himself. Pullmans were similarly down as the Saturday evening service had been suspended for the hectic month of August. Wittersham Road had now reverted to being the quiet wayside stopping place it had been for most of the previous century, again becoming almost a staff halt for the P.Way Department. The change has often reminded me of Edward Thomas's famous poem *Adlestrop* – No one left and no one came/On the bare platform......./only the name.

Although the aspiration of all, it was going to be some time before train services to Bodiam resumed. Work to restore the station had however been going on for some while; weeds had grown out of the platform and the track was almost lost beneath the undergrowth. In June, John Miller was asked to run a volunteer-led effort, Director Andrew Webb providing liaison with the Board. John accepted on condition that it was not proposed to radically alter the station for operational or commercial reasons. Working parties were organised at approximately monthly intervals, up to twenty people clearing the undergrowth and giving the station a 'cared for' look. There appeared to be a groundswell of opinion that Bodiam should be saved from 'development' and be preserved as an example of a genuine light railway station. However, preservation would not necessarily mean that nothing could ever be changed. Photographic evidence showed that with each passing decade this little station had undergone subtle alterations. The pragmatic view was taken that no site could become completely 'fossilised', and that to provide a run-round loop was one example of this approach.

John Miller concluded a *Tenterden Terrier* article on the subject by saying, 'Perhaps one day in the not too distant future a Terrier engine with two 1930s (or older) carriages will pull into Bodiam station and its passengers will really understand what preservation is all about. They may even realise that the Railway is of some historical importance.' There was more than an undertone here of the controversies which had surrounded the reopening of Northiam – and a sideways glance at the opinions of some of the volunteers.

The Bodiam working parties had done well to attract around twenty people, but as always recruiting and retaining these essential personnel in all areas of the Railway was of the greatest importance. An item by Allen Sinclair on this theme appeared in the *Rooter* for June 1990 and is worth quoting in full. It was titled 'Volunteer Crisis?':

'The percentage of members prepared to do anything is around 5 per cent.'

'Some volunteers have become such regulars as to seem like full time staff.'

Although they are from two entirely separate sources, these two quotes both highlight the same problem. One is from our own *Tenterden Terrier*, the other from the house magazine of another preserved railway in the South West of England. Both are from the editorials and both reflect the growing crisis within the preservation movement of the shortage of volunteer workers.

It is now over 20 years since the last steam hauled trains ran on British Railways. Consequently there is now a generation of teenagers with no concept whatsoever of what that form of traction meant. To really have appreciated the final era of steam hauled passenger and freight trains, one would now have to be in one's forties. Quite simply this means a decline in the number of fit young men who are willing to undertake steam in its preserved form. There was a hard core of ex-BR steam men who could correctly operate the disappearing breed.

The two editorials I have quoted from indicate that this shortage is not peculiar to the Kent & East Sussex but, with one or two notable exceptions, is a nationwide problem. Enginemen are available to the Bluebell in such profusion that their cleaners work shifts in the same manner as the firemen and drivers. But this is an exception and often the scene is one of engines in service that all too clearly show evidence of not having been cleaned for some time.

Our own Railway makes demands upon engines for a number of reasons. The notorious Tenterden Bank may be an ideal location for the photographer, but requires more work from both engine and crew than would be the case on a level line. The engines themselves are small, a requirement dictated by axle loadings in turn associated with tight curves and weak bridges. These factors place an additional strain upon footplate crews, who are already working flat out to maintain the demanding schedules imposed by a timetable attempting to keep pace with increased customer flows. Add the half hourly chore of running round (with its associated uncoupling and coupling up with a greasy screw link and a recalcitrant vacuum hose) and you are now beginning to get the idea that being an engineman is not all milk and honey. But that is not all, your engine crew will have been on duty from quite early in the morning, some may have preceded their duties with a 50 mile plus car drive before cleaning an engine or making up a fire or 'prepping' an engine. Only a complete idiot of 40 or more years would even think this was relaxation… let alone actually do it. Today's young volunteer is more likely to be a fan of diesels, where cleaning does not seem to matter and the damn thing starts at the press of a button.

Yet the facts are inescapable. The public wants steam trains not diesel.

There lies our dilemma. More steam trains are demanded travelling over greater distances. Fewer people are willing, or indeed able, to provide the steam engines to haul those trains.

I do not pretend to know all the answers. I do not pretend to know how to recruit new volunteer staff. But I do know that existing enginemen will leave not only the Kent & East Sussex but other railways unless and until there is a dramatic change in attitudes. The cavalier attitude, the rudeness and indifference, the lack of communication and the unreasonable demands that are the norm in some engine sheds will no longer be tolerated, especially by younger members. Lack of a career structure, indifferent or non-existent facilities and unprofessional line management are other features which will ensure the closure within the next five years of a preserved steam railway, not because of a shortage of passengers but because of a shortage of steam locomotive enginemen.

Most of the above related to footplate work, but it had implications for the wider K&ESR and heritage railway movement. The attitudes referred to in the final paragraph doubtless reflected a 'macho' culture and the defects of British management, left over from an earlier time and which ill-fitted the world of the early 1990s and indeed later years.

Although minds and efforts were now becoming increasingly focused on extending to Bodiam, the idea of going further and returning to Robertsbridge was also gathering support. Not only were the TRC Board looking at the possibilities – Mark Toynbee had been commissioned to undertake a feasibility study – but Network SouthEast, the then operator of the Tonbridge–Hastings main line, was showing interest. The Editorial of the winter 1990 *Tenterden Terrier* commented:

Vision or pipedream?

The feasibility study in connection with a possible extension back to Robertsbridge is an unexpected development. A link with the main line would establish us as a 'proper' railway in a way that we can never hope to achieve as an isolated section. For this reason alone, the concept is aesthetically appealing. As an engineering project, it is in no way so daunting as has been achieved elsewhere in the preservation movement; the capital cost, not so high as to preclude purchase through a separately launched company; the support – considerable and backed up by no less an ally than British Rail. At the end of the day, any negative factors may be essentially commercial. Although the additional three miles would open up a shorter route to Bodiam via Robertsbridge it would arguably add little of interest to passengers from Tenterden.

For Network SouthEast the financial benefits at the Robertsbridge end are obvious; for the Kent & East Sussex less so. A modest fare for a relatively short journey may constitute the bulk of revenues, given the thriving National Trust shop and restaurant at Bodiam Castle. The operating economics will no doubt be carefully considered, but as a charity, concerned primarily with preserving the whole of the Rother Valley Railway, should we be too concerned with these anyway?

The same issue of the house journal informed members that the summer services had taken their toll on the track and that most of the section from Wittersham to Newmill Bridge was in need of renewal – another mammoth job requiring all hands to help out. It was pointed out that this emphasised the scale of the task to be achieved before Bodiam, far less Robertsbridge, could be reached.

As was usual at that time, the *Tenterden Terrier* also carried a report from the Company Secretary, Raymond Williams. On this occasion, he began by telling members that a recent Board meeting had discussed the future of the Railway and continued with the somewhat world-weary comment, with an added undertone of surprise, that a subsequent volunteers meeting had very largely reached the same conclusions as the Directors. On a more routine note, 'The vexed question of lineside fires has taken up time at several recent meetings' and would continue to reappear at intervals far into the future. More significant straws in the wind which would have decided implications for the future of the K&ESR are also worth quoting:

> The two Finance Directors, Alan Robinson and David Felton, have continued in their efforts to make ends meet, with, if possible, an overlap. Their workload is probably the heaviest of all the directors. The full effect of this year's record business will probably not be seen until 1991. Meanwhile the effects of the extension project, influenced by continuing high interest rates, have tended to dominate the figures … In a largely voluntary organisation, relationships within the Company are important. Managers and directors do interact, but, to a small minority of working volunteers, the Board has been seen as too remote.

At this time, Raymond Williams was around half way through his ten years as the Tenterden Railway Company's Secretary. He was himself seen by many volunteers as a remote and aloof figure, this contrasting with some of the previous post holders such as Neil Rose, and was possibly explained by Williams having been a retired headmaster who did not however present as a physically intimidating figure. He would reportedly, and in company with the Chairman, inspect items such as Signal Box Registers – not on an exceptional basis during a crisis but as a regular routine. That was accepted practice then. Any such thing would now earn a rebuke from the relevant officers for not keeping to today's much more highly developed management chain and Safety Management System. Raymond Williams is particularly remembered for his considerable and effective work in connection with the Northiam extension as well as dealing with the legal issues, the routine and the minutiae that go with the position of Secretary. Andrew Webb, who as Administration Director was effectively Assistant Company Secretary, once told me that Williams was one of the few people who could tell David Stratton to slow down! His abilities also led to him holding similar responsibilities at a national level with the Association of Railway Preservation Societies (ARPS, later the Heritage Railway Association).

Beyond the Railway, 1991 was a year of much contrast with a deepening recession signalling the beginning of the end for the political era of the 1980s. The fall of the Berlin Wall less than 18 months earlier and the subsequent end to the Cold War had produced a sense of tranquillity and of finally arriving in Churchill's 'broad sunlit uplands'. This was undermined by the First Gulf War, although the international consensus and rapid Allied victory in that conflict eventually added to the perception of a New World Order. Rather more parochially, the spring 1991 *Tenterden Terrier* wondered if the international situation might lead to 'stay at home' holidays working to the Railway's benefit. (In the event this didn't happen, although the financial crisis which began in 2008 did.)

It was at this point that I finally began my own 'return to the Rother' and a little personal background is appropriate. By 1989, my close to 25 years employment in local government had reached an unsatisfying dead end. It was with some enthusiasm that I took up the opportunity to move to my employing department's publicity unit and use the skills I had developed writing railway and aviation books and articles. In my private life, I was by early 1991 sufficiently confident to attempt a book which it was widely held to be impossible to write – a book I had been thinking about for the best part of the previous twenty years – a book telling the story of how, between 1961 and 1974, the Kent & East Sussex Railway had been saved. Andrew Webb was of great help in getting this project off the ground and acting as a link with the Board – there was still some degree of apprehension about recording the details of those difficult years. A meeting to discuss the idea was held at my house on 16 January. This was the evening before the combat phase of the First Gulf War began, which for me gave a slightly unreal feeling to the occasion. Was this to be another quick victory like the Falklands, or the beginning of something much worse in which my proposed book would be lost as a triviality? Thankfully it was the former and I subsequently attended a meeting of the Maidstone Area Group where I was able to float the idea of the book to working members. It seemed to be well received and it was good to again feel the camaraderie of the K&ESR.

One of the straws in the wind mentioned earlier was picked up by Philip Shaw in his editorial for the spring 1991 *Terrier*. It was titled 'Light on the Horizon?'

> 1990 was, by any yardstick, a year of achievement. The ARPS award for excellence in January, followed by the opening to Northiam in May and culminating in a 17 per cent increase in passengers – another record. The price to pay has been the necessity to raise borrowings to record levels, and a higher fixed overhead to sustain the infrastructure of what has become a sizeable business. Track renewals alone on the operating section will cost £30,000 this year and we now have 11 people on the Company payroll. With a deepening recession in the economy, it would be easy to forecast a difficult year ahead.

Further on in the same magazine, Raymond Williams reported that Company Finance Officer David Felton was to step down, having managed the Railway's finances since 1974, through years of both difficulty and strong growth and progress. He could, it was said, 'sound notes of caution when overeager spenders have not always been appreciative of the fiscal responsibilities which must accompany sensible growth and progress'. David Felton intended to not relinquish the post until the next AGM and the Board was actively seeking a replacement. In the first instance it led to the appointment of Ray Collins and Philip Clark-Monks to cover the duties. Relatively routine matter though this was, it would indirectly begin a chain of events which would have profound consequences.

Chairman David Stratton's notes in the same issue provide an interesting 'snapshot' of the K&ESR one year into the new decade:

> As 1990 comes to an end, having been a most successful trading year with the opening to Northiam impacting well in all areas, we must now turn our thoughts to the future.
>
> Much needs to be done to improve our existing line, for instance Northiam needs to be finished. The permanent way requires expenditure and upgrading. Much of our carriage and wagon stock require expensive restoration as at present it is in depleted condition causing complaints from outsiders. Work needs to be done at the Wittersham Road site and finally Tenterden site, although much improved in certain areas, is open to major criticism for untidiness and poor storage of parts again causing complaints.

However on a more positive note let us turn to 1991 when we must NOT be seen to rest on our laurels. Exciting new projects are planned for this year making it more interesting both to working members and visitors, with the added bonus of a visiting locomotive from the Severn Valley Railway. With the depth of experience, expertise and knowledge that our railway possesses around me I view the future with more comfort than would otherwise be the case (elsewhere). Finally, however, in the event that difficult decisions have to be made, I hope that you will not find your Board and myself wanting.

Details were beginning to emerge of what an extension to Robertsbridge would involve following the feasibility study that was establishing the practicability of re-opening. *Tenterden Terrier* No 53 winter 1990:

> Since the demolition of that part of the line in the 1970s, and with British Rail's obligation to offer redundant railway land to the neighbouring landowners, the right of way had been sold off piecemeal. Ironically, but as it turned out beneficially, the last section, from Northbridge Street to Robertsbridge, had been disposed of to a speculator as recently as 1990.

The problems involved fell into four distinct categories: acquisition of the land, gaining statutory powers for the construction and operation of a new railway, the construction itself, and raising the necessary finance. The first six weeks of the feasibility study had been encouraging. The course of the Railway was by then in six separate ownerships and there were indications that two-thirds of the land required could be made available. At this stage it was thought that a half mile diversion round the site of Junction Road Halt would be needed, although this later proved to be unnecessary.

In an indication of how much things had changed since 1967, the positive support promised by British Rail Network SouthEast included interest in a cross-platform interchange at Robertsbridge. This aligned with the policy of encouraging the reconnection of private lines. Informal discussion with the National Rivers Authority had indicated that some existing bridges could be piped. Many local people had expressed support, not least because Robertsbridge had been literally 'by-passed' since the construction of the new formation for the A21. They only had to look a few miles across the county boundary to see how much the K&ESR benefited Tenterden. How the Robertsbridge By-Pass was to be crossed remained an open question.

What seemed almost unbelievable support came when Network SouthEast loaned Bo-Bo Electro-Diesel No. 73126 to the K&ESR for the official launch of the Robertsbridge project, the loco arriving via the usual delivery point at Wittersham Road on 21 May 1991. Various Class 73s were being named after heritage railways at that time and this one was to become *The Kent & East Sussex Railway* in a ceremony at Northiam on 23 May. The same occasion also marked the launch of the associated Rother Valley Railway Company, initially named the Rother Valley Railway (East Sussex) to distinguish it from a similarly named venture in South Yorkshire, to undertake the Robertsbridge scheme without putting the Tenterden Railway Company and its achievements at risk.

I attended the ceremony on 23 May – the first major K&ESR event I had been to for some years. The Railway was at its most buoyant and optimistic, and a far cry from the far-off days of the 1960s or even the 'austerity era' atmosphere of Wittersham Road a few years earlier. No. 73126 worked normal Tenterden–Northiam services for a few days – which raised a few eyebrows! This set something of a precedent in respect of medium-sized modern traction. The new company, which was not Limited by Guarantee, established its own membership and volunteer group, the Rother Valley Railway Supporters Association. This emphasised the arm's-length nature of the RVR, and there was by no means a complete overlap of membership with the K&ESR.

Robin Dyce, previously Forestry and Clearance Manager, joined the Board at this time. An ebullient character who sported a full beard and liked a pint, Robin worked as a senior highways engineer for Bromley Council. He was to play a prominent part in the next few years of the Railway. On the financial management side, the resignation of Alan Robinson (he was moving from the area) was added to that of David Felton, and a team of six took over led by Finance Director Paul Wilson.

The old ambition to run a vintage train, dating back into the formative years of the 1960s, was coming a step closer with the restoration of the GER six-wheeler nearing its conclusion. The L&NWR Inspection Saloon was also receiving repairs and completion of restoration which had begun several years earlier. In terms of bodywork, the floor and build rail to the balcony ends needed replacement. This involved lifting the body off the underframe and splicing in new sections, a task the department was to become familiar with on a number of vehicles over subsequent years. The original vacuum brake cylinder had to be replaced, as no spare existed for its obsolete rubber diaphragm. A rolling ring fitted cylinder from a BR Mark 1 was used instead, which meant that the brake rigging had to be completely redesigned. The vehicle was completed in the handsome livery of the London & North Western Railway. This vehicle entered service on Vintage Sunday, 21 April, together with District Railway Coach No. 100.

By the beginning of the 1990s, District Coach No. 100 had been in service for a decade, both on the 'Steam at Bodiam' events and in general service attached to the main carriage sets. It had proved popular with the public as something different. One could also argue, perhaps, that it met the expectations of a public led to have a certain view of heritage railways that owed much to the Welsh narrow gauge lines and the *Titfield Thunderbolt*. In anticipation of this, No. 100 was given an overhaul and repaint and also provided with electric lighting and steam heat. It subsequently returned to the C&W shed for adjustment of the springs – the vehicle's hard ride was proving a problem which would not be finally solved until some years into the twenty-first century.

The Great Eastern coach entered service on 28 July 1991 painted in GER 1919 Carriage Crimson. The K&ESR now had its vintage train of four- and six-wheeled coaches, reputedly the first in the standard gauge heritage railway movement. Among those involved in the project was Gordon Young, a volunteer of particular interest as, apart from coming from an old South Eastern Railway family, he was one of the few active members (he had joined the Preservation Society in 1961) who could actually remember the pre-nationalisation K&ESR. He had first visited the line in 1937. Hauled by either *Charwelton* the Terrier *Sutton* or the P Class, the Vintage Train, originally the Victorian Train until Edwardian vehicles began to be added, became a noted feature of the K&ESR – an innovation which, like so many Kent & East Sussex ideas, was to be widely copied elsewhere.

The Vintage Train did indeed prove popular with the public. It also reflected a growing enthusiasm within the Carriage & Wagon Department for the older vehicles, which was to have an impact on the management of the department in both the long and short terms. It also became a 'Northiam on wheels' with one side advocating that it was, with sensitive and pragmatic changes, what the public wanted and the other claiming that ex-BR Mark 1s were all that was needed. My first trip on the train, during the summer of 1992, was aboard the Balcony Saloon.

With *Charwelton* in fine form and making light work of this modest load, it remains among my memorable journeys on the K&ESR.

Locomotive variety had been enhanced, to a limited degree, in 1991 with the loan of a Robert Stephenson & Hawthorn industrial 0-6-0T, numbered 7597, which had had various homes in preservation and was then on the Great Central. It was not well liked by K&ESR footplate crews, a major complaint being the ride resulting from its coil springing – which had earned it the name 'Zebedee' after the spring-propelled character in *The Magic Roundabout*. This was to contrast with more promising developments the following year.

Mention of other heritage lines and TV programmes brings to mind the beneficial effect the still-popular series *Heartbeat* had from April 1992 on the fortunes of the K&ESR's friend and ally, the North Yorkshire Moors Railway. A year previously, the still occasionally repeated TV production *The Darling Buds of May*, based on H.E. Bates's novel of the same name, took to the air waves. The railway sequences had been shot at Tenterden Town. I have previously expressed the opinion that this series, whatever the shortcomings of the stories, captures to perfection the atmosphere of Tenterden's hinterland in the early, pre-reopening, years of the K&ESR preservation scheme. The Commercial Department duly launched an advertising campaign that the railway was 'the perfick day out.' It drew in many fans of the stories; coach companies from as far away as the Midlands arriving with parties of one hundred passengers every other Saturday throughout the summer.

Chapter 14

As so often happens following a re-opening, the 1991 passenger numbers were less than those of the year preceding, having declined from 81,934 to 68,469. The annual 'Tickets Please!' feature in the *Terrier* commented that it had been the year when the recession really hit the Kent & East Sussex Railway. The old problem of the Railway being Tenterden centred continued, with Northiam accounting for only 12 per cent of the traffic. The *Rooter* for November 1991 also summed up the position:

> Passenger numbers are 17 per cent down on last year's figures, but have improved from being 23 per cent down earlier in the year. The numbers are slightly up on the figures for 1989. The effects of the recession and the loss of last year's Northiam novelty have taken their toll. Two success stories have been the number of people taking up the option of paying 50 pence extra fare for First Class single tickets, and the popularity of the Victorian Train. In contrast to the passenger figures, the total membership of the railway has now passed 3,107, this representing a 5 per cent increase on last year's total membership of 2,955.

In the *Terrier* for the same period, the Editor, Philip Shaw, wrote in much the same way and touched on an issue which was to attract increasing attention over the next few years:

> 1991 was never expected to be a good year, given the severity of the recession. With traffic some 17 per cent down we could have been experiencing problems by now, but for the fact that we had budgeted for a downturn and set our expenditure targets accordingly. Not surprisingly, the activities that we do really well – the Vintage Train, the Rother Valley Limited, and the Pullman –, have come up to best expectations; – the normal service trains have seen lighter loadings. On a positive note, our assets are in good shape and we have a considerable flexibility in our operations so that we can set our overheads in line with income. Whilst operating surpluses of late have been good, the level of borrowings associated with the push to Northiam remain uncomfortably high. Cash generation must be a high priority in 1992 to improve the balance sheet.

Philip later reviewed (*Tenterden Terrier* No. 58, summer 1992) the Railway's financial performance in 1991 and his article is again worth quoting in full, highlighting a number of issues which were to set much of the tone for the coming decade:

> Following the excellent performance achieved in 1990, 1991 was the year when the recession really began to bite. Total income fell from £585,883 to £579,954, while expenses were up from £488,541 to £562,856. Interest payable was slightly down at £36,096, but

overall there was a deficit for the year of £18,998 compared with a surplus of £57,178 in 1990. In consequence, it was necessary to make redundant two paid members of staff – Paul Hatcher and Mike Barnes-Murfin – to take into account the constraints of the current economic climate.

On the income side, fares and charter receipts, by far our largest source of revenue, were down from £232,596 to £226,614 and buffet takings dropped from £54,526 to £48,276. There were also significant falls in filming receipts and sundry donations. By way of contrast Santa Special receipts achieved a noticeable rise from £70,458 to £86,914, and membership subscriptions were up from £14,036 to £18,135. Most of our other activities – Bookshop, Wealden Pullman, etc. –, produced results fairly close to the previous year.

Despite the generally less favourable figures, the net contribution made by these activities to the overall viability of the Railway should not be under-estimated. After deducting attributable expenses the surpluses were substantial and a credit to the volunteer managers and helpers who keep these departments running throughout the year:

Santa Specials £61,926 net surplus
Bookshop £35,879
Wealden Pullman £34,229
Buffet £24,817

Higher operating expenses reflected the fact that certain work programmes which had been budgeted prior to 1991 were allowed to continue; permanent way was up from £13,942 to £54,776, but repair and maintenance of locomotives fell from £74,935 to £65,734. These items are always subject to fluctuation from year to year, dependent on the number of major projects undertaken. With the exception of wages, up from £66,808 to £90,213, other operating expenses were contained at levels close to the previous year. Indeed rolling stock repairs were down from £23,354 to £15,482. Total administration expenses, telephone, printing, accountancy, magazine, etc., were up from £27,901 to £33,875. Although magazine expenses appear to have doubled from £7,538 to £15,433, this reflects mainly a change in the accounting allocation of postage and other items.

In an organisation such as ours, whilst we strive to make a surplus of income over expenditure, fairly substantial fluctuations from year to year are to be expected, given the discretionary nature of many of our expenditure items, which are carried out when time and money permit. As a registered charity without shareholders, our objective is to re-invest all income generated from running the Railway into the preservation and enhancement of the assets themselves. In this way we not only provide leisure facilities for our members but a service to the community – particularly to tourism in this part of Kent, carrying, as we do, some 75,000 passengers every year.

In the spring (*Tenterden Terrier* No. 57) issue, Chairman David Stratton further emphasised the financial position and added that a reorganisation of the Board responsibilities was in progress. This was then taken up by the Company Secretary:

The new Board on 30th May will comprise a majority of the existing directors continuing their service, but with specific designated areas of responsibility. They will be joined by new members, elected also to fill specific roles. This is the pattern for the future Board, with the expectation that directors are elected to direct and managers are appointed to manage. As this is being written (in January), the practical details are being worked out. Derek Dunlavey has taken away the drafting resulting from the Board discussions, for homework, and the final specification should be in place well before the AGM.

Whether it was intended or not, this organisational pattern resembled the Committee, elected Chairman and employed Chief Officer approach then universal in local authorities. There were doubts in some quarters as to whether it would work on the K&ESR.

It was during early 1992 that a planning application made to Ashford Borough Council caused consternation on the Railway. The proposal was to build an hotel in the field (known in recent years as Morph's Field) opposite the Carriage & Wagon Shed at Tenterden Town. This had of course been the site of the Steam & Country Fair and the development would have obstructed the glorious view from the station. The field was in an Area of Outstanding Natural Beauty (AONB) and was not scheduled for development in the Tenterden Local Plan. The proposed hotel would have had 25 bedrooms, conference facilities for 100 people, a 90-seat restaurant and a licensed bar open to non-residents. Two coach and 80 car parking spaces would have been provided. The Board unsurprisingly lodged an objection with Ashford BC and the Town Council also expressed their opposition.

The justification for this planning application in a protected area seemed to hinge on a phrase in the Tenterden Local Plan, which indicated that sympathetic consideration should be given to development proposals affecting the rural side of the railway line if these are 'in support of tourism'. An assumption had been made that this was in recognition of the restricted space on the Tenterden Town station site and was intended to help the Railway provide facilities for its visitors. Instead, it now appeared to have given grounds to any developer to put forward a scheme provided it has some connection with tourism, however tenuous. There was also a fear that, once permission had been given inside the AONB, ribbon development might occur on the north side of the line as far as Cranbrook Road and possibly beyond.

To anticipate events somewhat, the matter was finally resolved in 1993 through the planning appeals process when the application was turned down by the Secretary of State for the Environment. Supportive in this was a letter from the HM Railway Inspectorate pointing out that the level crossing was of the 'occupation' type for the benefit of the Railway's visitors (invitees) and the two north side land holdings which had existed before the K&ESR was built. The hotel proposal could not enjoy the benefit of this. A further point made by the Railway Inspectorate was that the Borough Council should have contacted the railway on grounds other than because it was a neighbour. Being a statutory undertaking it should have been formally consulted as the proposal would have increased the traffic over a crossing. The K&ESR was also indebted to Ashford Borough Council for its support in protecting the interests of the Railway. An important principle was established as a result of this case. The K&ESR marked the northern limit of development in Tenterden. It was the barrier which would protect the High Weald AONB.

Planning of a different kind was well in hand regarding the extension to Bodiam. The small group looking into its feasibility was led by Robin Dyce and initially operated under the title of Project Final Push. This was perhaps not the best of choices as the idea of going to Robertsbridge was beginning to grab the imagination. It came as no surprise when the notice on the Bodiam scheme's office door was unofficially amended to read 'Project But One Final Push'. In preparing a study for consideration by the company Board, the guiding principle was that the Bodiam scheme had to be cost-efficient. The line had to be capable of being operated using minimum demands on manpower, and promote and enhance Bodiam Station as an area to be preserved in the Colonel Stephens tradition.

With the then downturn in the economy and the greater reluctance of people to go and spend a day out, it was even more important for the railway to be cost-effective. It was not acceptable to run on track which required constant attention and upkeep with a consequent drain on resources. Morale would suffer with resources, particularly volunteer resources, being spread over a wider area. The Project Final Push working party considered that before a start was made on Northiam–Bodiam it was essential that major infrastructure works were carried out on the operating section. There was in particular a growing need to bring the permanent way from Tenterden to Oxney Straight up to the same standard as that from Oxney Straight to Northiam. The Bodiam scheme had to be seen in the context of the Railway as a whole and as fitting into the overall development plan, including proper financial planning for these developments.

The line from Northiam to Bodiam had been upgraded by British Railways in the early 1950s, the works including approximately some two miles of obsolete 91¼lb/yd rail on wooden sleepers from Northiam to a point just east of Pagham Farm, and 95lb/yd rail on metal sleepers from there to near Bodiam Station. Just before Bodiam Station the line reverted to heavier construction which had been completely re-sleepered by the Thameside Group in 1980. Spot re-sleepering had also taken place from Dixter to Padgham Farm. Flailing of the undergrowth in 1991, sponsored by the Maidstone Group, enabled the first impression of much of the track to be gained since the 1970s. Many drains had collapsed and landslips had altered both the horizontal and vertical alignments of the track in many places. The formation was ash throughout, and in general not suitable for modern safety and operational needs.

If the standards used for the Northiam scheme were to be continued, then this would be the biggest civil engineering on the Railway since the Headcorn extension had been built nearly a century earlier. The work would include over 15,000 tonnes of ballast; 530 × 45ft track panels (three times that of the Northiam extension); two bridges; 36 culverts and almost a mile of trackside drainage pipes. The project would be volunteer led but using contractors where appropriate.

There were some anticipated developments in the Bodiam scheme that either failed to come to pass or proved premature. For instance, it was proposed to extend the existing service much as it was (which did happen) but it was thought unreasonable to expect the Austerities to cope satisfactorily with the extra mileage (which in fact later proved to be no problem). It was therefore thought that 'suitable motive power' should be found but, in general, this was not pursued until a much later date. It was foreseen that there would be need for a passing loop at either Dixter or Ewhurst Green 'to maintain parity with the remainder of the railway and any extension to Robertsbridge'. This did not prove necessary once Bodiam was reached, and a loop at Ewhurst was still under consideration in respect of Robertsbridge in the second decade of the twenty-first century. The idea of a Northiam—Bodiam shuttle (for visitors to Bodiam Castle without enough time to travel to Tenterden and back) proved unnecessary.

There was a desire among various parties, particularly the local authority, that car-borne tourist traffic in Bodiam village be reduced. The K&ESR Board obviously saw this as an opportunity and supported a proposal by the newly established Rother Valley Railway Company for a Quarry Halt to the west of the existing station. The adjacent Quarry Steam Centre (a collection of traction engines) already had a large car park. In the event this was another idea which came to nothing as the Steam Centre closed down not too long afterwards. Public car parking was not going to be possible at Bodiam Station and it was seen from an early stage that passengers would be parking at Tenterden, Northiam and to a lesser extent at the Castle.

Early on, it was estimated that the Bodiam extension would cost £1million and that grants or loans would be needed, preferably the former, although with the then economic situation it was difficult to know where these might come from. Overall, it was thought that the extension might be ready for the year 2000.

Meanwhile, down at Robertsbridge, the Rother Valley project had actually organised working parties which had started clearing the section of track bed between the main line station and Northbridge Street. Between Boxing Day and the New Year, twenty years of overgrowth was removed sufficiently to allow foot traffic and bridge inspection. Visitors were nonetheless warned that either activity could be hazardous, as the decking was missing from the several bridges on the section. Promising as all this sounds, it reads, at this distance in time, as typical of the initial burst of enthusiasm that accompanies the embryo stage of any heritage railway scheme. It was however the beginning of a very long road the end of which was only coming into sight by 2020.

Despite these developments, the *Terrier* Editorial for summer 1992 claimed that the season was proving to be unexciting:

> At the time of writing (late May) it seems to have been an uneventful, even a dull and boring year on the Railway so far. With the two major annual events planned for mid-summer or early autumn, the spring has seen little to report on, or new topics to photograph. Plans for the extension to Bodiam and beyond are still at a formative stage. Visiting locomotives are planned, but nothing is here yet. The lack of news is reflected in these pages with some departments apparently having little or nothing to say at all.

In the same issue, the Chairman commented that the recession was proving very challenging for the Kent & East Sussex. The Company Secretary continued the theme:

> It is clear from the Railway Press that others beside ourselves in the Preservation movement have felt the strains of the severe recession which at present afflicts the country. Your Board will continue to take such steps as are necessary to maintain the sensible governance of the Railway.
>
> Your Board of Directors has remained steadfast in not rushing headlong into impossible situations. Board deliberations over Operation 'Final Push' to Bodiam have determined that it will never be allowed to become a final 'push over' which could endanger, if not sink, the K&ESR. When the result of the feasibility study is published, members will be able to judge for themselves whether Robin Dyce and his associates are talking sense about the way to get to Bodiam. Having said that, a provisional timetable towards the fulfilment of the project has been written, and costings are being looked at. Relationships with those engaged on the Bodiam to Robertsbridge section are being carefully strengthened: clearly there must be a dovetailing of the plans for constructing both sections of the extension to agreed standards.

Dull though the *Terrier* Editor considered the year to be, there were nonetheless some memorable events and developments.

Off site, between 30 May and 7 June, the K&ESR participated in Ashford 150, a celebration of the arrival of the South Eastern Railway in that town. That the Railway was able to participate to the extent that it did was probably due to the good relations established with Network South East at the time of the launching of the Robertsbridge project. The K&ESR's P Class No. 1556, which had been built at Ashford Works, was to be one of the exhibits amongst a cross-section of motive power ranging from modern 'Networkers' to Deltic Diesels, restored Hastings Diesel Unit power car 60000, and King Arthur class No. 777, *Sir Lamiel*. The Kent & East Sussex also had a sales stand in the main works exhibition hall and on Saturday 6th and Sunday 7th June, Class 73 No. 73126 *Kent & East Sussex Railway* was the motive power used for the shuttle service from Ashford Station to Chart Leacon Works. Sunday was also notable for the Severn Valley Railway's Class 4, 75069, hauling the Ashford–Hastings steam shuttles, and on one of these trips K&ESR regular driver, John Baker, took the regulator, dressed for the event in his Kent & East Sussex overalls. Long years before, John had been among the footplate crew from St. Leonard's Depot who worked the legendary 'Schools' Class on the London–Hastings service. In 1986, when the Hastings Diesels were withdrawn, he had driven the final enthusiasts' special into Charing Cross on a spirited and still-talked-about run.

Particularly significant was the first 'Thomas the Tank Engine' event to be held on the Kent & East Sussex Railway. This was greeted with apprehension by some – until they saw the financial benefits. Thomas events continued, as many as three times a year, on the K&ESR and for decades proved to be as vital a part of the income stream as the Santa Specials or the August traffic. In fact, just under ten years later, Thomas was to prove to be of the most critical importance. That first event was memorably described by Neil Rose ion the *Tenterden Terrier* for winter 1992:

Commercial Manager Graham Hukins telephoned me one evening earlier this year. He was straight to the point. 'We need a Fat Controller at our 'Friends of Thomas the Tank Engine' weekend in June. Will you take on the part?' I had noticed the event in the Railway's timetable and had mentally diarised to steer well clear of Tenterden. I had vowed a long time ago to have nothing to do with engines sporting silly faces.

Perverse really, my dislike of 'Thomas' events. I had enjoyed the Rev. W. Awdry's books as a child and had read many stories to my own children. Graham must have been persuasive for I heard myself saying yes. Against my better instincts, but a bit of me likes acting and I suppose I could not resist the challenge to dress up and show off a bit. To my family I expressed surprise that I was considered to have the right build for the role but they had no such doubts: after all I had a passing resemblance to a certain red coated gentleman who travels on the trains at Christmastide.

Putting my doubts to one side, I embarked on a rigorous training programme to ensure that I was in good physical trim for the weekend. I was to share the task with Chris Wood who would keep the Railway in order on the Saturday, whilst it would be under my care on the Sunday. The Weekend was months away and I dismissed it from my mind until Chris telephoned me to ask my vital statistics. I was somewhat relieved when he assured me the measurements were for our outfits. Perhaps wisely I decided that this was not the occasion to breathe in to lose an inch or two around the middle; guessing my hat size was a mistake, I realised later.

With the event looming closer, I thought I had better do a little homework. Having almost forgotten the stories, I decided to reread them and so rescued our books from the loft. I was perhaps a little unwise to get them out one evening on the 18.25 from Cannon Street; I drew some very odd glances. Strange looks at work, too, when I was caught muttering 'Thomas is blue, James is red, Henry is green ...' Their suspicions about me were confirmed! My family tutored me until I was engine colour perfect and I knew enough of the stories to get by: questions from small people about Edward, Duck, Annie and Clarabel, Percy, Bertie the bus and other characters held no fears.

Saturday 27th June. I called in at Tenterden to spy on Chris, to pick up some tips for my performance the next day. It was super weather, plenty of visitors and a somewhat perspiring, red-faced Fat Controller greeted me. He appeared to have the Railway under firm control; trains were running on time.

But shock! Horror! No Thomas. No Gordon. No sign of any of the other engines and vehicles I had carefully rehearsed! Where were they? Chris patiently told me to look at the posters – Friends of Thomas the Tank Engine Weekend. He explained that the copyright holders only allowed engines to be called Thomas, or any of the other named characters, if they appear identical to those illustrated in the books. Our engines did not fit the image, so they became Thomas's friends.

I checked out the friends. 'Holman' and 'William' (Nos. 23 and 24) had come from the army – no surprises there. 'William' had hayfever, sneezing from his cylinder cocks. 'Linda' (No. 26), sister to the army engines, used to shunt troublesome trucks at a South Wales coalmine; I bet she didn't wear lipstick in front of her wagons there! *Sutton* (No. 10) was too much of an old engine to change names for the weekend. On the other hand, No. 14 had no objections to being called 'Charlie'. Just in case the steam engines needed a hand, diesel D9525 'Teddy' was on pilot duty. 'Rolvenden' (No. 27) watched the proceedings from his siding, rather wishing he had a hot fire and steam inside him so he could pull trains, instead of having children climb over him rattling his levers. 'Diana' and 'Barbara' spent their time working up and down the line. In the yard 'Smithy' the coach looked a little lonely behind a bouncy castle, while 'Validus' the traction engine rested in the shade of a tree, gently puffing away to himself.

Before I left Chris told me that someone had complained that there were too many children milling around the station! If the Saturday was fine, the Sunday was a wonderful summer's day. It was a scorcher when I arrived at Tenterden and I was hot by the time I first stepped onto the platform, just before 9.30am; by lunchtime I felt like a greasy blob!

My image was slightly spoilt by the early realisation that my hat had to be stuffed full of paper to keep it up; without the padding only my ears stopped it from covering my eyes. I really should have tried it on earlier. I was glad I did not know then that I would still be dressed up ten hours later, with barely a quarter of an hour's rest.

By mid-morning all the engines had assembled, as had a good throng of visitors. Most seemed to be children under five, with parents in tow, showing varying degrees of enthusiasm. Although 'Thomas' was not there in person, he appeared everywhere; on tee-shirts, dungarees, hats, clutched flags and toys. Some children even carried toys that appeared suspiciously like me. There were several stalls with 'Thomas' goods and, seeing the brisk business, I wished I had a commission on sales.

We were fortunate to have the company of Christopher Awdry, for whom the stories were first written by his father and who nowadays pens them. He said he gets ideas from events such as ours. He seemed well impressed by our show and organisation. He put me right on one point. As devotees will know, Thomas's railway is centred on the Isle of Sodor: I now know the proper pronunciation is as in whisky and soda.

Off the platform children were bashing the sides out of the bouncy castle and enjoying the sideshows. A children's' roundabout gave rides and the Punch 'n' Judy shows were very popular, as was the Jester. I was a little surprised to see a popgun gallery, given the young tender age of most of the children. Not surprisingly, the buffet/refreshment tent did a roaring trade all day. The Fat Controller must have been the only person there who resisted the temptation of an ice cream – it did not fit the image.

Quite apart from the slick train operation, advance bookings proved their value. At least one courteous young person in uniform was at hand at each coach to show passengers to their seats and trains were not jam packed with sullen standing passengers. The booking arrangements also had the benefit of staggering visitors' arrivals through the day, which meant the station area was comfortably busy without being a mad scrum. An extra train was run in the morning for people without reservations; unfortunately there was no room in the timetable to squeeze in another service mid-afternoon.

My instructions were simple. Walk imposingly up and down the platform, talking to children and engines. Even if the faces on the smokeboxes didn't answer back, their drivers were not short of a succinct comment or two! I'm sure the engines appreciated being told their work was very satisfactory after puffing up the bank with fully loaded coaches behind them. 'Teddy' spent his day clanking troublesome trucks in the yard. With commentary ably broadcast by Ben Ramsden, I am glad to say that my PA announcements were limited to reminding passengers to board trains promptly so they could depart on time. After all we were running a well-regulated Railway.

Kodak's profits were boosted as children were snapped with the Fat Controller. Conversations with the junior fan club members generally followed the same routine: 'Where's Thomas?' 'He's on his branch line today and is sad he can't come to Tenterden. But he is happy all his friends are here instead.' 'But I wanted to see Thomas.'

Advertising had spelt out that it was the Friends of Thomas Weekend, but the message did not come across to younger visitors, some of whom were obviously disappointed. As was one visitor of pensionable age who hadn't read about the weekend either. He complained to me that while it was good to see so many engines, why did they have to wear such silly faces. I wonder who he thought I was! Several visitors obviously thought I was in charge from their questions – which engine is on the next train? When does the train arrive at

Northiam? I've lost my camera/child! – but I probably knew least of anyone what was going to happen next. And I didn't have a single question about engine colours!

How I envied the visitors who all seemed to be wearing very little. I was dressed up to the nines and by lunchtime I was fantasising about long cool drinks in the shade. Eventually Mrs Kyndley brought me a basket containing my lunch, fortunately mainly liquid, and 'Charlie' took me away in the LNWR inspection saloon. At the top of the headshunt I could at least remove my topper and slake my thirst. All too soon it was back to work.

During the afternoon 'William' had another bout of hay fever. Fortunately the 'tall stationmaster' was on hand to produce a large towel for his nose. This seemed to do the trick, much to general amusement.

It was not until sometime after 7pm that the last visitors departed and I was able to stagger off duty, a somewhat dehydrated and lighter Fat Controller. Did that first beer at home taste good! I now have a model Fat Controller on my desk at work to remind me of a fun weekend. Sadly, no-one addressed me as Sir when I next visited the Railway!

Over the weekend some 4,600 people visited the Railway, of whom 4,100 travelled on the trains. It was a welcome booster for the Railway's finances. Most importantly, it generated a good spirit of co-operation and fun amongst the many staff who helped make the weekend a success. If we have a similar event next year, and I am told the provisional dates set are 26/27th June, count me in.

Many people put in a lot of work to make the weekend a success. Special thanks are due to Britt Allcroft for the big 3-D glass fibre faces for the Austerities, which made them look very 'human' engines; to the Bluebell Railway for lending faces for *Sutton* and *Charlie*; and to the Buckinghamshire Railway Centre for providing faces for 'Teddy' and the troublesome trucks. Finally, two Fat Controllers are most indebted to the Savoy Tailor's Guild, Tenterden, for supplying the morning coats, striped trousers and toppers, not forgetting a rather splendid yellow waistcoat. I missed the spats though!

Chapter 15

The South Devon Railway put its Pannier Tank No. 1638 up for sale during 1992 and this locomotive was duly acquired, thanks to the generosity of David Stratton (who initially wished to remain anonymous in this respect). The 16XX Class was BR Western Region built but of pure Great Western design – and totally appropriate for use on the K&ESR, having been used on Colonel Stephens' reconstructed Burry Port & Gwendraeth Railway in South Wales. Furthermore, as a branch line engine rather than a shunting locomotive, it proved to be capable of handling anything that the K&ESR could ask of it. The locomotive arrived on 1 July 1992 and was unloaded at Wittersham Road the following day. In more recent years it has become the property of the Company.

Saturday, 24 October 1992 saw the arrival of the heritage era K&ESR's One Millionth Passenger, although it can now be told that this was, perhaps predictably, a public relations exercise. It was certain that the millionth passenger travelled around this time, but the person who was given celebrity treatment on the strength of this was picked at random from the Tenterden booking office queue. Still, it never hurts to make some publicity mileage out of this sort of thing.

A 13 per cent rise in passengers during the year, with the August figures increasing by as much as 21 per cent, was remarkable against the background of economic uncertainty. The downside of this was that attendant costs had been substantial, and membership fell for only the third time since TRC was formed in 1971. Visiting locomotives were claimed to be the reason for the increase in passenger numbers although one would doubt this. The locos in question would have meant little to anyone outside the enthusiast fraternity – which often makes up around 8 per cent of the visitors on any heritage railway. One of the locomotives referred to was Great Western 0-6-2T No. 6619 from the North Yorkshire Moors Railway which would, in the fullness of time, find a home on the Kent & East Sussex. The loco arrived on 16 July. After some initial problems with heavy scale in the boiler, two lead plugs, four superheater elements and the right-hand driving spring, it worked very successfully for a total of 31 days and covered in excess of 1,000 miles during that time. 6619 returned to North Yorkshire on 9 September.

It is worth mentioning in this context that there has been a regular, albeit informal, exchange of footplate staff between the NYMR and the K&ESR for many years in addition to one-time links between the two railways' Carriage & Wagon Departments. The Moors Line and the Kent & East Sussex might appear to have little in common, but they are, in their different ways, 'hard roads' and this has brought about a mutual respect. Another visiting locomotive was a diesel, Class 25 (D7672) *Tamworth Castle*, on hire to the Railway from the North Staffordshire Diesel Group. This followed on from the precedent set by the visit of the Class 73 in 1991. D7672 arrived on 12 July and was used on a number of occasions throughout the summer.

By the end of the year, passenger figures had climbed from 1991's 68,469 to 74,588 – a 9 per cent increase during a period of severe recession which showed that the Railway was continuing to attract visitors. It had however been necessary to run additional trains to achieve the increase; the average loading per train had remained stubbornly constant at 68. The number of Santa bookings at 11,791 was 7 per cent down on the previous year, but June figures were up by a remarkable 30 per cent thanks to the success of the Friends of Thomas Weekend. The Wealden Pullman was up by 27 per cent – the number of covers had been increased to 72 – but total Pullman passengers were below the records achieved in the late 1980s.

The writing of *Holding the Line – Preserving the Kent & East Sussex Railway* led me to be in Tenterden fairly often at this time and, unsurprisingly, the volunteering bug began to bite again. I had been away a long time and, with it being known that I had the book under way, was perhaps making a more high profile return than I might have wished. I remember discussing with Derek Dunlavey the possibility of returning as a volunteer. When he asked what sort of work I was interested in, I said that I would avoid anything to do with the operating side as I wasn't a railway professional and had not been around to be trained up as a volunteer during the interim. 'That's the preserved railways of 25 years ago,' Derek replied, 'We can't afford to do that now.'

With family growing up it was easier for me to volunteer again, and initially I did various odd jobs for the Gift Shop and S&TE (Signals & Telecommunications Engineering). The discussion with Derek had obviously changed my mind because I soon remembered having taken an interest in guards duties during the 1960s. This was unfinished business and I applied to become a Trainee Guard.

I found that I had returned to the K&ESR just in time. There were still people around who remembered me and the last fading echoes of the Railway I had known in its pioneering days of the 1960s were still to be felt. The SE&CR 44ft coach body on the platform still provided a night's rest and pleasant evenings were to be had in the pub. My old friends eased my introduction to the people who had joined in the meantime. The Railway had of course changed, as it is always changing; those last echoes of the early days finally ebbed away over the next few years and for me it was a good time to return and watch that transition.

Towards the end of 1992, the Board reviewed how the railway was being operated to ensure that profit levels could support future investment. After the hair-raising possibility of cutting back to a 1974-style weekends only, entirely volunteer operation had been rejected, a decision was made in favour of a modest expansion of services in the summer months. The 1993 service was nonetheless particularly ambitious with 1230 scheduled passenger trains running on 185 days. Doing this was something of a calculated risk, as the national economic position remained uncertain. This approach also attempted to resolve the perennial matter of the heritage era ignoring the Railway's roots. In place of increasing the number of coaches on trains to meet demand, there was to be a more frequent service of more authentic two-coach formations hauled wherever possible by the small, historic locomotives. Enterprisingly, a three-coach Hastings Diesel Unit was to be hired from the restoration group at the erstwhile St Leonards Depot and a pilot bus link was arranged to run on Sundays and Bank Holidays only from Robertsbridge to Northiam – the cost of the bus service, for which a charge was made, being underwritten by the Rother Valley Railway. Lastly for 1993, a full-time Catering Manager was to be employed. The creation of this post was to be of long-term importance. None of the other innovations mentioned above were however particularly successful.

1993 began with major civil engineering as rabbit infestation in the embankment immediately north of Rolvenden led to the formation having to be rebuilt in minestone for a distance of 300 yards. The formation was also to be strengthened to allow higher axle weight engines. This was expensive in terms of both money and general resources, but it left that section in very good condition. This episode even achieved an unlikely degree of fame when it formed the basis of a subsequent 'Thomas the Tank Engine' story appropriately called '*Rabbits*'.

Heritage railway volunteers can be long suffering as a group, but they can also be assertive when pushed too far. Something like this happened in the K&ESR's Carriage & Wagon Department in the early months of 1993. C&W had been under the control of the same supervisors since before reopening, although it had acquired other long-term and regular volunteers as the years went by. Those who had run the department for so long certainly had achievements to their credit – the provision of a fleet through the times of passenger growth, some notable goods vehicle restorations, the transfer of C&W to the new carriage shed and the introduction of the Vintage Train.

It was that last feature, the four- and six-wheel carriages, which brought matters to a head. Despite this use of vintage stock, there was a body of opinion, echoed in wider heritage railway circles, that the K&ESR was over-reliant on its less-than-immaculate Mark 1s – something emphasised by their use with the Austerity locomotives – to the exclusion of interest in restoring pre-nationalisation and pre-grouping stock. This was particularly keenly felt among the Carriage & Wagon 'shop floor' volunteers, who were of the view that the department's management style had grown stale. The volunteers had nonetheless started work during 1992 on restoring the SE&CR Family Saloon No. 177, in the open and in the face of opposition which had told them 'No one will ever want to ride in that heap…' and also denied them shed space.

Eventually, a mass walk-out was threatened because of the vintage carriages issue, an alleged unwelcoming atmosphere in the shed and declining morale. These concerns were brought to the attention of the Company Chairman. Shortly afterwards the (volunteer) management was changed, perhaps by over-reliance on the absence for volunteers of the sort of legal protection enjoyed by paid staff. What was flippantly referred to as 'Mutiny in the Carriage Shed' was effective but left scars in some quarters that took a good few years to heal. The former supervisors and their minority support decamped, initially to the new site at Robertsbridge, accompanied by various items of stock, many unrestored, which belonged to an owning group which they ran and which was itself asked to leave the K&ESR. Charities legislation was in this latter instance the basis for Tenterden Railway Company's action. This caused needless alarm among volunteers in other departments, some of whom ought to have known better, who imagined that the core fleet was departing. Once this impression had been corrected things quietened down.

By the time of the C&W report in the July *Terrier*, the department had become the scene of considerable activity with its slowly increasing workforce performing well in keeping up with demands imposed upon it by both restoration and routine maintenance work. Nonetheless, more volunteers were, as ever, needed and it was suggested that potential recruits attend the department's Working Week, the second of these to be organised and which was to run from Saturday, 31 July until Sunday, 8 August. The main focus of activity was to be Maunsell CK No. 5618.

Meanwhile, the SE&CR Family Saloon, which had been moved into the shed, was progressing well. A major figure behind this project was Andy Fielder. The vehicle now had the signwriting and lining completed on one side and presented a most impressive sight. Restoration of the interior of the main saloon was also progressing well, with most of the wooden panels and mouldings having been reinstated. Work on the vacuum brake pipes had also been completed, although a fair amount of minor work remained to be carried out on the running gear. On 1 July 1993, in a further move – again with Andy Fielder as the driving force and which indicated future developments in carriage policy – two four-wheel coach bodies were lifted out from behind the Buffet where they had been in store since 1986. They were placed on PMV underframes and moved to the Carriage Shed sidings. These were the two bodies which had been rescued from a bungalow in Kingsnorth Road, Ashford, by the Ashford Area Group. They had been completely enclosed and kept dry since 1921.

Passenger figures held up reasonably well during the first part of the year, the total having increased by August from 55,903 for the same period in 1992 to 56,373 despite the recession and the curtailment of services at the beginning of the year due to the rabbit warren repairs to Tenterden Bank. Total fare income however amounted to £83,979 compared with £84,870 the previous year, and it was noted that costs had to be kept in check.

In September Bernard Sealy, a Chartered Accountant who was already involved with another heritage railway, was co-opted as a Director to strengthen the financial presence on the Board. Mr Sealy would also join the existing finance team. These aims were met as intended but became part of the chain of events which had begun with the resignation of David Felton and were, at the turn of the century to lead to one of the greatest crises in the Railway's history.

Three weeks later there was a second co-option to the Board, the co-optee on this occasion being Graham Smith, a retired career railwayman who had developed an interest in the heritage movement. Although his involvement elsewhere had led to him being known to the Directors, he was totally unknown to the wider K&ESR membership. Matters were not helped when an ineptly worded notice containing little detail was circulated announcing the new appointments. This famously led to the Tenterden mess coach copy being endorsed with the comment 'Who the **** is Graham Smith?' and him immediately becoming known as 'Mr Who'.

Smith's brief was Operating, including safety, something fundamental to any railway. At that time, heritage railways in general were about mid-way between the informal attitudes of the earliest (often pre-reopening) years and the Safety Management Systems of the second decade of the twenty-first century; with Smith's working background his approach was much nearer to the latter. It is neither possible nor desirable to argue with this except to add that in implementing these systems, the present-day regulatory authorities have recognised that these have to be proportionate to the activities of heritage railways. They are not 80mph main lines. To be fair to the man, it has been pointed out to me that Graham Smith was ahead of his time. There is however an art in persuading, rather than forcing, volunteers into any mould. In this respect he was regrettably unsuccessful. The resulting disquiet, added to concerns about the financial position, had a detrimental effect on the Board's relations with the working members which ran on until the following year's Annual General Meeting.

November 1993 was a time of very mixed fortunes for me and, in retrospect, something of a turning point. It was during that month that *Holding the Line – Preserving the Kent & East Sussex Railway* was finally published by Alan Sutton Ltd. To paraphrase Lord Byron, I woke up one morning and found I had written something of a success. The book was well received on the K&ESR and favourable reviews appeared elsewhere, including in (of all places) the Ffestiniog Railway's magazine. I was interviewed on Radio Kent and even my employers were impressed. The icing on the cake came when *Railway Magazine* made *Holding the Line* its book of the month. Every silver lining has its cloud, however, and at this point it is necessary to digress, firstly on the subject of diesel traction.

The year had begun with the hire of the three-car Hastings unit. Although of some novelty value, this did not prove particularly popular with the public probably because, although well restored, it had all the (then) unappealing features of a Mark 1 without the compensation of a steam locomotive at the front. The two-car 'Derby Lightweight' Class 108 diesel mechanical multiple unit (DMMU) which arrived the same year proved, with its 'observation car' ends, to be much longer lasting and invaluable for less heavily trafficked services. The only hitch was that the 108 had been allowed on to the Railway without Board authority, this leading to the original version of the detailed procedure now in use. Purchase of the DMMU was undertaken by the Tenterden Railway Equipment & Traction Company, a new stock-owning group of mainly K&ESR members which later became the main diesel traction provider to the Kent & East Sussex. I was part of the crew for the 108's first outing in passenger service and recorded the event in an article for the *Tenterden Terrier*, from which the following is adapted.

I volunteered for a trainee guard turn on the first day of Diesel Weekend, Saturday, 6 November 1993, more out of a sense of duty than with any keen anticipation. The only bright spot this (non-steam) day seemed to offer was the genial company of the guard, Alastair Forbes. But I must admit that when, on arriving at Tenterden during the previous evening, I was told we were rostered for the 108 my interest was unexpectedly aroused. This was, after all, to be the unit's first revenue-earning trip on the K&ESR.

Saturday morning came, one of those steely grey dawns so typical of the Weald in winter. I was blearily munching my way through a bowl of muesli when gricers – as opposed to our usual visitors – started to be seen around the station. But where was Alastair? With immaculate timing he then arrived, having left Preston at some unheard-of hour, and with enough of a margin in hand for us to sign on, draw a guard's bag from the station office and set off for Rolvenden. The working timetable indicated that we were 'Special D' and that the Class 108 was to leave Rolvenden ECS (empty carriage stock) at 10.40. When we arrived, the DMMU was ticking over just beyond the platform and was about to be brought into the station by Mike Grimwood of the owing group accompanied by Loco Foreman Simon Long. 'It's the same as the Hastings Diesel,' said someone, 'except it's got vacuum brakes.' This was more-or-less reassuring news.

Alastair and I had both previously worked on the EP-braked Hastings unit, but otherwise didn't know too much about the Class 108. Once inside the seemingly huge brake van (located in the middle of the unit) there was indeed the familiar and comforting sight of a red vacuum brake handle but, like the Hastings unit, no hand brake. At cant rail level, above the inward opening door, was to be found the switch for operating the Guard–Driver communication bell. Our next move was to test the brake from the rear cab where, by combining the Hastings and steam train routines, we used the cab buzzer to alert Simon and Mike and dropped the cab brake handle to destroy the vacuum – which was then promptly recreated to show that all was well. Once everything was in order we were ready for the off and instead of sending the trainee to do the gates, Alastair, like the gentleman he is, went and opened them himself. This meant that I got to give the right-away for the DMMU's first trip in anger (albeit empty). Once over the crossing we stopped to pick up Alastair, made a brisk climb to Cranbrook Road – albeit the DMMU was only running on three out of its four engines – and despite the slack over the new embankment at the rabbit warren. Then it was my turn to get down and see to the gates.

At Tenterden, and in accordance with a suggestion by Simon, we conscripted our travelling ticket inspector and proceeded to strip all the safety gear and spares out of a Wealden Pullman BNO. There wasn't a single item on the 108 and we were, after all, about to invite the public aboard. I then had to rush off to a planning meeting for Volunteers' Day, which meant that Alastair was guard for the first passenger carrying trip, the 11.00 Tenterden–Northiam.

Promptly at 12.25 the Class 108 returned. TRC Director Andrew Webb had thoughtfully arranged the business of the meeting so I could make my contribution, grab something to eat and be ready to rejoin Alastair. By this point in the day, it was becoming apparent that Diesel Weekend was proving a success. Unlike during ordinary services, the Hastings unit had already been seen to depart packed to the gunwales and looking like a rush-hour train on the Dartford Loop. The combination of the Class 03 and one coach looked very 'light railway' indeed, and that well-known species, photographer, had taken root all the way up Tenterden Bank. 1pm rolled round and Alastair handed the brake van over to me (while of course keeping an expert eye on what I was doing). The gates were open, the Tyer's No. 6 token was delivered to the cab and the platform end starter came 'off'. The Station Master raised his hand (station work complete), a look to front and rear to ensure the doors were closed correctly and not on the catch, two on the bell to the driver, two to my bell in return and we were away. Once at Cranbrook Road I saw to the gates again, and then made a complete idiot of myself by trying to open the rear cab door the wrong way (it opens outwards), assuming it was locked and then walking all the way back to the brake van again! By the time we reached Rolvenden, a great advantage of DMMUs had become obvious – the superb forward view. 6 November was a freezing cold day, the heating was working well and all that was necessary when spotting signals and keeping a general watch on progress was to open the connecting door and look ahead. No need to crane one's neck out into the sub-zero airflow beyond the window.

We picked up two or three minutes at Wittersham Road (no passengers, intermediate stopping time advisory only) and then well and truly caught out the Northiam station staff. Class 108 is surprisingly quiet and, despite Mike sounding the horns for Cysters Crossing, there was no sign of the gates opening as we headed smoothly – the DMMU rides very well – towards the A28. They hadn't heard us coming and were only woken up by a double twin-tone blast! This was, allegedly, the second Northiam embarrassment of the day. On the first arrival of the DMMU, the announcer was rumoured to have gone into the usual routine: 'The train will be here for about 15 minutes. Passengers are welcome to watch while the loco runs...' and then remembered that the only thing running round would be the crew. There isn't much for the guard to do either on a multiple unit turn at Northiam – no need to work the ground frame or move the tail lamp – but at least you get a longer break.

The return trip, followed by the 4.00 train, went well and the Class 108 showed its ability to keep time. I eventually discovered how to get into the rear cab and how much easier this was than trying to climb into the brake van (as awkward as a Mark 1 but better than a Maunsell BNO). We found the light switches and also discovered they had a dimming facility. The DMMU seemed popular with the public, but we noticed that numerous members of staff were treating themselves to a well-earned ride in the new toy. We also received visits from various guard colleagues eager to find out what was what. After the final arrival back at Tenterden, we put all the emergency gear back in the Wealden Pullman and I managed to drop a bottle of first-aid eyewash under the unit. As a result, I dramatically announced I was 'going under' and disappeared beneath the DMMU while shining a Bardic into the gloom – only to re-appear half a minute later, clutching a small plastic bottle and feeling stupid for the second time that day.

We returned to Rolvenden ECS and ended the turn by parking the Class 108 on Sewage Works siding. Alastair and I locked up and found our way to the loco mess room by the light of our Bardic lamps. That 'end of the day' restfulness had settled on the line, the loco shed was silhouetted in the gathering darkness and the 08 diesel shunter was arriving as the final light engine movement. Class 108 may not be part of the railway's tradition, but somehow its presence on the K&ESR feels right. It fits the scene and doesn't seem out of place in either size or function. It is a direct descendant of the Ford railbuses of the inter-war years and shows how the railway's historic ethos can be successfully combined with a pragmatic approach.

This cheerful account describes a day which was something of an exception during my time as a Trainee Guard – an 18-month episode which proved to be a mistake. I include what now follows not out of anything as small-minded as grievance but to illustrate that, as so often in the world of heritage railways, initial defeat need not necessarily lead to long-term failure. It also provides another 'snapshot' of life on the K&ESR in the final decade of the twentieth century.

I had begun guard's training during the high season of 1992 and an immediate mis-match became apparent. Because I had a background on the K&ESR and had written about railways in general, it was assumed that I knew more than I did. For the same reasons, I was aware of the gaps in my knowledge. Not a good start. Most of the guards I worked with were nonetheless friendly, helpful and tolerant and the classroom sessions were informative and more than useful. Some of the small group who supervised the guards, however, displayed that chilly reserve which is more easily experienced than described and this set a few alarm bells ringing at an early stage. I could probably have coped with that had it not been for something it took me too long to realise. I had little aptitude for the work of a guard, ludicrous though this may sound when it comes to one of the more straightforward operating jobs.

Without going into the tedious details, I committed most of the classic guard's errors (the silly mistakes on the DMMU were trivial) without, I think, actually doing anything dangerous. Safety is, as pointed out earlier, the first consideration in railway operation. Most of the guards I worked with doubtless reported back in good faith, although in those days there was no formal written system for recording a trainee's progress. In paid employment, a halt would have been called after at the most six months but, this being a part-time voluntary organisation ever looking for willing hands, matters drifted on until the autumn of the following year. We now come to November 1993.

At this point, when I had accumulated enough of my own doubts about my capability, one of the supervising group approached me with unsettling criticisms and was at least honest enough to say that I would not be considered for passing out until well into the following season. Although this was perhaps to be expected, I was left feeling dejected and mentioned the matter to a very respected guard with whom I had become friendly. He subsequently confirmed that he had found that some of the supervisors were indeed expressing strong concerns about my performance. I was not interested in being second rate and maybe scraping a pass anything up to 12 months later. Such egotistical thoughts aside, there was the practical consideration that other operating staff would not have much confidence in someone who had taken so long to complete their training, which was not good in a safety-critical situation.

The attempt I had been making was not yielding to reasonable effort. An obvious option was to give up and find another job on the Railway (an opportunity had been developing). Doing this as a 'knee jerk' reaction seemed unwise and I decided to see how things went for a little longer but work on the assumption that I would be quietly shutting down my guard's training. I did a couple more turns and the season ended.

During the closed period, I was asked to attend 'Practical Day'. This was a routine part of guard's training which I had not already done and agreed, without much enthusiasm, as the on-track experience might come in useful for whatever I did next. I was not entirely sorry when it was cancelled. Not many weeks later, the Operating Department organised 'Training Day', an opportunity for the accomplished and promising in all relevant grades to fast-track their passing out and become available for the coming season. A notice was circulated about this but as I had realised by then that I didn't exactly meet the person specification I paid little attention to it. I was then asked to attend – under the supervision of my severe critic of the previous autumn. This was bizarre, although plausibly a mistake on the part of the person tasked with making the arrangements. As the most likely outcome would have been a humiliating failure in front of a lot of competent people, I refused, and didn't need to think about it much longer. I resigned as a Trainee Guard. I have never regretted it.

No experience is ever entirely without value, and there were positive aspects to this setback. The knowledge gained, both of the Railway and railway operation in general, was of great assistance in my later work for the K&ESR. Friendships and working relationships forged over that couple of years were also to be invaluable in years to come, but that was far from foreseeable at the time.

Chapter 16

My opportunity for other work was to join the resurgent Carriage & Wagon Department. Guards' turns had often seemed to end with a cup of tea in the C&W mess room, and it was here that I came to know such characters as Ken Lee and Andy Fielder and learned about the effort to restore and promote the use of the vintage carriages. From the 1960s there was Peter Carey as well as Andrew Webb, who was leading the team restoring the GWR Railcar. On days when I was not doing Guard training, I came to spend my time in Carriage & Wagon where there was no shortage of unskilled or semi-skilled work to keep me busy. The C&W volunteers were well aware that my attempt to become a Guard was not working out and in the early part of 1994, the Chief Carriage Examiner, Philip Whiteman, asked me what I wanted to do. This was around the time of the 'Training Day' and there was only one answer. I was to stay with Carriage & Wagon for the next 22 years.

1993 had ended with again only a minor increase in passenger numbers – 74,588 to 76,195 or 2 per cent. Eighty more trains had been run but average train loadings slumped to an all-time low of sixty-five. Ten years earlier, the average train loading had been eighty-four, and it had been ninety until as recently as 1991 when the figure dropped to sixty-seven. Santa passengers were down for the fourth year running, and the two 'Friends of Thomas' weekends only equalled the one event in 1992. The net effect had been to put up costs when revenue per passenger was falling. In 1991, the average fare per passenger (excluding Santa specials) was £4.05. This fell to £3.62 in 1992 and slumped again to £3.58 in 1993. Towards the end of the year there were changes in the Commercial Department; Mark Toynbee stood down as Commercial Director and also left the Board. He was replaced by former Finance Director and volunteer driver Paul Wilson. An innovation was the appointment of a paid Commercial Manager and Gillian Howie was recruited to this post from outside the Railway. Gillian recorded her initial impressions in the *Tenterden Terrier*.

> My first few months at the K&ESR have been fun, traumatic and an eye-opener, and have given the word 'challenge' an entire new meaning. Amidst Santa, Snowmen and Pixies, I have taken a little time to look at our Commercial services and to make outline suggestions for 1994. Maybe a good place to start is to throw some light on what the Commercial and Trading activities will be for the new season. The emphasis will be placed on rebuilding staff confidence in our various trading areas and ensuring that our services are profitable and efficient, and provide the level of service and high standards to meet passenger expectations. The key word will still be 'service' but more consideration will be given to ensuring that there are adequate resources, capital, equipment, facilities and most importantly, people. We are currently not maximising our revenue potential, but I cannot see how we can hope to increase our business or expand in 1994 unless we have the basics right.

Therefore the new year will be one of consolidation and assessment, and certain areas of trading that are not as profitable as one may have perceived have been reviewed. The principles for ordinary passenger services agreed in 1993 have been generally retained with a slight reduction during off-peak periods and some daily services. There is a slight increase in adult and group fares, whilst the child fare of £1.00 remains the same. The profitability of on-train catering has undertaken serious review and a major area of concern has been the 'Wealden Pullman'. The train has suffered a decline of standards resulting in customer complaints and staff dissatisfaction and, if the train is to continue to operate, it must be on a different understanding. 1994 will see the Pullman run from April throughout the year, with a maximum of 36 covers, and the voluntary position of Pullman Manager is now available. It will not be possible to run the Pullman throughout the season with the current level of staff and so many more volunteers are needed. If we have to introduce additional paid waiting staff again then this could be the last year of such a prime service. The 'Rother Valley' (Sunday Lunch service) will continue to be run by volunteers… with development of on-train catering services during the peak season. Private charter bookings and other special bookings including filming contracts will only be taken if they are profitable and within the resources available.

The role of the Commercial department will be to generate and maximise business of all the trading areas of the Railway and to ensure a significant level of revenue needed to sustain the continued operation and reduce our debts. Commercial activities will also be more concerned with staff views and how people feel about 'their' Railway. It will take time before any further changes or expansion of services can be implemented. We cannot work in isolation; the Commercial department needs full support from the membership and working volunteers to succeed and generate revenue for the future.

Despite the gloomy tone behind the assessments of 1993, this was the year that the K&ESR was joint runner-up in the Independent Railway of the Year award sponsored by the now-defunct Ian Allan Ltd publication *Railway World*. First place went to near neighbours the Romney, Hythe & Dymchurch Railway, and second place to the Ffestiniog Railway. The K&ESR shared the runner-up position with the West Somerset Railway. This was mighty company indeed, and one wonders what the West Somerset made of being coupled with a light railway of very different characteristics. Chairman David Stratton received the award from the Chairman of British Rail, Bob Reid, at a ceremony held at the Royal Society of Arts on 8th December.

The Carriage & Wagon Department started 1994 in fine form with morale good and volunteer numbers rising. After all the months of hard work, the restoration of the SE&CR saloon had reached a magnificent conclusion and the coach entered traffic with a test run attached to the back of a service train on Sunday, 13 March. The completion of this project was covered by the railway press and led to further interest in the Vintage Train, both in the C&W Department and throughout the Railway. The concept was, through necessity, part and parcel of preservation on the Isle of Wight, but other mainland heritage railways soon took notice of this development.

The strengthening of the Vintage Train came just as there was another round of controversy about the 'style' of the heritage era K&ESR. It began because Sir Neil Cossons, Director of the Science Museum, had claimed that the railway preservation movement had contributed little by way of original research and had not advanced public understanding of railways. He also suggested that an important goal would be to operate a railway to 'authentic historical and technical standards'. There was an immediate furore throughout the heritage railway movement, not least because the suggestions were widely held to be impractical and often not allowed under modern regulations. Locally, this led to another existential article by John Miller in the spring 1994 *Tenterden Terrier*. It was titled 'What are we?' and can be summarised by quoting the following two paragraphs:

> Long serving members will remember that with the K&ESR we were preserving a RAILWAY, not just a demonstration line on which to exhibit a miscellaneous collection of restored vehicles. All of which makes one wonder: What motivates volunteers to give of their time to run the railway? Is it to indulge their interests in playing trains, or just to socialise, or do they really feel they are playing a part in saving something for future generations?
>
> There seem to be two choices. Either we recreate the style of the K&ESR with authentic liveries, uniforms and job titles, and operate with economy and simplicity, or we simply become a tourist attraction, 'preserving' stock in an unrelated way, adding 'modern' diesels, and upgrading the line with costly heavy engineering.

The response was described as 'overwhelming', the *Terrier* probably receiving more letters on the subject than any in the journal's history up to that time. Points of view were expressed across a wide spectrum of opinion, and two letters anticipated the way things did eventually develop. Firstly, from my own contribution, although I make no claim that this had much influence on policy:

> Emotion abounds on this subject. A major part of the K&ESR's 'image' problem is precisely that it never was part of a Big Four company – we have no objective benchmark to work from. What we have instead is an 'anything goes' culture summed up by that overworked cliché 'If it had been available Colonel Stephens would have used it.' The result is, at the extremes of opinion, a wish to fossilise the Railway at some romanticised point in the past, and, in opposition, a desire for a generalised, overgrown train set. To make matters worse, the first view is championed by an influential group on the edge of the K&ESR 'establishment'. The second is the view of some (a minority, I think) of the more forceful volunteers. It gives me no pleasure to write in these terms; both groups include individuals for whom I have regard. The answer is to resort to something unfashionable for far too long – compromise. I implied this when I wrote, in connection with the class 108 DMMU, that 'the railway's historic ethos can be successfully combined with a pragmatic approach.' Fossilisation is undesirable; so is upgrading to main line standards. What is needed is sensible, sensitive and necessary development which contrives to retain that indefinable K&ESR 'feel'. Yes, we want steam (up to a moderate size) but there is room for appropriate diesels. Mk.1 coaches may be needed for the busiest days, but the public are as capable of distinguishing them from a vintage coach as they are a Model T Ford from a Cortina. A narrow gauge example may not make the best comparison, but look at the Talyllyn – they seem to have achieved something of the approach I suggest.
>
> Discussion is healthy, and I certainly welcome this one. But I also sound this warning. In *Holding the Line* I described the particularly nasty dispute of 1969, when the direction of the preservation project was resolved at the risk of a fatal split in the membership. In my

original draft I wrote (but later deleted) 'Let this episode act as a warning to those who would indulge in faction fighting.' Regretfully, there seems to me to be parallels with the present.

A slightly different approach was taken by member Vince Morris.

'What are we?' in *Tenterden Terrier* No. 63 has, to my mind, one simple answer: 'We' are the able successors to H.F. Stephens: we are running a railway on a shoe-string, using available equipment in whatever way necessary to maximise our revenues, and satisfy our customers. By seeing us doing that the public at large is gaining an accurate insight into the Railway and its history. Stephens did not start off with the intention of running a 'quaint' railway using antiquated stock gleaned from wherever. He started out with the intention of running a railway service, and the only way he could achieve that was to rent, improvise and experiment. Were he alive today I suspect that he would still be doing just that: not because he was an eccentric playing at running a railway, but because that was the way to get things done. If it was necessary to paint the opposite sides of a coach different colours he would have done it. I have no doubt that if the equivalent of a Mk. 1 from the North British were offered, at the right price and time to fill an operational need of the K&ESR in the early 1920s, Stephens would have taken it.

The Kent & East Sussex Railway is probably the closest aligned with its history of any preserved railway because it accurately reflects the approach its management of 70 years ago would have taken were it still in existence today. Of course Stephens would have had a DMU (or two), and probably a Norwegian loco as well. He would not have been constrained by an 'accurate representation of the past' from using what was available. History does not stand still; the K&ESR is an organic thing growing in a way that it would have done under Stephens.

Also, as a result of this debate former Chairman Peter Davis was commissioned by the Board to draw up a plan to enable the K&ESR to respond to the questions raised. Peter was regarded as one of the arch 'Colonel Stephens fundamentalists' by some which might have made him a questionable choice for the task. What he recommended was that an earlier idea – that each station should represent a different era – should be abandoned, as photographic evidence showed that the independent railway, like its heritage successor, had had a constantly changing scene. Instead, the policy adopted by the Board, on the basis of a discussion paper which had been circulated to Directors, was to re-establish the K&ESR's independent identity. The *Terrier* – which effectively meant Philip Shaw (ironically seen by some as one of the leaders of the 'High Street Mafia', a group of Tenterden residents rightly or wrongly perceived as the focal point of Colonel Stephens 'fundamentalism') – was of the view that the proposals offered a sensible and coherent strategy to work to, although the house journal acknowledged that there were alternative views.

This approach ultimately resulted in the Heritage Policy Document which is in its seventh iteration at the time of writing. It is worth looking at examples from the discussion paper to see what was adopted and what has continued to the present day.

Lighting – Stephens originally provided lanterns on wooden posts; Austen used concrete lamp standards. The former were used for the restoration of Bodiam and the latter remain in use at Tenterden. The position elsewhere is more varied.

Billboards – Historically both K&ESR and main line company boards were present. This has been recreated.

Station Running In Boards – Historically, enamel boards with white lettering on a blue background. This has also been recreated.

Platform Surfaces – Originally asphalt at Tenterden only, elsewhere ash. Today asphalt is used everywhere except Wittersham Road where there is a gravel surface.

Yards and Roadways – The old company used water macadam with crushed rock. Basically the same today (in varying condition). The public area at Tenterden now has asphalt but with granite setts in the Carriage & Wagon forecourt. The car park has water macadam with a roadway partly of concrete sleepers.

Signal Boxes – Historically, three very basic shed-like structures housing ground frames. The heritage era has followed SR practice, not without occasional controversy.

Signals – Pre 1954 a very mixed bag to standards acceptable neither in 1995 nor today. The heritage era has again mainly followed SR practice. A subject of occasional controversy, although the nature of present-day operations and regulatory requirements have made upgrading necessary.

Trespass Signs – These had originally been black and white enamel plates, replaced by Austen with a cast iron version after World War 2. 21st Century signs (both trespass warnings and for other purposes) are an eclectic mix including enamel 'Passengers Must Not Pass This Point' albeit in red lettering on a white background.

Station Colour Schemes – Originally purple brown woodwork with cream walls. The SR green and light stone scheme appeared after nationalisation. Purple brown and cream was decided on to accord with the independent identity. A minority have continued to advocate green and cream, sometimes vociferously.

Locomotive Liveries – A controversial subject which raises disproportionate emotion everywhere and not just on the K&ESR. The discussion document identified blue, various shades of green, black and BR liveries as appearing historically. This has been basically followed with some latitude to allow for owners' wishes.

Carriage Liveries – Another disputed subject although perhaps a degree less heated than the loco livery argument. Varnished teak, brown, ivory and brown, grey, bottle green, malachite green and 'blood and custard' were all mentioned by the discussion document. Ivory and brown, although used in the 1970s, has not reappeared post 1995 (other than Pullman livery) and grey has only been used briefly on a PMV. All the others have appeared plus LMS, LNER, SR and SE&CR liveries. Bottle green became much used for the Mark 1s to emphasise the K&ESR identity. There have been changes of shade and moves away from this scheme as it tends to become shabby and indistinct against the countryside when seen from a distance.

The discussion document then rammed home that railways were traditionally neat and tidy and that an untidy run-down appearance was a modern phenomenon that the K&ESR should avoid. (While this present chapter was being written a message appeared on social media detailing the latest attempt at clearing up.)

While issues of identity were being considered there was rising concern about the financial position of the Railway. Some might have argued that this was more important than debating the identity and appearance of the K&ESR, but in marketing terms the two things are of course connected. The *Tenterden Terrier* summed it up:

> …things will have to change. Unaudited accounts indicate that the Company lost around £43,000 last year – heady stuff which cannot be attributed entirely to the recession. We must make sure that the product is right otherwise the public will not pay; we need more active support from our members in a sensible and disciplined way, and just at the moment we need good housekeeping to ensure that bills are not paid out of money that we have not earned and that there is sufficient left to reduce our not inconsiderable debts.

The same issue of the house journal (summer 1994) included an article by Bernard Sealy, the then recently appointed Finance Director, which described 1993 as 'a year we must not forget'. The loss already mentioned compared with £4255 in 1992:

> This is clearly an unsatisfactory result, and the expenses are too high. Budgets were set to a level of expenditure necessary to sustain a high level of operation coupled with the investment in infrastructure demanded by such operation. With notably few exceptions, Managers controlled their expenditure extremely well with little significant overspend. The problems came about because income failed to reach projected figures and also the margins attained by the Pullman and Catering fell sharply. The Wealden Pullman, increased to 72 covers, became most unpopular with volunteers. This necessitated the employment of agency staff to fill the gaps with the consequent reduction in profit margin to a wafer thin 6 per cent, far short of the budget figure. A similar employment scenario on the Catering side led to low income areas being manned by paid staff, not even covering their own costs. Contractors were employed to clean the station areas at Tenterden, as well as the Wealden Pullman and Rother Valley trains, the total cost in 1993 being a staggering £14,894. Surely some of this work could have been undertaken by volunteers?

> Having recognised the problems, the Board has begun to introduce measures to reverse this trend. A certain amount of expenditure, principally in the advertising and publicity area, had already been committed during 1993 and could not be avoided. The newly led Commercial department has carefully scrutinised train services and made cuts where necessary to reduced running costs. Certain marginal days have been dropped altogether, allowing our hard-pressed permanent staff time to reduce excessive hours of overtime, an unfortunate feature of the 1993 service.

> The Wealden Pullman has been reduced to 36 covers, and already volunteers are coming forward to staff the train. Naturally, running it on a predominantly volunteer basis significantly increases the profitability, with the result that the 1994 budget figures are being attained.

> The Buffet at Northiam is being run by volunteers from the 'Friends of Northiam Station' supporting group. Whilst the income generated is not spectacular, it is surprisingly high and also makes an invaluable contribution to the financial situation.
>
> All site cleaning is carried out by our own staff within their day-to-day duties.
>
> It is my intention that the finances will show a much healthier position in 1994 so that we reduce our not inconsiderable debts to more manageable level.

This was accompanied by an item by Commercial Director Paul Wilson titled 'Facts Figures and the Future' and from which the following is an extract:

> In the last edition of the *Tenterden Terrier* figures were quoted in respect of average passengers per train and also for the average fare per passenger. On carrying out a more detailed analysis it transpires that many of the extra trains were formed by the Hastings Diesel unit, therefore the actual average passengers per steam train remained the same. There are numerous ways to calculate average fare depending on which figures are used, and this is further complicated by the formation of TRC Trading, (a wholly owned subsidiary company required under Charity law to undertake trading [static and on-train catering, gift shop etc] as opposed to railway operating activities) which also levies fares but does not pay them all to TRC. In 1993 the two Thomas weekends actually increased passenger numbers by 60 per cent. Examination of income figures in isolation is a serious mistake. There is no direct correlation between income and expenditure, therefore it is vitally important to monitor both together – if income is down then expenditure has to be cut to match, it will not automatically reduce in line. Two classic examples of ignoring the two aspects occurred in 1993. The first was the June service: this saw traffic increase by around 17 per cent yet the train service increased by more than 100 per cent. Thomas events, despite increasing income by 60 per cent, contributed less to profit due to 47 trains being run instead of 19 as in 1992. This increased all variable costs by over 100 per cent. It is also difficult to argue that the peripherals such as catering and the shop increased their business, as the capacity is very limited and passes saturation point on busy days.

Following Bernard Sealy's co-option to the Board operating costs had been broken down under direct and marginal headings. Previously there had been no realistic idea of train operating costs. An imperfect science it might have been, but the point where optimum returns could be obtained needed to be determined. [Bernard Sealy's email comment to me, January 2022].

> The Commercial department now keeps a close watch on the figures, monitoring the income on a daily basis using systems set up by Gillian Howie, our General Manager. On a monthly basis the Board compares these daily figures against the management accounts to verify the accuracy of recording, and at the same time reviews the expenditure situation. It is pleasing to note that the Company is presently in line with forecast, despite suffering at the hands of mother nature especially over the Easter period. This caused the fare income to fall short of budget, although sensible spending by the Managers resulted in outgoings reducing to more than compensate.

It seems that at present that we have an unfortunate tendency to dwell too much on the past, using it to fuel debate and argument about who or what was right and who or what was wrong. Inevitably there are those who use such detail to further their own ends without considering the most important overall subject – the future of the Railway. Whatever has happened in the past, let us learn from it, improve where needed and build on success. Our whole focus must be on the FUTURE.

The finalisation of the business plan sets out in broad terms the areas that need to be considered when seeking to drive the business forward. In 1991 the Board were persuaded that the best means of coming out of recession was to trade out and, by agreement, that commitment was given. Part way through 1993, it became evident that the business could not support such a policy, the strain on resources was immense and intolerable. The result of that realisation was the adoption of the 1994 budget, centred around a scaling back of the operation, with particular emphasis on profitability analysis. Pressure is still considerable, but the operation is more suitable for the amount of volunteer support that is available. The Bank is supportive of the policies that are being applied and have maintained their support for the Railway for 1994.

All too often we tend to criticise the shortcomings of the Railway, but pause a moment to reflect on how the visitors see us and what we do WELL.

In the spring of 1994 there were managerial changes resulting from criticism of communication, or rather the lack of it, between Board and staff. Although this was described as a 'historical' problem at the time it has been a persistent issue. Having been much involved with various communications in the meantime, I have sometimes had the feeling that the horse has failed to drink even when supplied with plentiful water. English social attitudes may well play their part as well. As in many organisations, and admittedly as a generalisation, the leadership has tended to be 'broadsheet' people and significant parts of the workforce to have a 'tabloid' outlook on life. This has inevitably been reflected in both the writing of information items and their reception by the intended readership. Efforts to improve matters, under way at the time of writing, appear to be achieving some success but have had to await the age of the internet and social media.

Management coordination up to the mid-1990s had also been perceived as having been poor. To achieve improvements, Gillian Howie was, as mentioned by Paul Wilson, appointed General Manager although continuing her existing duties in the Commercial Department. Regular meetings would be held with managers to monitor the business performance and she would attend the end of Board meetings to convey the views and problems of the Managers to the Directors and relay Board policy back to managers. Volunteer David Slack was appointed as Assistant General Manager. The appointment of a GM, a post almost universal on the larger heritage railways, was a significant innovation on the K&ESR. It established a pattern which, with breaks and sometimes different titles, was to be part of the way ahead.

Chapter 17

Despite the positive development of a General Manager being appointed, the financial position was giving rise to that familiar on the K&ESR feeling – a febrile atmosphere. I was nevertheless enjoying being back on the Railway, among volunteers, and hopefully making a modest contribution to the Carriage & Wagon Department.

I was sitting in the old mess coach on the platform one warm evening after work when Graham Hukins (then still a volunteer) came to see me with the news that, in view of the way the K&ESR was being run, a panel of candidates was being put together to stand for election with the objective of replacing a large part of the Board. In view of my known abilities as a 'communicator' (presumably my record as a writer) would I be interested in standing? My snap answer was, 'There are enough incompetents running this Railway without me adding my four pennyworth.' Not a bad one-liner on the spur of the moment, but very unfair! My more considered view was that, like many others, I might not be entirely happy with the way things were but that my varied experience did not necessarily make me fit for a directorship.

This was the beginning of the 'Gang of Five', a phrase originating in the overblown rhetoric of the Chinese Cultural Revolution of the 1960s. It had a revival in Britain as the 'Gang of Four' with the emergence of the Social Democratic Party in 1981 and was still current in popular usage nearly a decade and half later. Once again, quoting from a *Terrier* article by Neil Rose will serve to relate this more than adequately.

> A new member might be forgiven for thinking that the Tenterden Railway Company is unable to organise a straightforward general meeting. For this year's 23rd AGM there was a confusion over dates. The date set clashed with a 'Friends of Thomas' weekend, so it had as its sole agenda item a resolution to adjourn until a week later; even this second date had been altered from the one originally advised. Thus the meeting was convened on 17th September and those present voted for the adjournment but it is curious to conjecture what if they had not so agreed. Could 20 members, and proxies, have determined the outcome of the meeting, including elections, there and then? I rather think so, but fortunately for Raymond Williams, the Secretary, there were no upsets. Thus although it might have been an adjourned meeting, the AGM proper took place on 24th September.
>
> The 1993 AGM was also dogged by problems. The 1992 Accounts were unavailable for the meeting in June and were not considered until an Extraordinary General Meeting in January 1994 – when they were over a year out of date.
>
> The 1994 AGM followed hard on the heels of the EGM on 13 August this year at which the Directors wanted to reduce their numbers from ten to eight. Reasons for this change failed to impress the membership; they believed their views should be represented at the

highest level. This would be less likely with fewer directors. More than 50 members took the trouble to turn up and made their views quite clear by voting unanimously against the Resolution so that the number of Directors would remain at 10.

Another ineptly worded notice had suggested that members would not be interested in turning up for such a matter. This was like a red rag to a bull and the Board and Company Secretary soon realised that they would have to hire a large venue (the hall at the Tenterden Club) for the meeting. The proposition was actually quite reasonable, but the reaction to it was widely interpreted at the time as a 'shot across the bows'.

Neil Rose continued his account of the AGM as follows:

The main issue at this year's AGM was the state of the Company's finances. We knew they were going to be bad and the published accounts confirmed our fears. The Company had made a loss of £108,000 in 1993 on gross income of some £680,000 (shared between the Company and its trading subsidiary). Admittedly this included almost £61,000 to rebuild the embankment above Orpins Curve, which was regarded as one-off exceptional expenditure, but the loss compared very badly with the £4,000 shortfall a year earlier. By the end of 1993 the Company's debts, especially with National Westminster Bank, had increased alarmingly by over £110,000. This was seen as a very unhealthy situation which at least nine months earlier did need urgent remedial action. Concerns about the problems facing the Railway, an alleged lack of direction and poor communications, saw five members put themselves forward as candidates for election as Directors. Dicky Dyer, Graham Hukins, Richard Johnston, Chris Lewis and Mark Yonge conducted a carefully planned campaign, putting their views to the membership at large and ensuring their message was known to the working volunteers. Also in the contest were six existing Directors. David Stratton (Chairman), Andy Webb and Paul Wilson retired under the 'one-third' rule and offered themselves for re-election. Richard Osborn, Bernard Sealy and Graham Smith, as co-opted members during the year, offered themselves for election. Only Adrian Chapman and Robin Dyce remained as continuing Directors, but a week before the AGM the former resigned.

With eleven candidates for eight places, the weeks leading to the AGM were somewhat hectic. The merits and demerits of candidates were constant topics of volunteers' conversations. Lurid tales about the Railway abounded. Pieces for and against the candidates appeared in *The Smokebox*, the unofficial journal of the volunteer members. Posters and notices appeared and disappeared. All in all, it was a pretty robust contest. I don't know if anybody opened a book on the outcome but there were plenty of 'dead cert' tipsters.

After the excitement preceding the AGM the rather drab autumnal afternoon set the tone for the meeting as we gathered in the Tenterden Club. The hall was more crowded than any AGM I can remember: some 250 members were present with many standing throughout. Roadworks in Tenterden High Street caused delayed arrivals but fortunately the Secretary waited until 2.05pm to begin, giving time for latecomers to get their breath back. This gave an opportunity to study a consolidated balance sheet and financial statements for 1993, as well as the predicted out-turn for 1994, which were handed to us on arrival – information which should have formed part of the published accounts. The figures did nothing to alter the 1993 out-turn but the 1994 forecast was much more encouraging.

On opening the meeting, David Stratton passed the Chairman's job to Robin Dyce who was the only Director whose position was uncontested. It is very much to Robin's credit that he maintained good order throughout what could have been a very fraught afternoon. Having established that there were no press present, the formal business began, starting with the minutes of recent meetings which were quickly despatched.

We listened attentively to the Chairman's Address. It was not an easy presentation for David Stratton and emotion was never very far from the surface. Whatever their personal opinions, those present must have felt some sympathy for him and the other Directors as the preceding stressful months had clearly taken their toll. An 'Annus horribilis' was how he summed up 1993. He outlined how in late 1992 the 1993 budget had been narrowly approved by the Board, with the support of the Railway's management. However, revenue did not meet growth targets and extra costs could not be recovered. He explained why it was decided to go for a complete rebuild of an embankment to minimise future maintenance costs. The Board had protracted problems with the Charity Commissioners over advertising and much time was spent in countering an extremely worrying planning application for a hotel complex near Tenterden station.

When the financial deterioration had become known, the Directors had kept the bank fully informed and had sought professional advice. The upshot was positive support and agreement of the Company's immediate funding arrangements and its longer-term Business Plan. David Stratton read out a confidential letter he had sent to all Directors in March 1993 in an attempt to address the deteriorating financial situation; there was to be no work contracted outside without specific approval, no visiting locomotives and a 20 per cent reduction in spending in all areas forthwith. On a more positive note, he spoke of the positive contribution made by Gillian Howie since her appointment as Commercial Manager. Finally, he mentioned that the 1994 budget prepared last November looked for an ongoing 25 per cent reduction in expenditure.

It was no surprise that the Chairman concentrated on the financial situation. He did not attempt to excuse himself or fellow Directors from responsibility but said that the problems had been recognised and addressed although the losses appeared to climb inexorably during 1993 despite this action. It was a sombre presentation, but the conclusion was heartening and the K&ESR is still in business.

Bernard Sealy, who had the unenviable task of taking over the Company's finances earlier this year when they were at their nadir, then presented the accounts. His use of an overhead projector was a good idea, but I doubt if the figures could be read from the back of the hall. As the published figures were already known, he sensibly concentrated on the consolidated figures and the projected results for 1994. Unfortunately, he presented the figures rather as if to a gathering of accountants and I doubt if many in the audience understood what he was saying. Much of the overdraft with the bank had been capitalised into a loan with regular repayments, instead of repayable on demand which could have led to the bankruptcy of the Company. He forecast that the borrowings would fall by £50,000 by the end of the year. After just one question (from me) the resolutions for the adoption of the accounts and the appointment of the auditors were both carried on a show of hands; seven members abstained on the former, four on the latter with one against.

The financial problems highlighted the lack of management information available on spending. The Company's inability to produce accounts until many months after the year end is also disturbing and I certainly hope this delay can be addressed in future: they should be ready in May.

The meeting moved on to the election of Directors, the obvious highlight of the afternoon. Robin Dyce sought clarification about Richard Johnston's statement that he wanted to serve the Railway in a non-executive capacity. Robin's view was that all Directors should have some form of executive position and that this intention was incompatible. Richard Johnston explained how he saw his role, providing a strategic overview, to the satisfaction of the meeting.

Then each candidate, bar Richard Osborn who could not attend, was asked to speak to the meeting. They largely followed the manifestoes that had been sent out to members so I will not repeat them here. Nor will I comment on who impressed in their delivery and who rambled.

Presentations concluded and at last came the time to put crosses on ballot papers and to hand them in for counting, which was to take very nearly an hour. Immediately after the papers had been taken out of the hall for counting, Robin Dyce asked whether the meeting should accept the election of nine Directors, not eight, given the additional vacancy caused by Adrian Chapman's departure. I certainly felt that everyone had completed ballot papers or proxy forms on the basis of eight to be elected and that it would be improper to alter the numbers now: I said so publicly with the full support of the meeting. The correct course was for the new Board to co-opt someone to fill the vacancy, although this meant no-one on the ballot paper could be selected.

The traditional Open Forum took place while the votes were counted and was remarkably free of contention. Perhaps everyone had half a mind on the election results. That it was noisy was entirely due to a rock group practising downstairs, an irritating distraction. Subjects covered included interference with internal post, Terrier policy specifically and locomotive restoration generally; centralised purchasing ('it won't work'); staff wages and seasonal employment ('we get far more out of staff than we pay them for'); Rolvenden land purchase – two fields cost £47,500, and earmarked for future locomotive and carriage works; a K&ESR '300 Club' promotion; and an appeal by C&W for help to complete repairs on two carriages in time for the Santa Specials – their non-availability could harm valuable income.

Next Robin Dyce presented the Railway's recently developed Business Plan taking us into the next century. In summary it envisages keeping the KE&SR in the forefront of tourist attractions, making it a welcoming place to visit with a diversity of trains to cater for the average visitor and enthusiast alike. Bodiam will have been reached. For Tenterden the 'Soweto' office block will have long since disappeared with a proper shop building erected in its place. The C&W Department will migrate to Rolvenden leaving its shed as a museum and office accommodation. The financial statements given a little earlier contrasted with the £2 million plus needed to finance these plans; they seemed over-optimistic even with the various fund-raising exercises envisaged.

Nevertheless, the Business Plan aims to improve the Railway and at the meeting it struck a positive note. I couldn't help feeling that by not having made it known to the members before, the old Directors had done themselves a disservice. It represented much thought and work, a positive planning statement. There was a danger of its authors being unrecognised.

At 4.40pm there was a stir at the back of the hall, the count was complete. The results were passed around those on the stage. Expressions were scrutinised to see if the winners and losers could be identified before the results were announced. Raymond Williams started to read off the results at a gallop, too fast for the audience's pencils. He started again. We learnt that 388 members had voted at the meeting and by proxy (surely a record), with the following results:

Elected: Chris Lewis, Dicky Dyer, David Stratton, Bernard Sealy, Graham Hukins, Mark Yonge, Richard Johnston, Paul Wilson.

Not elected: Andrew Webb, Graham Smith, Richard Osborn.

So the five newcomers had been elected (in Mark Yonge's case he has been a Director, and Chairman, before), three Directors re-elected and three ousted. The meeting was all but over' but not before from the floor Peter Davis expressed thanks and appreciation to those who had lost their seats, a sentiment that was endorsed with loud acclamation.

My overall impression? A much more subdued meeting than usual. A time for thought but not for recrimination. The company has gone through a difficult patch recently when financial controls had been weak. Things were improving and this was very clearly an occasion to put a line under the past and look to a more positive future. The old Board had been too introverted for the volunteer members; rumour and suspicion abound in the absence of hard news. So hopefully the new Directors will have learnt a hard lesson: communications are all important. It is vital to keep an ear to the voice of volunteers, make sure they are kept properly informed and, above all, give proper direction and leadership, thus gaining the confidence and loyalty of the workforce.

Andrew Webb afterwards admitted to being hurt by his personal result but later told me that it was really something of a relief after nine years of intense involvement. Graham Smith's failure to be elected was entirely caused by his fractious relationship with the working members. Following this he ceased all involvement with the K&ESR, unfortunately taking his expertise and contacts with him. The *Tenterden Terrier* commented that those who had expected the 1994 AGM to be a noisy, recriminatory affair, reminiscent of the notorious meetings of the late 1960s (yes, that included me), were to be disappointed. We would have to wait another seven years for an AGM filled with déjà vu of the formative era.

A summary of The Tenterden Railway Company Business Plan appeared in the *Rooter* for November 1994 and can be found in Appendix B. It should be noted that this included the first mention of twinning with a European heritage railway in order to obtain grant funding from the European Union.

In the aftermath of the AGM the Board decided that the Directors' roles should be less executive than in the previous set-up. The idea was of course to allow the Board to concentrate on policy and forward planning. It was however somewhat of a half-way house between the executive Board of the previous years and the substantially non-executive Board of more recent times. David Stratton continued as Chairman. Individual Directors were to be responsible for various area of activity – Finance, Operating, fundraising etc. – and would communicate the necessary policy and budgetary information to the Managers. Commercial matters would however be dealt with by the Board as a whole and Richard Johnston declined to take a specific brief, preferring to keep a strategic oversight. Paul Wilson felt he would be unable to work with the new leadership style and resigned on 15 October.

Tragically Dicky Dyer, seen as one of the most able of the new intake, fell seriously ill soon afterwards and relinquished his position. He died not many months later.

Matters got worse on the financial front. On the advice of the Auditors, the cost of substantial reconstruction of the permanent way was written off rather than being capitalised as an asset. As a result, the loss for 1993 increased from £43,264 to £60,815. In addition, the Company's total indebtedness on 31 December 1993 had been £560,371. For some reason, perhaps to emphasise the historical background, the wholly owned commercial subsidiary TRC Trading was renamed Colonel Stephens Railway Enterprises (abbreviated to CSRE) with effect from 6 October 1994. This had no practical effect on the operation of either the parent or the subsidiary company. It did however spark an almost predictable correspondence with a member about the absence of a possessive apostrophe after 'Stephens'.

A rather more significant development was the appointment of Norman Brice at this time to the routine post of administrator for covenants and bankers' orders on behalf of the Membership Secretaries. Norman had been a member for some years and also a signalman. It was some time later that he arranged and donated the cost of an automatic watering system for the hanging flower baskets under the canopy at Tenterden Town. This produced 'much ado about nothing' typical of the K&ESR when those unaware of Norman's generosity complained about a waste of money. The row is long forgotten; the watering system remains in use in the twenty-first century. These events however marked the emergence of someone who was to be a significant figure in the next sixteen years of the K&ESR.

Despite all the bright hopes for 1994, the year did not produce the looked-for results. Once more there had been an overall drop in passenger numbers, although the average number of passengers per train increased. Unfortunately, this welcome trend did not compare favourably with what had been achieved in the 1980s. Average fares per passenger, excluding Santa trains, nonetheless rose from £3.58 to £4.05. Santa trains showed an increase of as much as 8 per cent; however, this was achieved by much more intensive running which caused some operational problems. Staffing and management of the 'Wealden Pullman' had been tightened up during 1994, the chef now being the only non-volunteer member of the crew. The reduction of covers to 36 per train had helped with volunteer involvement.

Chapter 18

1995 dawned and with it the 21st year since reopening the first section of the Railway. The pattern of operations was similar to 1994, with trains running on Sundays in March and November, at weekends from April to October, on Tuesdays, Wednesdays and Thursdays in June and September and daily during July and August. To this, of course, were added the Santa Special and New Year trains. This was similar to, but exceeded, present day levels of service which, as we shall see, were determined following the reopening to Bodiam.

A series of celebratory special events were arranged to mark the 21st anniversary, starting with the return to traffic of the Norwegian locomotive No. 19 after many years out of service and a Steam Spectacular on 3/4 June, Friends of Thomas the Tank Engine on 1/2 July and a Festival of Steam and Song (whatever that was) over the weekend of 9/10 September.

An important innovation during 1995 was the introduction of Railway Experience Days. These were initially run on winter weekends when no public train service operated. This produced an income stream at a time when trading was sparse. Only the Tenterden–Rolvenden section was used so as not to affect the work of the P.Way Department. Participants on these one-day courses sampled each activity needed to run trains as well as receiving a brief introduction to the history of the railway and a visit to the locomotive and carriage sheds. The highlight for most was the two hours spent on the footplate, learning the art of firing and driving a steam locomotive. The income from Experience Days was certainly needed. The *Tenterden Terrier* for spring 1995 commented:

> It is hard to believe that 21 years have elapsed since the first mile of track reopened in 1974; the good news is that we are now running to Northiam; sadly the target of Bodiam still remains well into the future. What was not envisaged in those early days was the mountain of debt, now costing the Railway nearly £1,000 per week to service, which cannot realistically be repaid from existing revenues within the existing infrastructure.
>
> The options open to us are clear cut but limited. Either we scale down our overheads and are content to operate only a 'basic railway', or alternatively an appeal is made to members for donations to reduce borrowings to a more manageable amount – say one half of the present level.

The same edition of the house journal included an account of the annual meeting for volunteers and paid staff which featured a similar theme:

> At a packed staff meeting at the Vine Inn on 28th January many of the regular volunteers discussed future plans for the railway. A lively debate centred on plans for extending the railway to Bodiam, especially in respect of the challenging time-scale set for this project by Mark Yonge. It was pointed out that we have not paid for the Northiam extension

yet, with the total debt of the railway not much reduced from £550,000, far less finished the Northiam station site. This means the railway is still paying nearly £1000 per week in interest payments to the bank before even turning a revenue earning wheel. It was generally felt that the debt burden should be reduced first before extending. Indeed it was even queried as to why we wanted to go to Bodiam since not only is there a backlog of projects on the existing line both for the P.Way and concerning Rolvenden even before the necessary enhancements to the Tenterden site are contemplated. There is little point in reaching Bodiam, assuming you can find the capital, if you cannot transport enough passengers to make the venture economic. We are not able to raise fares in direct proportion to the length of the line, and this has meant that a Bodiam extension could be a bigger millstone around our neck than Northiam has proved. Despite the reality there was much emotion expressed that our eventual aim must be to reach Bodiam. The Board was left to agree what must be done having heard some forcibly put opinions and a consensus emerging amongst those present.

The eventual aim of reaching Bodiam had, of course, its roots in the Railway's history, both before and after 1961. Historical interest was expressed through the Colonel Stephens Railway Museum which still formed a small section of the Tenterden & District Museum in Station Road. Since that date more material had become available, much of which was placed on 'indefinite loan' and for display. Following the closure of the offices at Salford Terrace, Tonbridge, on nationalisation in 1948, W.H. Austen had retained much of the furniture from Colonel Stephens' old office and also many interesting records. These in turn passed to his son Holly Austen. Holly died in 1981 and, under the terms of his will, all the material not already passed to or given to Philip Shaw was left to a friend who placed it on loan to the 'museum'.

After 1981, the collection had expanded hugely. In the porch area of Bill Austen's house in Tonbridge was a large unopened wooden box which he had said contained items that his father (who died in 1956) had put aside when the Salford Terrace offices closed in 1948. When broken open, the box yielded immeasurably important paperwork and a huge collection of other items, which form the core of the present archive and many small exhibits. Other material had also been acquired and by the early 1990s great difficulties were being experienced in finding sufficient storage.

Following inquiries made by Ken Lee, the Board agreed to space being rented in No. 1 Unit of the Romney hut next to the Carriage & Wagon shed for use as a Museum and archive store. The Romney hut was the property of member and adjoining land owner Henry Edwards, who has proved to be a good friend to the Railway over many years. Planning permission had been received and the 277 square feet available in the Town Museum would be increased to no less than 1536 in Unit No. 1. The theme would continue to be centred on Colonel Stephens' career and the railways he promoted, engineered or managed. The building alterations were to be undertaken by contractors, but the exhibition was to be put together by a team of volunteers led by Alan Tebboth and John Miller.

Also a tribute to volunteer initiative was the previously mentioned return to service of the former NSB 2-6-0 locomotive No. 376 (K&ESR No. 19 (later named *Norwegian*) which had last been in traffic in 1977. The recommissioning ceremony on Sunday, 5 March 1995 was undertaken by His Excellency Tom Vraalsen, the Norwegian Ambassador. The locomotive had been brought to the UK by local landowner David Barham in 1971 and subsequently became the property of the Tenterden Railway Company. As TRC was unable to finance the necessary overhaul, ownership passed to the Norwegian Locomotive Trust which was formed in 1984. Work had started in 1987 and the project cost £40,000 to complete. There are many cultural and historic links between Britain and Norway, something which is reflected in the appearance of this locomotive. The original design of NSB Moguls is attributed to a 'private job' by David Jones of the Highland Railway, and it can perhaps be said that Norwegian looks rather less foreign than does the USA Class.

The Norwegian locomotive was joined by another Mogul for part of the season when Ivatt 2-6-0 Class 2 No. 46443 arrived on hire from the Severn Valley Railway. This relatively modern locomotive looked quite at home on the K&ESR, having been designed for use on the minor lines of the LMS. It also made for an interesting comparison with No. 19, it being essentially an updated version of the same design concept.

Significant restoration was not confined to locomotives. In June, one year and four days after work had started on SE&CR four-wheel coach No. 2947, the vehicle left the carriage shed and was attached to the back of a service train for its first run. This would not happen today. There would be a test run first, a special working that would not interfere with normal traffic in the event of problems. The Carriage & Wagon Department claimed this as a record at the time and it was never challenged. More recently, however, the TV programme *Railway Restorations* has claimed to restore bogie carriages in six months, albeit using rather different circumstances and resources. The K&ESR was earning a substantial reputation for vintage carriage restoration at this time, which for a while aided the morale of the C&W Department. This had led during the previous year to the formation of a new support group, the Friends of Vintage Carriages, the membership of which was largely from within Carriage & Wagon. I took up the post of Secretary to the Friends. Initial activity was entirely concerned with fundraising. This changed to include vehicle ownership when one of the Southern Railway PMVs on the line was offered in lieu of the Company repaying a loan which the Friends had made to enable the purchase of a machine tool.

In October 1995 came a remarkable recognition of the Carriage & Wagon Department's efforts when no less a line than the Bluebell Railway borrowed three of the vintage coaches to take part in the filming of *The Wind in the Willows*. The vehicles hired were No. 2947, the District Coach and the Great Eastern Brake. Ken Lee went over to act as 'minder'. This occasion helped establish a friendly relationship between the C&W departments of both railways, which continued subsequently.

There were some significant management changes during the year. Gillian Howie left to pursue her career elsewhere. Graham Hukins left the Board and resumed, this time on a salaried basis, the role of Commercial, but not General, Manager. After a decade as Chairman, David Stratton announced at the 1995 Annual General Meeting that he was standing down. This caused some hesitation at the subsequent Board meeting about who was to replace him, such had been the influence of David on the organisation. Eventually, Robin Dyce said he would do the job and he was duly appointed. There were immediate changes to the Board structure. Chris Lewis and Richard Johnson were by this stage the only remaining members of the 'Gang of Five' and, significantly, Norman Brice had been co-opted as a Director. The Board felt that their existing structure no longer reflected the business and operating needs of the K&ESR. It was essential that the Board should be able to address the challenges and changing needs facing the Railway. It was felt that too much had become concentrated on the Chairman and that what was needed was someone who would lead the team. Teamwork had not always been evident in the past. On the face of it, Robin was a good choice in this respect, local government at that time laying much emphasis on team working.

It was also thought that Board members had, in some cases, become too involved in the day-to-day operation of the Railway (the executive director approach) which was preventing managers from running their areas efficiently. This caused resentment and a lack of confidence in the Board. Having directors involved in day-to-day matters also gave rise to managers receiving conflicting advice in problem-solving. The Chairman's role was to lead on policy and strategy, and the Board would lead the Railway forward. It was also thought essential for a person to be appointed to co-ordinate the day-to-day management. Re-establishing the post of full-time General Manager was also considered, but because this could not be afforded Board member Chris Lewis was appointed as Managing Director. Under the new structure, the core Directors would be the Chairman, Finance Director and Commercial Director. Above all, the new Board had the perennial problem of reducing the Railway's debt with the bank.

Finance was of course also key to extending to Bodiam. To this end the possibility of grants from the National Heritage Fund (the National Lottery), the European Union and a Derelict Land Grant from the government were all considered. Progress had however been hampered by the lack of a person with suitable experience in this area. The problem had been solved on 17 November 1995 by the previously mentioned co-opting of Norman Brice to the Board. Norman worked for the Department of Trade and Industry and was well placed to advise on these matters, not least because his work included contact with the European Union in Brussels. I recall discussing with David Stratton the seemingly sudden rise of Norman Brice within the ranks of the K&ESR. David gave me one of his straight-to-the-point replies. 'He's the next Chairman.'

Members continued to be concerned about the Railway's financial position and at the end of the year the November 1995 issue of the *Tenterden Terrier* published an article titled 'How Much Money IS There in the Bank?'. This explained in its introduction that the AGM for that year had provided the membership with a great deal of information on the 1994 finances including, for the first time, consolidated accounts showing the combined figures for the Company and the subsidiary CSRE. This improvement had been introduced by Bernard Sealy. The remainder of the article consisted of an interview between Bernard Sealy and the Editor, Philip Shaw, and which is, in edited form, summarised here:

Did the railway make a loss last year?

Yes. The railway lost £21,945 last year, after paying interest charges of £47,638 on our considerable debts. It does represent a considerable improvement on the loss of £108,566 incurred in 1993.

What are the total debts of the organisation?

Bank debts amounted to £400,670 at 31st December 1994, compared with £389,131 in the previous year. The figures for both years do not include £171,240 resulting from the two bearer bond issues which are, in theory anyway, like any other debt. Fortunately many of the bond holders do not claim interest to which they are entitled.

Why did the company make a loss last year?

Apart from the considerable burden of interest on our debts which has to be paid to our bankers, a key factor is that our train services are not sufficiently profitable. The operating income of the Company was £402,979 excluding income from commercial (i.e. non-charitable) activities such as the bookshop, buffet, Pullman and special events. However, this does include membership subscriptions and donations of £52,906. If these items are excluded the total operating income from running trains was £350,073. Against this, operating expenses amounted to £353,818, leaving us with a deficit of £3,745, before general administrative expenses of £32,945 and depreciation of £12,651. The commercial activities generated a profit of £50,000.

What can be done to restore the company to profitability and reduce our debts?

Firstly, the inherent profitability of the company is too low. In order to generate more income we must attract more visitors as there is fairly limited scope to raise fares and other prices. Our costs could be reduced if more volunteers came forward to help us run the railway. Last year our wage bill amounted to £123,113 because of the necessity to employ 11 people. Secondly, the crippling burden of our interest charges. Even with careful housekeeping, we cannot hope to trade out of our debts and we must maintain the quality of our assets at a high level. We must seek grants and funding from sources, commensurate with our charitable status.

What are the prospects for 1995?

I think it likely that we shall make a loss again in 1995, although it will be lower than in 1994. This is because in line with other leisure businesses in the South East, we are feeling the effects of people spending less and our income is running below budget. However, it is some comfort that we are protected against rising interest rates on much of our debt as most of this is now at fixed rates.

Will our debts come down in 1995?

I think that we shall end the year at a similar level to 1994.

From among the paid staff, Locomotive Department Manager Bob Forsythe retired in the middle of the year. Bob was a most interesting old-time railwayman who had started his career as a premium apprentice with the LMS. He retired from BR service as Shedmaster at Cricklewood and brought to the K&ESR a wealth of knowledge of both steam locomotives and railways in general. Bob stayed involved with the K&ESR through his membership of Rolvenden Steam Enterprises and was succeeded as Loco Department manager by Lawrence Donaldson. Also significant was the retirement on 8 July, and after ten years in post, of Raymond Williams as Company Secretary. This provided my first association with that particular role and led to a minor saga worth relating as another illustration of how things sometimes happened in those days.

It had been known for some time that Raymond Williams wished to retire. The subject had come up in mess room conversations along with many other issues and I had attached no particular significance to this. Raymond gave the Board 12 months' notice of his intention to step down and had stuck to it. David Stratton had, at the 1994 AGM, mentioned the need to find a replacement and an advertisement for this volunteer post duly appeared in the following (November) *Tenterden Terrier*. I rejected the idea of applying after considering it for less than ten seconds. My qualifications were reasonably appropriate, as was some of my experience, but this was the sort of administrative work I had either been glad to get away from or simply had not done. It was difficult comparing a London Borough with a just-about-medium-sized business which ran a tourist attraction. Insofar as one could make a comparison, I just didn't have the experience that far up the organisational tree. Anyway, I had a full-time job, I lived 50 miles away and the post of Company Secretary looked very time consuming. Also, and although those around me seemed everything one would wish of colleagues, I wasn't entirely certain, despite the seeming popularity of *Holding the Line*, how much the guard's training debacle had damaged my credibility. Lastly, I had not that long returned as a volunteer. People do not approve of someone being 'parachuted in' at senior level. If I was to aim for something more senior in the Company, I needed to work my way up through the ranks.

Not long after the advertisement appeared in the *Terrier*, Duncan Buchanan, whom some saw as a possible candidate, surprised me by asking, early one frosty morning, if I was interested in applying. There was, apparently, an assumption in some quarters that I was going to get the job. I gave my full-time employment as a reason for not being interested. Duncan and I laughed at the notion, although I did later check with C&W colleague Ken Lee (who had friends 'in the know') if there was anything in Duncan's assertion. Ken had also heard of the idea. The post was re-advertised in the March 1995 issue of the *Rooter* and, when visiting the C&W mess room, David Stratton several times mentioned that the position had not been filled. Shortly afterwards, he offered me the job despite the fact that I had not applied. I refused for the reasons already given. I also said that I thought too much was being inferred from my record as a writer and that my experience in management was inadequate. David withdrew looking disappointed and Philip Clark-Monks was appointed instead. This was not to be the last I would hear of the post of Company Secretary.

On 16 September 1995, The Terrier Trust held its inaugural meeting at Tenterden Town Station. This was an important development in the continuing tension over the K&ESR's heritage. At that time no Terrier was in traffic and this new group had been formed by members concerned that the class should once again run on the K&ESR, which at that time, rightly or wrongly, was much associated with the Austerity tank locos. It was not without significance that the new organisation attracted a more than adequate degree of support. By that date, No. 3 *Bodiam* (32670) sat forlorn and minus its boiler on Orpins siding, *Sutton* was out of traffic although on display at Tenterden and *Knowle* continued in a disassembled state. There was a widespread feeling, and not just among traditionalists, that an essential 'essence' of the K&ESR was being ignored.

The Terrier Trust was granted recognition as a Registered Charity, an initial objective being to purchase No. 3 from Ron and Vic Wheele, the then owners, and then to raise the necessary funds to fully restore it complete with a new boiler. The longer-term aims were much wider, giving support and help in any way possible to the other Terriers on the K&ESR. This was reflected in its statement of objectives:

> To advance public education by the acquisition, preservation and restoration of locomotives of the 'Terrier' class designed by William Stroudley for the former London Brighton and South Coast Railway, and the exhibition thereof for the public benefit. Such locomotives will be domiciled on the Kent and East Sussex railway operated by the Tenterden Railway Company Limited, itself a Registered Charity.

The publication in the *Terrier* of the annual 'Tickets Please!' article revealed that 1995 had been yet another disappointing year; 61,406 was the lowest number of paying passenger numbers since 1987. Wealden Pullman numbers were down and even the Santa Specials had experienced a 2 per cent reduction on the previous year, although their income had been above budget. For 1996, a determined effort was to be made to bring in coach parties and there were to be added attractions such as the new Museum. It was hoped that the end of the recession would see many more passengers, higher income and success in bringing down the still daunting debts.

The Railway had however succeeded in turning its finances round during 1995, the 1994 deficit of £21,945 being replaced by a surplus of £29,837. It was stated in the *Tenterden Terrier* that there were three reasons for this. Firstly, the net income from operating trains actually improved by about £8,000, despite the drop in visitor numbers which was attributed to the warm summer which had been experienced. Secondly, filming receipts, always unpredictable, increased from £4,300 to £37,495. Thirdly, exceptional costs which dropped from £27,872 to £9,748. Operating costs had also been contained during the year. In particular, the Vintage Train – hauled by economical locomotives (*Charwelton* and the P Class) together with reduced A set (Mark 1) train lengths – saved £10,000 in fuel and water costs. In addition to the improved filming income, donations and catering receipts showed excellent growth from £68,000 to nearly £82,000.

There was nonetheless an increase in finance costs due to the higher charges that the banks were making for their services. Bank borrowings rose slightly to £411,525 as a result of higher working capital requirements. Overall, the objective was to reduce borrowings in 1996 and achieve a surplus of at least £50,000 per annum in order to build up reserves.

Another route to easing the financial position was to secure grants and donations. The opportunity to explore these options had begun by chance some two years earlier, in the summer of 1994, when Norman Brice had been en route to Paris. With the Channel Tunnel yet to open and as a change from flying, Norman had been on a train from Boulogne one Sunday afternoon. Glancing out of the window when passing through the small station of Noyelles near the north coast of France, he noticed a couple of metre-gauge steam locomotives shunting wooden-bodied coaches. This was the Chemin de Fer de la Baie de Somme (CFBS) – one of France's leading heritage railways. Although being metre gauge, the line had a section of mixed gauge track between Noyelles and St Valery. From this unexpected sighting, the K&ESR initiated a formal twinning with the CFBS as part of a strategy of attracting external funding for the new projects to which both railways aspired but could not then afford.

A formal signature of the resulting agreement between the K&ESR and the CFBS took place during the afternoon of Saturday, 27 April 1996 at Noyelles during the host railway's Festival of Steam – a major event in the French heritage railway calendar. The P class, which had shunted at Boulogne during the First World War, accompanied various K&ESR representatives to the twinning ceremony and actually ran on the CFBS. The whole expedition crossed the Channel on the P&O ferry *Pride of Burgundy*, a most appropriate vessel as volunteer driver Howard Wallace-Sims was her Engineering Officer. It was not the last time that there would be cross-Channel visits by CFBS and K&ESR personnel.

No one was under any illusion that the K&ESR could finance new projects from either additional borrowings or retained surpluses. The overriding objective had to be the reduction of bank borrowings and the consequent interest charges. Nor could any reliance be placed upon large-scale donations from the members or even the otherwise successful Bond sales – many of the Northiam issue remained unsold. It was against this background that the link with the CFBS came into its own. The 'InterReg II' programme of the European Commission aimed to regenerate border areas which might have suffered as a consequence of the introduction of the 'Single Market' a couple of years earlier. Though really intended to aid areas adjacent to land frontiers, eligibility for InterReg funding also extended to Kent and East Sussex, which were considered near enough to France to be 'borders'. A prime requirement of InterReg was that a project in one country be supported by a partner in an adjacent state. The project did not need to be a joint one, nor actually involve trans-frontier activity, but it did have to have the support of a body on the other side. For the purposes of InterReg, Kent was linked to the Départements (the equivalent of counties) Nord and Pas de Calais. East Sussex was linked to Somme and Seine Maritime. To qualify for InterReg the K&ESR needed a partner in any one of these Départements. The CFBS fitted the bill nicely.

There were numerous organisations willing to make grants available for specific projects, but it was difficult to determine who they were and what criteria applied to which grant. Norman Brice had identified many organisations which offered grants in Kent and East Sussex and who all had slightly different objectives. The key was to match the donor to the project. Despite the availability of such grants, the K&ESR had been able to take only limited advantage of them for some years because of the '50 per cent rule'. What this meant was that public sector donors, be they the EU, UK government or local authority, offered a maximum of half the eligible project costs. The Railway's difficult financial position meant that the Company had been unable to provide the matching half. There was however now a solution to this problem – the National Lottery. The Lottery had five separate Funds which disbursed grants: Arts, Charities, Heritage, Sport and the Millennium Fund. The Tenterden Railway Company, being a registered educational charity, was eligible to apply to both the Heritage and Millennium Funds. The former was aimed at preserving and restoring Britain's heritage. The Millennium Fund was intended for projects which would mark the turn of the twenty-first century. These projects had to be finished by 31 December 1999. Lottery funds could provide the half of the project costs which the public sector would not contribute. This was similar to the approach which the Ffestiniog Railway had used in undertaking the much larger and far more costly scheme to rebuild the Welsh Highland Line.

It was to be an approach which pointed the way ahead for the Kent & East Sussex and the Board decided that the Railway was in a position to go to Bodiam and tap the traffic potential of the National Trust's castle. Project Final Push became Bodiam 2000, the name of a temporary subsidiary company which was set up under the Chairmanship of Norman Brice to run the project. The Board then made the momentous decision to apply for Millennium Commission funding. More than two decades later, one has a recollection of life on the Railway moving up a gear during 1996. Although optimistic statements made at the time back this up, it might of course only be a subjective impression. It was nevertheless a time when I had settled back into the workforce and felt part of the K&ESR community. Well remembered are the glorious summer evenings of motor cycling down the old drove roads south of Maidstone and opening the throttle on the long straights of the eighteenth-century turnpikes as the Kentish Plain gently climbed on to the High Weald. This would invariably be a Friday evening, the K&ESR already having a feeling of welcome mixed with anticipation of the running weekend to follow.

The optimistic statements included one by the Chairman, Robin Dyce (*Tenterden Terrier* winter 1996) that a 20 per cent upturn in trade had occurred during the year. A significant development appeared on Saturday, 31 August when 200 cream teas were served to passengers from a cruise ship using the then-new terminal at Dover – the beginnings of a lucrative income stream which would grow in later years. By the end of September, 62,650 passengers had been conveyed, compared to 49,970 in 1995 and 59,334 the year previously. All this was to be welcomed but had only appeared after considerable effort by every department to ensure that all business opportunities were grasped and commitments met. It was hoped that at the end of the year a significant reduction could be made to the bank loan.

Chapter 19

On-site visitor attractions had been much enhanced during 1996 when the Colonel Stephens exhibits in the Town Museum were relocated to their new Romney hut location at Tenterden Town Station. Central to the displays was a replica of the Colonel's office at Tonbridge. This was fitted out with the original furniture and numerous other items which had come to the heritage-era K&ESR thanks to the foresight and generosity of the Austen family. In addition, the archives were moved from their temporary store in another part of the same Romney hut to a newly constructed mezzanine above part of the Museum area where they were to be made available to researchers. Work had commenced at the end of 1995, and, by the following summer, the first section was opened to visitors. The Museum's most substantial exhibit arrived on 20 February 1997 when Shropshire & Montgomeryshire 0-4-2T *Gazelle*, said to be the world's smallest standard gauge locomotive, was placed on loan from the National Railway Museum. Arriving one cold winter's afternoon, the locomotive looked if anything slightly silly sitting on a low loader which appeared big enough to take a Bulleid Pacific. An equally enormous crane then lifted it onto a temporary track which enabled this venerable survivor to be pushed through the Romney hut's roller shutter door. This door has only been opened twice since, the occasions when *Gazelle* left for, and later returned from, an exhibition in York.

During the early months of 1997, an interesting piece of industrial archaeology began at Tenterden Town Station. In the nineteenth century, Tenterden had been a thriving livestock market based in and around the High Street. In 1888, in connection with this, the Borough of Tenterden had installed a weighbridge with a small operator's hut on the south side of the High Street. Following the extension of the Railway to the Town station in 1904, the market itself was moved beside the goods yard. The K&ESR bought the weighbridge and hut for £10 in 1905 and arranged for their repositioning by 1907. The goods yard was extended about this time to add two extra sidings and the yard's still-extant second gated entrance built. The bulky weighbridge itself was installed where the containers at the rear of the offices now stand.

Livestock traffic had faded out by the early 1930s. The weighbridge may have been used for general weighing thereafter but probably fell out of use except for mineral traffic. It was slowly forgotten, disappearing under layers of coal dust and dirt. Henry Edwards nonetheless recalled where it was. At the end of February 1997, one of two waste paper skips positioned over the site was stolen and a small group took the opportunity to excavate the site. The corners and part of the weighbridge platform were located five inches down. After temporary reburial to protect the table, the team returned in the autumn of 1997, when they succeeded in lifting the heavy structure and transporting it to the far end of the Station Industrial Estate for storage. The weighbridge was identified as W&T Avery's special 'Farmers weighbridge', probably a model 145 No. 2, designed to weigh items up to five tons, and it originally had detachable railings to contain livestock. The balance platform was in reasonable condition but showed slight damage, perhaps evidence of an attempt at scrapping. The steelyard and its cast pillar were missing. The operator's office had, of course, long disappeared. An unsuccessful attempt was made to obtain a Millennium grant to restore the weighbridge, with a replica hut, on the site of the picnic area fronting the Museum. The huge components of the weighbridge are still in storage awaiting restoration at the time of writing. (*Tenterden Terrier* spring 2020.)

On the personal front once again, it was in the final weeks of 1996 that I took early retirement at age 50, like many others in local authority employment at that time. In answer to the suggestion that I should attend an early retirement course my boss replied that there was no need, 'He's got his life sorted.' As I had done on leaving school in 1965, the first thing I did was to head straight for the Kent & East Sussex Railway. These were the years when there were many early retirees, and the heritage railways were to greatly benefit from them.

The upbeat theme continued with the editorial to the Spring 1997 issue of the *Tenterden Terrier*, beginning with the editorial:

> The exciting news that we have moved forward to the long-listed stage in our bid for Millennium funding brings the Bodiam project one step nearer. Putting this into context, it means that we are one of 156 organisations from around 1900 original applicants bidding for a share of around £170 million available and we have a one in four chance of success. Furthermore, we are one of only two heritage railways to be included. Our crucial hurdle at this stage is to provide match funding, although this in itself will not guarantee success. So far only 10 per cent of the membership have indicated that they will support a bond issue, so the campaign must be both broadened and better publicised. It would be a pity to fail now, when there is so much to go for and so much has been achieved.

The same issue informed members that 1996 had proved to be a very good year for the Railway, with total passenger numbers up by 21.6 per cent overall from 66,751 to 80,528. In fact, if the Santa Special results were eliminated, then the rise was almost 24 per cent, the largest for over ten years and exceeding even 1990's (Northiam reopening increase) 22.5 per cent. Passengers joining the train at Northiam rose by 44.7 per cent, although this trend was not to last once Bodiam was reached. The twin aims of reducing borrowing and achieving an income surplus of at least £50,000 had both been met. The surplus was £62,784 and indebtedness fell by £52,942 to £358,583, thanks to a near doubling of profits from trading activities – particularly the contribution from catering and buffet services as well as from the gift shop. It was regretted that the margin obtained on running trains was low (3.7 per cent in 1996) but it was coming to be accepted that this core activity would always have to be supported by the other aspects of the business. Members were also told that the wages bill was up and that the Company now had thirteen employees. There was the usual plea for more volunteers.

The 'caravan' of the K&ESR might have been continuing on its way but the 'dogs' of national life were certainly barking away during the first few months of 1997. The whole political and social era which had begun with the General Election of 1979 was drawing to a close in sleazy discredit, and this was to be one of those landmark moments which plot the course of history. The General Election on 1 May 1997 not only brought a Labour landslide (although obviously not pleasing everyone) but a tangible pepping up of the country's morale. As a lighter aside to this, within two days of the election Britain had won the Eurovision Song Contest and England had beaten the Australians in a Test Match! Because of the later mistakes of the Blair government, it is sometimes forgotten that the bright sunny morning of 2 May was the beginning of a buoyant and optimistic period – comparable with the 1960s – which went on into the new century. It was against that background that the K&ESR enjoyed its commercial upswing and focused on reaching Bodiam.

The early months of the year saw the arrival of Class 33 Bo-Bo diesel-electric 33052 (D6570) *Ashford* following the initiative of several members who consequently formed a further owning group. Interest in medium-sized diesels, not least ex-Southern Region ones, followed on from the presence of 73126 during 1991. It had gained further impetus with the short-term visit during 1992 of Class 25 D7672 (25322) *Tamworth Castle*. This decidedly non-Southern diesel had nonetheless been popular with loco crews and led several members to purchase the unserviceable D7585 (25235). Although not lacking in controversy, that locomotive had languished out of use awaiting restoration. The presence of D7585 on the K&ESR and its possible restoration continued to be contentious for many years afterwards and had still not been entirely resolved at the time of writing.

D6570 was however immediately operational motive power, and there was an instant division of opinion. The traditionalist, basically pro-steam, view was expressed in a letter to the summer 1997 *Tenterden Terrier*. This was however not entirely anti diesel and recognised the value of this form of traction for shunting, engineers' trains and as reserve motive power. It particularly mentioned the K&ESR's Class 14 0-6-0s in this respect. The pro-diesel viewpoint saw the acquisition of a Class 33 as an extension of the rationale for the ex-Western Region machines. In addition, the moderate size of Class 33 (something it shared with Class 25) made the type acceptable in the context of the K&ESR. The offer of a Class 37 was later rejected on the grounds that it was too large.

I have an interest to declare in respect of both Class 33 and Hither Green Depot where D6570 had spent much of its time. My early published work was about these very subjects. The emotional appeal of the arrival of a 'Crompton' on my Railway was naturally considerable. Rather more rationally, I supported the arrival of D6570 on the grounds that it represented the upward size limit for diesel locomotives. 33052 arrived in rail blue but fairly quickly was restored to its appearance when new, albeit with the Ashford nameplates. It performed a useful role in the K&ESR's locomotive fleet for some years until an accumulation of defects led to it being laid aside. It was eventually sold to another group and moved to the Bluebell Railway on 1 July 2021.

The grant funding process, however, was dragging on. The Millennium Commission's decision had been put back because of the General Election, and then the selection process was changed. A decision was now expected around October. The K&ESR had provisionally been offered £150,000 from English Partnerships. This did not mean that work on the extension could begin, because it was necessary to have all the funding in place before the Railway could commit itself to the project. In addition to the various grants, Bearer Bonds were once again to be issued in various values up to £5000; this aspect of fund raising was also on hold until the grant funding was known. The wisdom of the decision to again resort to Bonds has been questioned in later years, particularly as they were being offered at the attractive interest rate of 8 per cent. It hardly needs to be pointed out that in addition to adding to the existing level of debt, they would ultimately have to be repaid, in this case in 2013. The anxiety raised as that deadline approached, and a proposal for tackling the issue, will feature prominently in due course.

The cost of the extension was rising, partially because of the intended greater use of contract labour, but also the need to bring in materials. The drainage along the route would have to be totally rebuilt, with the original clay pipe cross drains being time-expired and the longitudinal drains having silted up through the long years without maintenance. Even though the track had been cleared six years previously, the vegetation had regrown vigorously. This had occurred to such an extent that a team undertaking a drainage survey had had to cut their way onto the trackbed to try to find the cross drains shown on the old track plans. It would have been impracticable to expect volunteers to complete this task in time, so this was an area where contractors would be used to prepare the trackbed prior to the P.Way Department relaying the track.

The Millennium Commission further delayed the decision-making process and a pronouncement was scheduled for 12 November. The K&ESR's final stage in the process was to answer a Detailed Assessment Review following which the Commission confirmed on 11 October that all the information required had been completed satisfactorily. An application for £100,000 through the European Inter-Reg fund had been submitted, and Norman Brice travelled to France to get all the various documents signed by the CFBS and the Département Somme. The K&ESR was supported by the Government Office South-East.

The project was now effectively running nearly a year later than planned. As a result, it was decided to remove the old track materials between Northiam and Bodiam. This had to be done at the Company's expense, but the Millennium Commission had said that a retrospective claim could be made if the grant application was successful. Track clearance started on 28 August. A 360° digger was first sent through to clear the brambles and saplings before the P.Way gang removed the rail fixings. These materials were then carried back to a compound at Northiam. The digger then removed what was left of the sleepers and graded the track bed. Where the sleepers were supposed to be the wood had rotted away, although they were still intact under the chairs and every screw had to be taken out. Just after Padgham crossing, about 2½ miles from Northiam, the undergrowth was worse than ever. A tree stub had grown up round a fish plate and covered the whole joint. When the joint was uncovered, the nuts had rusted away to such an extent that no spanner would grip them. Although there was now an open route along the line, the whole line was classed as a construction site and for safety reasons it is was off limits to anyone not directly involved.

Despite the stiff competition, approval of a grant of £975,000 for the Bodiam extension was given in late 1997. The announcement of this was, for me, one of those outstanding Kent & East Sussex moments – I heard it form part of a list of such grants announced during a TV news bulletin – my wife, in another room, wondered what the whoop of delight was about! The K&ESR was, as mentioned, required as a condition to match this from other sources. Some of the money was raised through the Bodiam Bond issue, voluntary work valued at £275,000, the Derelict Land Grant and assistance from Ashford Borough and Rother District councils. The twinning arrangement with the CFBS now paid off because grant assistance was received from the EU under the Inter-Reg scheme. The CFBS received a FFr2million grant for a complementary project to relay the St Valery to Cayeux section, restore various items of stock, fit brakes to all passenger vehicles and install automatic barriers on road crossings.

A major issue of concern at the Volunteers' Meeting held on 31 January 1998 was about the requirement of the Millennium Commission to take some form of security over the K&ESR's assets – the Commission had a statutory duty to safeguard the public monies it was distributing. Following negotiations, the Commission took a third charge on the Company's land, though not its moveable assets (e.g. rolling stock). This third charge was to be after the first charge to the National Westminster Bank to safeguard its loan to the Tenterden Railway Company and the second charge to the Environment Agency (successor to the National River Authority) in respect of any damage caused – for example, by the collapse of a bridge. The passenger figures for 1997

(*Tenterden Terrier* No. 75, spring 1998) showed decidedly mixed results, with a small overall decrease in passengers carried – 72,775 against 73,365 in 1996. Ordinary passenger numbers had actually increased by 0.8 per cent but the Santa Specials reduced by 9.1 per cent. The number of foreign visitors – the Dutch have always been prominent among these – had continued as a trend, first noticed the previous year, despite the adverse effects a strong Pound was having on exchange rates. Another pointer to a future positive income stream was the experiment of running a service during the October half term. Whether it was realised or not at the time, this probably tapped the so-called 'grey market' of older people preferring to travel after the main holiday period and in this instance taking their grandchildren out for the day. Loadings were around a satisfactory 70 per train. This contrasted with 56 on ordinary services at other times of the year which was perilously close to the 55 per train of 1995 – an all-time low. The cause was an excessive number of trains: 300 more of them than in 1996. The obvious remedy was to run fewer trains the following year, a move which would also help the volunteer staff position.

1997 had however been marginally more successful financially, the surplus increasing from £62,784 to £68,062 excluding exceptional items. (*Tenterden Terrier* No. 76, summer 1998) The margin achieved running trains, calculated as a ratio of net to total income, improved from 3.7 per cent to 7.6 per cent, with 36 per cent arising from operating trains and 64 per cent from trading – compared with 15 per cent and 85 per cent respectively in 1996. These may sound like dry accounting statistics, but they illustrate the realities of running a heritage railway. The message informing members of these facts was an article by Bernard Sealy for the *Tenterden Terrier*. In later years, I was to hear at first hand variations of the theme from Philip Shaw as Finance Director, his emphasis on the importance of the trading income usually being accompanied by the pithy, although gentlemanly, comment, 'Running trains is a dead loss – and probably always will be.' Lastly, members were told that the average number of employees was now nineteen as opposed to thirteen in the previous year. Although this included staff taken on for the Bodiam project, it was an indication of the future.

Another staffing development with an eye to future years was the recruitment of apprentices. It said much for the growing maturity of the heritage railways sector that near the turn of the century they were able to provide engineering training both in traditional skills and those transferable to the wider railway industry. The first two recruited by the Kent & East Sussex were Ben Swan and John Waddington. Both were enrolled in a day release course funded by the government, through Kent Tech at the South Kent College in Ashford. They were to learn of the skills needed at Rolvenden both from the full-time staff and from the volunteer workers.

The growing number of paid staff sometimes led to disquiet among the volunteers. The subject was addressed by Chairman Robin Dyce in the *Tenterden Terrier*:

> The Kent and East Sussex Railway has long been proud of the fact that it is a volunteer-led railway. However, gradually this is changing as full-time salaried staff are employed in critical posts. In a number of cases it has been necessary to employ further staff to meet increased trading expectations.
>
> In embarking upon this policy of employing more paid staff it has been, and will continue to be, essential to ensure that the Railway is not being run just to pay for more salaried staff. It is the salaried staff who are increasingly contributing to the financial well-being of the Railway.

Put simply, the Railway cannot sustain the level of business now being attracted using volunteer input alone. If we are to offer a high level of business and reap the benefits, it is essential that delivery promises are met and quality maintained. By employing salaried staff in critical positions we can ensure that our promises can be consistently met. Despite these opening comments the involvement of volunteers will continue to be vital to the future success of the Railway.

The matter of paid staff would in time also involve me; meanwhile my involvement as a volunteer took a new turn. About three years previously, I had been trained by Philip Whiteman as a carriage examiner, carrying out a routine procedure on operational carriages on a two-month cycle to determine whether or not a vehicle was fit to run. Following Philip's departure for Birmingham University (where he is now a noted academic specialising in local government) I took over, as a volunteer, the running of that side of the Carriage & Wagon Department. The positive approach taken by C&W since 1993 was however beginning to run out of steam. This was partly due to personalities and personal relationships; it was also, unfortunately, due to criticism of the department, some of which was justified.

I kept notes between April and June 1997 which are often a catalogue of complaints as well as mechanical and electrical defects together with the efforts to rectify these. Read today these give the impression of a willing department trying to manage with too few resources. There was also the curious allegation – of unknown origin and never substantiated – that the C&W department, in its restoration work, was working to too high a standard! It says a lot for the camaraderie and generally friendly nature of the K&ESR that the Department held together at all, although morale was beginning to suffer. On the wider Railway, Philip Clark-Monks had resigned as Company Secretary in the early months of 1997. I was again offered the job (by Robin Dyce and without the position being advertised) but once more refused as I was fairly certain I was being tarred with the brush of C&W's problems. If that were the case, attempting to gain any respect or establish working relationships would have been difficult. I had also been retired for over 12 months and was on the look-out for paid work nearer home. I suggested to Robin that he offer the job to another long-standing member, Cathy Roberts (now Cathy Crotty). She accepted. Around the same time, Bernard Sealy asked me to stand for the Board. Gut instinct told me not to. I wasn't completely averse to doing more and took on the additional voluntary post of Rolling Stock Administrator to help David Stratton with vehicle ownership records and Hire Agreements.

Matters came to a head in March 1998 when, for the second time is just over a year, a paid Carriage and Wagon Manager stepped down. A few other C&W people left around this time but most of the volunteers kept going. To plug the gap until someone with an appropriate background could be recruited, I was appointed as paid Acting Manager. This was for three days per week, although I often worked more, and as I was already a part-owner of the latest (Mark 1 BCK) mess coach at Tenterden Town, accommodation was not a problem. I had learned a lot as a carriage examiner but was fortunate in having the highly competent Alan Brice as Workshop Foreman. It was an exciting and challenging three months during which I was able to draw on earlier, not always positive, experience as a Team Leader in local government. If I achieved nothing else, I did manage to revive the department's morale – they seemed to like working for me. Resources Manager Neil Sime later said I had 'pointed C&W in the right direction'.

Eventually, Clive Lowe was appointed as Manager, and I was asked to stay on as C&W Administrator (Depot Clerk in railway parlance). Clive had been (and is still today) a long-standing K&ESR volunteer and a professional railwayman with a solid background in practical engineering.

He had a well-known forthright manner and had been prominent among C&W's recent critics. On the face of it we were utterly different people. We had however previously – in the pub – discovered that we both had family backgrounds going back a couple of generations in Suffolk's Ipswich railway community. We were able to build on this and following a frank exchange of views – refereed by Neil Sime – we got on well (and still do).

On 26 April, the CFBS held its 1998 '*Fête de la Vapeur*' and, as part of the joint marketing programme, the K&ESR again attended with a locomotive. As the P Class has been withdrawn for a ten-year overhaul, the possibility of sending one of the USA tanks was considered, the class having worked in France after D-Day, but it was soon found that a 43 ton locomotive would be too heavy for the dual gauge track. *Charwelton* went instead, despite a ferry strike which was resolved just in time.

A significant stage in the Bodiam project was reached on Wednesday, 27 May 1998 when Director Norman Brice and Company Secretary Cathy Roberts put their signatures to the formal Agreement with the Millennium Commission for the £975,000 grant. It had now been decided that services would resume to Bodiam on 2 April 2000, the centenary of the day the Rother Valley Railway had opened between Robertsbridge and Rolvenden Station (named Tenterden until 1903). Now that work had started and the overgrowth cleared between the fence lines, contractors tendering for the job could clearly see what was involved. The main groundwork contract had been let to Roe Roads. Work began on 1 June and the transformation of the site is remembered as dramatic. Tasks included the replacement of all cross/longitudinal drains, cleaning out of all the ditches, renewing all the gates and fencing, levelling the formation, and Bodiam platform works. Interesting as all this might be to the average railway enthusiast, the whole site remained closed to everyone except the contractors and the P.Way Department. Visits required permission.

During the year, Footplate Experience Courses were developed from the Railway Experience Days, much greater emphasis being placed on the opportunity to drive a train. The help of Clive Groome was enlisted, this being a 'product' which he offered on other heritage railways. He demonstrated his approach to members of the Locomotive Department to enable them to run similar courses on the K&ESR. Other staff acted as 'guinea pig' participants. These courses, now again known as Railway Experience Days, have grown to such an extent both in popularity and profitability that at some points during the season's 'shoulder periods' it is worth running them instead of offering a public service.

On 22 May 1998 the Colonel Stephens Museum, by then fully established in its Romney Hut, was officially declared open. I was among the invited guests, in my case on the grounds that I was Acting Carriage & Wagon Manager and that the Department had made various contributions to the project. It was a fine if breezy afternoon and the opening ceremony was held on the gravel area in front of the building. The principal guest, who performed the ceremony, was no less than that controversial figure Sir Neil Cossons OBE, Director of the Science Museum. An opening 'works plate' (now displayed in the entrance to the Museum) had been mounted on a board and covered by curtains in 'company maroon'. The nameplate and crests of the then recently withdrawn No. 73126 *Kent & East Sussex Railway* were to be presented by EWS Railways, and these were also mounted and covered by a drape. The Vintage Train was in the station platform, headed by *Charwelton*, and from 2pm the 75 guests plus members of the media started to assemble.

In addition to Sir Neil Cossons, the great and the good were there in some force, local and regional dignitaries present including the Mayor of Tenterden, Councillor Mrs Jill Kirk; Yvonne Painter, President of the Tenterden Chamber of Commerce; Guy Purdy, Museums Officer, South Eastern Museums Service; and Fred Cubbage, Chief Executive of the South East England Tourist

Board. Among a number of distinguished railway guests was John Snell, Vice-Chairman of the Heritage Railway Association, a legendary figure regarded as the first heritage railway volunteer (with the Talyllyn Railway in 1951). I don't recall actually meeting Mr Snell on that occasion but was to have rather more to do with him a few years later. Helen Ashby represented the National Railway Museum, York, and Jean-Marc Page and Arnaud Girode the CFBS. The modern scene was represented by Simon Ball, Area Engineer EWS, and Barry Stephens, Contract Support Manager from the same company.

At 2.30pm, John Miller, the Honorary Curator, acknowledged Philip Shaw's initiative in starting the collection more than 25 years earlier. John then introduced Sir Neil who spoke of 'this extraordinary collection of materials, vividly telling the story of Colonel Stephens', before drawing the curtains aside to reveal the 'works plate'. Simon Ball then presented the nameplate and crests from No. 73126 to the Museum.

Refreshments were then taken in an adjacent marquee before, at 3.45pm, the Vintage Train departed for a trip to Northiam and back. I took full advantage of this special working, but not to 'network' with the notable railway historians and academics aboard. Sometime previously, C&W Department had discovered that two of the cast iron buffer shanks on the L&NWR Balcony Saloon were fractured. Specialist welding was available at Rolvenden and any available train was an obvious way of moving the defective items to the loco shed. I had moved one of the fractured shanks to the luggage compartment of the SE&CR Family Saloon earlier in the day and travelled with it down the hill. Thus it was that the distinguished guests had to wait at Rolvenden Station whilst the goatee-bearded scruff, who had at least had the decency to wear the company tie and stand at the back during the opening ceremony, struggled on to the platform with a 6ft long metal shaft complete with buffer head.

Progress on the Bodiam extension was dramatic during the summer of 1998, the contractors having completed work on the formation as well as at Bodiam station. The trackbed between Northiam and Bodiam level crossing had required substantial works to reverse the years when there had been no maintenance as well as the economical style of construction a century earlier. Every cross drain had now been replaced with spun concrete steel reinforced pipes bedded in on a concrete base. Where possible the pipe size was increased and the level dropped, to improve the drainage for the railway and the surrounding land. At Mill Ditch, twin 1.2m concrete pipes, each section weighing over three tonnes, were installed and the track level was raised by 400mm to disperse the loading of the trains over a greater surface area of the pipes. Despite these improvements, this site was unfortunately to be the cause of later problems. In addition to this contractor-led work, the K&ESR P.Way department had assembled the track in the Bodiam station area. There was a brief alarming episode when the contractor went bankrupt, but a replacement company was rapidly found.

Bodiam station presented a difficult balancing act. It was necessary to have a station which met passenger requirements and modern safety standards, but which had the look and feel of the K&ESR as well as honouring a pledge to local interests that the view from the castle would be unaltered. To meet the commercial needs of the heritage era, it was vital that the platform was extended to accommodate revenue-earning five-coach trains. To limit the length of the platform extension, the Northiam end loop point was relocated into the highway, thus allowing the clearance point on the loop to be beside the station building rather than 20m (approximately the length of a bogie coach) past the building towards Robertsbridge. K&ESR Engineer Peter Barber related an anecdote about local authority approval for the crossing in the *Tenterden Terrier* for winter 1998.

After the level crossing was laid the council came out to assess the new crossing. The (council) engineer arrived first and had some concerns about the levels on the crossing. When his clerk of works arrived he was asked to try the crossing out at around 35 to 40mph. A wry smile appeared on the clerk of works' face as he climbed into his van. With tyres smoking the van headed off at speed over the crossing towards Staplecross; the same was repeated in the Bodiam direction. Obviously not convinced, the van departed at breakneck speed hitting the crossing at a vast rate of knots, screeching to a halt spinning round and returning at equal haste. The van then squealed to a halt and the clerk of works appeared out of the smoke to say that the ride was not too bad if you didn't push it!

At the opposite end of the station the loop was extended to the furthest extremity of the yard, which effectively closed off the narrowest part where the turnout to the sidings had previously been.

During the reconstruction work the sidings were lifted but they were relaid in as near to original condition as possible, with a mix of spiked flat bottom and bullhead rail and a flat bottom turnout acquired from the Llangollen Railway. The yard was reconnected to the running line by an extended siding running behind the platform, this in turn requiring the acquisition of further land to the south of the yard. The original platform was of unreinforced concrete with a blue brick coping; the replacement was also concrete with the overhang cast into the face, making possible a replica brick coping. Platform lamps were replicas of the original acetylene lanterns mounted on wooden posts, but electrically illuminated. It was decided to provide public lavatories and these were designed by Humphrey Atkinson. To be as unobtrusive as possible these were after the style of a coal office and placed at the back of the yard to the right of the cattle dock. The contract for the construction of the toilet building was placed with Alan and John Brice of the Carriage & Wagon Department in between their paid work for the Railway.

A typical K&ESR service of the 1974 season; No 10 *Sutton* leads two Maunsell coaches down Tenterden Bank. *Rail Archive Stephenson*

GWR Railcar No 20 at Tenterden Town on 25 April 1974. *Brian Stephenson*

Early days at Rolvenden. Volunteers Philip Wheeler (left) and (before he was famous) Mike Hart.
Chris Mitchell

K&ESR No 22 Maunsell at Rolvenden with a solitary Brake Nondescript Open coach in the early days after the reopening of the Tenterden–Popes Cottage section. *Chris Mitchell*

The original Newmill Channel bridge. The location today bears little resemblance to this scene. *CSRM*

Bridge components at Rolvenden ready to be moved to Newmill Channel. *John Liddell Collection/CSRM*

Newmill Bridge components being craned into position. *John Liddell Collection/CSRM*

The replacement bridge which allowed the reopening to Wittersham Road. *John Liddell Collection/CSRM*

The first passenger train to Wittersham Road crosses Newmill Bridge. *Brian Stephenson*

Flooding at Wittersham Road in late December 1979. *John Liddell*

Volunteer Doug Lindsay serving aperitifs to Julian Morrell (former Catering Superintendent of the Pullman Car Company) and Frank Harding (former Pullman Managing Director) aboard *Barbara* on 18 July 1981. *Doug Lindsay Collection*

The Carriage & Wagon Shed at Tenterden under construction in 1981. *John Liddell Collection/CSRM*

The NRMs Rocket on Tenterden Bank during its 1981 visit. *Brian Stephenson*

The locomotive crews on the occasion of the visit of HM Queen Mother on 9 June 1982. L to R, top: Jack Hoad, Jack Davey, Paul Hatcher; bottom; Fred French, Adrian Landi. *Brian Stephenson*

Ivatt Class 2 No 41241 banked by Charwelton climbs Tenterden Bank on 2 January 1983. *Alan Crotty*

Hunslet Austerity boilered *Iron Duke* in Kensington Gardens on 2 April 1985. Left to right, Mark Stuchbury, K&ESR fireman; Pete Wensley K&ESR driver; Dick Hardy, retired senior BR manager; John Bellwood, Chief Mechanical Engineer, National Railway Museum. *Brian Stephenson*

The former Maidstone Bus Station re-erected as the Buffet (or Refreshment Rooms) at Tenterden Town Station. *Brian Stephenson*

On 8 August 1986, four wheel carriage bodies 3062 (left) and 2947 are lowered into their temporary storage position at the rear of Tenterden Town Buffet. *Stuart Philips*

A 1980s scene. The lifted section of track; photographed from Northiam level crossing, looking back towards Wittersham Road. *CSRM*

The Kit Kat poster as seen by the author, albeit in a different location to that described in the text. *Brian Stephenson*

Rolvenden signal box nearing completion on 7 May 1988. *Brian Stephenson*

The official opening of the Colonel Stephens Museum on 22 May 1998. Sir Neil Cossens, OBE, Director of the Science Museum is seated on the left of the picture. *CSRM*

Chapter 20

Writing in the *Tenterden Terrier* for spring 1999, the Chairman, Robin Dyce, said that the K&ESR had had another good year during the previous 12 months. Passenger numbers had risen marginally and the balance had shifted slightly from general family visitors towards group bookings and the lucrative charter market – a trend that was to continue over the following two decades. Final figures for the 1998 season revealed that 80,361 passengers were carried. The *Terrier* commented that this had been a satisfactory year at a time when many tourist attractions were experiencing difficulties and that numbers were largely static. Some modest improvements had been negated by falls in other areas and the service had been reduced by more than 100 trains with no apparent effect on passenger numbers. June, July and August, the main months for 'ordinary' passengers, saw a rise of 1.4 per cent. Despite this, the loadings per train continued to disappoint. The *Terrier* item (written by Finance Department member Ray Collins and influential volunteer Duncan Buchanan) concluded that although the opening to Northiam represented the high point for passengers, if one ignored the novelty element of extending the line, this suggested that the real peak had been in 1993. The passengers per train numbers had also peaked in 1990, but subsequently had been consistently lower than prior to opening to Northiam.

The *Tenterden Terrier* also informed members that whilst trading activities from the Shop, 'Wealden Belle' and Buffet had increased their income in total by 2½ per cent (in line with inflation), revenue from running service trains was down on 1997, in part due to the absence of certain 'one off' sources of income which had boosted the results for the previous year. Direct operating expenses were also significantly higher, as investment had been made in locomotives and rolling stock maintenance and repairs. It was anticipated that the year 2000 would give the K&ESR a considerable boost once the extension to Bodiam opened. Large items of expenditure were of course occurring in connection with the Bodiam project, but these were fully funded by the Millennium and other grants as well as from the new Bond issue which once launched had proved very successful.

During the early weeks of 1999, track laying was half a mile ahead of schedule. (*Tenterden Terrier* spring 1999.) The first mile out of Bodiam was in the bullhead rail previously on that section, the relaying proceeding at about 100m per day. The new flat bottom track required a steep learning curve on the part of the volunteer P.Way workers but progress at 100m per day was soon resumed, and exceeded on one occasion at 180m. Work was soon to start on extending the existing platform 1 at Northiam to allow locomotives to take water without uncoupling.

The restoration of the track was completed in less than a year, enabling a clearance train, headed by Class 03 shunter D2023, to run to Bodiam on 27 March 1999. As this was the first working over the newly rebuilt line, this movement was kept as a low key affair so as not to detract from the intended high-profile events of the following 12 months. The running of engineering trains was kept to a minimum until the track was ballasted and tamped to reduce the potential damage to the formation and permanent way. Externally, the station building at Bodiam was restored by contractors, but the Museum team took over for the internal works. None of the original internal fixtures has survived. Replacements were made using a July 1898 drawing for Northiam Station building; items included office counter, shelves, fixed bench seating and matchboard walls.

The structure of Northiam signal box, which had remained at not much more than brick base level since the extension of services, was completed by contractors and handed over to the S&T department for fitting out. This building brought a marked change to the lower end of the station and yard. Work on number 2 platform, unfinished following the 1990 reopening, commenced in mid-June and included surfacing the platform and building access ramps and a barrow crossing.

Ballasting of the track was a major logistical exercise. The granite ballast, which came from Cornwall, arrived by ship at Rye. The Environment Agency had to improve the harbour to facilitate this, although the work was also part of a long-term regeneration of the harbour area. The stone was then moved by lorry to Northiam, the first consignment arriving in early July. The extension required 18,000 tonnes or around 900 tipper lorry loads, and liaison with East Sussex County Council was necessary to ensure that disruption to normal traffic did not occur.

The Health and Safety Executive made its first visit to the extension on 14 May in the person of Stuart Johnson, the Kent Area Field Inspector. This went very smoothly; all the work had been done to standards equal to or above the requirements for a 25mph heritage line. A final inspection would be made later. Much work remained to be done and all departments now had at least some involvement with the extension. The summer and autumn were expected to put the largest strain on the railway as a whole.

The major project for the summer was the ballasting and tamping of the line, deliveries continuing through July and August and into September. To spread the amount of stone involved the K&ESR supplemented its two Dogfish hoppers by borrowing four more from the Bluebell Railway. One thousand tons were laid each day before the stone was pushed out by the Shark ballast plough. This item, which was acquired for K&ESR use by ever-enthusiastic volunteer and professional railwayman Frim Halliwell, had been renovated by the Carriage & Wagon Department ready for work on the extension. Tamping and ballast regulating followed, the use of machines for this work greatly assisting progress. The final ride was very smooth although there was a marked difference between the 95lb bullhead rail, which dated back to the 1930s, and 1990s flat-bottom rail; this was improved by rail milling some years later. The practice of welding every other joint, which had first featured between Wittersham Road and Northiam, was now extended to Northiam–Bodiam. This welding, using Thermite pots, was necessary to minimise future maintenance through a reduction in dropped joints.

Despite the focus on extending to Bodiam, 'service as usual' was continuing between Tenterden and Northiam. Most welcome was the entry into traffic during May 1999 of Terrier No. (3)2678, also known as *Knowle*, which had been rebuilt in the workshops at Rolvenden and which now appeared in black with Southern sunshine lettering. The signwriting was carried out in C&W by Meg Gooch. I recall walking into the shed one Thursday morning and, following the superb reconstruction, seeing what looked like a brand new Terrier. *Knowle*'s entry into traffic was especially fortuitous as it effectively replaced *Sutton* which, after some years out of service, was later moved by its owners to the Spa Valley Railway. This was followed in July by the arrival of replica pioneering French 0-4-0 locomotive *Marc Seguin* representing the CFBS at the celebrations for the K&ESR's 25th year since reopening. Once again, the National Railway Museum loaned the *Rocket* replica, the originals of both *Rocket* and *Marc Seguin* having been close nineteenth-century contemporaries. We should perhaps add that there was a degree of rivalry between British and French volunteer crews.

The account given thus far of the K&ESR in 1999 gives however little indication of an alarming crisis which had begun to develop during that year. Although obviously closely linked to the running of the Railway and the progress of the extension, this part of the story needs to be related separately.

Chapter 21

Despite the improvements to both passenger numbers and income compared with earlier times, when the Directors met for their September 1999 meeting, they agreed to the formation of a Finance Committee. (TRC Board Minutes No. 358 Min 7.3) The objectives of the Committee, whose membership included Bernard Sealy, the Finance Director, were:

- To advise generally on all matters relating to financial controls
- To examine the Company's financial reporting systems and make recommendations on changes and improvements
- To comment on financial budgets and make appraisals of actual levels of income and expenditure with those budgets
- To draw the Board's attention to specific items of income and expenditure that may warrant comment or investigation
- To advise generally on means of enhancing the profitability of the Company and its subsidiaries.

One of the new Committee's first recommendations was the appointment of a salaried Financial Controller. However, when *Tenterden Terrier* No. 80 was published on 20 November 1999, there was no direct indication of a major financial crisis building up. Instead the Editorial told members:

> Good housekeeping is good management. The decision of the Board to appoint a full-time Financial Controller is an essential move in the drive towards better decision making. With turnover likely to top the £1 million mark shortly, it is unreasonable to expect that this vital time-consuming function should continue to be handled primarily by a voluntary workforce. The objectives of cash management are to ensure that our assets are maintained in good order and that our resources are used efficiently. A corollary to this is that we keep our costs within carefully controlled budgets and that we measure the effectiveness of what we spend. Financial controls will ensure that the generation of income does not merely drive us along a route of profitless prosperity. More financial information will ensure that the Board is able to make the decisions to keep the railway on the right lines.

A matching piece from Chairman Robin Dyce included the following:

> In preparation for the extension to Bodiam the engineering and commercial departments have been strengthened in terms of both manpower and resources. To deal with the resulting huge increase in workload it has also been necessary to strengthen the Finance Department. Bernard Sealy and the financial team have to be thanked for their hard work in supporting the development of the Railway that has required working long hours,

many on a voluntary basis. The strengthening has been achieved by the introduction of a Finance Committee headed by Philip Shaw with support from Bernard Sealy, TRC Finance Director; Kim Richardson, Development Director; and Roy Ellis, a Director of Bodiam 2000 Ltd. The first recommendation of this Committee, accepted by the Board of the Tenterden Railway Company, is the appointment of a full-time Financial Controller. To this effect an advertisement was placed in the *Daily Telegraph* on 21st October 1999.

On 13 November, a week prior to the publication of the *Terrier*, at TRC Board meeting No. 360 the Finance Committee reported that the recruitment process for the Financial Controller had narrowed the applicants down to a shortlist of two. The Committee also reported that it had set itself the objective of making annual cost savings to 'meet the cost of employing the Finance Controller and alleviating the unsatisfactory financial position of the Company'. Some of the directors and managers were of the view that a paid book keeper was needed rather than a Financial Controller. The Committee conceded that this warranted investigation.

The committee's report also made two highly controversial suggestions. The first was that the Railway's advertising should be cut and the second was that holding the February 2000 Thomas event could be high risk in terms of profit (or loss) and should be reconsidered. Projections for the Bodiam project had indicated a cash flow pinch point between November 1999 and April 2000 which was of course why a potentially profitable Thomas event was being planned, albeit for the first time in February. It was agreed to reduce the advertising budget subject to later review. There was no immediate decision regarding Thomas and in the end it was decided to hold the event, which in view of all that happened subsequently was just as well.

At this stage, Bernard Sealy was both Finance Director and Managing Director. He had held both positions during 1998 and 1999 although it had originally been intended that this should only be for six months. In the event this unusual dual role had drifted on for two years and it was during the Board meeting of 13 November that Mr Sealy resigned as Managing Director, stating his reasons to be business commitments and the difficulty of trying to cover both posts. Board member Kim Richardson took over as MD. The Board met again on 27 November specifically to discuss the likely financial outturn for 1999 but also the crucial budget for 2000. Also on the agenda was a discussion about the Finance Controller appointment. Tim Leigh, previously a private school Bursar with experience of working for a Registered Charity, was subsequently appointed to the post.

The Board met further on 11 December 1999 and was much concerned with the considerable expenditure, and over-expenditure, on the overhaul of the Pannier Tank, Terrier *Bodiam* and Pullman Car *Barbara*. Bernard Sealy had a conflict of interest regarding the overhaul of *Barbara* and has stated that he did not take part in the relevant discussions. All this work was being undertaken by contactors, a different firm being used in each case and there was, unsurprisingly, concern that the Tenterden Railway Company might be trading while insolvent and therefore illegally. The meeting had not commenced until 12.25pm and during the earlier part of the morning Robin Dyce, Kim Richardson and Philip Shaw had met with the Company's Solicitor to discuss these issues.

The month of December of course included the vital Santa Special traffic. Passengers for these were however 4 per cent down compared with the previous year, and overall numbers for 1999 slumped to 75,917, a 6.4 per cent decrease. ('Tickets Please!', *Tenterden Terrier* Spring 2000.) None of this, as well as the foregoing financial issues, had entirely escaped the attention of the working members. Even when details were confidential, they inevitably leaked and rumours, with all their potential for inaccuracy, were running rife. A strange atmosphere was developing. On the one hand there were the celebrations of the coming new Millennium and anticipation of opening the newly rebuilt extension, and on the other, – in contrast to a growing sense of optimism in the country at large – increasing anxiety about the Company's finances and management. As I have written before, the K&ESR has a capacity to exist on these two contradictory levels. It was something I had seen as far back as the 1960s and this time it seemed as profound as during the most difficult periods of the formative years. Amongst the Company records is a letter written on 2 January 2000 to the Chairman, Robin Dyce, by the late Douglas Edwards. No comment is made as to the accuracy of some of the statements, but the message illustrates the feeling which was around the Railway:

> As a bond holder, a K&ESR member and a volunteer I am writing to you because of the way the Railway is going.
>
> I have no doubt that what I have to say will be raised by other people at the meeting on 5th February.* There is a lot of unease amongst volunteers.
>
> At the time of writing, rumour has it that we lost custom and profit on the Santa Specials. We had built up a reputation with our Santa trains and people came back year after year and told their friends. Once we lose passengers we do not get them back. 1999 looks as if we have priced ourselves out of business and the buffet and the shop could also suffer from lack of passengers. The New Year's Eve train we charged 200 Guineas (£210) for the train ride and dinner, whereas rumour has it that the Mid Hants charged £40, filled their train and had a larger profit than the K&ESR.
>
> As to the future many people are worried about the timetable and fares between Northiam and Bodiam.
>
> *Annual Volunteers and Paid Staff meeting.

On 9 January 2000, Robin Dyce and Kim Richardson met with Bernard Sealy to discuss a number of issues of concern to the Board and the Finance Committee. These included a series of allegations including budgets being exceeded in 1998/99 without authority, unapproved expenditure, unresolved audit queries, applying for a bank loan without Board approval, late payment of the Auditor's invoice, and the CSRE accounts not being up to date between June and approximately September 1999.

At the Board meeting on 15 January Kim Richardson confirmed that most of the information requested had been supplied. Among comments made by Bernard Sealy following this were his statements that the bank loan had been put in place to rearrange the borrowing facilities and reduce the overdraft. This did not involve any increase in liabilities but instead the movement of an already agreed overdraft to a loan which could be paid off over a period of time. There was however an irregularity in the bank's procedures – proof of a TRC Board resolution agreeing to this should have been required – and this was to prove important. The CSRE accounts were now fully up to date. Sealy offered the explanation that the delay had had been the result of a volunteer in the finance team first offering to take these over and then withdrawing his offer when the Finance Committee was appointed. He stated that he has done his best with the resources at his disposal. No one had ever said that he could have the sum now to be spent on a Financial Controller. He went on to state that it was very unfair that he was being castigated in this manner and that he had undertaken work for the Railway to his personal detriment; it was not good that the Chairman and the Finance Director were at loggerheads and that one of them would have to go. Shortly after this Bernard Sealy chose to resign from the Finance post but remained a TRC Director as well as a Board member of CSRE and Bodiam 2000.

The Board next met on Saturday, 5 February – the day on which the Paid Staff and Volunteers meeting was due to be held. It was also the first Board meeting at which Tim Leigh, the Financial Controller, was present. To add to the 'churn' in personnel, Kim Richardson told the Board that his business commitments had changed and that he could not continue as Managing Director. He was later replaced by Graham Bridge. During the preceding days there had been further correspondence and discussions between the Chairman and Bernard Sealy. Following these, Sealy had said that he would prefer to resign as a Director 'without further ado'. (TRC Board meeting, 5 February 2000.)

To quote from the Board meeting minutes:

Since the Finance Committee had been put in he [Sealy] had become disillusioned and lost interest to a degree, and the amount of time he put into the Railway had decreased. He said that the Bodiam project showed a £30/40K overspend possibly due to the delay in receipt of information and he felt that a misunderstanding of the system had caused difficulties and a lack of communication. He took issue with the state of the books…

He accepted that there had been an overrun on some capital items but bearing in mind that other Board Members were responsible for those budgets, they should be bearing the blame. Considering the size of the Bodiam 2000 Project for which he was responsible and how close the out turn was to budget should have resulted in praise, not castigation. It was not unusual at this time to hear working members claiming that the Board had concentrated too much on the Bodiam extension that they had 'taken their eye off the ball' in respect of the rest of the operation.

Bernard Sealy signed a letter of resignation from all the directorships he held in the TRC Group of companies and left the meeting at 1.44pm. He ceased to be a K&ESR member in 2004. This episode in the Railway's history and the period which followed remain emotive subjects. Time has softened memories and Mr. Sealy has moved on to other interests. He nonetheless admits that recalling what happened can leave him feeling bruised. Much the same could be said by those of us involved in running the railway at the time; relating these events in an objective manner has been challenging.

During the remainder of the meeting, Philip Shaw was able to tell Directors that the bank was 'sympathetic' to the Railway's plight, and this was to prove crucial over the next few months. Philip added that he felt that this was because the bank's own procedures had been lax regarding the new bank loan. As a result of these developments, a reduction in the number of paid K&ESR staff was now seen as regrettable but unavoidable.

In the early evening of Saturday, 5 February, Robin Dyce opened the Paid Staff and Volunteers meeting by bluntly stating, 'The position is precarious.' Even after a quarter of a century I can still recall what seemed a nervousness in his voice and the hushed chill which settled on the meeting as the audience's worst fears were confirmed. The atmosphere within the local hall where the meeting was held was a mixture of despair and cold fury. At one point Robin looked at the members, suggested that the Board might step down, and asked if some of those in the hall might wish to take over. The response was, in so many words, 'You made this mess, you sort it out.'

The immediate subsequent developments were summarised in an article written by Robin Dyce and titled 'Back From the Brink', which appeared in the spring 2000 *Tenterden Terrier*.

As all members will be aware, the Railway's overall financial position is far from satisfactory.

Since the start of the year the newly-formed Finance Group (sic) has been examining the Railway's finances. Firstly, the total amount of our debts had to be determined as without this the future of the railway could not be secured. Secondly, the 1999 records have to be 'reconstructed' to determine exactly how this situation arose. Thirdly, measures have to be introduced to ensure that this sort of thing can never happen again. Finally, a business plan has to be developed against which the future of the business can be effectively managed and monitored. From the initial process, it transpired that the records were in disarray, with many figures having no bearing on what the Board had been led to be the case. This has meant that the Railway was found to have substantially greater liabilities than had previously been declared.

From the start of the Bodiam project, the Board had been aware that with very large sums of money involved and inevitable time delays in receiving payment from grant agencies, there was always going to be a problem in monitoring our cash flows. However, the situation in which we found ourselves, following an injection of cash from the Bond issue, masked the underlying financial situation. However, I am happy to confirm that, as far as can be determined at the present time, the Bodiam 2000 Millennium Extension is not the reason for our financial problems.

As soon as we became aware of the serious financial situation, our bankers were invited to a meeting at which we made clear our understanding the position. The bank also expressed concern about the information that we put before them.

The bank then appointed a firm of independent reporting accountants, Grant Thornton, to undertake an assessment of the business, the outcome of which was that the bank has agreed to continue to support us. Many people have asked what does the bank and indeed Grant Thornton know about running a railway? I can assure everyone that both organisations understand the workings of a business – and that is what the Kent & East Sussex Railway is. Grant Thornton, in particular, understands the workings of a charity and also the interactions within a largely volunteer workforce. It advised the bank that we have a business worth saving. The agreement with the bank and Grant Thornton is that we have to develop a realistic and robust business plan by 30th September, to show by then that we are capable of operating a profitable business and, most importantly, that it is capable of repaying the bank's support for us. The continuance of the support will be dependent on our progress. The challenge has been accepted, so how do we get the railway back on its feet?

Following a staff meeting on 5th February, I launched a general appeal to members for funds to help save the K&ESR. I have been overwhelmed by the generosity of members, who collectively have subscribed £84,000 at the time of writing. I hope that you will understand when I say that that I cannot write individually, but I trust that you will accept my heartfelt thanks through the medium of this article. The money has been invaluable at a time of year when we can generate little income to sustain our basic overhead structure and pay off our debts. However, we are perfectly aware that it will not of itself solve our structural problems.

Grant Thornton highlighted a number of issues. A notable point is that the Board has to become more focused to give greater accountability and control of the railway's affairs. It was felt that, with a Board of ten members, accountability had become diluted, the real issues had become blurred and the business had suffered as a result.

Accordingly, I shall be recommending to members at the forthcoming AGM, that the Board be reduced from a maximum of ten to six directors. [This did not happen and the maximum number of Directors remains at ten at the time of writing.] The meeting will be held in September this year to give time to prepare detailed financial information for members on measures taken to ensure our recovery and also to set up appropriate systems. The accounts for 1999 are likely to show a substantial loss for that year.

I have had concern that for some time that our constitution allows directors to be elected purely on the basis of a 'popular' vote and accordingly it is not possible for the Board to request that a person with a particular qualification be elected. With this in mind, and following the undoubted success of the Finance Group, the Board has agreed that in future 'policy groups' will be set up to advise them directly in certain areas and on appropriate issues. These groups will have no executive powers, but the Board will take into account the recommendations of the policy groups when making decisions.

Grant Thornton also commented on the need for a review of the Company's management structure in order that our finances can never be permitted to run out of control again. This matter is being considered by the Board and I shall report to members on our decisions as soon as possible.

Our overall financial situation decrees that costs must be reduced and income increased. The annual wage bill at £390,000 is not sustainable and is similar to the projected income from fares. Even allowing for a reduction in project wages following the completion of Bodiam, we shall still have to find a further £100,000 in this area. Regrettably we shall have to make compulsory redundancies, as voluntary redundancies will not produce the required savings.

For some years passenger numbers have been falling and whilst, in monetary terms, the shortfall has been made up from charter operations, it is a trend that must be reversed. Marketing has been identified as an area in which we can improve our business. Following consideration of a paper on 8th April, written by Donald Wilson, the Board agreed to set up a Commercial Policy Group, similar to the Finance Group, to strengthen our commercial operations. Grant Thornton has suggested that university researchers may also be able to help in this area and this will be followed up. We shall also carry out market research to learn more about the needs and aspirations of our visitors and potential visitors and to ensure that we adapt to those needs. The huge success of the February Thomas event shows what can be done. What we now have to ensure is that we provide a quality attraction that is second to none, that our visitors feel that they have had value for money and will return again, perhaps with their friends.

I and my directors accept responsibility for the unacceptable state of the company's finances and we are facing up to our responsibilities by putting the house in order. On behalf of the Board, I believe that I can say, with confidence, that the situation from which we are now extricating ourselves, will never happen again.

These early weeks of the new century continued to have – to say the least – an uneasy atmosphere. News of the financial problems quickly became common knowledge in Tenterden, appearing in the local press; and before long the matter had reached the railway magazines. It was particularly worrying for those with full-time posts and families. Having an occupational pension I was fortunate in this respect, but the emotional impact of the threat to the Railway alternated between resignation and determination. At one really bad point in the crisis I recall trying to sleep in my mess coach bunk and wondering what exactly was going to happen the next day, and around the same time placing Dymo labels on third-party-owned rolling stock to safeguard it from the possible attention of bailiffs. I also recall discussing with a younger volunteer what to do if we found the Railway being taken off us by the bank and 'the powers that be'. It sounds melodramatic but we had both quietly made up our minds that if it happened, we would be on the premises and that we would have to be physically removed. We were also sure that many other people felt the same way.

Such occasions bring out a particular gallows humour in the British as an antidote to fear and anxiety. It can of course also be invaluable in maintaining morale. Thus it was that one evening during this period, the 'High Street crowd' met for a social gathering at someone's house. Although attempts were made to talk about anything else, a leading member of the Finance Department spent much of the time propounding Eeyore-like views about the gathering crisis. As the evening ended this person was still in full flood while, at the same time, the departing guests disappeared into the darkness singing the chorus from *Always Look on the Bright Side of Life*. This story soon got around and before long colleagues meeting each other would spontaneously sing the first line of the Monty Python ditty. That was when they were not impersonating Private Fraser from Dad's Army with cries of 'Doomed, we're all doomed'.

The appeal which the Chairman had referred to in the spring *Tenterden Terrier* was indeed an immediate and significant success. The correction of the cash situation was however spectacularly aided by that other positive matter mentioned by Robin Dyce – the success of the February Thomas. This was of course an event which had come dangerously close to being cancelled. This was the first time the K&ESR had organised a February Thomas, and it provided one of those situation-saving coincidences which have so often featured in the history of the Railway.

From Saturday, 19 to Sunday, 27 February, the K&ESR ran a continuous service featuring the late Reverend Awdry's Little Blue Engine (and friends). I had been in the C&W for my normal three days and returned home as usual. A day or two later my wife, probably noting that I was restless – and well aware of what was happening – asked if I ought to be going back early. I didn't need telling twice and half an hour later my Yamaha was heading down the M20. Maybe I was only going to do my routine work, but this was a crisis where instinct said that the Railway needed us all there. The weather was exceptionally fine for the time of year, there was little competition open and during those nine days 11,500 people came to the Railway. Day by day the cash income was equally gratifying. If the K&ESR was not clear of the rocks, it was at least to remain afloat for the fight-back that was to follow.

Thus the Kent & East Sussex Railway reached the end of February 2000 with a month and a day to go before the opening of the Bodiam extension. On 15 March the Railway featured in the BBC's *The National Lottery: UK* programme. This followed a request for a human-interest story which in this case centred around the demolition train of 1955 on the Headcorn section, when long-standing member Doug Lindsay (then aged 14) rode on the locomotive with the crew during his school holidays. Filming was carried out on 6/7 March, with Jonathan Marsh playing the part of the youthful Doug and featured Locomotive No. 25 with a flat wagon and brake van, representing the demolition train. The four-minute film was broadcast from BBC Manchester on 15 March. Following this positive publicity and the success of the Thomas event, morale began to cautiously improve. I nonetheless remember making some optimistic remark to David Stratton and receiving a reply that there might be euphoria surrounding the extension but that there were 'storms ahead'.

Two days before the reopening, in a manner typical of an English spring, the weather deteriorated resulting in drizzle on the evening of Saturday, 1 April. This coincided with a Tenterden–Bodiam staff special intended to allow the 'regulars' to enjoy the extension without the responsibilities of being on duty. This was eagerly taken up and No. 19 *Norwegian* and the Mark 1 'A' set headed south west under a damp and overcast sky. It was the first time those of us not involved with the P.Way Department had seen the new extension, and in my case, it was the first time I had travelled over that section of the line for 33 years. With driver Michael Harman at the regulator, No. 19 tackled the 3½ miles in spirited fashion and soon the magical sight of Bodiam Castle emerged from the greyness of the evening. I recall leaning out of a window to find, further down the train, CFBS President Jean-Marc Page grinning happily back. The 'A' set would be in service next day and a concluding recollection is of André Freeman of the Catering Department assertively collecting any rubbish his colleagues might be in danger of leaving behind.

Despite the weather of the previous day, the morning of 2 April 2000 dawned dry with the sun eventually breaking through. I was up early and for once was wearing a collar, tie and jacket instead of the more casual approach suitable for the carriage shed. In a very personal opinion, the atmosphere of that magnificent day can be evocatively recalled by James Horner's music *The Launch* from the film *Apollo 13*, perhaps because of the underlying theme of 'a close run thing' in both (very different) stories.

A crowd duly assembled and the opening ceremonies began ready for the 9am first departure from Tenterden Town, the Bond Holders Train, hauled by USA No. 65. This was for the just under 200 purchasers of £1,000 and £5,000 Bearer Bonds and their guests – in other words for a group who had been particularly generous in the fundraising for the extension.

The second departure of the day, the 9.30am VIP Train, was in many ways the 'real' reopening train. The locomotives for this were Terrier No. 2678 and Austerity K&ESR No. 25 *Northiam*, the latter locomotive carrying the Railway's original Oxford Blue livery. This train carried 100 specially invited guests to the Bodiam ceremony. That figure may or may not have included various members of staff who were accommodated in the Mark 1 Brake Second Open including Clive Lowe (as C&W Manager), John Brice (for his work on the Bodiam 'facilities') and me. I was fortunate in being included as John thought I should be present as his guest because of my long association with the K&ESR. Before departure, the Railway's President, Lord Deedes, who had been instrumental in saving the K&ESR, made a brief speech during which he apologised for being unable to travel on the train to Bodiam but also regretted that he had been a member of the Cabinet which had approved the Beeching Plan. Attitudes towards railways had certainly changed since the 1960s.

The Bond Holders' Train duly arrived at Bodiam, and was played in by the Battle Town Band. After the bond holders had received hospitality, No. 65 ran round its train and departed back to Tenterden. Around half an hour later the VIP Train arrived, the band again playing it into the platform. The locomotives then ran round and propelled the coaches back past the end of the platform thus allowing a view of the Castle across the valley. Robin Dyce opened the proceedings but part way through his address there was an unannounced fly-past low overhead of three light aircraft led by volunteer Sue Saggers. It was dramatic but I remember, somewhat ungratefully, wishing that it had been a Spitfire performing a victory roll. (And don't believe that because something hasn't occurred it won't happen eventually!)

It had been intended that Sir Alastair Morton would perform the reopening, but he was indisposed and his place was taken at short notice by Christopher Fildes, a member of the National Railway Heritage Committee. He was accompanied by Dr Heather Couper, the eminent astronomer, on behalf of the Millennium Commission, and Admiral Sir Lindsay Bryson, the then Patron of the K&ESR. The Tenterden Railway Company had achieved everything it set out to do when it reorganised the K&ESR project in 1971. But as Christopher Fildes said during his address, 'You cannot stop here.' He meant, of course, that the Railway should go on to Robertsbridge. There was then a ceremonial breaking of a white ribbon across the track before the VIP Train left for Tenterden Town at about 11.15am and at Northiam crossed the stock from the Bondholders train which was on its second run to Bodiam. Some distance towards Wittersham Road where the line curves to the left I glanced out of the window and saw that train still standing in Northiam Station. It occurred to me that it was probably a very long time since anyone had last had a similar view.

Chapter 22

It was with considerable relief for everyone that the upturn begun with the February Thomas event continued with the anticipated post-extension boost to traffic. Philip Shaw's Editorial in the summer 2000 issue of the *Tenterden Terrier* summed it up:

> As we struggle to clear our debts away from the Financial Fiascos of 1998 and 1999 ... the omens for 2000 are decidedly upbeat. Passenger numbers are running 78 per cent up and we are now in the enviable position of being a 'destination' railway rather than a ride to nowhere. So what should be our priorities? How will we achieve financial stability and avoid the seemingly quinquennial disasters of the past? Firstly, we must settle our paid staff and working members into the new business structure; secondly, generate cash to provide funds both for investment and for working capital through next winter; thirdly, we must direct cash into projects where there is the prospect of a high commercial return. Change may not please everybody, but come it must – our bankers and Bond investors will dictate that there is no time left to play trains or indeed politics.

The Commercial Report in 'Lineside News' added:

> Passenger numbers up to the end of June – (excluding Wealden Belle and Charters) were 46,167 – no less than a 78 per cent increase on the 25,853 carried in the corresponding period of last year. Our business is, in fact, changing noticeably, with visitors using the railway as a 'destination' route to Bodiam rather than just as a day out for a ride on a train. This has brought with it certain problems, noticeably over-crowding on the later trains from Bodiam to Tenterden as people return from a day out at the castle. We have also noticed an adverse effect on takings at the shop at Tenterden, as some of our visitors have spent money in the National Trust shop at the castle. These matters are being addressed as a matter of urgency. Bodiam Station itself is undoubtedly our most attractive site, beautifully restored and merging gently into the heritage village of Bodiam itself.

This same issue of the *Terrier* included a significant change in the listing of officers and staff. Tim Leigh, who had of course been engaged as Financial Controller, was now in the post of Business Manager. The matters of redundancies and revising the Board and management structures had been discussed at Board meetings in March and April and were raised again in May. Voluntary redundancy was to be offered at this stage, it having been reported two months previously (TRC Board Meeting 366 March 2000) that some casual employees has been persuaded to continue as volunteers. At the same meeting, the management structure was the subject of a report produced by non-Board members and introduced by volunteer and senior civil servant Simon Marsh, who became Chairman many years later. This contained various ideas, not all of which were adopted; significantly it did mention the need for an overall Catering Manager.

At the first of two May Board meetings, on 6th of the month, Norman Brice replaced Robin Dyce as Chairman. This had of course been predicted by David Stratton, who himself now became Managing Director in place of Graham Bridge, who had to resign for reasons which were not related to railway matters. The second meeting, on 13th, was able to discuss returning control of the budget to the departmental managers, an indication of the improving financial position.

At the Board meeting on 10 June, Tim Leigh was able to report more than glimmerings of hope in the financial position. Both monies owed to creditors and the Company's overdraft had been reduced and passenger figures appeared to be about five weeks ahead of the previous year. Also at the June meeting, the legendary John Snell, whom we have already met in connection with the Museum, was appointed to the Board of TRC subsidiary Colonel Stephens Railway Enterprises. As well as being credited with being the Talyllyn Railway's first volunteer he had later been General Manager of the Romney, Hythe & Dymchurch Railway. More about Mr Snell in due course.

On Wednesday, 5 July 2000, HRH The Duke of Gloucester made a return visit to the K&ESR, this being to officially open Bodiam Station and the following account of the Duke's visit is adapted from the late John Miller's much more detailed article which appeared in *Tenterden Terrier* No. 82, summer 2000. The Duke arrived by car at Tenterden Town at 12.15pm and was given a civic welcome similar to that when he officially opened Northiam Station. Norman Brice escorted His Royal Highness for the remainder of the visit. He first called at the Museum, where Board members Bob Forsythe, David Stratton, Graham Bridge and John Snell were presented, followed by David Morgan, Chairman, Heritage Railway Association; Jean-Marc Page of the CFBS; and Henry Edward's wife Felicity. Inside, Philip Shaw conducted the royal party, which included the Duke's Private Secretary and Lord Kingsdown, Lord Lieutenant of Kent, around the Museum.

The next stop was at the Carriage and Wagon shed after which the royal party went to the platform where the 'Wealden Belle' set was boarded for the journey to Bodiam. It departed at 12.50pm with *Norwegian* leading the three-coach set and *Charwelton* as assisting engine at the rear. The party was joined by Lord Kingsdown, David Morgan, Philip Shaw, Jean-Marc Page and the Board members in the Pullman set's RU No. 69 where they were served with a light lunch.

At about 1:35pm the royal train could be seen in the distance and at 1.40pm the Duke alighted opposite the running-in board. He was welcomed to East Sussex by the Lord Lieutenant, Mrs Phyllida Stewart-Roberts, who then presented various local worthies before Norman Brice resumed his role of escorting the Duke around the Station. After further introductions it was time for speeches, Norman beginning by saying that the day was the culmination of 30 years of imagination and hard work to finally reach Bodiam. He also referred to the environmental benefits to the Rother Valley, to visitors to the Castle travelling by rail, and to the contribution to tourism and economic growth that the railway makes to the district. Norman then invited His Royal Highness to say a few words and to unveil a commemorative plaque. Speaking without notes, the Duke began by expressing his pleasure at arriving in Sussex from Kent 'using your splendid railway', and 'collecting all these funds from the lottery and elsewhere'. During the remainder of his speech, the Duke congratulated the K&ESR on maintaining the Railway and keeping it going through good times and bad before unveiling a commemorative brass plaque. Following a short footplate ride on *Charwelton*, the Duke left by car to round off his trip with a visit to Bodiam Castle.

The issue of the *Terrier* which recorded these events also carried a poem written by Alastair Forbes, inspired by Gray's *Elegy* and with perhaps a nod to Betjeman's *Dilton Marsh Halt*. This was not, as one might have expected, about Bodiam but was instead set at Wittersham Road. It is reproduced as Appendix C. It elegantly captures the atmosphere on the K&ESR at the time.

Chapter 23

Optimism regarding finance continued at the Board meeting on 15 July. Tim Leigh reiterated his comments at the June Board about the payment of monies owed and the reduction in the overdraft. In fact, he was able to report that everything on the income side was above expectations. Grant Thornton had particularly noted these positive developments but reserved the right to attend the AGM if they felt it was appropriate. The profit and loss figures to the end of June showed TRC making a profit of £13,000; this revelation led to Philip Shaw reversing his usual mantra and stating that he never expected to make a profit out of running trains!

The July Board meeting then turned to the vexed subject of the 1999 accounts which Philip had been reconstructing. He said that this was 'no mean task given the state of the books'. He had rewritten the accounts for CSRE and Bodiam 2000 and was trying to make sense of those for TRC. As was expected, the K&ESR had made a substantial loss. By way of stark contrast, at this point in 2000, and in the usual wake of a reopening, the passenger figures were continuing to rapidly climb past those of the previous year.

The Annual General Meeting for 2000 was held on 10 September in a marquee on the newly acquired open ground adjoining Bodiam yard. The venue was of course appropriate to the year and had originally been planned for one of the modern buildings at the castle. After the Notice of Meeting had been sent out, it was realised that said modern building was too small and recourse had to be made to the marquee at the station. There was therefore the rigmarole of members being told to go to the station while the Board went to the castle, opened the meeting and adjourned it to the marquee.

Considering the traumatic nature of the preceding year, the meeting was remarkably quiet and well behaved. Prior to the AGM, the Board had considered a letter received from the Company's accountants, Messrs Day Smith & Hunter, which, among other things, contained the following passage regarding their difficulties in auditing the K&ESR's perilous financial position.

> The majority of the problems which had arisen stemmed largely from the fact that the accounts function was spread amongst a number of volunteer/part time staff and there was no proper co-ordination of their work. Also, the rapid growth of the company's activities was a contributory factor. My recommendation throughout was for the company to employ a full-time accountant with the necessary experience.

And there, for the moment matters rested as, with Charlie Masterson at the controls and driving at a sedate pace, those attending started their journeys home on the Class 108 DMMU, the company having arranged an AGM special from Tenterden where members had of course been able to park their cars.

The Board next met on 7 October, newly elected Board members Carol Mitchell and John Weller attending for the first time. John was, like me, an early retired local government officer. Unlike me, he retained an interest in local government and later became a member of Tenterden Town Council and eventually Town Mayor. Carol had been Guards Training Officer during my failed attempt in that sphere, although not the person who had 'expressed their displeasure' with me! Each of us had previously been unaware of the other but subsequently discovered that we had grown up about 500 yards apart in South East London and had had overlapping social networks – proof of that old saying that it's a small world.

That 7 October Board meeting was advised by Tim Leigh that Grant Thornton hoped to cease their monitoring of the K&ESR's affairs at the end of the year. It was more than good news that matters had improved thus far. Five days later a serious and unexpected problem occurred.

Chapter 24

As explained in an earlier chapter, much of the Rother Valley below Bodiam had been navigable waterway until relatively recent centuries. Serious flooding was known to occur on an occasional basis and there had been a few instances during the K&ESR's post-1961 heritage era. Climate change has however increased the possibility of such occurrences. Exceptionally heavy rains led to another inundation of the Rother Levels during 12/13 October which exceeded the Environment Agency probability of a once-in-a-100-year flood. As a result, the K&ESR suffered two washouts around Mill Ditch on the Bodiam extension and several small ballast shifts on the same curve. Both washouts were around 15m long and 1.5m deep, with the spoil being deposited in the surrounding fields.

The speed of the flood was at the time described by Peter Barber as 'incredible' in the *Tenterden Terrier* for winter 2000, from which this account is adapted. The water level had reportedly risen 600mm in under half an hour, and to higher levels than had been recorded previously. This left over a mile of track under water up to a depth of 1.6m. The K&ESR was fortunate to get away with relatively little damage. The washout 200m on the Northiam side of Mill Ditch was caused by sheer weight of water and a blocked cross drain. This made the railway formation act as a dam holding the water back until it ran over the top, eroding the formation. The second washout was at Mill Ditch itself. This waterway had flood banks constructed to the same pattern as those on the Rother, to contain flooding when water backed up from the river. These works had been undertaken during the long period when the Northiam–Bodiam section was dormant; balance pipes had been put under the railway and the banks extended to run parallel to the track over the ditch. During the storms, the majority of the rain fell on the upstream side. When the Rother burst its banks, the largest volume of water came from the Bodiam direction. With Mill Ditch acting effectively as a dam, the railway was the lowest point. With the difference in level being some 600mm, there was a strong flow of water running from the Bodiam flood plain to the Northiam one, and the sheer weight of water blasted away a section of track formation. The embankment, as originally constructed, contained a layer of beach ballast. Once the water got into this, the structure would have disintegrated under the forces very quickly. The minor ballast shifts were caused by the strong currents flowing through the surface ballast.

During the first inspection on 15 October, the K&ESR's engineers found two pieces of track suspended over large pools of water. Dipping with a stick revealed the true extent of the damage. This was four days after the storms, and still the track was only just passable with wellington boots. Not everyone made it back with dry feet! As the valley flood protection scheme was designed to keep the water out, it also stopped the water draining off the flood plain. The majority of the water had to be pumped over the flood banks and into the Rother, which was a slow task. With the onset of winter, the breaches in the Railway had to be filled as quickly as possible to reduce the damage to the compacted base of the embankment.

The main problem with the two large washouts was that the eroded spoil was saturated and unsuitable to reform the embankment. Fill had to be imported to the site to reform the structure, and it had to be a stone granular fill that would not 'pudding up'. The suspended track had firstly to be removed for safe working and to free access. At the washout furthest from Mill Ditch, two 600mm spun concrete cross-drains were installed to act as balance pipes. These would reduce the potential damage in the event of another severe flood. The embankment would then be reconstructed with the granular fill compacted in 100mm layers. This was wrapped with a sheet of geo-grid to hold it together and give it greater strength. The track ballast and permanent way were then replaced. The cost of the repair work, using existing resources, was provisionally estimated at around £25,000, later revised the bulk of the labour to be provided by volunteers supplemented by some specialist plant operators.

An unfortunate side-effect of the Mill Ditch washouts was that Bodiam would no longer be available on 21 and 22 October for the first, and innovative, Hoppers Weekend. Northiam was used instead, its resemblance to Bodiam on this occasion being fortuitous (and a change from it occasionally confusing passengers!) This was a celebration of the K&ESR's long association with hop growing and hop pickers, both of which had in times past brought much traffic to the Railway. The initiative had its origins in the 'Delivering the Goods' weekends of earlier Octobers, but which had produced very limited public interest. As a new departure, beer was an obvious candidate for development once the decision to proceed was taken – only six weeks prior to the event! Planning began, led by Sandra Marsh of the Commercial Department and John Brice as Chairman of the Special Events Committee.

The plans had been ambitious, involving the provision of a beer tent at Tenterden by the local branch of the Campaign for Real Ale (CAMRA), hopping displays and veteran hop pickers at Bodiam station, plus the transport of hops along the line, with transhipment – via steam crane – from rail to a boat on the Rother at Northiam. Then came the floods and the need to move the Bodiam-based part of the weekend to Northiam. Unfortunately, the Rother remained swollen, and the intended steam crane and boats contribution had to be abandoned. The beer tent at Tenterden was however open all weekend selling a variety of real ales. The whole weekend was regarded as a successful experiment, although visitor numbers were affected by the continuing poor weather and last-minute publicity for the beer and hopping attractions.

A further matter related to heritage was raised at the Board meeting on 18 November when it was reported that The Terrier Trust was in a position to purchase the Terrier *Knowle* from its previous owner, Rick Edmondson. (*Knowle* was of course the Southern Railway/BR-owned locomotive to have served longest on the K&ESR.) Also at that meeting it was agreed that the Cavell Van, which had been amongst the stock removed to Robertsbridge and had been purchased by John Miller, should be returned to the Railway. This vehicle was of exceptional historical importance having been not only the prototype of the ubiquitous Southern PMV but the vehicle in which, on separate occasions, the remains of Nurse Edith Cavell, The Unknown Warrior and Captain Fryatt been taken from Dover to London following the end of the First World War.

The same meeting also received a report from Philip Shaw about the progress made in righting the Railway's financial position. This was later published in the *Tenterden Terrier*.

> Following last year's financial fiasco, when the Railway was almost terminally bankrupt, the Board has decided to release regular statements to members in order to keep them fully appraised with the Company's financial fortunes.

Unaudited figures for the nine months to 30th September 2000 show a consolidated profit of £231,229, includes £115,403 for The Tenterden Railway Company itself, which encompasses our train operations and membership activities, including subscriptions & donations and £231,323 from Colonel Stephens Railway Enterprises, which reflect our commercial operations. From this is deducted finance costs of £115,497 which include interest, bank charges and audit fees.

Members will recall that figures for the six months ended 30th June 2000, previously circulated, showed a profit of £135,610, so we have more than maintained progress in the third quarter.

Passenger numbers have been exceptionally good and … were 64 per cent up over the corresponding period of last year. This has been the main reason for the rise in fares income, although our commercial activities have also traded strongly. Our strong cash flows have enabled us to pay down the backlog of trade creditors, but we still have tough targets to meet in reducing the overdraft to levels demanded by the bank.

The final quarter of the year will not be anything like as profitable, indeed we are likely to record a loss. Santa bookings are coming in fast (£20,000 raised in advance bookings by the third week in October) but this is now the traditional low season and revenues will not pick up significantly until the early spring. We shall have to meet the cost of flood damage – estimated to top £30,000 – whilst our substantial fixed overheads still have to be met.

The opening to Bodiam has changed the focus of operations quite considerably. We are now a 'destination' railway and a large proportion of passengers use us as a convenient method getting to Bodiam Castle, whereas in the past, a trip to Northiam was a ride on a train to nowhere. Charter traffic continues to expand and there are plenty of untapped opportunities for joint promotions with the National Trust at Bodiam. Levels of expenditure will be kept under close scrutiny in 2001, with capital expenditure being kept approximately in line with depreciation. Some of our resources will be directed to improving the quality of the station sites at Tenterden and Northiam, which are fairly run down in appearance. Bodiam is a shining example of what can be done to present an attractive terminus. We also need to expand our computer systems to incorporate the bookings side of the business, which is presently manually administered. The new accounting systems installed at the beginning of the year are now providing adequate financial information, which we never had in the past. A revised management structure is now in place, bar the appointment of a catering manager to supervise activities in this area. An announcement is, however, expected shortly.

The year 2000 is likely to the most profitable in the Company's history, but we are still saddled with loans and overdrafts well in excess of £1 million, which for a Company of our size is unacceptable. Furthermore, the results have been boosted to the tune of £73,206 by the very generous response from the members to our appeal for funds in the early part of the year. It will be noted that the whole of the 'profit' from the Tenterden Railway Company in the nine month period was gulped up by finance costs. Our heavy level of financial gearing leaves us very little room for manoeuvre in the event of a downturn in the economy or any other events that crop up beyond our control. What would have happened if our bridges had been washed away in the floods? So, we are on the mend and trading well, but we must exert extreme vigilance on costs throughout 2001 if we are really to learn from the lessons of the past.

By this stage the bank was much happier with the Railway and no longer classified it as a high risk. It did however want Grant Thornton to continue monitoring until Easter 2001 to complete a full year. In addition to the improvements in the K&ESR's performance and Natwest's leniency in acknowledgment of their own procedural deficiencies, it has been plausibly suggested (my conversation with Norman Brice) that the bank took into account the likely effect on Tenterden in the event of the Railway failing. It has also been cynically suggested that Natwest did not want the negative publicity which would most likely have resulted!

An interesting item, which was entered in the minutes as a 'Part 2' confidential item and not widely known at the time, involved the proposed further extension to Robertsbridge. This recorded that sometime previously, the Rother Valley Railway had approached Chairman Norman Brice with a view to the Tenterden Railway Company taking over RVR. This had earlier led to the creation of a new company, Robertsbridge 20/20, for the purpose. He now asked the TRC Board to approve his choice of persons from both TRC and RVR to be directors of RB 20/20. The resolution of that item does not appear to be recorded.

What was recorded in the minutes was deep unease at the idea of TRC taking on debts amounting to £39,000 and other liabilities together with the potential for additional financial risk to the Tenterden Railway Company. The Rother Valley Railway had made relatively little progress by this time, and while the Robertsbridge project had its supporters on the K&ESR, many involved with the day-to-day running had deep doubts about the viability of the idea and the continuing 'embryo project' appearance of activities in Robertsbridge yard. In the event, TRC did not take over RVR. Robertsbridge 20/20 continued a dormant existence (with directors from both sides) for several years until absorbed into the TRC group to facilitate liaison with RVR at a later stage in the latter company's development.

The Board met again on 9 December 2000. This was unusual, as meetings were generally suspended during the resource-stretching Santa season; and indicated, despite the prediction of £100,000 profit for the year, the ongoing concern about the viability of the Railway. It was particularly noted that planned redundancies had not taken place because of their likely effect on service provision. The matter of redundancies was one of the issues which would dominate the two years which followed.

Chapter 25

The year 2000 had indeed ended with record passenger figures, 112,154 been having been carried – a record for the heritage era, and almost equal to 1913's all-time total for the K&ESR. A profit of £100,000 was still anticipated; indebtedness had been reduced, there had been a 7 per cent increase in Santa traffic and the Pullman service remained a valuable bulwark to the trading position. There remained however the issue of reducing staff costs and the consequent redundancies.

On a less sombre note, it was anticipated in February that capital expenditure, which had of course been out of the question throughout 2000, could be resumed. The renewed optimism which had continued into the New Year, including another successful Thomas event in February, however, came to an abrupt halt in March. This was in large part due to a factor external to the Railway – the outbreak of Foot & Mouth Disease.

Although the farms of Kent and Sussex had been little affected at that stage, the Board considered the implications on 17 March. The National Trust and English Heritage were closing properties and, the public having been warned by government about travel in rural areas, the question was asked whether the K&ESR should do the same. There had been no regular running at that point in the year and it was difficult to assess what the impact on the Railway might be. One outcome was that the planned military-themed 'War on the Line' event was cancelled, fortunately little having been spent on preparations. The same meeting discussed at length a proposal, which Tim Leigh had first raised with the Board in January, to lease part of the Northiam site for use as a garden centre. Despite the urgent need to raise finance, Board members were deeply uneasy about the idea, which hung around for some time but was eventually not proceeded with.

The Board met again only ten days later. The reason for this was a deterioration in the financial position up to the end of February. Norman Brice was, however, at pains to point out that this was not a cause for panic. The problem had in part been caused by a possible clerical error by HM Customs and Excise who had not paid monies due to the Company. In addition, there was a delay in grant payments, income forecast in the budget had been allocated to the wrong months and, now that the regular service had re-started, the effects of the Foot & Mouth outbreak. The situation had fortunately been eased by receipt of some grant money, some trading income and what was described as a 'relaxed attitude' on the part of the bank. Concern was expressed about the continuing high staff costs.

There was nevertheless still positive news, the spring 2001 issue of the *Terrier* announcing that the K&ESR had received recognition from the wider world of railways for its achievements. Two awards had been made, both associated with Ian Allan Ltd, which was then still a major force in railway publishing. In the first, which did not require anyone to submit an entry, the K&ESR was runner-up for having ridden out its serious financial storm and for having achieved the extension to Bodiam. The second was the *Railway World* Award which did require heritage lines to submit entry forms. The Kent & East Sussex submitted the Bodiam extension and received a 'Highly Commended'.

Looking to the future, the Railway had by this date that twenty-first-century necessity – a website, together with separate sites for the Operating Department and the Museum. This aspect was of course to grow in importance over the years, e-mail and mobile phones having arrived around the same time. One could not help speculating that Colonel Stephens with his love of communicating by telegram would have approved. It was not long before a modern feature of business life set in and staff around the Tenterden site started e-mailing each other rather than making a phone call, writing a memo or arriving at someone else's office in person.

Further positive news announced in the spring issue of the *Terrier* was the return of the Steam & Country Fair. The following unattributed item was in fact written by me, shortly after I had added the post of Secretary to the Special Events Committee to my other duties:

> *Terrier* readers with long memories will recall the K&ESR's Steam & Country Fairs of the 1970s and early 1980s. The Railway ran several of these highly successful events, which attracted thousands of people to a site adjoining Tenterden Town Station. Income was for several years substantial and used, among other things, to pay for the cost of building the Carriage & Wagon shed.
>
> Plans are well under way to revive these popular events, and the first Steam & Country Fair of the 21st Century is to he held on 21st and 22nd July 2001. The Railway has, of course, developed greatly over the past 20 years, and in acknowledgement of this the Fair is to be held in a field next to Northiam Station.
>
> Organisation is in the hands of the Special Events Committee, a fairly informal body which maintains liaison between everyone involved, the Chairman being steamroller owner and Carriage & Wagon fitter John Brice. John has had long experience of such events elsewhere in the preservation movement, and under his guidance contact has already been made with owners of traction engines, commercial vehicles, vintage and classic cars, motorcycles and buses. The interest shown to date has been most encouraging. There will be an old-time fairground, country crafts and trade stalls, and CAMRA will be involved with an appropriate beer tent. It can take several years for such events to establish themselves in the public mind and while the 2001 Fair is not intended to be as large as some of its legendary predecessors, we aim to make it as varied and interesting as possible. Success breeds success and a good result in 2001 will surely lead the way to dizzy heights in years to come.
>
> The Railway will be operating an enhanced service during the Steam & Country Fair with combined train-fair tickets on offer.
>
> There will, of course, be running costs; and this has had to be kept firmly in mind following TRC's financial difficulties during 2000. From the outset it was made clear to the organisers that the Steam & Country Fair would have to be made self financing. A substantial boost to the funds was received from the raffle run by the 300 Club and drawn at the 60s weekend in September. To this has been added a steady income from a series of Sunday boot fairs held in the car park at Tenterden Town. Various firms have been approached regarding the possibility of sponsorship and this too is, at the time of writing, beginning to produce results, including a significant promise of help from a major brewer. Further help in this respect will still be more than welcome nonetheless, and a sum as

small as £250 would, for instance, enable an extra traction engine to attend. Assistance will be acknowledged in the event programme and there is the possibility of purchasing further advertising space.

There will also be every opportunity for the ordinary TRC member to get involved. Volunteers will be most definitely needed. Whether you are an existing volunteer who will not be involved in running the Railway that weekend, or someone who would like to help for the first time, we need to hear from you.

The site was to be the Cyster family's field immediately to the north of Northiam Station. The Cysters owned various tracts of land in the area – hence the eponymous user-worked crossing on the other, Tenterden, side of the A28. The Committee's first site visit in connection with the Fair had taken place three months earlier on 14 January. The still-flooded valley had the K&ESR in 'Hayling Island' mode; the temperature was below zero and the event field was under about 6ft of frozen water with ducks sitting on top. Summer had seemed a long way off.

Board meetings continued to be frequent at this time. On 12 April, the effects of the Foot & Mouth outbreak were considered. At that point there had been few operating days, and although there had initially been a significant reduction in passengers (compared with 2000) numbers had picked up and it was suggested that the epidemic might not be affecting the K&ESR too badly. There was again a discussion on staffing levels and the need to reduce overheads. Both these topics were returned to on 21 April. It appeared that Foot & Mouth was affecting tourism in rural areas more than coastal locations – the Romney Hythe & Dymchurch had not seen a reduction in traffic but the Bluebell Railway had, like the K&ESR, experienced a poor Easter. Most of the meeting was devoted to finance, and it was regarding this that Paul Wilson revealed that he had discovered flaws in the 2001 budget.

The Board met yet again on 3 May, by which time Paul Wilson had made further progress in revamping the budget. He anticipated a £35,000 profit for the year before a £6,000 item relating to the flooding was stripped out. This was however dependent on a high catering forecast, and there was some concern over whether this could be achieved. Redundancies were now almost certain and, although these were seen as undesirable during the season, there was a definite need for them after the end of September. To make matters worse on this front, an item about staff cuts had appeared in the local paper the previous week and was having the predictable effect on morale. There was to be a meeting with the bank on 15 May and the tone of the minutes does not indicate that it was anticipated that this would be easy. Six days later concern was expressed about a continuing lack of financial control; among other issues cheques had recently been issued without funds to cover them.

There was debate about proposed revisions to the management structure and whether or not the Finance Controller should come under the General Manager – as and when someone was appointed to the latter, now to be revived, post. The span of control of the GM was discussed and in the course of this Derek Dunlavey pointed out that historically the heritage-era K&ESR had evolved engineering departments from a very early stage but that the commercial function had been set up in a hurry when proper trading started. This had resulted in an 'instant chasm', the two sides had remained separated, and there been a major problem ever since. It was of course intended that the re-establishment of the post of General Manager would close that gap. It is my opinion that although there has been better co-ordination of these two aspects of the Railway in later times the influence of this fundamental division has continued.

Despite the annual Volunteers and Staff meeting having been held in the early months of 2001, a leaflet was circulated advising that a meeting, organised by a number of volunteers, was to be called on the evening of 12 May (later changed to 19) to discuss the current state of affairs. This initiative achieved some credibility as it was to be chaired by the respected Neil Rose, a JP and former Company Secretary. The Board met on the morning of 19th to discuss their approach. At the evening meeting, Norman Brice made a pre-arranged presentation which was followed by a question-and-answer session. Peter Davis made a lengthy speech, which included allegations of breach of fiduciary duty, and there was a call for the retirement of the longer-standing directors. Norman Brice later countered this by writing a document titled 'Fact or Fiction' which he now asked the Board to approve him sending to Peter Davis and circulating to the working members. Articles also appeared in *Heritage Railway* and the *Kentish Express*, both appearing to have been written before the meeting took place. The potential for fireworks at the meeting may, to continue the metaphor, have been something of a damp squib – I did actually attend, but had totally forgotten it until my memory was jogged while researching for this book! The meeting was nonetheless a precursor to later activities by its organisers intended to provide salvation, but which many saw as a threat.

The frequency of Board meetings then decreased, with the Directors' next meeting being on 26 May. There was further discussion about paid staff reductions as well as deficiencies in the budget and its variance from the Railway's actual performance. By the meeting of 23 June, a redundancy programme had been agreed and, with regret, meetings with the individuals concerned began.

The next Board was on 14 July, one week before Tim Leigh was due to leave by mutual agreement. This meeting was attended by Peter Bourne of Day Smith and Hunter, the Company's very supportive auditors, to discuss the accounts for 2000. Mr Bourne commented on the remarkable turn round in the Railway's financial position – from a deficit of £296,467 in 1999 to a surplus of £75,030 in 2000. But it was not enough. He continued to be concerned about the £1million debt, including the Northiam Bonds, although on this occasion he had not found it necessary to qualify the accounts as had been the case in previous years. There are many reasons for qualifying an audit, but usually it is a sign that the auditors are not fully content with what they have seen either on a procedural basis or future ability to trade. Mr Bourne then made a particularly important observation. A dedicated accounts manager (Tim Leigh's original brief as Financial Controller having been subsequently widened) would have avoided the recent errors and anomalies in financial matters. The need for an accountant on the staff would however soon be addressed. Recruiting a replacement for Tim Leigh was considered but there was some feeling that this might be insensitive in view of the forthcoming redundancies.

It was during this meeting that John Snell said that financing the Railway was impossible with all the interest and debt due. He then went on to add that the K&ESR had to get away from this system and go for recapitalisation, and that the charitable status was a problem. It was a view which existed among the group who had called the meeting on 19 May. 'Recapitalisation' referred to the issuing of shares – something which TRC as a Company Limited by Guarantee, and more crucially as a Registered Charity – could not do.

The other types of company then existing in UK law were the Private Company (of which CSRE was an example) and the Public Limited Company (PLC) whose shares could, although not necessarily, be quoted on the Stock Exchange, and which could be freely bought and sold. PLCs were also able to pay annual dividends to shareholders, although they did not have to do so. The great advantage of raising money by the sale of PLC shares, which a number of heritage railways were resorting to, was that the sums obtained for debt repayment and capital investment never had to be paid back. The disadvantage of this was that floating a PLC would, in the case of the K&ESR, create a body with a strong controlling interest. There would be no guarantee that it would overlap in either membership or aspirations with TRC, which was of course the organisation for the active supporters. All this was controversial, and another issue which would dominate the next couple of years.

As ever, the day-to-day life of the Kent & East Sussex Railway continued whatever the crises being played out at Board meetings. In my case this now included the work of the Special Events Committee which, fortunately, I had no trouble fitting in around my paid duties. When I became the Committee's secretary, Charlie Masterson, speaking from his involvement with the 1980s Fairs, told me, 'You'll know when you've done it!' In other words, stand by for some intense pressure. He wasn't wrong.

Although the Foot & Mouth crisis continued (it was not finally resolved until November) it was possible for the Steam & Country Fair to take place, albeit without the animals which had been a feature in the 1980s. Organising the event in the months leading up to the weekend of 21/22 July kept everyone busy enough but the weekend itself took everything to an intense pitch. Clutching a sleeping bag, I arrived at Northiam by train sometime during the preceding Friday afternoon to find the atmosphere of an old-time country-fair-cum–traction-engine event already establishing itself on the floor of the valley. Intruding modernity into the scene, the mobile phone had become well established by this time and proved invaluable to the organisers on site throughout the weekend. All seemed to be going well until in the early evening a problem arose with approving the electrical installation for the site. It briefly looked as if the whole enterprise was doomed until someone contacted a suitably qualified mate who 'sorted' the problem. Those of us involved with the organisational side could have done without that.

For the first time in decades, I slept under canvas that night. Fortunately, the weather was mild and the experience didn't seem too spartan compared with the fairly basic comforts of a mess coach. Thankfully the next day and the Sunday were a roaring success against the background of the operating Railway. Centrepiece, as in the 1970s and 80s, was the Harris Brothers old time fair incorporating their famous 'Southdown Gallopers' and other vintage rides. The wider Fair included a range of exhibits – portable engines, traction engines, steamrollers, motor cars, motor cycles, tractors, commercial vehicles and buses. Musical entertainment was provided by three street organs, there was a wide range of country crafts and stalls, and there was an air display by a Mustang fighter aircraft. (Still not a Spitfire – which had originally been hoped for – but getting close.) The Fair was a great success, making a profit, if not a vast one, but nonetheless leading to significantly higher-than-average ticket sales on the railway from visitors who travelled to Northiam by train. At the same time, it brought added goodwill and publicity to the Kent & East Sussex Railway.

Despite this success there was still the reality of recovering from the crisis of the previous year. The summer *Tenterden Terrier* appeared around the same time as the Steam & Country Fair was held and contained an article by Philip Shaw, entitled 'How are the Railway's Finances?'

> The Kent & East Sussex Railway suffered badly during the early months of this year from the unprecedented bad weather, which resulted in the worst floods in the region for a century. This was exacerbated by the Foot & Mouth crisis, and tourists simply stayed away from the countryside. Other attractions in Kent were similarly affected and the recovery has been slow and difficult. At one stage our income was around one half of what we had anticipated.

Up to the end of May passenger numbers in 2001 were 23 per cent down on last year, but the month of May itself was only 7 per cent lower, and the recovery has been progressive. However, this is not the whole story. Our cost base had been rising substantially throughout 1999 and by the end of 2000 had reached a level which is totally unsustainable for the volume of business that we are likely to achieve. The audited accounts for last year to be presented to the members at the October AGM will show that we achieved a modest profit of around £75,000 – rather lower than we had originally anticipated – on a turnover of some £1.25 million. This was a year in which passengers were literally standing in the aisles on some peak days, but it masked an underlying weakness in our administration which, with hindsight, should have been addressed somewhat earlier.

Several years ago the Railway adopted a policy of widespread daily running. In 2000 we operated on 235 days and ran 1233 trains, excluding Pullmans and charters. Even then some 45 per cent of the traffic was conveyed in the months of July to September, including a 'Thomas' in September, but many of our trains – then and now – have been running largely empty. The sight of a Terrier and two coaches simmering in the sunshine at Tenterden with scarcely anyone in sight or sound apart from the staff was commonplace; beautifully authentic as a light railway in a time warp of the 1950s, but uneconomic to the point of absurdity. We did not monitor daily income data closely; had we done so it would have drawn attention to the inadequacies in our strategy.

Although the Railway has been established for over a quarter of a century, it has never been a high volume carrier and anyway its sites are somewhat limited for space. In fact, passenger numbers had shown no real growth for more than a decade. In an attempt to address the situation, expenditure on advertising was raised by no less than 140 per cent between 1995 and 1999, but this provided little obvious benefit and passenger numbers continued to track downwards. The push to Bodiam in 2000 gave an initial and welcome boost to traffic and a logical destination, but the financial benefit was dragged down by an overblown overhead structure and massive debts, which had and still have to be serviced and ultimately repaid. The level of volunteer assistance has also been below what we would have liked, although our members have been generous in their financial support.

The railway has tended to rely more and more on paid staff and the wages bill, which was £152,384 in 1997 had risen to a massive £360,463 in 1999 and a similar level in 2000.

We spend some £100,000 per annum on coal and oil, and another substantial item is finance costs – nearly £100,000 – which to a large extent are a reflection of our massive debts. Quite simply, we are living beyond our means.

So what is being done to restore the Kent & East Sussex to viability and ensure its existence? Well, quite a lot. Firstly, the timetable will be radically reviewed and running days reduced for 2002. It is virtually impossible to introduce changes before then, without the risk of offending passengers who have the existing published timetable, which has been widely distributed. Furthermore, we are now approaching the peak of our trading season. However, as part of the overall review, fares may have to be increased next year. Our advertising expenditure, already substantially reduced, is being targeted at key areas, where we perceive that there will be a measurable benefit, particularly when we organise special events. We are getting good free publicity through filming activities and editorial coverage.

We are going all out for group business, in many cases with a catering offering. A trip on the train to Bodiam Castle with tea and scones served is an attractive package, which appeals to coach parties. Our customer base also seems to be changing, with older people predominating over the traditional turn-up-and-go family passenger. Special events such as 'Thomas', 'Santa Specials' and the 'Steam & Country Fair' are highly profitable and will be pushed aggressively. Our greatest growth area is probably in the area of special catering trains – the Wealden Pullman, Sunday Lunch and Special Charter trains, where our new chef is already achieving a reputation for superb cuisine, boosted by editorial publicity in local newspapers and journals. Our gift shop was revamped at the beginning of the year and, under Brian Janes' watchful eye, is achieving higher turnover from a wider and more imaginative range of merchandise.

However, difficult decisions that have been made still have to be implemented. It is likely that the Company will achieve an overall loss on its operations during 2001, even if there is a substantial increase in business during the latter part of the year. We must return to profit in 2002 and this autumn we must show our bankers that we are capable of both servicing and reducing our debts in the short term. This can only be done by reducing our overheads. We are carefully managing our trade creditors, with each item requiring authority of the finance department before items can be ordered. Tim Leigh will be leaving us at the end of July and, in the short term, the department will be administered by me with Karen Bridge, under the overall authority of Paul Wilson, our Finance Director. Paul has direct responsibility for setting the public timetable and the financial budgets, and dealing with the bank; and he is also monitoring income levels on a daily basis. I produce monthly accounts for the Board from data supplied by our book keeper, Karen Bridge, monitor day-to-day expenditure with departmental managers, and keep an eye on the office.

Of the 35 years in which I have been associated with the Kent & East Sussex Railway the last two have been particularly challenging. Nevertheless, if all the necessary measures for revitalising the business come into place, I shall look forward to the future with optimism.

The redundancies eventually began after the due processes required by employment law had been observed and, at no great surprise to myself, I was made redundant towards the end of the summer. I nevertheless continued to turn up as a volunteer, particularly to keep the admin side of Carriage & Wagon running. Financially this wasn't too much of a problem. I had since 1998 been working in my spare time as an electoral registration canvasser for my home London Borough. Redundancy had come just at the right time of the year – the months when the annual updating of the register required additional office staff. When I phoned the relevant Council department to ask if there was any part-time work going the reply was, 'Can you start tomorrow?' Thus it was back to local government for a few months, although this was to prove a rather useful refresher course in electoral practice.

Chapter 26

Thus we come to the 2001 Annual General Meeting, which was held on 13 October – the following is based on the minutes of the meeting, *Tenterden Terrier* 86 Winter 2001, my own recollections and those of Norman Brice, together with input from Paul Wilson, Doug Lindsey and David Morgan. It had been hoped that this would unite the railway at a time of very considerable difficulty. In the event, a degree of unity was achieved, although it was not exactly what had been intended. Morale had, one way or another, held up during the preceding financial crisis, but that was of course an emotional buttress. Underneath it all, and particularly in some quarters, feelings were running very high.

There were two vacancies on the Board, and Graham Bridge was standing for re-election to one of these. A second and unsurprising candidate (I was among his nominees) was shop manager and Museum volunteer Brian Janes. There were however no fewer than nine other members standing, all of whom had nominated each other. They overlapped into the group which had called the 'unofficial' volunteers meeting on 19 May and which, as previously explained, was advocating a legally problematic recapitalisation by way of a share issue. They were standing with the aim of, hopefully, getting two of their number elected to the Board where they would presumably have acted in the manner of an opposition. We shall not name them, but it is appropriate to say that they were a very mixed bunch, some being better known than others. One has to comment that by fielding nine candidates, even if their attempt had proved positive, they were bound to split their own vote and that a more effective strategy might have been to only nominate two people.

As the Railway's members gathered in the eighteenth-century Assembly Room of Tenterden Town Hall (scene of the infamous rowdy AGMs of the 1960s) an unexpected stranger was noted. It was no less a person than David Morgan, Chairman of the Heritage Railway Association, who had been approached by a volunteer and asked to act as his proxy in accordance with the provisions of the Companies Acts and TRC's Articles of Association. A well-to-do solicitor, every inch the establishment figure and writer of forthright columns in the railway press, Morgan's presence caused a subdued apprehension amongst those who recognised him. My personal recollection is that it seemed like Cromwell arriving to dismiss the Rump Parliament.

The meeting started promptly at 2.30pm with the Chairman's report, which covered much of what has already been said related in foregoing chapters. It can be summarised by the statement that although '2000 had been a year of engineering success, 2001 will have been a turning point in the fortunes of the company'. The Accounts for 2000 were then adopted, surprisingly with no queries raised, a solitary vote against and four abstentions. Three amendments to the Articles of Association were then considered, the first being the closing date for Board nominations, the change from six to twelve weeks prior to the meeting being accepted without much ado, although David Morgan made the first of his interventions by asking when the date of the AGM was decided. Although, as described earlier in this book, AGM dates have occasionally been changed, the usual practice has been to decide when the meeting would be held considerably in advance of the closing date for nominations, in this case in March. The change from six to twelve weeks was to allow adequate time for the administrative arrangements. The second and third amendments, to membership categories and voting rights, were also approved. This time David Morgan spoke up to suggest 'a legal review of membership', to which proposal Norman Brice was able to respond that the Membership Committee was to further consider the membership categories. David Morgan has told me that, as a solicitor, his concern was that any review or subsequent changes should be within the provisions of the Memorandum and Articles of Association and the Companies Acts.

As has remained customary, each of the candidates for Board membership was given the opportunity to address the meeting outlining what they felt they could offer the Company. Once this got under way the meeting threatened to descend into chaos as, to quote the minutes, 'Derogatory comments were addressed to the existing Board'. To the consternation of many, Paul Wilson (Finance Director) and David Stratton (Managing Director) walked off the platform and left the meeting, furious, following their efforts to put the Railway's finances back on an even keel. Former Company Secretary Neil Rose raised a Point of Order as to whether the Board still had Managing and Finance Directors. Norman Brice responded that both remained in post until written letters of resignation had been received by the Company Secretary, a formality which duly happened later the same day. To add to the mayhem, one candidate for the Board told the meeting that he had obtained (different) employment, no longer wanted to be considered and was withdrawing his candidature. He was told that he could not; postal ballots might already have been cast in his favour and they had to stand. If elected, he would have to resign.

It had been the practice for the previous seventeen years that candidates for Board places had to attract at least 50 per cent of the votes cast rather than simply receive more votes than their competitors. The purpose of this was to prevent, particularly if vacancies equalled or exceeded the number of candidates, persons with little or no support being elected by default. This arrangement had never been queried. The subject was however raised when a questioner from the floor asked whether candidates might be co-opted onto the board if the requisite 50 per cent of votes cast had not been attained. Norman Brice replied that they would not (as it was, and is not, the practice to co-opt those who have failed to be elected).

David Morgan then fired a veritable broadside by stating that the 50 per cent rule was illegal under the Companies Acts. This was the statement recorded in the minutes and which I personally recall. When this was discussed with David Morgan in 2020, he explained that the 50 per cent rule would have been legal if it had been incorporated into the Mem & Arts. In this instance, the two candidates with the highest number of votes should automatically be elected. Raising this on its own this might have been seen as a genuinely arguable point. After the foregoing furore it was not unreasonable to wonder if this was part of a co-ordinated attack. David Morgan has however assured me that this was not the case, that he was trying to assist the Tenterden Railway Company to keep to correct procedure and that he was in no way hostile to the K&ESR or its members. By this time there was a palpable feeling of disquiet in the assembly room and Norman Brice was wondering whether to adjourn the meeting. He nonetheless decided against.

The voice of Neil Rose was then again heard, this time asking where the 50 per cent rule was written down, and was told by Philip Shaw, who had drafted the original version of the Mem & Arts, that it was not. He added that there had originally been a 10 per cent rule, that the Board had increased it to 50 per cent in 1984 and that the membership had been informed of the change at the AGM that year. David Morgan then stated that the Board should accept what the members required and Norman Brice made the pragmatic decision that the election should continue with the two candidates with the most votes being elected. He added that the matter would be looked at further with legal advice being taken if necessary. During these exchanges, one of the Board candidates appeared to lose his temper, made further derogatory remarks and threatened to consult his solicitor.

When the result of the poll was declared, Graham Bridge and Brian Janes had been elected, with the others a significant distance behind. Some had received very few votes and one individual (neither the temper loser nor the now-reluctant candidate) appeared to have little better than the votes of his sponsors and himself.

Following the formal business, presentations were put to the meeting on three possible means of raising longer-term capital. The proposals were:

- The formation of a Public Limited Company (PLC) or in other words recapitalisation by way of a share issue. As The Tenterden Railway Company was a Company Limited by Guarantee and a Registered Charity, it was unable to raise share capital as distinct from debt. A PLC would take over the running of the railway and enter into a lease or licensing agreement with the TRC which would retain ownership of the land and track. The new company would have a separate board of directors appointed by its shareholders and the Tenterden Railway Company would be reduced to being a supporters organisation. The consent of the Charity Commission would have to be obtained and the bank and bondholders would have to be satisfied that TRC would be provided with sufficient resources to meet its obligations to them.
- A zero coupon bond issue from TRC; a variation on the previous Bond issues. In this instance holdings would not attract interest but be redeemed at a premium of 15 per cent after 15 years providing, with a few exceptions, that they were held by the original applicant to maturity. This would not require the consent of the Charity Commission or the bank. If the proceeds were used exclusively to reduce the bank loan interest savings would be more than sufficient to repay the debt plus premium on maturity.
- An appeal. This would not add to the debt of the Company, would have valuable and immediate tax concessions in the form of Gift Aid and require no authorisation from any organisation. It would however require the whole hearted support of TRC's members.

A 'straw poll' taken at the end of the presentations indicated a preference for a share issue from the members present. No decision would be taken on any of the options without debating the various issues and consulting the membership.

Having been involved with the adoption of the PLC option on other heritage railways, David Morgan had spoken in favour of this course of action. At one point someone asked him who the new shareholders would be. His reply was to wave his arm around the room in a theatrical gesture indicating the members present. Sitting in the body of the meeting, my impression was of a somewhat underwhelming response. In view of the undertone of hostility that Morgan had attracted by this time, his intervention made the result of the straw poll a little surprising although the proposed further consultation did make the decision safely tentative. Other railways which had gone the PLC route already had a (Private) owning company and a separate although obviously linked Preservation Society for the volunteers and supporters. In such instances the culture change would most likely have been less than it would for a basically democratic Company Limited by Guarantee.

David Morgan is on record (*Railway Magazine*, November 2006 as later quoted in *The Railway Preservation Revolution* by Jonathan Brown) as believing that 'volunteers have maintained an independence of spirit'. Following the K&ESR's 2001 AGM, that independence manifested itself, not in respect of the TRC Board, which was directly accountable to members, but towards their, in effect, national leader with whom they had, rightly or wrongly, taken considerable umbrage. In the weeks that followed there were calls – although wisely not acted on – for the K&ESR to leave the Heritage Railway Association. A number of normally assertive people wondered why they had not said something during the more contentious parts of the AGM, and reluctantly concluded that they had felt intimidated. When told about this in 2020, David Morgan expressed disappointment, insofar as members' reaction had related to him, and reiterated that he had borne no ill-will to the K&ESR. He had merely been trying to help.

Some time later there was a sequel to this story when it became known around the mess rooms that someone called 'Morgan' had been co-opted to the Board. By that time I was in a position to nip the resulting stirrings of discontent in the bud. I replied to the e-mail from the spokesperson for the affronted with the news that the appointee was in fact Bill Morgan, Station Master and C&W volunteer, who was bringing a wealth of experience from the Army and British industry to the Directors' deliberations.

Chapter 27

In the aftermath of the AGM, the immediate need was to appoint a Managing Director in order, among all the other reasons, to maintain the validity of the Safety Case. Derek Dunlavey had been unable to attend the meeting but, as a Board member, a professional railwayman and one of the K&ESR's most experienced volunteers, was offered the post. He accepted. At around the same time, the position of Company Secretary again became vacant. It was advertised on a voluntary basis and this time, feeling that I had gained enough experience of how the K&ESR worked, I decided to apply. Acting as Secretary of the Special Events Committee had been an instructive 'dry run'.

Also advertised – in the railway press – was the paid post of General Manager and, rather to my surprise, I had been told – during an interview about my redundancy – that an application from me would be welcome. There was a long enough delay after the closing date for the matter to be reported in one of the enthusiast railway magazines, along with all the latest on the K&ESR's troubles. For some reason copies of the magazine issue involved seemed hard to find, and I finally tracked one down on the book stall at Inverness Station during a railway holiday in Scotland; 500 miles from the Kent & East Sussex, and on the concourse of a station maintained with due regard to its heritage, I read that three people known to the Railway had applied for the job.

Back at Tenterden I was examining coaches on No.1 road one Saturday morning when Norman Brice approached and offered me the post of Company Secretary (I was apparently the sole applicant). My immediate reply was that I thought it might be appropriate if I had a formal interview first. Once this had been organised, I was appointed with effect from 3 November 2001 – the date of the first Board meeting I attended in my new role – experiencing my first of the necessary treks up Church Path, carrying a bundle of books and papers, to the then usual venue in the local Day Centre. Much of the meeting set the tone of Board business for many months to come. The Railway's finances continued in an improving but marginal manner; it was projected that the profit/loss outturn at the end of the year would be £90,000. There was to be a visit from the bank on 15 November which would be handled by Norman Brice in person. This sounded ominous but was probably routine.

The PLC option for refinancing was inevitably on the agenda, Graham Bridge reminding the meeting that the AGM had given a 'steer' towards that option. Various aspects of the idea were discussed and the Chairman stressed that no decision had been taken. There was a general feeling that all options should be explored, and that there was a tendency to keep going over the same for and against arguments. Despite the events at the AGM, David Morgan had offered to make no charge for legal advice until a decision had been made; but, as Norman Brice pointed out, no decision could be made until advice had been given. None of the Board was in a position to do this. It was decided to concentrate on the PLC and Bond issue options for the moment and drop the general appeal.

An interesting if regrettable money-raising move at this time was the sale of an additional Austerity locomotive which had not yet arrived on site. This was ex-LNER J94 Class No. 68078 which had been purchased in mid-1999 from the GWR Preservation Group Ltd at Southall. In January 2001 the locomotive left Southall, but as there was no space at Rolvenden, it was delivered to Hope Farm, Sellindge, Kent, home of Bulleid Pacific restorers Southern Locomotives. Work was to be undertaken by the 68078 Association which had been formed by interested K&ESR members. Not long after arrival the Group was informed that the TRC intended to sell No. 68078 because of the K&ESR's financial situation. As a result, the locomotive passed into the ownership of Kent Locomotives Ltd with restoration continuing to be progressed by the 68078 Association. A fuller account of this project, including details of the kind of effort that heritage railways often involve, is to be found in Appendix D.

Another recent appointee at the November Board meeting was John Cobb, who now occupied the part-time salaried post of Accountant in the finance office. This was the dedicated accounts manager suggested by Peter Bourne, and the creation of this position was widely welcomed by both managers and volunteers. John was a management accountant by profession who held his K&ESR post as one of a portfolio of similar jobs in the Tenterden area. His background was in industry and he was possessed of both a waspish sense of humour and an often forthright manner. He was efficient at his work and fitted in well with the workforce. Sometime later, John, probably unintentionally, demonstrated the common ground with his peer group when he purchased one of the then current range of Triumph motor cycles.

A few weeks after I became Company Secretary, interviews were held for the General Manager's job. I went through with this as I didn't see any reason against someone holding both positions. If I had been successful it would of course have been the end of my involvement with Carriage & Wagon. I also realised that this was likely to be my last opportunity for a post at that level with any employer. In the event it was all academic – David Lloyd was appointed.

David was an interesting character. He was a career railwayman very much in the tradition of the 'Black Macs' (hands on managers) of the pre-sectorisation era and had worked for British Railways and its successors as well as with London Underground – particularly on the Metropolitan Line, a railway which keeps having unlikely connections with the K&ESR, starting as far back as Colonel Stephens' apprenticeship. LT had not too many years previously been controlled by the Greater London Council, and when David produced a draft Equal Opportunities policy, I recognised it as an old friend that the GLC had passed on to the London boroughs. Similarly, after I sent him a draft job description on one occasion, his comment was 'I've rewritten it so it's not in the Council style'! David commenced paid employment with the K&ESR on 10 December 2001.

The final Board meeting of 2001 was held on 8 December., and a number of critical issues were discussed. Legal matters included an end siding at Bodiam (which would in time grow into the Junction Road extension) and mention of the registration at Companies House of something new – a Kent & East Sussex Railway Company Ltd.

The last-mentioned matter came as a complete, but pleasant, surprise. Norman Brice and I had a matter of weeks beforehand discussed the possibility of creating a similarly named company with the aim of recovering the Railway's historic title which, as has been explained in the Preface, had been lost to George Pickin in the early 1960s. (Once the name was secured it would be a relatively simple matter to swap the TRC and K&ESR names over.) Imagine my amazement when on making an online check of the name's availability with Companies House,

I discovered that Director John Weller and K&ES Locomotive Trust Treasurer Boris Perkins had already, recently and with benign intent, got there before us. To quote the relevant minute:

> John Weller declared his directorship of the Kent & East Sussex Railway Company Ltd. He has, together with Boris Perkins, formed this limited by guarantee company with the object of securing the Railway's historic title. It had recently been ascertained the name was available. The new company will be offered to TRC at an appropriate moment.

Finance was as ever critical, and John Cobb reported that the cash position was looking a lot better, in part due to the pick-up in Santa business. The profit/loss out-turn for 2001 was however now projected at £100,000, although minus some old (i.e. outstanding) PAYE and VAT and redundancy money this would have looked lower.

The meeting had earlier commenced with a 'Part 2' confidential discussion, the details of which have not previously been made public. It must also be added that the following concerns the activities of, among others, John Snell. Mr Snell died in December 2013. It is uncomfortable for an author to have to record events concerning a distinguished and respected person, deceased within relatively recent years, when these events may not be seen as entirely complimentary. During the previous month, the small group advocating the contentious idea of a share issue had morphed into a PLC Supporters Group. Norman Brice, Brian Janes and Paul Wilson had attended a meeting with them on Sunday, 2 December which was chaired by John Snell. Norman Brice had later become aware of a press release (issued by the Supporters Group but not written by Snell) which had resulted in a newspaper report of the meeting. In the opinion of K&ESR Board members, it was debatable whether the press release was supposed to be speaking for the Supporters Group or the Railway, and the article reflected this – it could have been inferred that TRC wished to float a PLC. As a result, Norman Brice had written to John Snell asking for his resignation from the Board of CSRE. John Snell had refused. Norman Brice then asked for his comments as he considered there to have been a fundamental breach of trust and collective responsibility in addition to a conflict of interest. He was backed up in this opinion by Graham Bridge.

John Snell replied that he favoured a particular course of action, but was not pursuing it, and asked if the TRC Chairman was saying he did not have the right to make public statements. Brian Janes said there was nothing to prevent comment except about things which had been said in confidence – everyone needed to work together, Board members should be able to speak, and comment should not be censored. Carol Mitchell disliked the existence of a group of people who were trying to make her mind up for her and John Weller commented that the Board were to look at the options. They were prepared to be persuaded, not to be told, but the latter seemed to be the case. John Snell replied that the PLC Supporters Group was neither issuing dictats nor telling people what to do.

Derek Dunlavey considered the PLC Supporters to be a pressure group and also disliked being pressurised. He however saw no reason why people should not express differing viewpoints. Norman Brice then made it clear that it was the manner of the pressure – the matter was in the papers, via the media. John Snell was back-tracking by this stage and expressed the nuanced opinion that the release should have said it was hoped the Railway would launch a PLC.

When Graham Bridge reiterated his opinion that there was a conflict of interest, John Snell again disagreed, saying everyone should work towards the preservation of the Railway. Graham then made the significant statement that, in his opinion, the people in the Supporters Group were unacceptable to TRC members. John Snell replied this was unfortunate as all concerned should be building bridges. Graham Bridge had reasonable grounds for saying what he did, as he had previously been Volunteer Liaison Officer and was now receiving numerous phone calls and e-mails from working members. The general tone of these was that the PLC Group appeared elitist and aroused suspicions that the proposed organisation would reduce or dispense with the need for volunteers. Reasons for this were that John Snell was associated with the Paignton & Dartmouth Railway, which had dispensed with volunteers almost entirely, as well as the Romney Hythe & Dymchurch where he had been Managing Director. The latter was seen as being heavily reliant on paid employees. (My conversation with Graham Bridge in 2020.) It has to be pointed out, however, that it had been stated, in my presence, that in the event of a PLC taking over TRC would, in effect, act as an 'employment agency'. This would, of course, have been seen by many as no substitute for the 'common ownership' ethos of a Company Limited by Guarantee.

John Snell and Norman Brice then exchanged views on whether the charity or the charitable object was being put first. Mr Snell thought it was the charity but if he was wrong, he apologised. He was of course correct that charity law places the object before the organisation. The thrust of this argument nonetheless overlooked the mutually dependent relationship, referred to in chapter 2, between a railway and its supporters. Any charity by definition needs supporters but, in the case of a heritage railway – with all the cultural issues involved and a group loyalty resembling the close-knit railway communities of the steam era – the position is more complex. John Snell's background was in railways with a company–supporters group structure, famously the Talyllyn as well as the Romney Hythe & Dymchurch. This more closely resembles the traditional employer–employee relationship of the wider world than a Company Limited by Guarantee where the workers are in a very real way stakeholders in the enterprise. Norman Brice again said that John Snell's position was incompatible with membership of the CSRE Board. John Snell replied that he had heard the Board's annoyance and the incident was regrettable, but repeated that everyone should move forward.

The meeting later returned to the subject of the PLC during the non-confidential part of the agenda. Norman Brice began this by stating that he had asked the AGM if they wanted the PLC option explored and repeating his view that this approach had been misrepresented in the Press. No PLC could take over without the agreement of the TRC's Board and, at a General Meeting, members. From the press release and reports, the Support Group appeared prepared to launch a PLC themselves. During the meeting on 2 December, a minimum subscription of £250,000 had been indicated. This would only raise £200,000 after start-up costs had been deducted. They doubtless hoped more would be subscribed, but TRC's debts amounted to £1.4million. Norman Brice had asked for a written confidentiality agreement from the Supporters Group as he was unwilling to release information not previously in the public domain without such an agreement. John Snell regarded this as a 'gagging' order.

It was possible that the minimum subscription to a PLC flotation might not meet what TRC would demand as the premium for a lease. Day Smith & Hunter (TRC auditors) were of the opinion that this should be between £600,000 and £750,000, a mismatch of at least £400,000. Norman Brice was not prepared to act against the advice of the auditors as to do so might make Trustees personally liable. (There was murmur of agreement around the table.) He then read an extract of a letter from John Snell stating that a TRC premium estimate of £800,000 to £900,000 was too high.

The TRC Chairman thought that both the PLC and Bond issue options should still be explored. His own judgement was that flotation of a £600,000 PLC issue would probably fail. Day

Smith & Hunter were of the opinion that the Charity Commission would not approve the transfer of the Railway on the basis of a 99-year lease. John Snell at this point appeared to be agreeing with the Board members when he said that the K&ESR would require considerably more than the minimum a PLC must declare as necessary for its objectives. To this, Norman Brice pointed out that if the PLC took 12 months to raise the money, TRC would meanwhile be in limbo and could not issue bonds at the same time. Snell replied that to set an impossible objective was 'obstructive'. After further comments and discussion, Brian Janes made the practical suggestion that TRC would have to set a date some time during 2002 for a PLC to raise the necessary money. The debate ended after Norman Brice pointed out that the notion of a PLC and the Supporters Group were different things. Consideration of the PLC and Bond options was to continue.

January 2002 is an appropriate point to make mention of the K&ESR's connections with the two great rail engineering projects of modern times. During the construction of the Channel Tunnel a decade or so previously, various items of freight rolling stock had been hired to the contractors and various K&ESR members had been involved through their full-time employment. This was repeated on a larger scale during the building of the Channel Tunnel Rail Link (CTRL), now High Speed 1. During the early phases of CTRL, David Stratton and Bob Forsythe, the owners of the K&ESR's two Class 14 diesel hydraulic shunters, obtained the Board's permission to move their locomotives to the temporary marshalling yard at Beechbrook Farm near Ashford. This was being run by Victa Railfreight, itself an enterprise run by K&ESR member Neil Sime. On 7 January 2002, David and Bob formed a small company, Stratrail Ltd, for the purpose and invited me to join them as a Director and Company Secretary. (I handled most of the business administration.) Various wagons were directly hired to Victa Railfreight by TRC and many of us from the K&ESR, in our private capacities, became involved in one way or another with the building of the first British main line for over a century. In fact, on visiting Beechbrook Farm and its control tower, a significant part of the site seemed to be occupied by staff from the Kent & East Sussex.

The Board next met on 26 January 2002. It was the first such meeting attended by David Lloyd, and on this occasion the other managers had been invited as well.

Brian Janes presented a paper about volunteering, and made the interesting observation that if volunteers wished to work, they had to persist. Following my experience with guards training this had a decided resonance. Consequent to the issues raised at the AGM, I presented my conclusions about voting procedures. Norman Brice had sought the advice of TRC's solicitors; I had asked Philip Whiteman (by then working with the Institute of Local Government at Birmingham University) to refresh my memory about voting methods and also discussed the matter with former Company Secretary Neil Rose. It appeared that the 50 per cent rule would need to be incorporated into the Articles of Association if it were to continue in use. I was (and still am) of the opinion that Single Transferable Vote might suit the fragmented range of views on the K&ESR. Proportional Representation is however complex, and would have produced difficulties in reaching a result during the course of a meeting. I therefore recommended the use of 'First Past the Post' voting except where the number of candidates was equal to or fewer than the number of vacancies. In the latter situation, and at Neil Rose's suggestion, members would be able to vote against, as well as for, candidates, this provision being necessary to prevent persons with no support attaining Board seats by default. It was agreed this was the best course of action

John Cobb's report revealed that the draft profit/loss out-turn for 2001 was settling down at approximately £75,000. £30,000 had been spent on staff restructuring or, in other words, redundancies. In general, the cash flow position would be dependent on the success of the

Thomas event. This was critical in the wake of the earlier difficulties although the early months of the year had been, and would continue to be, a recurring challenge.

At the conclusion of the open part of the meeting the managers left. Shortly after, the CSRE-relevant parts of the meeting having concluded, John Snell was asked to withdraw. While leaving the room he commented that no-one involved with the PLC Supporters Group was hostile to TRC. Whatever the veracity of this I sensed scepticism among those around me.

Norman Brice had received a letter from the Charity Commission in response to an enquiry from him regarding the PLC option. This spelt out that getting a derogation to facilitate a share issue would be difficult; there were insuperable legal obstacles in the way. In the meantime, TRC had to deal with the PLC Supporters Group who, in Norman's opinion, had done nothing, probably could not raise the minimum subscription, and did not seem worth treating with. He added that, on the basis of the Charity Commission's advice, a 99-year lease to a PLC was not an option. There followed a unanimous vote of those present that on that basis a 99-year lease to a PLC, however composed, was not a feasible option and that Norman Brice should write accordingly to a named member of the PLC group. The Board then considered the alternatives of a Bond Issue and/or the flotation of CSRE as a freestanding company but noted the risks inherent in a PLC that TRC was unable to control. There was unanimous agreement not to pursue further the option of Tenterden Railway Company itself floating a PLC but instead to consider the principle of a Bond issue.

Around this time, a part-time salaried vacancy occurred in the Commercial Department, for which I applied and to which I was appointed. This was only for a couple of days a week and I was still able to continue with much of the C&W admin work in the evenings as well some carriage examining at weekends. The Stratrail work was done at home, together with a fair slice of the Company Secretary duties. All this was possible thanks to the existence of the internet and the fact that I had a long-suffering wife; but overall, I had rarely been busier. After a few months I was transferred back to C&W paid staff which helped focus my efforts.

During February, the PLC Group held a meeting in the Leisure Centre at the other end of Tenterden to explain their ideas to K&ESR members. It was poorly attended, Board members and 'hangers-on' being the majority of the small number present. The term 'hangers-on' was used in my presence and doubtless intended to (accurately) include me. Philip Shaw, a Finance Committee member also attended. The atmosphere was one of mutual suspicion. It appeared that the Railway's membership had 'voted with their feet', a fact confirmed when feedback from volunteers was discussed at a Board meeting on Thursday, 21 February. The PLC Group was known to have made unofficial requests to the Joint Membership Secretaries (Pam and Sheila Stevens, who rejoiced in the self-inflicted, if apt, soubriquet of 'Hinge and Bracket') for the membership list but had been told to contact me under the provisions of the Companies Acts. I had received no such request at that time although this was later made, the information being promptly and efficiently supplied by Pam and Sheila. It is also worth noting that the request for details of the Membership Register came from Roy Seabourne, a wealthy backer of the Rother Valley scheme. There was at that time discernible common ground between the advocates of a Robertsbridge extension and the PLC Group. This must be balanced by stating that such linkage diminished in later years.

There followed a discussion on how much might be raised by a bond issue, how much it might cost and the various ways the resulting capital injection might be used. It could have been that by June or July the cash flow requirements would be significantly different. Indeed, by the time of the Board meeting on 24 February, it was noted that trade creditors were the lowest for several years. Norman Brice added that, in the light of the advice received from the Solicitors and the Accountants, and while acknowledging the cash flow problem, he was satisfied that the Company was not insolvent. It was up to each Director to make up their own mind about this. No one dissented from that view.

During the meeting, the renaming of the company was progressed by TRC agreeing to nominate a number of Directors as members of the K&ESR company. Once they 'dominated' the Board I would take over as Secretary for the new company, which would henceforward be part of the group along with the parent organisation and CSRE. Norman Brice expressed the Board's gratitude to John Weller and Boris Perkins for their initiative in the matter and the TRC Board unanimously agreed to the proposed course of action.

The publication of the *Tenterden Terrier* on 16 March 2002 informed members that the anticipated fall in passenger numbers had indeed occurred, although the figure remained at a very healthy 98,669. Concern about the financial position continued, and the overdraft stood close to the limit agreed with the bank – although this was near the close of the non-trading months, as always a difficult point in the Railway's year. John Cobb had since his arrival put much effort into putting the Railway's financial records into good order and, together with Philip Shaw, was able to tell the meeting that the K&ESR's total indebtedness at that point amounted to £1.4million. The Board rightly thanked John for the work he had done since joining the Company. Preparations for the 2002 Steam & Country Fair were well under way by this time and an appropriate item had appeared in the spring *Tenterden Terrier*. It was hoped to build upon the success of the previous year's event, and Northiam was again to be the venue. On this occasion, the fair was to occupy a larger 25-acre field on the opposite side of the road to the station. There was to be an aerobatic display by a vintage Second World War aircraft, possibly a Mustang, and the article included the usual plea for volunteer help.

The first of two April Board meetings took place on 20 April. Early on in the agenda, Philip Shaw made a remarkable statement, in fact one that marked a turning point in the history of the Kent & East Sussex Railway. After presenting the cash position, he was able to say that there had been an improvement in the overall position and that the Company was no longer in jeopardy. Having sat through several months of sometimes dispiriting news it gave me considerable pleasure to record this in the minutes. Philip hoped that the Company would be out of the worst by May. Income in advance was not included in the figures but was running at £1,000 per day. Although the trade creditors were lower and the cash flow good, Norman Brice rightly pointed out that problems were nonetheless being stored up as expenditure had been severely restricted. Philip Shaw's further statement that he was 'quite comfortable' with the financial position compared with 2001, and with David Lloyd emphasising that expenditure restrictions had not compromised safety, ended this part of the meeting on a positive note.

Amidst the concern about the financial position at that meeting, the Board considered a vital marketing issue for the Kent & East Sussex Railway – its image as presented to the public. There had recently been a survey of members' comments via a letter distributed at the AGM and with a *Terrier* mailing. The response had principally come from 'armchair' members with working staff in a minority and the 'Genuine Rural Light Railway' option was clearly indicated by the stated preference. It was suspected that the reason for the poor response from volunteers was in the nature of the people on the Railway. Many volunteers only wanted 'A Railway'. One outcome of this exercise was the adoption of the K&ESR logo still in use at the time of writing. The new device was a happy combination of elements from the Railway's past, the heraldic belt of 1904 and a second design from the 1960s which incorporated the arms of Kent and East Sussex plus a Terrier silhouette.

Away from Board issues, my other main area of K&ESR life was seeing more changes, with Clive Lowe resigning to take up a position with Victa Railfreight. He was replaced by John Brice who held the post until the autumn of 2004.

On 28 April, the Chairman told the Board that the PLC Group had not met since before Easter and no future dates of Group meetings had been provided to him. He had been meeting with the Group on behalf of TRC and had asked Brian Janes to join him, which would seem to have been a wise move. Brian, like Norman, had been a senior Civil Servant, well used to the manoeuvrings of politicians. It was understood that the PLC Group was likely to meet with the North Yorkshire Moors Railway in the near future, that line already having formed a PLC, with the intention of learning from their experience.

Then, on 3 May 2002, following the appropriate action by members of the PLC Group, The Kent & East Sussex Steam Railway Company PLC was registered at Companies House. I cannot now recall whether or not TRC had rapidly became aware of this, but it was certainly not discussed at the Board meeting on 11 May.

Finance continued to form a weighty part of the agenda at this time, although John Cobb was able to report that the cash flow in April and May had shown a dramatic transformation, with a satisfactory reduction in the overdraft, and that the Railway was in a much healthier position. The profit/loss account for the first quarter of 2002 was budgeted for a loss of £25,000. It was in fact just £3,000. John Cobb's stewardship of the K&ESR's finances was becoming widely appreciated, and during the meeting Philip Shaw congratulated John on the way the Company's finances were set up.

The financially optimistic theme continued at the meeting of 9 June, the first of two that month. Philip Shaw was able to say that there had been a substantial improvement in the current cash position; cash inflow was £95,000 ahead of budget, £65,000 of this being Thomas and £10,000 Gift Aid. The latter was becoming an increasingly important part of the K&ESR's income. Gift Aid allows UK income tax payers to complete a short declaration after which their donations to a charity (e.g. the K&ESR) are treated as being made after deduction of income tax at the basic rate and the charity can reclaim the basic rate income tax paid on the gift from the government. For a basic-rate taxpayer, this added approximately 25 per cent to the value of any gift made under Gift Aid. A device used by many charities that charged for admission, including the K&ESR, was to ask visitors to regard the price of their ticket as a donation.

It was anticipated at the meeting of 25 June that that the Railway would move into profit during that month, the Thomas event having proved highly successful with the shop enjoying one of its best days ever. It was predicted that the overdraft would be eliminated during July and that it was possible to look forward to a reasonable profit for 2002. In the meantime, Norman Brice had secured an additional grant of £39,525 from the Millennium Commission. This occurred at around the same time that it became known that the Company was to receive a very generous sum from the estate of the late Alan Merrills, who had been a member of the Ashford Area Group. It was the wish of Mr Merrills' executors that this should be applied to a major project; the new grant and the bequest were combined and this was the beginning of the scheme to restore Pullman car *Theodora*.

Philip Shaw found a new adjective in July for the financial turn-about when he described it as 'dramatic'. In his typically cautious manner, he nevertheless informed the same Board meeting that heard that statement that he was concerned about the prospects for the consumer economy in 2003, and that this could prove difficult. A very firm grip should be maintained on costs, particularly in relation to staff numbers.

That July Board meeting later dealt with some formal business preliminary to the proposed renaming of the Tenterden Railway Company as the Kent & East Sussex Railway Company Limited. This was before attention was turned to contentious developments involving the PLC Supporters Group. What follows has not previously been public knowledge (a 'Part 2' Board item), although available to K&ESR members in the company records and is related in some detail as it very much reflects the feelings surrounding the whole issue of the PLC at the time.

I had previously circulated to Board members a report (from which the relevant following paragraphs have been adapted) which Norman Brice had prepared about his meeting with John Snell, representing the PLC supporters Group, on 26 June. Snell had wanted to discuss legal advice the Group had received that TRC's Trustees (the Board members are Trustees under Charity legislation) had the power to sign a 99-year lease to a PLC, provided that certain formalities were observed and that the deal was considered by the Trustees to be better than could be achieved by not entering into the agreement.

Snell then said that the PLC Group had three options: to work in co-operation with the TRC Trustees, to mount a hostile take-over, or to do nothing. Which they adopted would depend to a large extent on TRC's financial position and the attitude of the Trustees. He continued that he had a right, under the Companies Act, to see a list of TRC's shareholders (i.e. members) and the Group could send out a statement which was issued jointly with TRC or their own statement proposing a PLC flotation.

Norman Brice observed that Snell was apparently complaining of a lack of co-operation from the TRC Board, which he rejected. He had offered to accompany him and others to meetings with the North Yorkshire Moors Railway and a solicitor, but his offers had not been take up. Further, if necessary, he could publish letters confirming his willingness to meet any of the Group and to provide information which might help them prepare a Business Case. He would do just that if the allegation of non-cooperation were to be repeated publicly. Norman Brice had also drawn attention to the PLC Group's Newsletter No. 1 dated January 2002 which had stated an intention of launching a flotation in the spring of that year. It was now June and the only progress apparently made had been a visit to a solicitor and the formation of the dormant PLC. John Snell accepted that the spring date had been seriously erroneous and misleading.

The two men than debated (again) the relative merits of charitable and PLC status. While it was true that a successful flotation would reduce bank borrowings and hence repayments, there would be compensating losses. Payments to the bank (interest and capital) probably ran at some £80,000 a year, but membership subscriptions and Gift Aid were in the region of £70,000 a year. There was also the question of the PLC's minimum subscription and its relationship with the annual lease that TRC would charge. Unless the PLC raised £1.4million at flotation, commonly accepted as highly improbable, it would have to meet TRC's lease from a combination of share proceeds and improvements to the business. TRC's published book assets (i.e. what the railway had cost to build) were very close to £3million and debts were £1.4million, all repayable over the next ten years. The debt alone gave a lease cost of £150,000 a year, disregarding the underlying asset value. Stripping out membership and Gift Aid, how could the PLC demonstrate to the Trustees' satisfaction that the business of running trains and the ancillary trading could generate £150,000 a year more than the existing operation could manage? The way forward was for the PLC Group to prepare a Business Case and obtain a Valuation from a firm of Chartered Accountants. There would then be a further meeting when TRC had had the opportunity of reflecting upon the Group's arguments.

Norman Brice then told the Board that he had maintained a relationship with the PLC Group as he had consider it to be in the best interests of the TRC and Trustees to do so, for three reasons:

- TRC required capital for debt repayment and new projects, and the plc might be able to offer such funding on terms acceptable to the Trustees. The Board had a duty to consider such offers;
- so far most of the 'debate' had been on emotional terms. He wanted to see a properly argued economic and business case for the PLC; and
- the Group had threatened a hostile bid. He would like to explore whether there were grounds for dialogue, rather than confrontation.

There was continuing concern about the apparent conflict of interest John Snell had between his membership of the PLC Group and his Directorship of CSRE. By his references to 'We can mount a hostile bid…' he had clearly aligned himself with the Group. Norman Brice therefore considered Snell's threats to mount a hostile bid against TRC to be incompatible with his continued presence at Board meetings. In addition, the matter of a company called the Kent & East Sussex Steam Railway PLC was then raised. As this name was close to TRC's long-established marketing title an objection was to be made under the Companies Acts.

After quoting the 'hostile take-over' remarks, which John Snell said had been taken out of context, Norman Brice asked if the PLC had prepared the suggested business plan; however, he received the reply that various details were in delayed first class post, although this was only a first step. Norman then stated his not unreasonable opinion that there was nothing to talk about because there was nothing on the table.

In response to a question from John Weller, Mr Snell then informed the meeting that, in spite of having earlier declared an interest, he was neither a Director nor a shareholder of the PLC but was speaking 'on behalf of that company'. Norman Brice pointed out the PLC Group had been moving in the direction of the present position since the previous October, in response to which John Snell spoke of 'misunderstandings' and that delays had occurred because of the involvement of third-party consultants. He confirmed that the TRC Chairman would be involved in discussions with these consultants 'at the next stage' and also explained that the PLC was now examining the possibility of a jointly owned TRC/PLC subsidiary. Norman Brice confirmed that he was already aware of this and that TRC Trustees would have to consider any offer.

John Snell then made what must have been an attempt at reconciliation with the TRC Board when he said that some PLC people had been saying things he 'did not accept'. When Norman Brice added that hostile publicity had been put out, John Snell indicated that he wished to '"back away" from this'. He was reminded of the concept of collective responsibility.

Towards the conclusion of these exchanges, Norman Brice expressed the view that the TRC Board could not go to their AGM with an 'unquantified hostile approach' by the PLC. He was however happy to talk to the PLC with their professional advisers, but that John Snell's 'hostile' statement was inimical to his continued presence at the Board table. Unsurprisingly, John Snell did not agree. Norman Brice would not accept any responsibility for the cost of meetings with the PLC's professional advisers and said that it should be made clear that any such consultations were not a joint approach. Snell replied that the PLC Group was working towards the emergence of a joint proposal, and if there was failure to agree 'something else might be done'.

Chapter 28

In his editorial for the summer 2002 *Terrier*, Philip Shaw told readers that following the unpleasant but necessary decisions of the previous year income was running comfortably ahead of budget, and that a much more profitable future was anticipated. With initiatives from volunteers and paid staff, particularly in the Commercial Department, pre-booked parties, catering and charter services were all going from strength to strength, with special events being the 'icing on the cake'. The journal's regular 'Lineside News' feature continued this upbeat theme by adding that the Weekend at War figures had been very good and that bookings for the June Thomas were very healthy. The Santa Specials were already selling and a number of filming contracts were in hand.

The new season saw the introduction of several changes to the Pullman services, which by the time of the magazine's publication were 70 per cent booked. Sunday luncheon trains now ran from platform 2 at Northiam Station to overcome the pathing problems of trying to run the Pullman between the ordinary scheduled service trains. The Pullman trains were again going from strength to strength. The redoubtable Meg Gooch became Pullman Chef around this time and has been a feature of the service ever since. She later became Pullman Manager, an appointment which has not prevented her from using her artistic skills as the K&ESR's signwriter, particularly on behalf of the Loco and Carriage & Wagon Departments.

On-train catering demand on the scheduled 'A' set service also remained high, sometimes outstripping the ability to provide the required standard. The 'kitchen' on the set was a converted PMV with a gangway installed at one end. This was a British Standard gangway, not the Pullman type as found on all the other 'A' set stock. The two designs were compatible with the use of a series of clips. Following unfortunate 'incidents' with the clips, disconnection of the gangway was only to be undertaken by C&W staff. The procedure was loathed nearly as much as the destructive results of it not being correctly followed. The PMV was far from ideal, but an Restaurant Miniature Buffet acquired from the Llangollen Railway soon replaced it. The initial replacement in fact took place sooner than expected after the PMV was derailed when the Rolvenden crossing gates were incorrectly operated. Damage to the underframe resulted, and the vehicle has been static as a store in Bodiam yard more or less ever since.

When the previous year's figures were finalised, it was found that the Tenterden Railway Company had incurred a loss in 2001 – which was disappointing compared with the profit achieved in the previous year, but lower than had been indicated to members earlier. Furthermore, this was incurred after the exceptional flood damage expenditure and the redundancy costs. Without these items, the loss would have been modest. There was every expectation of a return to profit in 2002, with a significant reduction in bank borrowings.

The same weekend that the summer *Tenterden Terrier* was published, the 2002 Steam & Country Fair was again held at Northiam. This time, and as already mentioned, the venue was the field on the Wittersham side of the road, but still with easy road access and the Railway running in the background. The customary range of attractions was on display including Harris Bros Gallopers, traction engines, steamrollers and vintage farm implements. Musical entertainment was provided by three organs. Craft stalls demonstrated their skills while working exhibits included a threshing drum, a blacksmith display and a rack saw bench. Other displays included vintage toys, models of steam engines, old and new AA vehicles and hop-picking items. About 200 classic cars and motorcycles came to the show, the majority dating from the post 1950 period, as well as a number of buses, stationary engines, kit cars and tractors. Unlike the previous year, shire horses were able to attend and give rides around the site. There was an aerial display, once again by a Mustang fighter aircraft, which brought the spine-tingling sound of a Merlin engine to the Rother Valley. Although the gross income from the event was around £26,000, profit only amounted to £4,700, less than had been hoped for. There was nevertheless the increased traffic on the Railway and the intangible benefits of publicity and goodwill. With my increasing duties elsewhere in the Company, 2002 was the last year that I was involved with the Steam & Country Fair, but it had been a worthwhile experience. As Charlie Masterson had predicted, I nevertheless knew that I had done it.

On 13 September there was a meeting with the Bank, Norman Brice later reporting to the Board Meeting of 15 September 2002 that this had been entirely satisfactory. He did not have any reason to believe that an adequate overdraft for the period January–April 2003 would not be forthcoming. The Bank had mentioned that they considered the Railway to be 'embedded' in the community. The following weekend, 14/15 September, K&ESR held that year's Hoppers Weekend, this time at Bodiam Station. The weekend event on the area's traditional theme of hop-picking was becoming established and was destined to continue as a regular feature of the Railway's calendar. Indeed, by the early twenty-first century, Bodiam Station had become one of the few tangible reminders of the hop gardens and the Cockney hop pickers who once arrived by train for what, for many, had amounted to a paid holiday.

The issue of the PLC Group and their newly formed company continued. (Minutes of Board meeting 12 October 2002) On 26 September, Norman Brice, together with Brian Janes and Paul Wilson, no longer a Director but present as a member of the Finance Committee, had met with representatives of the Group and their professional advisers at the offices of a Canterbury-based firm of accountants. Also present were John Snell, Steven Bennett (a PLC Group member), a manager from the accountants, and a solicitor representing both the PLC Group and Roy Seabourne, the wealthy and influential RVR member who had previously contacted me about the K&ESR Membership Register. The first hour of the meeting was taken up by John Snell yet again explaining the advantages of a PLC. Norman Brice then pointed out that there was no precedent for a heritage railway charity becoming a PLC, as opposed to running in parallel. He gave the accountants' representative a copy of a letter from the Charity Commission commenting on the obstacles involved in a charity becoming a PLC – it was the first time that the accountants had seen this. They responded by asking for an agreement by the time of the TRC Annual General Meeting on 12 October, a request which Norman Brice quite rightly said was unreasonable. What looks many years later (and to those who took part in it at the time) to have been a rather pointless meeting concluded with the obvious statement that both parties agreed that they had the common objective of raising money in the most debt-free way.

The Annual General Meeting, once again held at Tenterden Town Hall, passed off without any of the 'excitements' which accompanied the event in 2001. The new voting system worked well, Norman Brice being re-elected for a further three years and Paul Hutchinson, who had been co-opted to the Board in July, receiving the endorsement of the membership. Happily, the proposal to rename TRC as the Kent & East Sussex Railway Company was also approved by the meeting. I commented in the subsequent *Tenterden Terrier* that not only would the Railway be reunited with its historic company name, but it would bring an end to all those irritating conversations with suppliers who had Tenterden Railway Company down as K&ESR (or vice versa) and claimed never to have heard of us! The changeover was pencilled in for some time during 2004.

The year was ending well, as David Lloyd reported in the General Manager's contribution to the winter issue of the *Tenterden Terrier*:

> The change in the Company's fortunes this year has been exceptional. We started off with a substantial overdraft and creditors running into six figures; this now seems a distant memory. What has happened to change things? Firstly we had to impose severe spending constraints which caused managers to look closely at the way in which they were running their departments and also the fact that a General Manager was monitoring their progress. The change was immediate and the financial impact on the Company's finances has been dramatic. Coupled with excellent advance bookings in catering and special events we survived a difficult winter and moved forward through a successful season to an autumn of exhaustion but with much more financial security. Critics will say that our problems are not entirely over and they may be right, but we have built upon solid foundations with a tough but workable budget and gained valuable experience from it to set next year's budget. Some of the decisions that had to be made were not popular, but they have been effective and the managers have had someone to turn to. 2002 was a year of many changes with a reduction in full time staff and a reduced timetable, but it still stretched our volunteer resources to the limit. They responded magnificently and I am proud of every one of them. Spare a thought also for the paid staff who toil relentlessly, often giving far more hours than they are paid for. The commercial office has been under great pressure with extra bookings for our most successful ever Thomas event and now booking for the Santa Specials.

This upbeat theme continued through the next few Board meetings. On 24 November, Philip Shaw reported the cash position to be in credit, which represented a turnaround in the bank position of £100,000 since the beginning of the year. The creditors' position was also much improved. The latest development in the saga of the PLC Group was discussed, a letter recently from their accountants offering £1 per year for a 999-year lease plus terms for possible debt repayment; John Snell thought this was a good offer. The TRC Board members thought otherwise and approved an appropriate reply from Norman Brice. At the December meeting, the Board concluded that there was not much point in continuing the debate with the PLC. After that, with the K&ESR's improving finances, little obvious support among the membership and later good fortune, the idea faded away. The (renamed) Tenterden, Bodiam and Robertsbridge Railway PLC still existed as a dormant company in the early 2020s.

Publication of the 2002 passenger figures in the spring of the following year initially appeared worrying, showing a decline from 92,346 to 86,570. The focus had however moved to running a profitable service rather than relying on revenue. The key statistic was passengers per train, which had reached 87 for the first time since 1990. Some trains had not been carrying sufficient passengers to justify their retention and a 24 per cent reduction had proved cost effective. As Paul Wilson put it at the time: 'We might as well have stood at the barrier and handed everyone a

£10 note.' Pre-booked passengers now accounted for a healthy 47 per cent of traffic, up from 36 per cent the year before. The Santa Specials, in their best season since 1991, had carried 12,100 passengers; Thomas events had continued their success and the Wealden Pullman continued as a major contributor to revenue.

By February it had been possible to report that the Company was no longer considered to be at risk and that the bank account (previously in 'special measures') was being moved back to the Ashford branch. By January it was possible to discuss proposals for a carriage shed extension and carriage storage shed at Rolvenden. Both schemes were to be achieved in later years. A month later, at the Board meeting of 8 March 2003, it was stated that the finances were in a healthy position with £72,000 in the bank and creditors at £74,000. This compared with a combined creditor and overdraft of more than £250,000 at the same point in the previous year. The Editorial to the spring 2003 *Tenterden Terrier* related similar sentiments to the wider membership:

> The news that the Tenterden Railway Company moved strongly into the black last year, with profits in excess of £70,000, is welcome indeed given the losses that were incurred in the previous year. Our success has, in the main part, been due to the tailoring of costs to expected and achieved levels of income, but our charitable status has been of immense benefit to us, with the Government chipping in Gift Aid of £40,000 and local authorities granting us exemption from industry's ever-rising burden of business rates. So what of the immediate future? 2003 has got off to a good start with the Winter Thomas event achieving income levels well in excess of budget. Careful cash management should ensure progress, whilst new infrastructure projects will improve the quality of our business and our assets.

The positive direction the K&ESR was now taking was matched by another centenary celebration, this time of the extension 'up the hill' to Tenterden Town Station. This event took place on Sunday, 16 March (100 years to the day) with a civic parade of Town Council members along Tenterden High Street and down to the Station. The event was well attended and the Mayor of Ashford (successor authority to the Borough of Tenterden) was also present. This community involvement was more than appropriate for a town which for so many had become synonymous with the Kent & East Sussex Railway.

The following weekend, 22/23 March, the K&ESR once again took part in the biennial *Fête de la Vapeur* at the CFBS. The usual expedition headed for Saint Valery-sur-Seine, this time taking the P Class with them, the locomotive again making a return to France where it had shunted Boulogne docks during the First World War. Also attending was Alan Brice's Wallis and Steevens Advance steam roller, making its way to the event on the back of a lorry. It was on the autoroute which runs west from Calais that the French police noticed some technical infringement under the local law and promptly impounded the vehicle and its load at the roadside! I became aware of this when my phone in the C&W office rang at the start of a series of frantic cross-channel calls. The lorry (and load) were subsequently released when Norman Brice, who was in France at the time, paid the resulting on-the-spot fine.

There was a relaunch ceremony on 10 May for the Pannier Tank, No. 1638, following an overhaul and the re-entry onto traffic of Maunsell BNO brake No. 4432 after extensive bodywork repairs. The Board heard the same day that the year generally was looking good with Easter income well in excess of budget and that the first three months had all been ahead of both budgeted income and passenger numbers. The TRC group profit in 2002 was now known to be £77,000, although this included a legacy which, if deducted, could be viewed as making the position look less rosy. Brain Janes commented, quite accurately, that few other heritage railways were in any better position. During this discussion Board members revisited the growing realisation that they must start setting money aside for repayment of the Northiam Bonds.

There was a similar mixed message during the Board meeting on 7 June when it was reported that income was much greater than anticipated and included £50,000 in legacies and £8,000 transferred from the Steam & Country Fair account. Fares were £22,000 in excess of budget excluding advance income, but overall costs were more than £50,000 ahead of budget.

The same meeting included an intriguing discussion which illustrated the sometimes bemusing attitudes of volunteers in their relationship with the Railway's leadership. Managing Director Derek Dunlavey began this when he said that the managers would like Directors to visit them and spend more time out and about chatting. What were the Board going to do to find a subtle way of developing this? David Lloyd added that the managers had told him that volunteers would like to know who the Directors were. Brian Janes quite aptly responded that this was a baffling comment as most people around the Board table worked on the Railway, some in several departments. I recall that as I wrote this down, I found myself in agreement with Brian. Many people seemed to know who I was, so why not their elected representatives? Both then and in subsequent years, Directors could be found in the Carriage & Wagon mess, whether as volunteers or visitors, and members were not usually reluctant to question them. Years later, Philip Shaw made a comment which would have been equally applicable in 2003. He said that if he called at the C&W mess room during a tea break, he could find out what he needed to know simply by sitting and listening.

The controversy over the PLC issue took an almost predictable turn at the Board meeting on 9 August 2003 when Norman Brice reported John Snell's resignation as a Director of CSRE. Mr Snell's letter of resignation was read by the Directors present. Right to the end, and indeed afterwards, Snell maintained that although the financial situation was improving, the K&ESR would eventually fail at the 'cliff edge' of the Bond repayments. He was to be proved wrong. The same meeting also heard that following the recent collision and derailment on the neighbouring Romney Hythe and Dymchurch Railway on 3 August which had resulted in the death of Driver Kevin Crouch, a minute's silence on his memory had been held at Tenterden Town Station at 11.35pm the following day. With the RH&DR still closed for the recovery and necessary investigation, the K&ESR handled the Romney's group bookings for the 4th but did not keep the resulting income. That was sent on to the RH&DR.

On 6 September, John Cobb reported continuing improvement in the financial position with £146,051.21 in the bank compared with a £3,000 overdraft at the end of August the previous year. But there was no room for complacency; in June and July the Railway had broken even on trading, the difference being in donations and legacies. The budget allowed for an £18,000 loss but there was in fact a £46,000 profit. In later months these improvements led the Board to consider the thorny matter of the Northiam Bond Redemption in 2007 and the Bodiam Bonds at the then seemingly distant date of 2013. By November it had been decided to set aside £50,000 from the 2003 accounts with a further review in June 2004. The implication was that this sort of sum would need to be reserved annually. Brian Janes dissented from this decision and stated during research for this book that, in his view, using Bonds for the Bodiam extension had been a mistake. He was, however, by this stage not attracted to the PLC option on offer.

The 2003 AGM was held on 11 October and was once again relatively uneventful – an outcome for which, as Company Secretary, I was always particularly grateful. I had no wish to experience the events my predecessor had had to endure in 2001! In his Chairman's Statement, Norman Brice told the meeting that, within reason, the K&ESR was doing well. The cost reductions introduced in 2001, difficult though they were, proved well justified, as did the policy of a better balance between services offered and passenger demand. The Railway had fewer passengers but was trading more profitably. The headline figures for 2002 were a surplus close to £76,000, coupled with a reduction in borrowings of £203,000, a very creditable performance which reflected well on the efforts of everyone involved. Norman however sounded a cautionary note: however sound the financial performance, there was need to guard against being over-confident and complacent. As ever the biggest risk was lack of adequate volunteer manpower. 2002 had been a good year and 2003 showed signs of being the same and possibly better. With continued support from volunteers and staff the Kent & East Sussex Railway could go forward with a degree of confidence.

Grants continued to form an essential element of working capital and with the successful completion of the Bodiam scheme, the Millennium Commission looked favourably on a further application for funds. This was in connection with the restoration of the ex L&NWR 'Woolwich' four wheeler (K&ESR No. 67) and Pullman Car *Theodora*. Both these vehicles had of course been present on the K&ESR since the 1960s. It was almost a point of honour that these vehicles which had languished for so long should enter revenue earning traffic.

Some private money had already been provided for No. 67 which had enabled work to commence, and it was fully intended that the coach would be ready for traffic during 2004. By the time the November *Terrier* was published, work to the underframe wheels and running gear was substantially complete and the remains of the body were retrieved from the far side of the yard by steam crane on 20 October. The task of reconstruction remained and involved the extensive use of new material. The same grant was also to be used to enhance the bequest left to the Railway by the late Alan Merrills for the restoration of Pullman Car *Theodora*. This project was scheduled to overlap the work on the Woolwich coach, with late 2004 as a target date for completion.

December brought with it echoes of the past. News came of the death of Peter Benge-Abbott, who had been Chairman in the aftermath of the failure in 1967 to obtain a Light Railway Transfer Order. Much of the credit for keeping the K&ESR project in existence at that time was due to Peter. He had been awarded an Honorary Life Membership in 2001 in belated recognition of his contribution.

Another matter from the past also reached its climax as 2003 came to an end when I sent the necessary paperwork to Companies House renaming Tenterden Railway Company as the Kent & East Sussex Railway Company Limited. I had timed this, using my cynical knowledge of the public sector, with a view to the change occurring during 2004, the centenary of the original adoption of the title. Never assume anything! When, shortly after Christmas, I received the new registration certificate it was dated on what I would have imagined to be the least likely date – 24 December 2003, Christmas Eve! I felt privileged to have made the practical arrangements for the change and put right something which had seemed so wrong for so many years. It was also quietly satisfying to show the new certificate to Robin Doust, the original Secretary of the K&ESR Preservation Society, when he arrived in England for his annual book-buying visit on behalf of Bulawayo Public Library. I knew only too well that he had been among those of us who had regretted the loss of the company name in the 1960s.

In terms of finance, 2003 appeared to be ending reasonably well although, overall, finances remained tight. There was however a very large cloud on the horizon. In his pre-Budget statement, the Chancellor of the Exchequer had announced that Gift Aid on donations in lieu of entrance fees was to be withdrawn under the 2004 Finance Act. The implications were that this effectively reduced the Railway's 2004 budget by £32,000 and that the Company would go into 2005 with a £2,500 cash balance and an £80,000 cash outflow. There was an immediate howl of anguish throughout the entire British heritage industry, and not just on steam railways. This matter, and objections to it from many quarters, continued for some time until the Blair government gave in to the pressure and withdrew the proposal. During the course of the protests, our Management Accountant, John Cobb, attended a meeting of the outraged and reported back to the Board. His verbal account of the event included the comment that most of those attending had been from zoos and wildlife parks. Without batting an eyelid, Director Paul Hutchinson dryly commented, 'You must have felt at home, John.'

The December 2003 Board meeting included a presentation by Locomotive Manager Lawrence Donaldson and his volunteer colleague Chris Greatley. They were there to explain the need for a reverse osmosis plant, an installation which would produce treated water for steam locomotives. Chris, an industrial chemist by profession, had a talent, shared with one or two Radio 4 presenters, of being able to make highly technical matters deeply fascinating. I was later told by a C&W volunteer who had once been on a conducted tour of Dungeness B Nuclear Power Station, that Chris Greatley had been the guide and had made it a more than memorable occasion. This was useful to say the least as Chris persuasively enlarged on a previously circulated cost effectiveness report and other handouts following his investigation into this method of water treatment. Both he and David Lloyd considered its installation to be a high priority for revenue protection, with benefits too numerous to list. By the end of the meeting, the Board were sold on the idea and set about seeking the necessary finance; the cost was eventually met through the generosity of the Norwegian Locomotive Trust.

The December Board meeting also included mention of the sort of dispute which probably occurs on most heritage railways but has at times seemed prolific on the K&ESR. In this instance the subject was the platform width at Tenterden Town. Although the platform been extended to five-coach length during the heritage era, the original section near the station building was none too wide and could become alarmingly crowded on the busiest days. Watching from the brake van during guards training I experienced for myself the unnerving sight of passengers appearing to be dangerously near the edge as a train approached Tenterden. The answer was to cut back the flower beds and extend the platform width. This was duly done, only to be followed by bristling indignation that an 'original' feature of the station had been destroyed. The resulting emotion bubbled around for a while until Museum Curator John Miller produced a photograph of the station which indicated that the platform had been restored to its approximate width in Colonel Stephens' day! It may be surmised that the flower beds had themselves been widened at some point (wartime digging for victory? the BR era?), when passengers were few and there was time for station gardening.

Chapter 29

We now come to 2004, when on 3 February the Kent & East Sussex Railway reached the 30th anniversary of the partial reopening of the line. Presentation of the financial outturn for 2002 included John Cobb once again being congratulated for his stewardship of the Railway's finances. In addition, when Day Smith & Hunter subsequently conducted the annual audit, they stated that they were impressed with the good order of the financial records. This appreciation was not confined to the Board and the auditors; at the annual volunteers and staff meeting, following an explanation of the company's financial position, John received a hearty round of applause from those present. A rare accolade for a senior finance officer in any organisation!

Total passengers carried in 2003 had increased by more than 4 per cent over 2002 to 96,580, which was also close to those achieved in 2001, but still below the record-breaking 2000 figures. The number of running days had increased but the key statistic in measuring profitability was the number of passengers carried per train, which improved from 87 to 89. This also compared favourably with 83 per train in 2000. The 2003 figure would have been significantly better but for the steady decline in the number of Thomas passengers. This may have reflected one of the periodic declines in interest in the Little Blue Gent, and it had been felt necessary to cut back the number of operating days during the February event to lessen the risk to finances in the event of inclement winter weather. Thomas was nevertheless still very good business, although the best occasions seem to reflect his appearance on TV. It appears that with each succeeding cohort of toddlers, fascination with the railways of the past reignites, and that some of those who come to a heritage railway as small children reappear in later years as volunteers.

When the Board met in January, Philip Shaw advised that debt had been reduced by £126,403 during 2003 and that the cash position at 23 January 2004 stood at £152,402 (including monies set aside for Bond repayments). The unaudited profit at the end of 2003 was £74,798 – very close to the figure for 2002. However, without the legacies the profit would have been the much lower figure anticipated in the budget (approximately £4,500). In his typically cautious fashion, he nonetheless drew attention to 'drift' in the level of salary expenditure, particularly in the employment of casual staff. To this Derek Dunlavey replied that expenditure would have been less if fewer people had been employed – but to the detriment of income generation. It is appropriate to end this review of the financial position at the beginning of 2004 with the 'glass half full' message which Norman Brice gave to the Volunteers & Staff Meeting in February. He said that on 1 January 2000 the TRC Group had a liability of £750,000 and an overdraft of £259,000. On 1 January 2004 the K&ESR Group had £152,000 in hand; in other words the position had been pulled back £630,000. If this could be continued, the Railway would be comfortable but not well off.

An unfortunate issue involving Terrier No. 10 *Sutton* was coming to a regrettable conclusion at this time. The locomotive continued to stand out of service at Tenterden Town, the financial position having prevented any possibility of it being overhauled and returned to traffic. It was strongly suspected that the owners, the London Borough of Sutton, Wished to take the locomotive elsewhere. It was believed that the ownership was actually vested in the LB Sutton Pension Fund, an arrangement common among local authorities but usually involving paintings or other valuable artefacts. The Council required the overhaul to be completed within two years and £100,000 to be deposited with the authority, conditions which were little short of impossible for the K&ESR to meet. Norman Brice and Derek Dunlavey had held discussions with officers from LB Sutton and the Board discussed the possibility of attempting to raise the required sum by appeal or alternatively hiring the locomotive back for specific periods if it was overhauled elsewhere. A letter from LB Sutton was awaited but the general sentiment was, reluctantly, to recognise that LB Sutton was intransigent.

Sutton was eventually moved to the Spa Valley Railway where it remains. As this was a locomotive that had been on the K&ESR since the 1960s and which had worked the first steam service on 3 February 1974, there was, as a result, apprehension as to how the workforce might take its loss. There was however no need to be concerned; the reaction that came back from Rolvenden was, 'Oh well, that's one we won't have to overhaul.' With other small locomotives available and the service tending to require heavier types, losing *Sutton* made little operational difference. A long-standing volunteer nonetheless offered to finance the return to the UK, and to service, of Terrier *Waddon*, LB&SCR No. 54, which British Rail had donated to the Canadian Railway Museum. As the locomotive was known to be in need of attention it was hoped that this move might be successful, but the Canadians wished to hold on to the *Waddon*. The locomotive was subsequently cosmetically restored.

Another rolling stock proposal was, on the face of it, more difficult to address, involving as it did multiple issues about the culture of the K&ESR. In this instance a member, acting on behalf of a group, approached the Company asking for permission to bring in a Class 205/207 'Thumper' demu, which at that time were being withdrawn from Network service. A number of other Southern heritage railways were taking on 'Thumpers', and one of the enthusiast magazines had jumped the gun and included the K&ESR in a listing of these.

The proposal appeared to have originated with the younger and more assertive element among those holding 'pragmatic' views. On the face of it one of these units had a better claim to be on the K&ESR than the Class 108 that was in use. Classes 205/207 were the Southern Region's version of the same concept, and on still evenings at Tenterden their English Electric engines could be heard at Appledore on the Marshlink service. Their technology was nonetheless more complex (albeit with similarities to the line's Class 08 shunter) and they lacked the marketable 'observation car' ends of Class 108. The Board was unable to support this proposal and the group's spokesman was to be informed accordingly. I drafted the necessary letter, sent it off and waited for the indignant explosion. Surprisingly, nothing happened. Many years later one wonders if refusal was the right decision. The Spa Valley Railway has a Class 207 which appears to run quite adequately between Tunbridge Wells West and Eridge. Then again, Tenterden Railway Equipment & Traction Company needed the income from hiring the 108 to the K&ESR to maintain their unit, although on the other hand a 'Thumper' might have been useful when the 108 was not available.

In the meantime, the possibility of extending to Robertsbridge and the Rother Valley Railway had not gone away; the project was in fact experiencing new impetus. A key factor in this was the involvement of Mike Hart whose notable career had in the years since he left the K&ESR, among other accomplishments, taken him to the Chairmanship of the Ffestiniog Railway. Those accomplishments had included the rebuilding of the Welsh Highland Railway, a scheme whose history was even more convoluted than that of the heritage era Kent & East Sussex. With that outstanding project having reached a significant point, and having stepped down as Ffestiniog Chairman in 2001, Mike again turned his interest to the K&ESR and the Robertsbridge scheme in particular.

Managing Director Derek Dunlavey had been in discussion with Mike regarding the Rother Valley Railway. (K&ESR Board meeting 20 March 2004) Following this, a joint K&ESR/RVR meeting was suggested and Derek was tasked with determining what such an extension would do to the Railway's finances. I was to arrange the meeting, which I duly did, and following the problems with the PLC proposal it was to be on the understanding that any consequent publicity would only be on the basis of an agreed statement to appear after the event.

The meeting with the Rother Valley Railway took place immediately following the K&ESR Board meeting on 17 April 2004, RVR representatives including Mike Hart and, from the K&ESR's own recent past, Peter Davis. One of the first items was the explanation of the RVR management structure. This involved the Rother Valley Railway Trust which acquired and managed land, and owned the RVR Company, in which it had a majority shareholding. The Company was responsible for managing and reconstructing the railway. The Rother Valley Railway Supporters Association co-ordinated activities of the volunteers and had a licence to develop the line between Robertsbridge and Northbridge Street. This complex structure of course contrasted with the unitary approach plus support groups of the K&ESR. It was more like that of some heritage railways elsewhere.

Mike Hart next outlined the RVR aspirations and objectives. These were to rebuild Robertsbridge–Bodiam at no cost to, and in co-operation with, the K&ESR. This was essentially a restatement of the original 1991 intentions although Norman Brice pointed out that a completed Bodiam–Robertsbridge extension was then to be handed over to the K&ESR Company. Was that still the business model? Mike replied that he had no knowledge of the situation ten years earlier (it was in fact thirteen by this point) but that the question could 'be sorted out over the next few months'. For the RVR David Felton (whom I subsequently got to know as their Company Secretary) said that they needed a partnership to access the K&ESR's experience of operating and also in dealing with the authorities. He said that the RVR was not looking for cash contributions from the K&ESR but that the two sides needed to keep in touch. There was also some discussion as to whether the extended Railway would be likely to be run as one section or two, there being a consensus that it was only viable to run the Railway as one.

The discussion then returned to the matter of communication between the two sides, it being said that it had been better on a personal than on a corporate level. Norman Brice suggested that Robertsbridge 20/20 should be used as a vehicle for co-operation and a reorganisation of that company with equal representation of both sides under a K&ESR Chairman and this was eventually decided on. The meeting included a statement of what was to be the K&ESR approach thereafter: that the Kent & East Sussex Railway would go to Robertsbridge if it were economically justified.

In the summer 2004 *Tenterden Terrier*, Mark Yonge explained how the Rother Valley Railway, with which he was active, was making it possible to improve the operating arrangements at Bodiam station and also outlined the longer-term plans for the re-instatement of the line between Bodiam and Robertsbridge:

> Readers of this journal will be aware of the existence of Rother Valley Railway Ltd, an independent company formed to rebuild the link between Bodiam, the present terminus

of the line, and Robertsbridge. In furtherance of this, the RVR has been acquiring or leasing parcels of land as and when they become available and collectively they account for about one third of the three-mile route length. Planning permission has been obtained to rebuild the whole section; a Transport & Works Order will be required in due course. The Kent & East Sussex Railway Company land ownership terminates at a point some 300 metres from Bodiam level crossing and is marked by a buffer stop. Beyond this, the RVR owns most of the half mile section of line to the site of junction Road (B2244) halt terminating short of the halt, at the boundary of Udiam Farmhouse, which extends over the trackbed at this point. Beyond this, the main physical barrier to re-instatement is the Robertsbridge by-pass, which breaches the trackbed and is incorporated in the re-routed A21 road from Hastings which meets the M25 at the Sevenoaks interchange. The Railway originally crossed the old A21 through the village on the level, and from this point the RVR owns the trackbed to Robertsbridge station itself.

As a result of a recent initiative, the RVR has agreed to make available to K&ESR some 200 metres of formation that it owns beyond Bodiam so that the track can be re-instated. This will be done in August by the K&ESR Permanent Way department and will enable parked rolling stock to be re-located from existing sidings and thereby enhance the visual appearance of Bodiam station, which is the key heritage site. The cost of the track materials is being met by a generous donation from the K&ESR Maidstone Area Group.

Concurrently with the development, the RVR will also re-instate the embankment beyond this point, utilising contractors. This is necessary because some 600 metres of route were ploughed out and returned to nature by the owner of Quarry Farm. The contractors will also remove some closely wooded areas along the route and, as a result, the track formation will be completely restored to a point some 90 metres from Udiam Farm and near to the former Junction Road halt. The original formation went through Udiam Farm but the planning consents are to divert northwards over the River Rother and pass the B2244 on the level on the other side of the river. This will, of course, involve considerable engineering works. A landscaping scheme for this option has been submitted to Rother District Council for approval. There are no immediate plans to re-lay track at this stage. The remaining formation between Udiam to a point east of Salehurst remains reasonably intact. Plans have been made to re-instate bridges in the Robertsbridge area. The key issue of the A21 crossing has been the subject of much discussion. A level crossing is a possibility, but the ideal solution would be to tunnel under the road itself. This would be very expensive if undertaken as a single project, but less so if incorporated into any plans to make the entire southern section of this busy road a dual carriage way.

The Robertsbridge project in its entirety is essentially a long-term one and as such no time frame can realistically be put on it at present. The plans have been formulated and drawn up by Mike Hart, Peter Barber and Gardner Crawley, and works completed so far have been funded by donations. The participants are keen, energetic and enthusiastic. They will keep interested parties abreast of developments.

In the years that followed, the problem of land ownership at Udiam Farm was overcome and the line restored up to the B2244 (the eponymous Junction Road) using the original alignment.

K&ESR volunteers assisted with the construction, or should it be reconstruction, of the Bodiam end siding. For various legal reasons this had to be in their private capacity as members of the RVR Supporters Association, a pattern which was repeated later when the reconstruction work was extended to Junction Road. I obtained a Licence to Occupy (a form of simplified lease) and the new end siding was soon used for the storage of disused rolling stock. (Historic Artefacts Awaiting Restoration – or HAARs, as Norman Brice later dubbed them.)

During the summer the Carriage & Wagon Department made substantial progress with returning two such 'HAARS' to traffic. The vehicles involved were of course the Woolwich Coach and Pullman Car *Theodora*, which were the recipients of the further grant from the Millennium Commission. The Woolwich Coach was test run to Bodiam and back on Tuesday 13 July 2004 and entered service, on the Vintage Train, one week later. The official launch took place on 6 August.

Sue Kinnear of Meridian Television, accompanied by a film crew, performed the launching ceremony and Andrew Duck, who had been liaising with C&W during the project, represented the Millennium Commission. The launch received plenty of good publicity, Sue's report appearing on the local news the following Sunday. There was also coverage in the railway magazines and the local press. The lady reporter from the latter cornered me looking for a quote, and I quickly came up with 'The coach was delivered when I was in the sixth form. Now I've taken early retirement it's finally been restored.' This somewhat two-edged summary of 40 years of the coach's history, which both the reporter and I instantly realised was what she wanted, duly appeared in the local paper. Finally, a degree of friendly rivalry had developed with the Bluebell Railway C&W which was on the point of completing a Stroudley four-wheeler. The K&ESR promptly claimed to have beaten them by a few days, though the Bluebell would no doubt have argued otherwise.

Back in the carriage shed, Pullman Car *Theodora* was progressing rapidly, the bogies having been returned from overhaul at Sellindge and preparations were being made to refit them. The all-important drinks bar was in the latter stages of construction and interior and exterior panelling was well advanced. Wiring (including circuits to allow for use as a conference coach) was also progressing, and the contract for construction of Pullman-style seats was about to be let.

Chapter 30

On reaching the autumn of 2004 we come to this book's rather arbitrary cut-off date in the history of the Kent & East Sussex Railway. It nevertheless marks the completion of the first 30 years since that bright and hopeful February morning which had seen the end of the beginning. The Railway had survived, at times prospered, and, after the problems of 2000/2001, was beginning to look secure. But as ever the glass was 'half full or half empty', depending on which way you looked at it. Chairman Norman Brice's address to the Annual General Meeting on 9 October 2004 neatly sums up the position as another running season was nearing its end:

> The first thing I did when preparing this address was to go back and read what I said here a year ago and ask myself the question: What has changed in the past 12 months? We have achieved a lot, both financially (of which I will speak later) but also in improving the product we offer our visitors, those kind people who pay for our hobby.
>
> Improvements include: completing the Woolwich coach, with considerable financial support from the Millennium Commission; completing loco 25; improvements to Tenterden site; opening up access; new, improved signs at stations – much funded by a grant from InterReg; and we have now placed a contract for the new food store for Tenterden. Also, Railway Experience Days and footplate tasters are proving that we can introduce and develop new niche products. Organisationally, bringing the Thomas and other events catering 'in-house' has increased revenue by no less than 26 per cent.
>
> But what is more interesting, and often much more challenging, is what has not changed. We are still not profitable as a business; each year we have to be rescued by our charitable status and donations/bequests. Despite a variety of marketing and event initiatives, we seem to have a plateau of around 80,000 visitors, with all that means for revenue. Managers consistently ask for more budget than we can afford – this is not a criticism but a reflection of the high fixed costs of the business and the very modest amounts we can make available for improvements. At the same time, Managers must now be congratulated on their much stricter adherence to budgets – vital financial discipline which was less obvious in times past. As a business, our planning and control mechanisms are incomparably better.
>
> We remain a largely volunteer organisation: this is a short-term strength but, as I remarked a year ago, it is our biggest worry for the future. Changes in the nature of society seem to mean fewer people volunteer for any unpaid activities, and the current volunteer force grows older. As the demand for labour increases and the available pool dwindles, there are constant calls for posts to become salaried. If the business were growing, that would

not be a problem; but with our relatively fixed income, it is a trend we must watch most carefully indeed.

Sometimes the answer is not even money, but the lack of skills. We cannot recruit certain mechanical skills, even if we have the money, so we have gone down the alternative route of training our own apprentices. This is long and expensive but ultimately more rewarding as we are ensuring the long-term existence of that skill base. More broadly, since opening to Bodiam four years ago, we have been consolidating our financial position, with some considerable success. From being a whisker away from bankruptcy, we have repaid close to half our debt. In 2003 we made a profit around £60,000, reduced our creditors from £104,000 to £60,000, and repaid £29,000 of our long-term bank loan, as well as putting aside the first £50,000 towards the Northiam Bond redemption in 2007. For the current year we will again turn in a modest surplus, and generate more than enough cash to enable us to set sums aside for bond redemption. Having consolidated, we now have the opportunity to look again to the future and at the ever-evolving nature of the tourist market in which we compete. Compete we have to. Customer expectations are ever higher – what we could get away with a few years ago is no longer acceptable. There are ever more ways to spend the leisure pound.

Over the past couple of years we have developed a number of plans and strategies: ten-year locomotive and carriage plans; an Image Policy; and, more recently, a Stations Strategy. We have identified clear needs to improve the infrastructure, or the running of the Railway, as well as for improving the attractiveness of what we offer the public and to discharge our obligations as an educational charity. A few examples will suffice: the locomotive shed at Rolvenden is wholly inadequate for the joint tasks of restoring locomotives and keeping the running fleet going. We desperately need covered accommodation for the historic wooden bodied carriages. Our 'offices' are life expired and occupying a prime position on the Tenterden site.

All of this will need a lot of detailed feasibility studies, planning and costing. We have all the different plans but they need to be made inter-dependent and prioritised. Then we must find sources of funding. Bearing in mind what I said a moment ago, you may well be wondering how we can afford to undertake all these expensive works. The answer, as ever, is with the best sort of money – somebody else's! Potential funding sources include InterReg and Heritage Lottery, and much work will be needed to develop sound, fully costed project plans for these bodies.

Your Board is developing a long-term plan which we hope to be announcing in due course and, as ever, volunteers to help produce this would be greatly welcomed. Thereafter we will have a period of consultation because, ultimately, everybody has an interest in how the railway develops. A balance has to be drawn between absolute historical accuracy and what will generate revenue – a difficult balance, but one where we have to succeed. The short term has been secured, and now we can look forward with greater confidence thanks to the efforts of everybody who contributes to the Kent & East Sussex Railway.

The 2004 AGM was also the occasion of David Lloyd's retirement as General Manager, although he became a Board member for a while. He was replaced by Graham Baldwin, who came to the

Railway from the hospitality industry and, as a local resident, was seeking a job which did not take him away from home. This change also led, once the new GM had settled in, to Derek Dunlavey stepping down as Managing Director, that post then being abolished.

2004 itself ended with passenger figures having dropped from 90,757 to 86,375, with average passengers per train at 80 as opposed to the previous year's 89; although this was still substantially better than 1999's average of 58. There were however some positive points re-emphasising the K&ESR's continuing strengths. Santa Specials continued to improve, with 2004 the best year since 1990. August passenger numbers showed a consistently high figure: 15,500 in 2004, whereas before extending to Bodiam this was more variable and typically around 14,000. The Pullman, as always, remained the jewel in the crown, the service being further enhanced when *Theodora* joined the train in the spring of 2005.

Although this book has set out to relate the story of the Kent & East Sussex Railway between 1974 and 2004, it is more than necessary to round out the account with a summary of some of the notable events in the years up to the time of writing. Sadly, one has to begin by recording that, following no Steam & Country Fair at all in 2004, the second run of these events came to an end the following year with a smaller-scale fair adjacent to Rolvenden Station. K&ESR spectaculars were far from over, however, and the most notable event of 2006 was the Terrier Gala of 6th/7th May which, thanks to the co-operation of the heritage lines involved, saw most of the serviceable members of Class A1X handling that weekend's service. Particularly significant on this occasion was the K&ESR's own No. 3 *Bodiam* which had recently re-entered service thanks to the financial assistance of its majority owner, The Terrier Trust. The following years have continued to feature a series of Branch Line Weekends and Spring Galas and it is pleasing, in an organisation with a rising 'age profile', that these have been substantially manned by a number of highly committed and able younger members.

A most definitely special event the following year was the routeing of the English stage of the 2007 Tour de France cycle race through Tenterden. This involved the closure of a number of public roads in the area, effectively isolating the town for several hours. The public nevertheless wished to both come and go, and view the race from the High Street. For the first time since 1954 the K&ESR provided a proper public service, this proving to be so popular that at times the operation of the Railway resembled a miniature version of the legendary 1950s Summer Saturdays in the West. Furthermore, the television coverage, which included a shot of No. 3 standing with the Vintage Train at Cranbrook Road, went round the world and brought the K&ESR much publicity.

2007 was of course the year that the Northiam Bonds were due to be redeemed. The last letter I saw from John Snell, some time after he left as a CSRE Director, acknowledged that there had been 'some improvement' in the K&ESR's affairs, but still warned of the 'cliff edge' of the Bond repayments. Despite his dire warnings, repayment to Bond holders was made from within the Company's own resources, a process much aided by many members not asking for their own Bonds to be redeemed. From a personal point of view, 2007 was also the year that added the post of *Tenterden Terrier* Editor to everything else I was doing. It was the only K&ESR job that I had ever coveted, but I never thought it would come my way. It did so when, 12 months after having replaced Philip Shaw, Brian Janes unexpectedly stood down and the post became available again.

The loss of another significant figure from the early heritage era occurred in March 2008 when Robin Doust died in far-away Bulawayo at the early age of 66. His health had been declining for some time, but one could not help feeling that the chaos then overtaking the failing state of Zimbabwe had been a contributory factor. A memorial service was held in Ashford soon afterwards which was attended by representatives of the K&ESR. I was greatly honoured to be asked to present a tribute on behalf of the Railway which he had played such a pivotal role in saving.

These years saw a number of varied initiatives including the construction at Rolvenden of the reverse osmosis plant mentioned earlier. This proved not only successful in reducing the intervals between boiler wash outs but also capable of providing water for coach batteries that was superior to the commercial product. Rolvenden Works also completed the overhaul of No. 14 *Charwelton* during 2008, this effort having been notable for the participation of the 'Saturday Gang' – a group of teenagers whose enthusiasm enabled vital skills to be passed on to another generation.

The Carriage & Wagon Department officially launched the SE&CR 'Birdcage' (K&ESR No. 61) on 13 July 2008 following a protracted restoration. C&W were also involved with three appeals during this period, the first being in aid of GWR Railcar No. 20 which had been the subject of an ongoing restoration for some years. The second appeal, which would ultimately help meet the objectives of the first, was to raise money for a substantial extension to the Carriage Shed at Tenterden. The first phase of this project was completed in January 2011 and the official opening was celebrated on 4 March. The third appeal, aided by Heritage Lottery Funding, was of national as well as K&ESR significance. This involved the full restoration, by contractor and to 1920 condition, of the 'Cavell' SE&CR Parcels and Mails Van No. 132. The Cavell van project had of course been made possible because former Chairman John Miller had first secured the vehicle for the K&ESR and then generously gifted it to the Company. The restoration, which attracted considerable interest in the media and among ex-service and nursing organisations, had been ably co-ordinated by Norman Brice, this proving a fitting climax to his Chairmanship of the Company through ten, at times difficult, years. He stood down from the post in November 2010 and was replaced by Geoff Crouch, a local businessman and volunteer and formerly the Permanent Way Manager.

In the wider world, 2008 marked the beginning of the international financial crisis which proved to be greater than any since the 1930s. Ironically for the K&ESR, which had weathered so many financial difficulties of its own, this proved to be something of a blessing in disguise. It produced the phenomenon (and awful word) of 'staycationing' or a holiday boom within the UK. This increased both passenger numbers and income, lasted for several years, and was to the benefit of all heritage railways – not just the Kent & East Sussex.

The 2011 season got off to a remarkable start and proved to be one of the best and most memorable years I had experienced on the Kent & East Sussex Railway. There were no fewer than four major Galas, two of great historical significance and two which were an outstanding commercial success. Six years after the Bodiam End Siding was built, and again with the assistance of K&ESR volunteers, that project became the seed which grew into a full-scale restoration of the line to Junction Road, the first stage of RVR's newly determined efforts to reach Robertsbridge. As a result, Kent & East Sussex services were temporarily extended to Junction Road – although there remains no platform at that site – for the weekend of 19 and 20 March 2011. To those of us with long memories of the K&ESR, the sight of a heritage era passenger trains at the site of the former halt was something which we once thought we would never see. The actual first train was a Pullman special which had run the previous day for invited guests as well as officers of the K&ESR and RVR. It was 44 years and 4 months since I had last travelled that part of the line, the previous occasion having been as a 19-year-old volunteer on a Wickham trolley. I travelled down again the following day, accompanying Geoff Crouch in the brake van of the Woolwich Coach with *Charwelton* hauling the Vintage Set. This combination of rolling stock heading for Junction Road seemed, like the renaming of the Company, to be the righting of wrongs from the 1960s.

Then between 30 April and 2 May the K&ESR was visited by no less a locomotive than *City of Truro*, something that, like so much of what was now the heritage sector of the railway industry, would have been unimaginable 40 years earlier. It was the first of that year's commercial successes, and many asked how we could possibly top that. Two weeks later the Railway did precisely that, when the Saturday of 40s Weekend featured a spine-tingling display by the Battle of Britain Memorial Flight. At last, I was to see a Spitfire perform a victory roll over the K&ESR, and furthermore to be seen on the day that was said at the time to have been the busiest in the Railway's entire history. Then on 11 June the K&ESR marked the 50th anniversary of the line's closure in 1961 and the occasion was distinguished by the presence of three BR-black Terriers – the Railway's own Nos. 32670 and 32678 again joined for the occasion by Bressingham's No. 32662, otherwise known as *Martello*. Then again, it was not the anniversary of the end, it was the anniversary of the beginning – the beginning of the heritage era.

Also during 2011, the Rother Valley Railway began rebuilding the five bridges in the short distance between Robertsbridge and Northbridge Street. Four of these single-track steel spans were formerly on the Tonbridge–Ashford line at Staplehurst. They were sent to a specialist restoration company at Lamberhurst for shot blasting and painting before being brought back to Robertsbridge. In addition to these spans, two longer single-track bridges were sourced from Network Rail at Reading. 2011 proved to be the third year in the K&ESR's entire history when over 100,000 passengers were carried (100,341 in fact), the outstanding events of the year having certainly helped to achieve this.

The year was further notable for the emergence of a scheme to bring GWR 42XX class 2-8-0T No. 4253 to the K&ESR. This locomotive, although preserved in South Wales for many years, was in totally unrestored condition. Volunteers, particularly those based at Rolvenden, were very much behind this project, which emerged as 4253 Ltd. The aim – to provide, at no cost to the K&ESR, a locomotive suitable for the longer run to Robertsbridge – would have been met by a GWR Prairie tank but as these were scarce and expensive a 42XX was an acceptable substitute. The project was very much promoted on the ethos and what had become the traditions of 'railway volunteering' and proved highly successful, particularly in terms of fundraising. No. 4253 arrived at Rolvenden in the first half of 2011, the owning group soon starting to better their own best estimates of progress. Two of the leading lights in this were Bryan Atkins, who later joined the K&ESR Board, and, in the tradition of the erstwhile Thameside Group, Charlie Masterson, who was, to say the least, a driving force behind the fundraising effort. Restoration work continues to be well under way at the time of writing.

A suitable Prairie tank may not have been available, but no sooner was the 4253 project under way than GWR 56XX Class 0-6-2T No. 6619 came on the market. This locomotive was well known to the K&ESR, having visited from the North Yorkshire Moors Railway on two occasions and considered highly suitable for both present and future needs. No. 6619 was eventually secured through the efforts of 6619 Ltd which, although in some ways similar to other volunteer-led owning groups, had a significant capital input from the K&ESR Company. Volunteers raised the £100,000 needed to secure the purchase in little over six months, with K&ESR underwriting the future share issues with the stated intent to own more than 50 per cent of the issued shares. No. 6619 arrived on the Railway in November 2012 and was soon in service, although withdrawn from traffic a few years later when its ten-yearly overhaul became due.

As the years have gone by it has become a sad but inevitable fact that long-standing and respected members of the Kent & East Sussex Railway have reached the end of their lives. Peter Benge-Abbott and Robin Doust have already been mentioned, and many were grieved when in 2011 Museum Curator John Miller passed away. To attempt listing all would risk making omissions, and to select only some would be invidious. One occasion which should be recalled, and perhaps stand for all of those who have gone before, was the funeral of Driver and volunteer of many years standing Christopher Mitchell, who died on 15 April 2011.

Chris was buried in the cemetery beside the Railway close to Cranbrook Road level crossing, and was lowered to his rest as a Terrier stationed near the crossing sounded its whistle. This was a well-attended ceremony that combined the fraternal bonds of the railway communities of old with the traditions of country funerals such as Thomas Hardy might have described. John Emmott, the K&ESR's Chaplain, later told Chris's widow Carol that this had been one of the most memorable services he had conducted. Prior to the interment a service had been held in St. Michael's Church where the hymn *He Who Would Valiant Be* had been sung with great gusto. Carol had chosen this because it had been the school song of Christopher's youth. As we joined our voices in Ralph Vaughan Williams' rousing setting to those inspiring lyrics it occurred to me that they were apt, not only for our late friend and colleague who had known many health problems in his life, but for the determined resilience of those who sang. This seems all the more so if one considers John Bunyan's original seventeenth-century version:

> ...One here will constant be,
> Come wind, come weather
> There's no discouragement
> Shall make him once relent
> His first avowed intent...
> ...Whoso beset him round
> With dismal stories
> Do but themselves confound
> His strength the more is.

Surely sentiments not just for the Kent & East Sussex Railway but for the whole heritage railway movement.

There was a foretaste of things to come during the May 2012 Spring Gala when GWR 2-8-0T No. 4247 – sister locomotive to No. 4253 – loaned by the Bodmin & Wenford Railway, demonstrated the potential this type had for the Kent & East Sussex. This event also featured the Gresley Society's Great Northern Railway N2 Class No. 1744, thus adding to list of 0-6-2Ts which have run on the K&ESR and shown the suitability of this wheel arrangement for the Railway. At the other end of the season, the Hop Pickers' Weekend featured further use of the extension to Junction Road. We had, with the RVR, worked out a procedure for the K&ESR making short-term use of the Bodiam–Junction Road section with the Kent & East Sussex taking a short-term Licence to Occupy for each period it was to run services. This was necessary to extend the K&ESR's Rules, insurance and safety procedures over a section of line which the company did not own. Like all such things, this seemed cumbersome at first; but David Felton, the RVR's Company Secretary, and I got this organised to a point where 'running rights' could be granted at very short notice.

2013 was a year of old memories and echoes of early ambitions. To begin with, the Sentinel–Manning Wardle hybrid *Gervase*, which was fondly remembered by volunteers from the pioneering days of 50 years earlier but had languished dismantled in Rolvenden yard, reached the end of a very thorough restoration at Elsecar Steam Railway in South Yorkshire. To mark the 50th anniversary of her first steaming on the K&ESR, this quirky locomotive made her first return visit for the May Gala. Mike Hart was to be thanked for enabling this nostalgic occasion and, amazingly, it was possible for six of the original 1962/63 restoration team to be present.

The other 'return to the beginning' was the Return to Robertsbridge event held on 21/22 September 2013, with trains running between Robertsbridge Junction and Northbridge Street. The work achieved by the Rother Valley Railway over the previous year had been nothing short of amazing. Prior to the beginning of 2013, the track along the embankment from Northbridge Street had been laid across Bridge No. 1 and around the curve to connect up with the old track layout and the 'new' station area, and the site had been completely cleared and levelled.

The scene then changed dramatically, with the new platform well under way. Track was laid to form the new main line, joining the check rail curve and the new run-round crossover points. The loop had also been laid from the run-round points to the loop/main point near Bridge No. 1, and this included what is thought to be the longest set of points in preservation. Installation of this track layout was a task which had mainly been carried out by volunteers from the K&ESR Permanent Way Department, who had divided their time between the works at Robertsbridge and the rather more routine inspection works on the K&ESR. August saw an increase in the pace, however, as firm details of just what was wanted in readiness for the mid-September event were identified. This included ballasting and tamping in order to present a completed railway for the 'Return' Weekend.

Having first come to the Rother Valley via this very section of line in 1901, Terrier No. 32670 stood coupled to a three-coach rake of the K&ESR's vintage four-wheeled carriages, all of which had been brought down by road. This attractive formation provided a popular 'push pull' service throughout the weekend. For the first time since 1954 it was possible to arrive at Robertsbridge by train and buy a ticket for a journey, albeit a rather short one, on the historic route of the Kent & East Sussex Railway. As an RVR Trustee, Mike Hart, wrote in the *Tenterden Terrier*: 'This gala event has exceeded all expectations and it is a credit to all those supporters and backers who have enabled it to happen. We hope to be able to organise future events as the scheme to reconnect the railway progresses.' Following a much-delayed Public Inquiry into an application for a Transport & Works Order the necessary permission received ministerial approval on 9th May 2023. At the time of writing, further progress with the Rother Valley Railway is eagerly awaited.

Less dramatic, but also of great significance, 2013 was rounded off by the repayment of the Bodiam Bonds, an event which had been viewed with some apprehension over the preceding years as there was concern that the successful end to the Northiam Bonds issue could not be repeated. With great good fortune, a generous legacy played a significant part in achieving a satisfactory outcome (yet another example of fortuitous coincidence coming to the Railway's aid) together with the further generosity of Bond Holders who did not take up the option of reclaiming their money. It was also gratifying that the Railway's financial position had improved sufficiently for the bank to agree to a less onerous restructuring of the Company's other loan arrangements.

During 2014, the involvement of the Rother Valley Railway was again to the fore when a more-than-generous donation via the RVR enabled the completion of a new four-road carriage storage shed adjacent to Rolvenden station. The year also saw the retirement of General Manager Graham Baldwin, thus ending another era in the history of the K&ESR. The post remained vacant for a year until Shaun Dewey was appointed. Shaun had previously had a career in civil aviation and appointing someone from a cousin industry (with its own band of camera-wielding enthusiasts!) proved an appropriate move. After three months Shaun was reported to have said that he felt 'completely at home'. He was succeeded by Robin Coombes in 2022. There were also changes at Board level, Geoff Crouch stepping down as Chairman in February 2015. Ian Legg acted in the post until November of that year, when Jamie Douglas took over for two years. Ian Legg was then appointed as Chairman for a further 12 months until Simon Marsh took the Chair in November 2018.

I retired as Company Secretary and as a member of Carriage & Wagon paid staff when I reached 70 years of age, as well as for family reasons, in December 2016. I was able to continue as Editor of the *Tenterden Terrier*. For all the rough patches and occasional troubles, I didn't regret a moment of the previous 25 years.

A volunteer visiting from another heritage line is said to have remarked that the K&ESR is a big railway that thinks it is a little railway. He was of course referring to the line's light railway status and construction. It could, however, also be a comment on the way the Kent and East Sussex sees itself in a broader sense. The fact is that it is an historically important railway which, during the past half century, has had to fight hard, often against the odds. It has a great and significant past, both before preservation and in the years since 1961. Its history continues and develops, and there is more than can be said about the era described here. In the future there will doubtless be further stories to be told.

The Kent & East Sussex Railway has loyal and determined supporters who very much care about it, something that seemed particularly relevant as I completed the initial draft of this book at a time when the COVID 19 pandemic has disrupted normal life. The Railway had, like much else, been closed for lengthy periods, but in the resolute way of its tradition had looked forward to resuming services. It is no surprise that an important factor in this had been the manner that, thanks especially to the internet, those same loyal supporters had kept together and looked to the day when steam trains would again climb from the Rother Levels, through glorious and varied countryside, to the ancient town on the edge of the High Weald.

Appendix A

Rolvenden Steam Enterprises

The members of Rolvenden Steam Enterprises (RSE) first met as volunteers at Rolvenden Loco Depot in the mid-1970s. They all got on well and had the objective of securing a suitable locomotive for use on the Kent & East Sussex Railway. At that time, RSE comprised David Brailsford, Robert Forsythe, Alan Castle, Lawrence Donaldson, John Liddell and Richard Crumpling. In later years they were joined by Richard Stannard, who was also a volunteer at Rolvenden. Bob Forsythe died in November 2008 but the membership of RSE otherwise remains the same.

After about two years of trips and the examination of more than 80 locomotives, Richard Crumpling and Bob Forsythe found a suitable Hunslet Austerity, although built by Robert Stephenson & Hawthorn as their No. 7086 of 1943. Bob considered this would be within RSE's budget to purchase, transport and restore. They had not been specifically looking for an Austerity but by that time most of the alternatives had gone. It was intended that it should be called *Rolvenden*. Bob already owned an ex-NCB Austerity *Linda* (Hunslet 3781 of 1952) which was on site at Rolvenden. He was seeking partners to fund the overhaul, and to achieve this it was logical that RSE became joint owners of *Linda* which became K&ESR No. 26. This locomotive was later sold to the Mid Hants Railway where it was converted it into the Rev. W. Awdry's *Thomas*, in which guise it often returns to the K&ESR for the events which hopefully inspire new generations of railway volunteers. No. 7086 became K&ESR No. 27 but never entered service on the Railway. Some years later RSE and the Board of TRC decided quite fairly that it was surplus to requirements, and No. 27 was sold off the Railway to a new owner. It is now at the Embsay & Bolton Steam Railway, named *Norman* in memory of its late owner. It is available as a 4mm scale model.

In September 1977, the Army located its Hunslet Austerity *Sapper* (3797 of 1953) at Rolvenden with the intention that it should be a working locomotive. Two years later, when the Junior Leaders had been unable to undertake any restoration work, a group led by K&ESR member Tim Stanger was formed with the aim of purchasing *Sapper* from the MoD. RSE and the 'Northiam' Group were successful in this and, the *Sapper* nameplates not being available, the locomotive became No. 25 *Northiam* and a stalwart of the K&ESR loco fleet. In recent years, RSE bought out the 'Northiam' Group members as they wanted to move on to the restoration project for GWR No. 4253.

No. 23 *Holman F. Stephens* was formerly owned by Paul Sutton, a significant figure on the heritage era K&ESR who died far too young. Bob Forsythe bought the locomotive from Paul's widow Valerie. At the same time Bob let RSE purchase a 25 per cent share to give the group an interest in the loco. As the years passed, for security, Bob signed over 100 per cent of the loco to the care of Rolvenden Steam Enterprises (much to the then General Manager's relief on Bob's passing!).

David Stratton owned No. 24 *William H. Austen* but sold this locomotive to Bob Forsythe and RSE when *Linda* went to the Mid Hants. It was with no disrespect to the memory of the man who had kept the K&ESR running after Colonel Stephens died that No. 24 was afterwards renamed *Rolvenden*. When No. 24 came out of service, the K&ESR and other owning groups had alternative locomotives available and it was requested that RSE should sell No. 24 off the Railway. Thanks to some excellent work by David Brailsford, the first prospective purchasers bought it at the asking price. Hopefully it will one day be in steam again on a railway not too far away.

Rolvenden Steam Enterprises Ltd. now owns No. 25 *Northiam* and No. 23 *Holman F. Stephens* and it is RSE's intention to keep these running at the Kent & East Sussex as they are the last two Austerities on the Railway, and for many reasons they should stay and work on the line. Both have been on the K&ESR a very long time and are now very much part of the Railway's history. To keep these Austerities running many tools, machines and spares have been accumulated by the RSE group, which runs in parallel with Rolvenden Steam Enterprises Ltd.

Appendix B (See Chapters 16 & 17)

Summary of 1994 Business Plan

About two years ago the Board, while seeking sources of grant aid for the Bodiam extension, were left in no doubt by Kent County Council and East Sussex County Council of the need for a business plan if funding institutions were to be attracted to invest in the Kent and East Sussex Railway. Subsequently, following discussions with other funding agencies including our bank, the Board decided in 1993 to prepare a business plan which was to perform three basic functions.

Firstly, to set out policies for the next three years against which budgets could be prepared. This fairly basic function had never before been carried out on the railway which had tended, in common with most other volunteer organisations like ours, to prepare budgets on a yearly basis to no overall plan.

Secondly, to persuade financial institutions, including our bank, that we are worthy of support and particularly of investment in development schemes designed to improve our profitability so that an extension to Bodiam can be developed.

Thirdly, as a management tool against which to measure our successes or failures and to form a basis for future years.

During summer 1993 a series of meetings took place between managers and the Board to consider our main strengths and weaknesses and to lay the foundations for the future direction of the Railway. The appointment of Gillian Howie, now General Manager, enabled critical examination of the previous season's poor financial figures to be undertaken and unprofitable services to be identified. In particular, this work resulted in an approximate 8% reduction in timetabled services and a commercial programme which has already shown a dramatic improvement in net income.

However, the Business Plan does not concentrate on the purely commercial side of the business. The Railway is registered as an educational charity and, in line with the charity status, it is the aim of the Company to educate and inform the public of the history of the Railway, to preserve historic relics and to operate the Railway to demonstrate a light railway branch line. This is not to be confused with the aim of the business which is to provide a quality leisure experience for the public.

A major financial constraint on the Railway in that the most profitable and cost effective service may not be acceptable to either or both visitors and working Members. The Railway has in the past, and will in the future, balance the constraints and objectives but will not lose sight that, financially, 'books must balance'.

In both short and medium term the operation of the Railway will not be highly profitable, with only ancillary activities providing the profitability to renew and replace assets. Because of the need to protect the Railway's finances it is not possible to consider financing most of the future development schemes from revenue. It is proposed that funding should be sought from funding institutions to assist in providing the major finances necessary in the form of grants and sponsorship for these schemes.

As well as to our bank the Plan has been presented to Rother District Council, The National Trust, South East England Tourist Board, the Rural Development Commission, Ashford Borough Council, Kent County Council and East Sussex County Council. Much goodwill and several promises of grant aid have been achieved from the authorities approached so far.

The new East Kent Euro MP, Mark Watts, whose constituency includes the Kent part of the Railway, has provided considerable assistance in the Railway's application for European grant assistance.

One interesting 'spin off' is the need to investigate twinning with a railway or railways in northern France. It seems that European money may be more available if shared between similar organisations on either side of the Channel. Apart from the more social benefits it is an opportunity not to be missed. The intention of this article is to give members some idea of the work which the Board has been undertaking into planning for the future. The Business Plan is not written in tablets of stone and will be reviewed every year. Undoubtedly amendments will have to be made as circumstances change, but without the Plan the Railway could not prepare for the future with any certainty.

I hope that a more detailed article will appear in the next edition of the Terrier, at which time this year's performance can be reviewed together with a more detailed look at next year's plans.

My thanks to the other Board members and management team who helped in the preparation of the Business Plan.

Robin Dyce, Development Director

Appendix C

Elegy Written in a Country Station

The block bell sends the last train on its way,
The carriages wind slowly o'er the lea.
We staff will soon have finished for the day
But first I make another pot of tea.
A lonely Signalman, I view the scene
So tranquil 'neath the sun's declining rays,
And ask myself, what can this vista mean?
Has this old station e'er seen better days?
Was there a time when sweating rustics brought
Their wagon-loads of fragrant hops and hay,
And milk and cattle which the townsfolk sought
Were loaded on to trains and borne away?
Did country folk walk here from near and far
To catch the train, in which they put their trust?
Today their rude descendants go by car,
And must walk only when they really must.
True, locals still to London go by train
From Headcorn, or from Ashford it may be
They go by Eurostar beneath the main
To Brussels, Lille Europe or gay Paris.
But many years ago destruction's hand
Laid waste the northern section of our track
So Headcorn we can't reach, and buildings stand
Where once the slow mixed trains ran up and back
And politicians rashly put an end
To our connection with the Hastings line.
Such attitudes are hard to comprehend –
No wonder public transport's in decline!
The Station building here was swept away,
And weeds engulfed the platform's sad remains
But preservation brought reopening day
With crowds, Distinguished Guests and public trains!
This followed many months of labour grim
By teams of people striving to prepare
The platform, station building, garden trim,

The loop line, signalbox and crossing there.
But maybe all their efforts were in vain:
The booking office door stays locked and barred
Most operating days, when there's a train
The crossing gates are opened by the Guard.
Whenever passing moves are needed though,
The signalbox is open all day long.
You might think passengers would come and go
Using the platform here, but you'd be wrong.
Some people park their cars just to observe
The passage of the trains, then drive away;
Some think the picnic area will serve
To add enjoyment to their leisured day.
Though they could buy their tickets on the way
They seem to see no reason why they should.
"We love to see your railway," they might say,
"And if you don't change anything that's good!"
But any kind of visitor is rare,
Except for sundry animals and birds.
The sounds of chorused nature fill the air,
More beautiful than any human words.
Could brick and concrete be preferred to green
Do people for the countryside not care?
The flora and the fauna go unseen,
Wasting their sweetness on the desert air.
Far from the madding crowd the station sleeps
Waiting for passengers who never come.
Each signalman a lonely vigil keeps
Beside the little road to Wittersham.

Alastair Forbes

Appendix D

68078: Restoring a Locomotive in a Field

LNER No. 8078, built in 1946 with classification J94 and absorbed into British Railways as No. 68078, is one of only two genuine (as opposed to industrial) J94s to survive into preservation. The engine spent most of its time at Immingham shed until transferred to Langwith Junction in 1956. Withdrawal from BR service occurred in March 1963. In mid-1999 the then Tenterden Railway Company bought No. 68078 from the GWR Preservation Group Ltd at Southall, the locomotive strategy having identified the need for another Class 5 locomotive by 2010. Prior to the engine being based in West London it had, between 1963 and 1978, undertaken trip working for an open cast coal contractor, Derek Crouch Ltd, in the North East at Widdrington, Northumberland and in 1967 it received a major overhaul at Doncaster Works. In 1978, the boiler was due a ten-yearly exam and the loco was put into store pending a decision on its future. It was offered for sale in 1984. No. 68078 was thought to be the last ex-BR steam locomotive in service with British industry.

In January 2001, the locomotive left Southall, but as there was no space at Rolvenden it was unloaded onto a track panel in the lower field at Birch Estates, Hope Farm, Sellindge, Kent. Negotiations with Les Birch and Southern Locomotives led to the use of the field and its somewhat spartan facilities for a nominal rent. Work was to be undertaken by the 68078 Association which had been formed by interested K&ESR members. Bob Forsythe, as TRC Rolling Stock Director, was in charge of the project and in his usual meticulous way had written down a schedule of work required to get 68078 operational again. Work restarted again on stripping down, but the weather played an important role in what was achievable. Some work had already been carried out in the shed at Southall prior to the move. Any parts removed were stored in secure locations in Ashford, Swanley, Rolvenden or Staplehurst as we had no storage facilities on site.

Not long after arrival at Sellindge, the Group was informed that the TRC intended to sell No. 68078 because of the K&ESR's financial situation. Fortunately, a group of like-minded individuals managed to raise the money required and the locomotive passed into the ownership of Kent Locomotives Ltd in November 2001. Restoration continued to be progressed by the 68078 Association, with Kent Locomotives being responsible for the fundraising, an arrangement still in existence at the time of writing. Naturally the two groups overlap.

Efforts were concentrated on de-tubing the boiler and taking down motion parts. It was found that one of the boiler tubes had failed and that others were getting thin, a sure sign that the boiler needed a ten-yearly exam. Bob Forsythe always arrived on site with the back of his car full of the tools required for the job in hand, and the restoration team were able to use the gas cutting equipment from the Southern Locomotives site to free the boiler tubes. The first major hurdle was to remove the cab roof, cab front side sheets and saddle tank as access to the boiler was needed to remove the asbestos lagging. Southern Locos came to the rescue once more when they brought a crane in for one of their jobs. Storage of these large items was out in the open but on wooden blocks.

Having obtained a quote from a reputable contractor the lagging was duly removed from the boiler and the steel cladding sheets were cleaned up in May 2002 at a cost of £2530. Being in an isolated field out in the open had been of benefit on this occasion. The cladding sheets were then transported to a storage container at Rolvenden to await their turn for repair and restoration.

In 2002, Bob Forsythe decided it was time to get a 20ft container and there was at last somewhere we could put parts, tools and equipment. In addition, a 25 tonne load of crushed concrete was delivered which was used to level the site. Following that a rail contracting company wanted a training exercise so arrangements were made for them to add an extra 45 feet of track onto the existing panel, and then this had to be levelled out to provide a suitable working area. During all this infrastructure work the boiler was jacked clear of the frames, the bunker released from the back of the footplate and the pistons and rods taken out of the cylinders using a block and tackle attached to the smokebox door.

The aim had always been to get everything stripped down to the point where a road crane could lift the frames, wheels, boiler and bunker and re-arrange the site. All this was dependent on the ground being sufficiently dry to support the 50 tonne capacity crane safely. The boiler came off easily during a very hot day in July 2003 and placed on timbers on the site. The bunker was placed on the ground and then the frames and wheels were tackled. The leading and driving pairs came out without any problem, but the trailing set was another story. After much effort the volunteers and a crane driver finally got the axle to drop. It had been held in place by the build-up of rust between the horns and the axle box cheeks. The journals and crank pins were covered in Denso tape and greased up as well to avoid any corrosion setting in. The whole lot then had to be sheeted over and all the parts, axleboxes, springs pins etc. stored away.

In 2004, volunteer John Collard used his Fire Brigade contacts to enable the boiler to be washed out prior to it being sent for repairs. With a vintage fire engine on site scale was blasted out from the firebox sides and the boiler barrel. The boiler finally arrived at Chatham Steam's premises in Lower Higham, Kent in August 2004 although it was not to return to Sellindge until November 2013 as time was needed to raise funds for the repairs. Covered accommodation was now important if any progress was to be made. Richard Stannard provided the necessary in the form of a number of polytunnel hoops. These were secured to scaffolding poles that had been driven into the ground at the required spacing. Tarpaulins were then secured to the framework and they in turn were fixed to the ground with sleepers. The tarpaulins were rather lightweight and the whole assembly required regular attention to ensure that it did not get ripped to pieces during storms, even if it was something of a wind-tunnel. Disaster struck in the spring of 2009 when a fierce storm demolished and deformed the structure. By August of the same year there was a brand new substantial one-piece sheet in place that would also allow the height of the structure to be raised as the loco was put back together. Some work on the loco had been possible during this period, but much effort had again been put into infrastructure maintenance.

The restoration team managed to work on the loco with snow on the ground, thanks to the tent and a brazier, but had to make sure that the snow did not build up too much on the tent structure.

Initially power supply came from two portable generators, and this enabled the cleaning down of the frames and various other parts with rotary wire brushes. Later a cable reel was run down the field from the Southern Locomotive's premises, but this had to be laid out and cleared away each time the team were on site. To enable welding to be carried out a second-hand diesel-powered welder generator was bought. This single cylinder Lister engined machine was started using a handle; it never once failed to run but it was difficult to get going in the cold. Later more modern technology was acquired to improve the quality of the welding needed. The restoration was able to use the small array of machine tools that Southern Locos had assembled on the site, but the volunteers preferred to use Mike Whittingstall for all machining needs until his untimely and sad demise in early 2019.

Painting was only possible when the atmospheric conditions permitted. There were days when the metal surfaces ran with moisture due to the differences in temperature. Some days it was just too hot and the paint dried so quickly that a good finish could not be obtained; this was particularly the case when the finished tank was painted in the open. One pair of wheels was cleaned down in the field prior to painting, the other two were done at the premises of the tyre turning contractor. The building was spotless: that was until with their permission all the muck and old paint was removed – onto the floor. Clearing up took some time.

Once the trueing up of the axleboxes and frames was finished, they needed to be jacked up so that the wheelsets could be positioned underneath with their newly refurbished springs, axleboxes, links and pins. To facilitate this task four concrete pads had to be cast, one at each corner of the front and rear buffer beams. Re-wheeling of the frames was completed in October 2012. 2014 saw the cleaning down and repainting of the boiler out in the open, at the same time as preparing the boiler for its insurance hydraulic test following repairs. The insurance surveyor passed the boiler, which allowed the project to move onto the next stage.

In 2016 and 2017, work concentrated on the boiler cladding sheets and the associated frame that they sit on. New sections had to be rolled and mig welded into some of the barrel sheets while the firebox sheets were renewed. Fitting them was carried out in the open on some very warm summer days. 2018 saw a few changes take place: the landlord, by then the Sellindge Locomotive Group, offered the opportunity to move into their larger, better-equipped tent at the top of the site. They wanted to extend a siding, which would mean moving 68078's restoration base at a very reasonable cost. The movement of the locomotive and equipment was delayed until April due to wet ground. The move permitted a permanent electricity supply to the container, there was power and lighting available in the big tent, and the compressor was easily accessible. The boiler and tank still sat outside but in close proximity to the frames. A new ashpan was manufactured by Sciss Ltd and Hop Engineering, and the volunteers equipped it with the damper doors and operating mechanisms.

In 2019, work had to be suspended for two weeks in order to allow Bulleid Pacific *General Steam Navigation* to leave the site for a new home on the Swindon and Cricklade Railway.

The loco was on the same track as No. 68078 but behind it, so its frames and boiler had to be moved to allow 'GSN' to be moved out. Advantage was taken of the crane that was on site to assist with the move to install the bunker and cab parts on the loco. The LNER three-ton bunker assembly was completed and bolted firmly to the frames together with steam heat and vacuum pipework. At the time of writing – the difficult year of 2020 – a list of things remained to be done, but there was every confidence that the project would be successful.

(Based on information supplied by David Brailsford and Richard Stannard for an item in the *Tenterden Terrier*, summer 2020.)

Sources and Suggestions for Further Reading

In writing this book much use has been made of information published in the *Tenterden Terrier*, the house journal of the Kent & East Sussex Railway since 1973, together with the Board Minutes of the Tenterden Railway Company (name changed to the Kent & East Sussex Railway Company in 2003).

Suggested Further Reading

Brown, Jonathan, *The Railway Preservation Revolution;* Pen & Sword Transport
Garrett, S.R., *The Kent & East Sussex Railway*, Oakwood Press
Janes, Brian, *Colonel HF Stephens - The Man and His Railways,* The Colonel Stephens Museum
Janes, Brian, *Tenterden's Railway,* Lightmore Press
Pallant, N., *Holding the Line - preserving the Kent & East Sussex Railway*; Alan Sutton Publishing

Index

AC Railbus W79978, 59, 79, 80
Allen, Dr Ian C, 28
Annual General Meetings, 78, 85, 138-142, 147, 176, 189-192, 204, 216
Area Groups
   Ashford, 124, 200
   London, 29
   Maidstone, 73, 109, 213
   South East London, 26, 57
   Surrey, 30
   Sussex, 91
   Thameside, 57-59, 68, 74, 78, 80, 83, 85, 91, 219
   Tunbridge Wells, 26, 29, 30, 38
Ashford Borough Council, 74, 75, 115, 155, 226
'Ashford' Coach Nos 2947 & 3062, 84, 146
Association of Railway Preservation Societies, 103, 108, 109
Austen, William Henry, 12, 133, 134, 145
Austen, William Holman, 39, 145
Awdry, Christopher, 120
Awdry, Rev W, 118, 170, 223

Balcony Saloon, 111, 159
Baker, John, 118
Baldwin, Graham, 216, 221
Barber, Peter, 159, 178, 213
Barham, David, 20, 145
Barnes-Murfin, Mike, 114
Barker, Gary, 98, 100
Bearer Bonds, 56, 57, 60, 61, 91, 92, 154, 171, 185, 197, 207, 217, 220, 221
Beck, Gerald, 100
Benge-Abbott, Peter, 16, 208, 209
Bennett, Stephen, 18, 20, 31, 37, 39, 44, 56, 204

Bilsby, Derrick, 40
Birdcage Coaches, 17, 18, 19, 25, 43, 64, 65, 66, 72, 86, 218
Bluebell Railway, 13, 18, 24, 29, 63, 68, 69, 72, 73, 86, 88, 94, 106, 121, 146, 154, 162, 184, 214
Bodiam 2000 Ltd, 151, 165, 167-168, 176
Bodiam Castle, 44, 57, 72, 107, 116, 171, 174, 180, 188
Bodiam Station, 15-17, 30, 32-33, 36, 41, 44, 47, 49, 51-52, 54, 57-58, 59, 62, 70, 71-75, 78-80, 93-95, 98, 103-105, 107, 111, 187, 194, 203, 204, 212-214, 218
Bourne, Peter, 185, 194
Brailsford, David, 223, 224
Brice, Alan, 157, 206
Brice, John, 160, 171, 179, 183, 200
Brice, Norman, 143, 146-147, 150-151, 155, 158, 174, 181-182, 185, 189-190, 193-202, 204-208, 210-212, 214-215, 218
Bridge, Graham, 167, 174, 189, 191, 193, 195-196
British Railways Mark 1 Coaches; 41, 55, 64-66, 68, 79, 82, 84, 87-88, 95, 103, 111, 124-125, 127, 157, 171
Brydon, Lawrence, 87, 103
Bryson, Admiral Sir Lindsay, 172
Buchanan, Duncan, 149, 161
Burry Port & Gwendreath Railway, 122

Canterbury & Whitstable Railway, 54
Carey, Peter, 130
Carriage & Wagon Department & Tenterden Carriage Shed, 27, 66, 68, 77, 87, 111, 115, 122, 124, 130-131, 134, 138, 144-146, 158, 160, 162, 171, 183, 188, 194, 203, 206, 207, 214, 218, 222

Carriage Storage Shed, Rolvenden, 206, 221
Castle, Alan, 27, 223
Castle, Rt Hon Barbara MP, 16
Catering Department, 47, 171
Cavell Van, 179, 218
Chapman, Adrian, 139, 141
Chemin de Fer de la Baye de Somme (CFBS), 150-151, 155, 158-159, 162, 171, 174, 206
Clark, Peter, 43
Clark-Monks, Philip, 109, 149, 107
Class 108 DMMU, 125-127, 132, 176, 211
Class 205/207 DMMUs, 211
Cobb, John, 194-195, 197, 199-200, 207, 209-210
Collins, Ray, 109, 161
Colonel Stephens Railway Enterprises (CSRE), 17, 143, 147, 166, 167, 174, 176, 180, 185, 195-196, 198-199, 202, 207, 217
Colonel Stephens Railway Museum, 37, 84, 145, 152, 158
Commercial Department, 46, 112, 130-131, 135-137, 164, 179, 198, 203
Companies House, 194, 200, 208
Company Secretary, post of, 148-149, 157, 193-194, 197, 222
Cook, Keith, 52
Coombes, Robin, 221
Cossons, Sir Neil, 131, 158
Couper, Dr Heather, 172
Cranbrook Road Level Crossing, 31, 34, 42-43, 64, 67, 82, 84, 88, 115, 126-127, 217, 220
Crawford, Roger, 20
Crawley, Gardner, 13, 213
Crotty, Alan, 24
Crouch, Kevin, 207
Crouch, Geoff, 218, 222
Crumpling, Richard, 223
Cyster Family (landowners), 184

Dalton, Jonathan, 95
Darling Buds of May (TV programme), 112
Davis, Peter, 16, 18, 25, 67-68, 92, 93, 133, 142, 185, 212

Day Smith & Hunter (Auditors), 176, 185, 196, 210
Deedes, Rt Hon William MP, later Lord Deedes, 16, 20, 80, 104, 171
Deacon, Dick, 29
Denty, Norman, 26
Department of the Environment, 33, 97
Derelict Land Grants, 97, 147, 155
Deverell, Colin, 38
Dewy, Shaun, 221
Dining Car K&ESR No 69 *Diana*, 47, 55, 66, 103-104, 119
District Coach, 58-59, 86, 111, 146
Dixon, Alan, 30
Dixter Halt, 59
Donaldson, Lawrence, 148, 209, 223
Douglas, Jamie, 222
Doust, Robin, 13, 16, 20, 95, 208, 217, 219
Dunlavey, Derek, 21, 70, 103, 115, 123, 184, 193, 195, 207, 210-212, 217
Durrant, John, 98
Dyce, Robin, 111, 115, 117, 139-141, 146, 151, 156-158, 164-168, 170, 172, 174

East Sussex County Council, 68, 104, 162, 225, 226
Edmondson, Rick, 70, 73, 76, 95, 179
Edwards, Colin, 27, 76
Edwards, Douglas, 16
Edwards, Henry, 74, 145, 152
Edwards, Phil, 75
Ellis, Roy, 165
Emmott, Rev John, 220
English Partnerships, 154
English Tourist Board, 8, 77, 97-98
Environment Agency, 97, 155, 162, 178
Esau, Mike, 93
European Union, 143, 147

Family Saloon, 124, 159
Farmers Line (newsletter), 102
Felton, David, 30, 108-109, 111, 125, 212, 220
Ffestiniog Railway, 82, 125, 131, 151, 211-212
Fielder, Andy, 124, 130
Fildes, Christopher, 172

Finance Committee, 164-169, 198, 204
Fletcher, Eric, 37
Flooding, 29, 53, 62, 83, 178-181, 184, 186, 203
Foot & Mouth Disease, 182, 184, 186
Forsythe, Robert, 77, 148, 174, 197, 223, 229-230
Fox, Jack, 30
Freeman, Andre, 171
Friends of Vintage Carriages, 146
Fulcher, Kevin, 67

Garrett, Stephen, 37
General Manager, post of, 136-137, 147, 184, 193-194, 205, 216, 221, 225
Gravesend West Branch, 83
General Elections, 153, 154
Gift Aid, 191, 200, 201, 206, 208
Girode, Arnaud, 159
Gooch, Meg, 162, 203
Grant Thornton, 168-169, 176-177, 181
Great Central Railway, 86, 112
Great Dixter, 59, 73
Great Eastern Coach, 86, 111, 232
Great Northern Railway (Ireland), 38, 49, 51
Great Western Railcar No 20, 15, 17-18, 53, 79, 130, 218
Greatley, Chris, 209
Green, Simon B, 21, 29, 38, 43, 51
Grimwood, Michael, 126
Groome, Clive, 158
Guards Training, 123, 125-129
Gulf War One, 108

Hart, Michael, 23, 27, 36, 70, 211-213, 221
Hastings Diesel Units, 118, 123, 126, 136
Hatcher, Paul, 68, 114
Hawkhurst Branch, 11, 38
Hazeldine, David, 87, 98, 99, 103
Headcorn Extension, 12, 116
Heath, Rt Hon Edward MP, 39-40
Heritage Policy, 133
Heritage Railway (magazine), 185
Hickmot, Kevin, 99
High Speed One (Channel Tunnel Rail Link), 83, 197

HM Queen Elizabeth the Queen Mother, 68
HM Railway Inspectorate, 17, 31, 38, 42, 58, 77, 84, 93, 103, 115
Hocking, Tony, 13, 40
Hodson's Mill, 2, 16
Holding the Line, Preserving the Kent & East Sussex Railway, 9, 13, 123, 125, 132, 149
Holiday Which? (magazine), 84-85
Hoppers Weekend, 179, 204
Howie, Gillian, 130, 136-137, 140, 146, 225
HRH The Duke of Gloucester, 104, 174
Hukins, Graham, 118, 138-139, 142, 146
Hutchinson, Paul, 204, 209

Ian Allan Ltd, 131, 182
InterReg EU Funding Scheme, 150-151, 215-216
Isle of Wight Steam Railway, 38, 131

James, Mike, 40
Janes, Brian, 188, 189, 191, 195, 197, 200, 204, 207, 217
Job Creation Programme (JCP), 31, 32, 36, 38, 40-41, 77
Johnson, Richard, 146
Johnson, Stuart, Heath & Safety Executive, 162
Junction Road, 31, 32, 36, 38, 40-41, 77
Junior Leaders Regiment, 32 223

Keighley & Worth Valley Railway, 24, 70
Kent County Council, 31-32, 36, 38, 40-41, 77
Kent & East Sussex Locomotive Trust, 13, 73, 95
Kent & East Sussex Railway Association, 15
Kent & East Sussex Railway Company Ltd, 14, 194-195, 201, 205, 208
Kent & East Sussex Railway Preservation Society, 13
Kent & East Sussex Steam Railway PLC, 200, 202
Kent Locomotives Ltd, 194, 229
King's Wimbledon School, 13
Kit-Kat Van, 86

Laming, Gordon, 29, 68
Lawrence, Peter, 67, 103
Lawson Finch, Maurice, 13
Lee, Ken, 130, 145-146, 149
Leigh, Tim, 165, 167, 173-174, 176, 177, 182, 185, 188
Legg, Ian, 222
Levett, Dave, 68
Lewis, Chris, 139, 142, 146-147
Lewis, Tom, 43
Liddell, John, 27, 29, 223
Light Railways Act 1896, 11, 61
Light Railway Orders, 15,17, 208
Lindsey, Doug, 171, 189
Llangollen Railway, 160, 203
Lloyd, David, 194, 197, 199, 205, 207, 209, 216
Locomotives
   03 Class BR No D2023, 126, 16
   Adams Radial Tank No 488, 69
   Arthur K&ESR No 17, 19-20, 23
   Ashford, Class 33 Diesel Electric No D6570, 154
   Baxter, Fletcher Jennings No 158, 73, 86
   Bodiam, K&ESR No 3, BR No 32670, 14, 20, 27-28, 54, 77, 86, 149, 19, 221
   City of Truro, GWR No 3440, 219
   Clan Line, BR No 35028, 24
   Class 14 locomotives, 103, 154, 197
   Class 73 Electro Diesel No 73126, 110, 118, 154, 158-159
   Dom, K&ESR No 11, 13, 14
   Fenchurch, LB&SCR No 36, 63, 69, 86
   Gazelle, S&MR No 1/ K&ESR No 1, 152
   General Steam Navigation, BR No 35011, 231
   Gervase, K&ESR No 10, 13, 220
   GNR N2 Class No 1744, 220
   GWR 0-4-2T No 1466, 86
   GWR 2-8-0T No 4253, 219-220, 223
   GWR 2-8-0 T No 4247, 220
   GWR 0-6-2T No 6619, 122, 219
   Holman F Stephens, K&ESR No 23, 23, 39, 63-66, 119, 223-224
   Hastings, K&ESR No 15, 13
   Hunslet Austerity 7086, K&ESR No 27, 223
   Hunslet Austerity BR No 68078, 194, 229-231
   Iron Duke (replica), 86
   Ivatt 2MT 2-6-2T No 41241, 70
   Ivatt, 2MT 2-6-0 No 46443, 146
   Knowle, K&ESR No 8/SR No 2678, 95, 149, 162, 170-171, 179, 219
   Linda, K&ESR No 26, 119, 223
   Marcia, K&ESR No 12, 13, 31, 54, 58-59, 73
   Marc Seguin (replica), 162
   Martello, BR No 32662, 219
   Maunsell, K&ESR No 22, 23, 31, 57, 63
   Northiam, K&ESR No 25, 69, 86, 171, 223-224
   Norwegian, K&ESR No 19, 16, 20, 26, 38, 70, 144, 145, 146, 171, 174
   Pannier Tank BR No 1638, 122, 165, 206
   Pannier Tank GWR No 7752, 86
   P Class, K&ESR No 11/SR No 1556 (formerly *Pride of Sussex*), 13, 89, 104, 111, 118, 150, 158, 206
   Rocket (replica), 63, 162
   Sir Lamiel, SR No 777, 118
   Sutton, K&ESR No. 10, 14, 16-17, 20, 31, 39, 72, 80, 86, 89, 104, 111, 119, 121, 149, 162, 210-211
   Tamworth Castle, Class 25 Diesel Electric No D7672, 122, 154
   U Class SR No 1618, 23-24
   'Ugly', K&ESR No 29, RSH No 7667, 23
   USA Class BR No 30064, 69
   Waddon, LB&SCR No 54, 211
   WH Austen/Rolvenden, K&ESR No 24, 39, 223-224
   'Zebedee', RSH No 7597, 112
Locomotive Department, 77, 148, 158
London Brighton & South Coast Railway (LB&SCR), 12, 57, 94-95, 149
Long, Simon, 126
Longmoor Military Railway, 17-18, 84
Lowe, Clive, 57, 94-95
Lumley, Joanna, 58

Mann, Terence, 28
Manpower Services Commission (MSC), 32, 57, 82, 94, 95

Marsh, Jonathan, 171
Marsh, Sandra, 179
Marsh, Simon, 51, 173, 222
Marshall, Tom, 69
Masterson, Charles W, 58, 83, 176, 186, 204, 219
Merrills, Alan, 200, 208
Mid Hants Railway, 94, 166, 223
Mill Ditch, 159, 178-179
Millennium Commission, 151, 154, 155, 158, 172, 200, 208, 214, 215
Millennium Fund, 151, 153
Miller, John, 37, 40, 60, 62, 78, 85, 89, 90, 105, 132, 145, 159, 174, 179, 209, 218, 220
Mitchell, Carol, 177, 195, 220
Mitchell, Christopher, 27, 220
Moore, Roger, 61
Morgan, Bill, 192
Morgan, David, 174, 189-193
Morris 20 Railcar, 14
Morris, Vince, 133
Muston, Brian, 26

Nationalisation, 12, 95, 134, 145
National Lottery, 147, 151, 171
National Railway Museum, 37, 63, 86, 152, 159, 162
National Rivers Authority, 110
National Westminster (Natwest), Bank, 139, 155, 181
Network South-East, 107, 110, 118
Neame, Robert, 75
Newmill Channel Bridge, 13, 19, 26, 28, 32, 36-37, 39-41, 45, 53, 107
Norman, Clive, 75
North Yorkshire Moors Railway, 48, 59, 112, 122, 200, 201, 219
Northiam Station, 13, 60, 62, 91, 97-100, 102-104, 127, 136, 145, 162, 172, 174, 183-184, 203

Official Reopening June 1974, 20
Olver, Major Peter, Railway Inspector, 103-104
Operating Department, 103, 128, 183
Osborn, Richard, 139, 141-142

Page, Jean-Marc, 159, 171, 174
Perkins, Boris, 195, 199
Permanent Way Department, 45, 59, 87, 98, 213, 221
Petros (coach), 68
Pickin, George, 14, 194
PLC Proposal, 185, 186, 191-207
Popes Cottage P Way Hut, 13, 25, 35, 36, 75
Popes Cottage Derailment, 75-77, 80-81, 87
Pullman Car *Barbara*, 15-16, 24, 27, 39, 41, 54-55, 104, 119, 165
Pullman Car *Theodora*, 15, 45, 47, 87, 200, 208, 214, 217

Quarry Steam Centre, 116

Railway Grouping 1923, 12, 84, 124
Railway Magazine, 121, 191
Ramsden, Paul, 27, 120
Registered Charity status, 17, 114, 149, 165, 185, 191
Reid, Bob Chairman British Rail, 131
Richardson, Kim, 165-167
Rice, Anneka, 101
Roberts, Catherine, 157-158
Robertsbridge 20/20 Ltd, 181, 212
Robertsbridge Station, 11, 13-15, 17-18, 51, 107, 110, 117, 123-124, 172, 179, 181, 212-213, 219, 221
Roesen, Jo, 68
Rolvenden Shed, 66, 85
Rolvenden Station, 11, 53, 58, 76, 158-159, 217, 221
Rolvenden Steam Enterprises, 223-224
Romney Hythe & Dymchurch Railway
Rose, Major C, Railway Inspector, 38, 58-59
Rose, Nick, 13
Rose, Neil, 66, 108, 118, 138-139, 185, 190, 197
Rother Bridge, 19, 44-45, 56, 60-62, 77, 98-100
Rother District Council, 155, 213, 226
Rother Valley Railway (1896), 11
Rother Valley Railway Company (1966), 15, 17, 25
Rother Valley Railway Company (1991), 107, 110, 116, 123, 181, 211, 219, 221

Rother Valley Railway Supporters Association, 111, 212
Rother Valley Railway Trust, 212

Saggers, Sue, 172
Santa Specials, 24, 37, 39, 43, 47, 56-57, 88, 92, 96, 103, 114, 118, 130, 141, 144, 150, 153, 156, 165-166, 188, 203, 205-206, 217
Seabourne, Roy, 198, 204
Sealy, Bernard, 125, 135-136, 139-140, 142, 147, 156-157, 164-167
Searle, Robert, 30
Severn Valley Railway, 94, 110, 118, 146
Shark Ballast Plough Brake Van, 162
Shaw, Philip, 16-17, 21-22, 37, 45, 71, 91-92, 109, 113, 133, 145, 147, 156, 159, 165, 167, 173-174, 176, 179, 186, 190, 198-200, 203, 205, 207, 210, 217
Signalling, 26, 28, 32-33, 34, 38, 41-42, 45, 48-49, 50-52, 62, 67, 75, 78, 83, 95, 108, 134, 162
Signals & Telecommunications Department (S&TE), 42, 45, 123
Sime, Neil, 103, 157-158, 197
Sinclair, Dave, 68
Sinclair, Allen, 105
Sittingbourne & Kemsley Railway, 18
Siviour, Dr Gerald, 88
Slack, David, 137
Smith, Graham, 125, 142
Smokebox (satirical newsletter), 139
Snell, John, 159, 174, 185, 195-198, 201-202, 204-205, 207, 217
South Devon Railway, 122
South Eastern & Chatham Railway (SE&CR), 12-13, 25, 84, 86, 92, 123-124, 131, 146, 159, 218
Southern Railway/Region, 12, 30, 31, 40, 49, 50, 55, 68-69, 92, 94, 95, 154, 162, 179, 211
Southern Railway Maunsell era coaches, 15, 17, 19, 21, 41, 55, 64, 72, 95, 104, 124, 127, 206
Southern Water Authority, 32, 53, 98
Spa Valley Railway, 162, 211
St Michaels Church, 220

St Mildred's Church, 21
Standard, Richard, 223, 230
Steam & Country Fairs, 40, 47-48, 55, 62-63, 66, 69, 71, 73, 77, 81, 115, 183, 186, 188, 199, 203-204, 207, 217
Steam Lines South East, 18, 24
Stephens, Holman F, 11, 12, 17, 22, 25, 33, 37, 38, 43-45, 48, 53, 69, 77-78, 89, 90, 92-94, 98, 116, 122, 132-133, 145, 159, 183, 194, 224
Stevens, Pam & Sheila, 198
Stirling-Baker, Rex, 98
Stratrail Ltd, 197-198
Stratton, David, 59, 78, 83, 85, 88, 89, 93, 96, 98, 101, 103, 104, 108-109, 114, 122, 131, 139-140, 143, 146-149, 157, 171, 174, 190, 197, 223
Sutton, London Borough of, 31, 211
Sutton, Paul, 39, 89, 94-95, 223
Swan, Ben, 156

Talyllyn Railway, 132, 159, 174, 196
Tebboth, Alan, 99, 145
Tenterden (history of), 11
Tenterden Bank, 21, 31, 61-63, 70, 83-84, 87, 98, 106, 125, 127
Tenterden Club, 139
Tenterden Station Buffet/Refreshment Rooms, 87-89, 114, 120
Tenterden Town Council, 74, 177
Tenterden Railway Company, 17, 18, 28, 59, 78, 82, 88, 108, 110, 124, 138, 151, 155, 165, 172, 181, 190-191, 198, 201, 205, 208, 229
Tenterden Railway Equipment & Traction Company (TREATS), 126, 211
Tenterden, Bodiam & Robertsbridge Railway PLC, 205
Tenterden Terrier (magazine), 18, 20-21, 25-26, 29, 31, 33, 36-37, 44-45, 50, 52, 54-55, 58, 60, 67, 71, 76, 78, 80, 84, 88-89, 94, 98, 101, 103, 105-108, 110, 113, 114, 118, 126, 130, 132-133, 135, 136, 142, 144, 147-148, 150-151, 153-154, 156, 159, 161, 164-165, 168, 170, 173-174, 178-179, 186, 189, 199, 203, 205-206, 212, 217, 221-222, 231

Tenterden Town Station, 11, 13, 31, 35, 37, 74, 77, 82-83, 88, 91, 112, 115, 143, 149, 152, 171-172, 174, 183, 206-207, 209-210
Terrier Gala 2006, 217
Terrier Trust, 149, 179, 217
Thatcher, Rt Hon Margaret MP, Prime Minister, 39
Thomas events, 118-121, 123, 130, 136, 138, 144, 165, 170-171, 173, 182, 187-188, 198, 200, 203, 205-206, 210, 215
Tonks, Eric, 25
Tour de France Cycle Race, 217
Toynbee, Mark, 85, 91, 100, 102, 107, 130
TRC Trading, 136, 143

Victa Railfreight Ltd, 187, 200
Vidler, Paul, 67
Vine Inn public house, 81, 144
Vintage Train, 55, 78, 86, 111, 113, 124, 131, 150, 158-159, 214, 217
Volunteers & Paid Staff Meetings, 144, 166
Vraalsen, Tom, Norwegian Ambassador, 145

Waddington, John, 156
Wealden Pullman, 15, 27, 44, 54-56, 66, 70-71, 74, 80-81, 85 87, 91 114, 123, 126-127, 131, 135, 143, 150, 189
Webb, Andrew, 69, 76, 85, 97, 103, 105, 108-109, 126, 130, 142
Weighbridge at Tenterden Town, 153
Weller, John, 34, 36, 177, 195, 199, 202

Welsh Highland Railway, 22, 151, 212
Welshpool & Llanfair Railway, 17
Westerham Valley Railway Association, 15
West Somerset Railway, 48, 95, 131
Wheele, Ron & Vic, 149
Whiteman, Philip, 130, 157, 197
Whiteman, Stephen, 42
Wickham Trolleys, 14, 36, 38, 218
Williams, Raymond, 104, 108-109, 138, 142, 148
Wilson, Jim, 30
Wilson, Donald, 27, 31, 73, 89, 167
Wilson, Paul, 27, 87, 98, 100, 111, 130, 136-137, 139, 142-143, 184, 188-190, 195, 204-205
Wine & Dine Train, 25, 28, 31, 39, 44
Wittersham Road Station, 13, 19, 25-26, 29, 30, 32, 36-39, 42, 45, 49-50, 51, 53, 57, 60, 61-62, 64-65, 676-68, 70, 73, 75-76, 82-83, 87, 91, 96, 99, 104-105, 109-110, 122, 127, 134, 175
Wood, Christopher, 118
Woodcock, Laurie, 76
Woodham Brothers, Barry Scrapyard, 23, 53
Woolwich Coach, 14, 31-32, 208, 214-215, 218
Wright, George, 57-59, 78, 85, 91, 95

Yonge, Mark, 40, 48, 56-57, 74-75, 78, 139, 142, 144, 212
Yorke, David, 33
Young, Gordon, 111